REASSEMBLING MOTHERHOOD

REASSEMBLING MOTHERHOOD

PROCREATION AND CARE IN A GLOBALIZED WORLD

EDITED BY
YASMINE ERGAS, JANE JENSON,
AND SONYA MICHEL

Columbia University Press
New York

Columbia University Press
Publishers Since 1893
New York   Chichester, West Sussex
cup.columbia.edu
Copyright © 2017 Columbia University Press
All rights reserved

Library of Congress Cataloging-in-Publication Data
Names: Ergas, Yasmine, editor. | Jenson, Jane, editor. | Michel, Sonya, 1942– editor.
Title: Reassembling motherhood : procreation and care in a globalized world /
edited by Yasmine Ergas, Jane Jenson, and Sonya Michel.
Description: New York : Columbia University Press, [2017] |
Includes bibliographical references and index.
Identifiers: LCCN 2017005586 (print) | LCCN 2017022195 (ebook) |
ISBN 978-0-231-53807-7 (e-book) | ISBN 978-0-231-17050-5 (cloth : alk. paper)
Subjects: LCSH: Motherhood. | Human reproductive technology. | Child rearing. | Families.
Classification: LCC HQ759 (e-book) | LCC HQ759 .R425 2017 (print) | DDC 306.874/3—dc23
LC record available at https://lccn.loc.gov/2017005586

Columbia University Press books are printed on permanent and durable
acid-free paper.
Printed in the United States of America

Cover design: Milenda Nan Ok Lee

Cover image: Eva Hesse, H+H. June 1965. Hauser & Wirth Collection / © The
Estate of Eva Hesse. Courtesy of Hauser & Wirth Collection.

TO RACHEL (RIKKI) MIHAELOFF ERGAS

CAIRO, JULY 3, 1927—NEW YORK, JULY 30, 2014

IN LOVING MEMORY

CONTENTS

AFTERWORD: CROSSING INTO THE FUTURE

ALICE KESSLER-HARRIS

287

ILLUSTRATIONS

ACKNOWLEDGMENTS

This book began with an intuition: motherhood as a set of practices and understandings is being transformed by the convergence of globalization, reproductive technologies, and shifts in gender relations. The book examining this transformation has benefited from the expertise and support of many whom we wish to acknowledge here. Yasmine Ergas organized an interdisciplinary workshop at Columbia University, called Deconstructing and Reconstructing "Mother": Regulating Motherhood in International and Comparative Perspective, which met twice in 2012. We are grateful to the scholars who participated in that workshop; their contributions to the discussions helped to inform the papers that ultimately became chapters in this book.

Peter Bearman, then director of the Institute for Social and Economic Research and Policy (ISERP), now of the Interdisciplinary Center for Innovative Theory and Empirics (INCITE), and Elazar Barkan of the Institute for the Study of Human Rights (ISHR) at Columbia University supported this endeavor from the start. Without their confidence, this project could not have happened; thank you, both. Invaluable logistical help and advice were provided by Ariella Lang (ISHR) and Michael Falco (ISERP). Jennifer Hirsch (Columbia's Mailman School of Public Health) played a key role in preparing the ISERP grant application, and Alessia Lefebure (Alliance program, Columbia University) provided additional financial support. We are grateful to you all.

At Columbia University Press, we thank Anne Routon, the editor who saw the potential of this book from the beginning, and her dedicated staff. We also acknowledge the help provided by the external reviewers, who generously gave invaluable feedback and careful, knowledgeable, and insightful comments.

Inevitably, working on motherhood harks back to our personal experiences. As it happens, we all have daughters. One of them became a mother herself as this book was being finalized. From our daughters and sons, we learn how to be mothers. Together with our partners, they help us to "think" motherhood; together, we invent and reinvent its practices. Luckily, we also laugh together. Yasmine is especially grateful to Lenny and Sofia for their patience and good humor through many conversations over the meaning of what, after all, is a role that they might have just expected her to fulfill. Jane thanks Bridget and George for their help in understanding one of life's most rewarding roles. Sonya thanks Josh, Colin, and Nadja for introducing her and Jeffrey to the joys of grandparenthood.

Before our own mothering begins—and, if we are lucky, even as it is ongoing—we learn from our mothers. Yasmine's mother, Rikki Ergas, attended the first meeting of the workshop. We are grateful she was there to help launch this project.

REASSEMBLING MOTHERHOOD

INTRODUCTION

NEGOTIATING "MOTHER" IN THE TWENTY-FIRST CENTURY

Between Choice and Constraint

YASMINE ERGAS, JANE JENSON, AND SONYA MICHEL

"**M**other" as an identity and a role is undergoing rapid change. There long have been multiple avenues to motherhood, including adoption and fostering, yet conventionally a "mother" has been understood to be a woman who both bears and cares for a child. Today, however, the status of mother may be conferred on a person who fulfills only one or even neither of these roles. Changing social norms, reproductive technologies, including assisted reproductive technologies (ARTs), and the possibilities offered by globalized personal services all have led to the creation and expansion of markets in both procreation and care. As a result, women who previously could not bear children may now do so, and those who cannot or do not wish to physically reproduce may foster, adopt, or engage a surrogate mother who will bear a child on their behalf. Men, too, may access the markets in procreation and advance claims to being "mothers" rather than simply parents.[1] In addition, global as well as local labor markets now provide childcare workers, without the women who hire such workers ceding any of their status as their children's mothers.

In other words, as increasing numbers of women who are not going to be considered mothers give birth and care for children, and as women who claim the status of mothers perform only one or neither function, neither parturition nor care is either necessary or sufficient to define a mother. Instead, large social processes are at work, creating chains of procreation and chains of care. ARTs are redefining who may procreate, whether by direct gestation or through surrogacy, and with what or whose genetic material, while states struggle to define which of the new pathways to procreation should legitimately endow a woman with the status of "mother." At the same time, paid care workers are assuming a major presence in the lives of children, while public policy shapes the means and ends of care.

Changes in social norms and public policy as well as in legal rights and technologies, and the development of markets in both procreation and care, mean that motherhood has become a choice for more women. In this sense, there is what we might think of as a "liberalization" of motherhood. But the new panoply of choice is not, of course, available everywhere and to everyone. Motherhood has not been fully "democratized." The possibility of choosing how to mother is not equally available to everyone, either within any one society or across different countries. Compulsion and coercion, exclusion and privilege persist; the opportunity to decide to bear children (or not) or how to organize the care of those children is unevenly distributed. Restrictive policies, socioeconomic disadvantage, cultural mores, and discrimination founded on multiple bases force some women into motherhood while preventing others from either bearing or caring for their children. The chapters in this volume examine the inequalities that affect the distribution of choice as well as the ways in which more choice has been generated within the two chains of procreation and of care.

DISMANTLING BARRIERS, EXPANDING CHOICE

There is no denying that many barriers to motherhood are being dismantled. While geographic, socioeconomic, and racial or ethnic variations continue, more individual women can choose motherhood and more categories of women can do so. As medical advances render female bodies more reproductively malleable, the groups previously included among the "medically infertile" are being whittled down. Women without viable oocytes, women approaching or in menopause, and women without wombs, among others, need no longer be classified among those who cannot bear children. As with women whose partners have low sperm counts, these women may choose assisted reproductive technologies or surrogacy as well as adoption.

At the same time, the legality as well as the legitimacy of exclusions based on discriminatory criteria are being challenged nationally and internationally. Forced sterilization of indigenous women in the 1990s in Peru, for example, provoked outrage, leading to the end of the practice (Boesten 2014). Collective mobilizations and legal proceedings have contested and at times halted forced removals of the children of indigenous, Roma, or African American women as well as those with disabilities or nonconforming sexual orientations and gender identities and political dissidents.[2] In numerous jurisdictions, restrictions on adoption have been loosened. Some permit single women, whether heterosexual, lesbian, or transgendered, to adopt. Some permit adoption by LGBT couples. And some jurisdictions allow women to effect second-parent adoptions of nonmarital partners' children to whom they are not biologically related. As all of these examples illustrate, access to motherhood has broadened.

At the same time, women also have been empowered to limit their childbearing and child-rearing or to forego these options altogether. The ability to engage in heterosexual relations without risking undesired pregnancy has increased as a result of improved availability of contraception and abortion (Alkema et al. 2013). The unmet need for contraception has declined, and over the past two decades abortion has also been legalized in more than two dozen countries.[3] The Center for Reproductive Rights reports that more than 60 percent of the world's population now lives in a jurisdiction with liberal abortion laws.[4] Indeed, social norms legitimating women's decisions not to reproduce have been strengthened and, with them, voluntary childlessness.[5]

INEQUALITIES IN ACCESS TO MOTHERHOOD

Despite the reality of expanded choice, long-standing barriers and forms of coercion endure while new ones emerge, creating as well as maintaining inequalities in patterns of mothering. The obligation to bear and raise children has long been a marker of "good" womanhood. The value-laden conjunction of femininity and maternity that Katherine Franke (2001) terms "repro-normativity" persists in the continuing stigma attached to (perceived) infertility and voluntary childlessness (see also Jansen and Saint Onge 2015). Infertility and childlessness can lead to consequences ranging from matrimonial dissolution to insecurity in old age.[6]

Factors such as stigma, marital insecurity, and economic and social vulnerability reflect and reinforce strong and widespread norms equating women's identities with childbearing and child-rearing in ways that may overshadow other dimensions of their lives. As Jane Jenson documents in this volume, a "new maternalism" prevalent among international and domestic policy makers casts women as mothers and "writes out" women as independent subjects, along with their equality claims.

Coercion also follows from the fact that in many countries contraception or abortion are still prohibited or severely restricted, despite the improved access described above. In a seeming paradox, the restrictive abortion and contraception regulations that are legitimated as promoting the right to life contribute to the most significant exclusion from motherhood that persists today: maternal mortality. Illegal and botched abortions are a leading cause of the high rates at which women continue to die in pregnancy and childbirth (World Health Organization 2011). To be sure, such rates have declined significantly in the past two decades, but there remains a significant gap between the objective of a 75 percent reduction by 2015, set by the United Nations Millennium Development Goals in 1990, and the 45 percent decrease actually achieved (United Nations 2015a).

As many of the essays in this volume attest, long-standing legal forms of exclusion from motherhood also persist. These include discriminatory application of parental fitness standards and termination of maternal rights, as Dorothy Roberts documents, and induced and even coerced renunciations of maternal rights in the context of adoption, as the chapters by Pien Bos and Carol Sanger describe. New examples of exclusions from motherhood come from the contracts that transfer to others the child a woman has borne. Claire Achmad and Yasmine Ergas document this exclusion via commercial reproductive surrogacy, while Letizia Palumbo assesses restrictions that limit access to assisted reproductive technologies, such as occurs where adequate medical facilities are lacking or obstructive legal and administrative norms apply.

Difficulties in reconciling work and family obligations also erect barriers to motherhood, barriers that women of means can negotiate more easily than those with fewer resources. When the pursuit of careers has led to the postponement of childbearing, better-off women can afford to access ARTs, to take significant breaks from paid employment, and to purchase high-quality nonparental care. But for poor and low-income women, especially those from developing countries, the opposite is true. As Helma Lutz and Sonya Michel and Gabrielle Oliveira document in their chapters, many of those women must commute or migrate to find paid employment, often caring for the children of others while leaving their own children behind.

From maternal mortality to maternal expropriation to unwilling renunciation and migration, social inequalities shape patterns of access to motherhood and the two chains of procreation and care. Although chains of procreation and care cater to different needs, they are both based on the segmentation and commodification of functions once associated with "mother." Fetuses, for example, are viewed as separate from the bodies of the mothers who bear them, as Anne Higonnet's chapter illustrates, and that separation, Yasmine Ergas contends, informs a view of childbearing as a marketable function. Care may become a form of work, a set of tasks performed by members of a specialized labor force, who may even acquire the requisite competencies through specific training, as Sonya Michel and Gabrielle Oliveira discuss. And yet, as all the chapters in this volume show, to the extent to which chains of procreation and care, and the processes of segmentation and commodification associated with them, tend to redefine "motherhood," they also give rise to intense contestation. Such contestation reflects ongoing tensions over who may be a mother and who must or must not.

PROCREATION AND CARE: MULTIPLE ISSUES

While motherhood is denied to some women, it is imposed on others. This difference often follows from the relation between embodiment and procreation: women are simultaneously regarded as embodied subjects and yet disembodied bearers of fetuses and then children. How can this be? The foundation of Western political and civil rights lies in the embodied self and in the notion that the rights of personhood are, in the first instance, grounded in the indissoluble nexus between the person and her physical being. The right to contraception constitutes women's habeas corpus claim to self-possession, as Geneviève Fraisse (2013) argues. But what are the boundaries of the self when it comes to pregnant women? Does the process of multiplication entailed in gestation—the physical process through which one person becomes two (or more)—call into question the notion of a unitary physical self? Anne Higonnet recounts how imaging techniques such as ultrasound may be utilized to sever the representation of the fetus from the maternal body. This capacity to delink the pregnant woman from the fetus she is carrying is reflected in the relative paucity of attention paid to the consequences of assisted reproductive technologies. As Linda Kahn and Wendy Chavkin show in their chapter, concentration on the production of children overshadows concern for the women who bear them.

The issue of embodiment also pervades the practices of surrogacy. Yasmine Ergas examines notions about where the pregnant woman ends and the possession/child of others begins. The "straight-line" assumption implicit in surrogacy discourse posits that the ownership of gametes seamlessly translates into being the parent of a child that another women bears. This assumption is necessary to enable a contractual relationship with the surrogate and the marketization of childbearing.[7] The chapter also argues that assigning rights in the fetus to someone other than the woman bearing it opens a door to rethinking the jurisprudence under which abortion has been legalized thus far, to the extent to which it has been based on the notion that the fetus is not only *in* a woman but *of* her.

The matter of embodiment also permeates debates on men's rights to childbearing, raising issues such as whether motherhood is exclusively an attribute of women or might pertain also to men. As Nara Milanich's chapter tells us, the assignment of parenthood—fatherhood as well as motherhood—is based on understandings of reproductive physiology that have proven highly labile over time and have become further complicated in recent decades with the emergence of ever more sophisticated and powerful ARTs. (This is also discussed in Kahn and Chavkin's chapter in this volume, and in Thompson 2005).

Motherhood is, of course, also closely associated with nurturance and care, but this pairing has been historically easier to disassemble than motherhood and procreation. Over time and across social boundaries, as Alice Kessler-Harris's afterword reminds us, the practices of nurturing and caring have frequently been assigned to persons other than the biological mother, mostly women such as wet nurses and nannies. In some countries, the tasks have gone to men as well.[8] Such practices open up a number of areas of instability in the representation of social relations. For example, caring for children counts as "work" when it is paid but not when it is unremunerated. If care involves an emotional connection as well as a custodial one, might not the law recognize a paid care worker's right to visitation when her employment comes to an end?

The distribution of care also raises issues about women's roles and rights more generally.[9] As Jane Jenson's chapter documents, social policies in several regions of the world have been altered since the mid-1990s, shifting from ensuring the rights and capabilities of all adults, including women, to framing women's needs as being based primarily on their functions in childbearing and child-rearing. This resurgent maternalism echoes the traditional gendered division of labor. But as Martha Fineman argues in her chapter, both the traditional devaluation of care as "not work" and the social ideal of autonomous, self-sufficient citizens obscures the reality of dependence as a constitutive rather than exceptional characteristic of social relations. We are all, she says, "vulnerable," and it is this vulnerability that ought to ground social policy.

Such shifts all have profound implications for the definition of motherhood. Renegotiations of motherhood are being provoked by tensions around embodiment as well as around care, which touch on matters as diverse as the "value" of women as individuals and as bearers of children, the framing of "mothering" as work or family (and the relationship between these two), and ultimately the claims of women to, simultaneously, be able to choose to mother and to not be reduced to mothering.

RENEGOTIATING MOTHERHOOD

At times, one woman's ability to mother depends on another woman's inability to do so: adoption, surrogacy, and nonfamilial caring might all be cast in zero-sum terms. But a broader view suggests that constriction and choice can interact in ways that produce new practices and patterns. When emigration leads a woman to leave her children behind in order to care for those of others, her mothering is constrained. This situation has led analysts to identify "care deficits" that are created by the pull of care workers from the Global South to the Global North and from east to west in Europe. Such migration patterns have sometimes, as Helma Lutz recounts in her chapter, generated public debates about the social consequences of maternal absence and have even led to "mother blaming." Numerous studies have shown, however, that women who migrate do not neglect their children but rather rearrange the structure of caring. Often this entails delegating children's care to migrants' female relatives or to other (even less well-paid) women. Each "mothers" in the other's stead (Hochschild 2000).

As the work of care is redistributed, contests over motherhood may arise. In their chapter, Michel and Oliveira provide an example of a nanny challenging her employer's claim to motherhood: she herself is, she contends, her charge's "real" mother. But viewed from the perspective of employers—in a context in which women's income is ever more central to household economies—fulfilling their responsibilities as mothers may entail providing children with the benefits derived from employment, including good substitute care. Indeed, as women, whatever their position in the care chain, reconcile paid work with family obligations, they are likely, as Lutz and Michel and Oliveira describe, to reformulate their understandings of what motherhood entails, shifting from direct caring to the overall coordination of child-rearing, providing financial support, ensuring long-distance supervision and, for those who migrate, working to realize the promise of immigration rights to family reunification.[10]

Adoption and surrogacy also are prompting renegotiations of motherhood. In her chapter, Carol Sanger analyzes legal cases involving women who, faced with the risk of having their maternal rights terminated, sought to bargain over the terms on which they would give up their children for adoption. These women signed contracts that promised continued connection with the children, having been persuaded to give up their children by the prospect that they would be able to hold on to a piece of motherhood. For the most part, however, especially where the birth mother could be represented in terms of racialized social disadvantage, the contracts were not upheld.

The process of "de-kinning" that birth mothers undergo during adoption can leave searing traces. In her chapter, Pien Bos describes birth mothers who, years after giving up children for adoption, still consider themselves to be the mothers of those children and await their return (see also Volkman 2005).[11] Amrita Pande (2014) has detailed the hopes of continued connection that surrogate mothers nurture despite having been repeatedly instructed that they are *not* the mothers of the children they will bear. Moreover, even as they cling to hope, they too are redefining the terms of motherhood—for instance, earmarking the compensation they will earn for their other children's education and care. Producing children on behalf of others may be a way to mother one's own.

BEYOND PRIVATE NEGOTIATIONS: MARKETS, STATES, AND GLOBAL GOVERNANCE

The meanings of motherhood are not individually negotiated only by birth mothers and adoptive parents, surrogates and intended parents, care workers and employers, and their reference groups, families, and communities. Rather, private and public institutions also play a crucial role. In the Indian state of Tamil Nadu, Pien Bos researched an adoption agency-cum-home for pregnant women that simultaneously provided accommodations for pregnant women in difficulty and coaxed them to yield their children for adoption. When pregnant women and women who had just given birth proved ambivalent, the institution worked assiduously to reassure them, seeking to convince them that keeping the child was not in the child's best interests or their own. The situation of the women on whom Carol Sanger focuses are also catalyzed by adoption agencies: birth mothers are persuaded to give up their children in exchange for promises of postadoption visitation.

Chains of care and procreation also are shaped by state action. The rights and duties of motherhood have long been organized by states. Conventionally considered to fall within the domestic jurisdiction of states (and sometimes their subnational jurisdictions) and thus to be free from external interference, designations of who may and who must become or remain a mother, the value assigned to "mothering" and its constituent aspects, how and by whom is it to be recognized and supported and, ultimately, who is to make the relevant determinations have all been the purview of national decision makers. In recent years, however, this relative autonomy of national states has been undermined by the diffusion of authority over practices and policies about motherhood and the involvement of institutions of international and supranational governance, including courts (see Ergas 2013 and the chapter by Palumbo, for example).

Perhaps even more consequential has been the emergence in recent decades of markets that structure the global chains of procreation and care. Markets in procreation involve selling gametes and selling the gestation and delivery of children, addressing the needs of women and men who cannot or do not wish to bear their own children. Markets in the chains of care involve payment for the performance of tasks such as nurturing, feeding, cleaning, safeguarding, accompanying, or supervising the education of children, catering to those who either cannot or do not wish to perform these functions themselves. Workers' and suppliers' entry into these markets is often controlled by agents and vendors of varying reliability and beneficence.

Both chains share some general characteristics. First, they are based on the disaggregation of "motherhood" into discrete elements that can be demarcated, commodified, and outsourced. Second, they promote a view of each of these elements—and, indeed, of the status of mother itself—as legitimately subject to marketization and hence to regulation as part of systems of commercial and contractual exchanges. If nonparental care has been recognized and regulated for many years, the disaggregation of procreation and its rules are less well established.[12]

Segmentation or disaggregation translates naturalistic views of "mothering" into specific and commodified goods, such as oocytes, and into services, such as homework supervision. Separately packaged and brought to market, these elements can be reassembled by their purchasers, who can source them on a worldwide basis. Such markets require material and legal organization of the processes by which the purveyors of the various goods and services transfer them to consumers. Specialized information disseminators (such as websites), brokers, transportation and hospitality operators, financial agencies, "handlers" and "fixers" adept at smoothing transitions between legal and illegal, familiar and foreign markets, connect potential parents to the suppliers of the goods and services that they require (Thompson 2005, as well as chapters by Achmad, Michel and Oliveira, and Palumbo).

These characteristics of chains of procreation, in particular, call into question the legal and policy framework within which the regulation of motherhood has conventionally been situated for centuries (Ergas 2013). Despite significant variations across countries and regions, it is possible to say that these frameworks generally have treated "motherhood" as a status, not subject to contract. Moreover, the functions and physiological elements associated with it have been treated as familial obligation, not as services and goods traded in markets. In keeping with this framework and with a general stance against human commodification, women, children, and body parts have been shielded from the regulations of commercial transactions. Moreover, to the extent to which they have been constituted as objects of exchange—via slavery, human trafficking, and so on—decommodification and removal from market processes have been a primary objective of international as well as national regulation. Nonetheless, with respect to procreation, these strictures have proven hard to apply: the lines demarcating that which may be bought and sold from that which may not, that which pertains to status from that which is grounded in contract, are not only contested but persistently circumvented. Along with other markets for human beings, including brides, sex workers, and indentured workers, a thriving "business in babies" has emerged (Spar 2006).

To a significant extent this market in babies and children is frankly illegal. Child traffickers worldwide notoriously organize and profit from a prohibited albeit flourishing trade in children. But these markets also operate in a gray zone, one in which the lines between de jure prohibitions and de facto acceptance blur. The international convention on adoption, for example, bars any "improper gain," incorporating a resolutely anticommercial stance to the transfer of children. But it also allows for "costs and expenses" (Hague Conference on Private International Law 1993, articles 8, 32). Uncertainty about the term "reasonable expenses" raises issues about whether women may be legally paid to provide children to adoptive parents. Tellingly, the U.S. courts that Carol Sanger discusses in her chapter do not generally enforce contracts for postadoption rights between birth mothers and prospective adoptive parents, on the grounds that gifts may not be contracted. And for the same reason, U.S. courts are also often reluctant to order a birth mother who changes her mind to repay amounts that she has received from prospective adoptive parents while pregnant. Nonetheless, some courts have enforced these contracts, as Sanger also recounts, and some have allowed for payments in exchange for future concessions of adoptive babies to be recovered.

Care is also marketized. As Alice Kessler-Harris documents in her afterword, nonparental and paid childcare is far from new. Employed women have historically engaged other women to care for their children, while even non-employed mothers with substantial means have long engaged nannies and governesses. Did these employees see themselves, and did their employers cast them, as "workers"? It seems reasonable to suppose so. Yet the intense struggles employees have had to wage to gain recognition as workers suggest that their labor has been imbued with a naturalizing aura that prevents its recognition as a form of work requiring adequate compensation (see, for example, Boris and Nadasen 2015).

In recent years, such struggles have catalyzed the emergence of global as well as national civil society organizations of domestic workers that have included childcare providers, and international labor federations have also begun to organize the representation of such workers (Boris and Fish 2014). As a result, the national governments of some "sending countries" of domestic workers have sought to improve the treatment of their citizens in "receiving" states. And such movements have prompted international action: in 2013, the International Labor Organization's (2011) Domestic Workers Convention came into force. While the convention found early supporters among governments who "export" such workers, some "importing" states have also acceded to it. This convention marks the success with which domestic care workers—and domestic workers more generally—have been able to define themselves and organize as workers entitled to bargain over the terms of the services they provide, including compensation and working conditions. This means that nonparental childcare, when provided within households, increasingly will be recognized as a form of work and will be sufficiently compensated and subject to regulation as such.[13] Indeed, there is now an international conversation about "unpaid work" in general; the recently approved United Nations Sustainable Development Goals (United Nations 2015b) include "recognize and value unpaid care and domestic work" among their targets.

In all of these ways, it is clear that "motherhood" is in transformation: more accessible, yet still restrictive; more subject to choice, yet still also a locus of coercion. This collection highlights sites of contestation that have emerged as chains of procreation and care have simultaneously generated greater liberty and new forms of constraint, promoted market relations and prompted new intersections among institutions of global governance, national governments, and civil society. While most of these issues are far from being resolved, the chapters here lay the groundwork for further thought and deliberation.

NOTES

1. Opening up the possibility that "mother" may be a quality of "men," such claims call into question conventional uses of "mother" as a signifier of "female" and highlight perspectives that view the maternal—and the feminine—as purely performative.

2. See, for example, the reports of forced removal of indigenous children in Australia (Commonwealth of Australia 1997) and in Canada (Truth and Reconciliation Commission of Canada 2015).

3. Nonetheless, provisions for mothers to safely give up their children are still necessary (Sanger 2006; Oaks 2015).

4. See Center for Reproductive Rights, *The World's Abortion Laws 2015*, http://world abortionlaws.com, accessed December 11, 2015.

5. Significant differences still exist, however (Eicher et al. 2016). Franke (2001) describes persisting stigma attached to perceived involuntary childlessness.

6. On childlessness as a cause for matrimonial dissolution, see Rosenblum (2013). For a review of risks entailed by childlessness in relation to old-age dependency and the solutions to which it may give rise, see De Vos (2014).

7. In practice, however, this process is not seamless; it requires a complex "ontological choreography" on the part of biomedical personnel and clinics, among others (Thompson 2005).

8. In colonial India, for example, male servants frequently looked after children (Banerjee 2016).

9. This contradicts states' obligation to ensure that maternity does not constitute a basis for discrimination against women. See the Convention on the Elimination of All Forms of Discrimination Against Women (CEDAW, UN 1979), articles 4 and 5.

10. The term "global care chain" was formulated by Hochschild (2000). For an early recognition of the idea that mothering includes financial support, see Segura (1994).

11. For a cinematic representation of birth mothers who continue to identify as mothers, see the 2013 film *Philomena* (Frears 2013), based on a book of the same name by Martin Sixsmith (2013).

12. France, for example, legislated around wet-nursing at the end of the nineteenth century (Jenson 1986). For the regulatory story of childcare in the United States, see Michel (1999, chap. 7).

13. Nonparental care outside the home has been paid and recognized as work, perhaps not sufficiently, but protected nonetheless (see Michel 1999, chap. 7; Jenson and Sineau 2001).

REFERENCES

Alkema, Leontine, Vladimira Kantorova, Clare Menozzi, and Ann Biddlecom. 2013. "National, Regional, and Global Rates and Trends in Contraceptive Prevalence and Unmet Need for Family Planning Between 1990 and 2015: A Systematic and Comprehensive Analysis." *The Lancet* 381, no. 9878: 1642–52.

Banerjee, Swapna M. 2016. "Subalternity and Manhood: Male Care Workers in Late Colonial India." Paper presented at the American Historical Association Meeting, Atlanta, GA, January.

Boesten, Jelke. 2014. *Sexual Violence During War and Peace: Gender, Power and Post-Conflict Justice in Peru*. London: Palgrave.

Boris, Eileen, and Jennifer N. Fish. 2014. "Slaves No More": Making Global Labor Standards for Domestic Workers." *Feminist Studies* 40, no. 2: 411–43.

Boris, Eileen, and Premilla Nadasen. 2015. "Introduction: Historicizing Domestic Workers Resistance and Organizing." *International Labor and Working-Class History* 88, no. 2: 4–10.

Commonwealth of Australia. 1997. *Bringing Them Home: National Inquiry into the Separation of Aboriginal and Torres Strait Islander Children from Their Families*. https://www.humanrights.gov.au/sites/default/files/content/pdf/social_justice/bringing_them_home_report.pdf.

De Vos, Susan. 2014. "Biologically Childless Women 60+ Often Live in Extended Household Families in Latin America. *Journal of Cross-Cultural Gerontology* 29, no. 4: 467–80.

Eicher, Véronique, Richard A. Settersten, Sandra Penic, Stephanie Glaeser, Aude Martenot, and Dario Spini. 2016. "Normative Climates of Parenthood Across Europe: Judging Voluntary Childlessness and Working Parents." *European Sociological Review* 32, no. 1: 135–50.

Ergas, Yasmine. 2013. "Babies Without Borders: Human Rights, Human Dignity and the Regulation of International Commercial Surrogacy." *Emory International Law Review* 27, no. 1: 117–88.

Fraisse, Geneviève. 2013. "The Habeas Corpus of Women: A Double Revolution." In *The Female Body: A Journey Through Law, Culture and Medicine*, ed. Brigitte Feuillet-Liger, Kristina Orfali, and Thérèse Callus, 339–45. Brussels: Editions Bruylant.

Franke, Katherine. 2001. "Theorizing Yes: An Essay on Feminism, Law, and Desire." *Columbia Law Review* 10, no. 1: 81–208.

Frears, Stephen (director). 2013. *Philomena*. The Weinstein Company. Film.

Hague Conference on Private International Law. 1993. *Convention of 29 May 1993 on Protection of Children and Co-operation in Respect of Intercountry Adoption*. https://www.hcch.net/en/instruments/conventions/full-text/?cid=69.

Hochschild, Arlie Russell. 2000. "Global Care Chains and Emotional Surplus Value." In *On the Edge: Living with Global Capitalism*, ed. Will Hutton and Anthony Giddens, 130–46. London: Jonathan Cape.

International Labour Organization. 2011. Domestic Workers Convention, 2011 (No. 189). http://www.ilo.org/dyn/normlex/en/f?p=NORMLEXPUB:12100:0::NO::P12100_INSTRUMENT_ID:2551460.

Jansen, Natalie Anne, and Jarron M. Saint Onge. 2015. "An Internet Forum Analysis of Stigma Power Perceptions among Women Seeking Fertility Treatment in the United States." *Social Science and Medicine* 147: 184–89.

Jenson, Jane. 1986. "Gender and Reproduction: Or, Babies and the State." *Studies in Political Economy* 20 (Spring): 9–46.

Jenson, Jane, and Mariette Sineau. 2001. *Who Cares?: Women's Work, Childcare, and Welfare State Redesign*. Toronto: University of Toronto Press.

Michel, Sonya. 1999. *Children's Interests/Mothers' Rights: The Shaping of America's Child Care Policy*. New Haven, CT: Yale University Press.

Oaks, Laury. 2015. *Giving Up Baby: Safe Haven Laws, Motherhood, and Reproductive Justice*. New York: New York University Press.

Pande, Amrita. 2014. *Wombs in Labor: Transnational Commercial Surrogacy in India*. New York: Columbia University Press.

Rosenblum, Irit. 2013. "Being Fruitful and Multiplying: Legal, Philosophical, Religious and Medical Perspectives on Assisted Reproductive Technologies in Israel and Internationally." *Suffolk Transnational Law Review* 36, no. 3: 627–48.

Sanger, Carol. 2006. "Infant Safe Haven Laws: Legislating in the Culture of Life." *Columbia Law Review* 106, no. 4: 753–829.

Segura, Denise A. 1994. "Working at Motherhood: Chicana and Mexican Immigrant Mothers and Employment." In *Mothering: Ideology, Experience, and Agency*, ed. Evelyn Nakano Glenn, Grace Chang, and Linda Rennie Forcey, 211–36. New York: Routledge.

Sixsmith, Martin, with Dame Judi Dench. 2013. *Philomena: A Mother, Her Son, and a Fifty-Year Search*. New York: Penguin.

Spar, Debora L. 2006. *The Baby Business: How Money, Science, and Politics Drive the Commerce of Conception*. Boston: Harvard Business School Press.

Thompson, Charis. 2005. *Making Parents: The Ontological Choreography of Reproductive Technologies*. Cambridge, MA: MIT Press.

Truth and Reconciliation Commission of Canada. 2015. *Final Report of the Truth and Reconciliation Commission of Canada*. Vol. 4, *Canada's Residential Schools: Missing Children and Unmarked Burials*. Montreal: McGill-Queen's University Press. http://www.myrobust.com/websites/trcinstitution/File/Reports/Volume_4_Missing_Children_English_Web.pdf.

United Nations. 1979. Convention on the Elimination of All Forms of Discrimination Against Women (CEDAW). http://www.un.org/womenwatch/daw/cedaw/text/econvention.htm.

———. 2015a. *The Millennium Development Goals Report 2015*. New York: United Nations.

———. 2015b. *Sustainable Development Goals: 17 Goals to Transform Our World*. http://www.un.org/sustainabledevelopment/sustainable-development-goals.

Volkman, Toby. 2005. *Cultures of Transnational Adoption*. Durham, NC: Duke University Press.

World Health Organization. 2011. *Unsafe Abortion: Global and Regional Estimates of Unsafe Abortion and Associated Mortality in 2008*. 6th ed. http://apps.who.int/iris/bitstream/10665/44529/1/9789241501118_eng.pdf.

1

CERTAIN MOTHERS,
UNCERTAIN FATHERS

Placing Assisted Reproductive Technologies
in Historical Perspective

NARA MILANICH

In their foundational volume on the global politics of reproduction, Faye Ginsburg and Rayna Rapp (1995) asked, "What's new about the new reproductive technologies?" In the succeeding two decades, the burgeoning interdisciplinary scholarship on assisted reproductive technologies (ARTs) seems to have answered: just about everything. A recurring but generally unexamined refrain is that the advent of assisted reproduction heralded a discrete rupture in patterns of human reproduction and in the social meanings, relationships, and identities attached to it. In vitro fertilization, surrogacy, artificial insemination, and other practices "challenge our most established ideas about motherhood, paternity, biological inheritance, the integrity of the family, and the 'naturalness' of birth itself" (Shore et al. 1992, 295), producing a "transformation of the boundaries of family" (Satz 2007, 523). Such changes are said to be destabilizing, to have "shaken the unshakable" (Stumpf 1986, 187), and to have unsettled roles and identities once assumed to be transparent, self-evident, and stable. New technologies are thus "deconstructive in introducing ambiguity and uncertainty into kin relationships, including the fundamental categories of motherhood and fatherhood" (de Parseval and Collard 2007, cited in Inhorn and Birenbaum-Carmeli 2008, 182). One gleans from the literature the sense of a fixed and unambiguous "before" and a brave, new "after," with ARTs as the critical watershed between them.

On one level, this narrative makes sense. The technoscientific novelty of ARTs as well as the creative social and legal adaptations and reformulations they have engendered seem indisputable. But what if, rather than framing their emergence as rupture, we considered ARTs as part of a longer-running and dynamic process in which law, science, technology, culture, religion, the state, and social practice have shaped and reshaped constructions of kinship and identity, maternity and paternity? For, as the ART literature itself shows so well, these are all malleable social categories, subject to profound reinterpretation and resignification within changing political and technological contexts. What if, then, we view ARTs as not the first, but merely the latest, reformulation of categories and identities that derive from and shape reproduction?

This chapter attempts to do that, exploring enduring tensions and synergies among social, legal, and scientific constructions of parentage. Such a historical exercise helps to place contemporary debates about who counts as a father or mother in a broader perspective, showing that ambiguity and contestation long predate the emergence of these new technologies. More specifically, even as one signal contribution of the scholarship on ARTs is to question facile assumptions about the social and the biological, the narrative of rupture tends to reify unwittingly not only the past as a foil to the present but also the binaries of certainty/uncertainty and ambiguity/unambiguity that signify a reproductive "before" and "after." Invoked to make a point about the unprecedented novelty and disruptive potential of ARTs, notions of ambiguity/certainty themselves go unrecognized as social and legal constructs.

Invocations of past and present, certainty and uncertainty are common not only in the ART literature but also in assessments of another domain of technoscientific practice said to have revolutionized reproductive roles and identities: DNA paternity testing. But biological paternity has historically been constructed, in binary opposition to maternity, as intrinsically uncertain. Thus, if ARTs have rendered maternity ambiguous, genetic parentage testing has done precisely the opposite: made knowable that which had previously seemed inscrutable. As one scientist on the cusp of the DNA revolution declared, "Motherhood has always been a biologic certainty; now fatherhood will be as well" (Shaw 1983, 2537). And as with ARTs, this development tends to be framed in historical terms, in order to highlight its unprecedented novelty. "As society enters a new millennium, the age-old problem of determining paternity is finally being eradicated" is a typical refrain (Shapiro, Reifler, and Psome 1992, 2).

Juxtaposing DNA testing with ARTs highlights how notions of certainty and uncertainty help to define maternity and paternity and to define them in opposition to one another. Indeed, the relationship between these two roughly contemporaneous technoscientific developments has been expressed in precisely these terms, perhaps most provocatively by feminist scholar of science Charis Thompson (2005, 68), who has suggested, "The new reproductive technologies . . . made biological motherhood uncertain just as DNA testing was beginning to make the notoriously uncertain facts of paternity more certain." In other words, notions of maternal certainty are constructed against complementary notions of paternal ambiguity, and the past is posed against the present, to argue that recent developments in reproductive and genetic science have in effect reversed the signs, rendering maternity ambiguous and paternity certain.

Notions of certainty/uncertainty have a remarkably long historical genealogy in the domain of what scholars have referred to as Euro-American kinship (Schneider 1984; Strathern 1992), and indeed in Western legal and social thought more generally.[1] I begin with a brief historical appraisal of these ideas in law and culture and go on to survey various historical scenarios that demonstrate how social and legal ordering produces them. I then assess the impact, beginning in the early twentieth century, of new scientific technologies on notions of parentage, with a focus on early paternity testing. I argue that, even as they promised to reveal the incontrovertible truth of paternity, new technologies arguably rendered paternal identity more ambiguous than ever. If ARTs and DNA testing have unsettled older social and legal categories, as many scholars have noted, the categories they unsettled are themselves the product of earlier interactions between law, state policies, social practices, and scientific developments. Given its length, this essay can only sketch this evidence in the broadest of strokes; still, restoring some texture and specificity to history before ARTs, even anecdotally, allows us to address anew Rapp and Ginsburg's query, "What is new about the new reproductive technologies?"

CERTAIN MOTHERS, UNCERTAIN FATHERS: A BRIEF HISTORY

The notion of biological maternity as certain and biological paternity as uncertain is a long-standing trope of Western law and culture. Roman law, for example, held "mater semper certa est" (the mother is always certain), because the fact of maternity could be clearly and unambiguously attributed at the moment of a child's birth. Notions of maternal certainty were in turn constructed against complementary notions of paternity as ambiguous. "Pater semper incertus est," held the accompanying Roman dictum: the father is intrinsically uncertain, because nature had drawn an "impenetrable veil" over the fact of paternity (Fuchs 2008, 52).[2] But Roman law then went on to establish a qualifying principle: "pater est quem nuptiae demonstrant" (the father is he whom marriage indicates); that is, the husband of the mother is always, by law, the father of her children. If marriage renders paternity certain, the corollary, of course, is that the father necessarily remains uncertain in the case of unmarried mothers. That is, paternity is made "knowable" by marriage, even as it is effaced outside of it.

This cluster of legal principles concerning certain maternity, uncertain paternity, and the so-called presumption of marital legitimacy traverses a variety of legal traditions ancient and modern, religious and secular, Western and "non-Western." Present in Catholic canon law and Jewish and Islamic legal traditions, they also are found in Anglo-American law and the civil law of continental Europe as well as in Latin American and some Middle Eastern legal systems. While undergoing evident modifications in emphasis and interpretation over time (some of which are outlined below), today these tenets continue to exercise considerable weight across diverse legal jurisdictions. As one author has suggested, marital legitimacy, and the accompanying principle of paternal uncertainty outside marriage, is "as close to a cultural universal in law as we get" (Stolzenberg 2007, 345).

Such ideas are not just the province of law. Disparate fields of knowledge have elaborated on the principles of maternal certainty and paternal uncertainty and theorized about the significance of these seemingly natural facts to the origins of human societies, psychic development, cultural difference, and gender inequality. In the mid-nineteenth century, diverse strains of social theory attributed critical significance to the fact of paternal unknowability. Evolutionary accounts of the origins of human civilization from Friedrich Engels to Lewis Henry Morgan, for example, posited a primordial stage of familial promiscuity, uncertain paternal origins, and matrilineal descent. Johann Bachofen's account of the defeat of "mother right"—the early stage of human society characterized by primitive matriarchy—hinged on the discovery that paternity could be made certain through monogamous marriage. Later, Sigmund Freud discussed the psychic impact of children's dawning knowledge of human procreation and, in particular, their realization of their own indeterminate paternity, in "Family Romances" (1909). By the 1930s, anthropologists such as Bronisław Malinowski had embarked on a heated debate about whether contemporary "savages" understood the concept of physiological paternity (Allen 1999; Coward 1983; Delaney 1986). More recently, sociobiologists and primatologists have dwelled on how paternal indeterminacy shapes selection strategies among male and female primates. And even as they espouse a very different intellectual and political project, some strains of what has been labeled essentialist feminism have begun with a remarkably similar premise, arguing that the fact of uncertain paternity lies at the heart of patriarchy and its institutions (O'Brien 1981).

Such widely held and deeply rooted convictions about the "natural facts" of procreation form the backdrop for contemporary assessments of reproductive technologies. In a word, what is new about these new technologies is that they appear to have utterly revolutionized these facts. For the first time in human history, science has rendered maternity ambiguous, even as paternity has become certain and knowable. The naturalness of these facts constitutes the basic premise against which to assess the transformations wrought by reproductive technologies, from ARTs to paternity testing.

But are they, in fact, natural facts? I suggest that the principles of maternal certainty and paternal uncertainty, enshrined in law and elaborated in social theory, sit uncomfortably with the historical record of cultural practice. The role of legal fictions—that is, presumptions created by law because it is socially and legally convenient to assume they are true—are a widely acknowledged dimension of the legal architecture of paternity, and I will return to this issue. First, however, I want to suggest, less conventionally, that there are equally powerful and enduring, but less recognized, legal fictions at work in this construction of maternity.

The dictum of certain maternity implies, first, a natural, physical, or biogenetic basis for maternal identity. Second, it implies that the fact of this natural relationship is unambiguous: over the course of a mother's or child's lifetime and beyond, the fleeting moment of birth imparts a clear and indelible link between a parturient and her progeny, despite eventual physical or social separation. A central pursuit of earlier generations of anthropological inquiry was the study of "non-Western" societies whose kinship systems or child-rearing practices operated according to a logic other than this physical or biogenetic one. But we need venture no further than Euro-American history to encounter a plethora of social scenarios in which this logic was normative rather than descriptive. In fact, the notion of maternal certainty fixed by and at birth seems utterly at odds with a wide array of child-rearing, familial, and labor practices in diverse Euro-American societies historically—societies, of course, governed by legal systems that nevertheless embraced the juridical logic of maternal certainty (and paternal uncertainty). These include the widespread practice of child abandonment, which dates from Roman history and stretches into the nineteenth century; the ubiquity of wet nursing and fosterage arrangements (Sussman 1982); and other cultural practices of child circulation, placement, fosterage, adoption, labor, and sale (Gager 1996; dos Guimarães Sá 1995).[3] In different ways, all of these practices belied a fixed, stable, or singular maternal identity.

Significantly, these were not exceptional practices that existed on the margins of law or social custom. Rather, in particular times and places, they became widespread, ritualized, and institutionalized mechanisms for unmooring children from their natal identities and, when they survived, effecting their transfer to alternative kin and caretakers. Examples include *oblatio*, the donation of a child to a monastery, a practice that may be as old as Christianity itself (Boswell 1998), and its subsequent incarnation, the ritualized practice of leaving children on the steps of a church.

But the iconic "foundling wheel" is perhaps the most widespread example of the institutionalized effacement of identity. This contraption allowed an infant to be committed to an orphanage while preserving the anonymity of its natal kin and, especially, its mother—sometimes in contravention of their desire to retain or remain known to the child.[4] Economically underwritten and ideologically sanctioned by both state and religious authorities (especially the Catholic Church), foundling wheels date from the thirteenth century and functioned in Europe until well into the nineteenth century. In Latin America and even in Europe, they continued to operate in some places into the twentieth century. At the height of their usage in the eighteenth and nineteenth centuries, abandonment in some European cities reached astonishing proportions: in Madrid, Dublin, and Warsaw, up to one-fifth of newborns were consigned to foundling homes; in Milan and Florence, as many as one-third; in Vienna, one-half. Such statistics led historian David Kertzer (1994) to characterize this as the era of "mass abandonment," which characterized Catholic Europe in general. Diverse Latin American societies have exhibited parallel patterns, although in that region extra-institutional forms of child abandonment and circulation predominated.

Indeed, in some societies, informal practices of fosterage, adoption, and other procedures by which children moved across households and kin groups were equally if not more common, though they may be less visible and harder to trace. Their outcome—the effacement of natal, including maternal, identity and its substitution for alternative identities and kinships—was often the same. In other instances, the logic of accretion rather than substitution prevailed. In poor communities in Brazil, in which circulating children are often said to have more than one mother, social practice does not efface maternal identity so much as pluralize it. The question of who is the mother implicates not only biological ties but also relations of affect, responsibility, and support. It may also be deeply contested and reflect the unequal access to power of different claimants—poor biological mothers and wealthy foreign adoptive ones, for example (Fonseca 2002).

In the face of such ubiquitous, persistent, and deeply institutionalized social practices, the principle of maternal certainty, which attributes to a fleeting moment of physical propinquity a permanent, indelible, unambiguous, and exclusive association between two individuals, seems a powerful legal fiction. "Mater semper certa est" is more normative dogma than a descriptor of a social, much less a natural, reality. The point is not just that maternity is historically more ambiguous than we might assume but that, in the face of this evidence, we can better appreciate the extent to which the doctrine of maternal certainty is a social and legal construct.

REINVENTING PATERNITY

If the legal fictions that operate in the construction of maternity are largely unacknowledged, those that structure juridical understandings of paternity have in contrast frequently been acknowledged and critiqued. For example, the legal effacement of paternity outside marriage—the notion that the extramarital child is a *filius nullius* who has no father—is often cited as a classic legal fiction, insofar as it forecloses the very existence of an individual who, while perhaps unknowable, is at least known to exist.[5] So, too, is the principle of paternal certainty in marriage. Sometimes, useful fictions became patent absurdities; skeptical jurists were fond of citing the so-called four seas doctrine of seventeenth-century English common law, a particularly rigorous expression of the presumption of marital legitimacy. The doctrine held that if a husband was located within the four seas of England at the time of his wife's conception, he was legally the father of her child.[6] Whereas historical practices reveal maternal certainty to be more normative dogma than social or natural fact, legal fictions have a different function in the case of paternity. Rather than *undermining* the principle of paternal uncertainty, legal fictions are deliberately generated in response to uncertainty. That is, the fictions written into the law of paternity are understood as a necessary, if occasionally awkward, strategy for contending with the immutable verities of nature.

But once again, if maternity has under certain historical conditions been decidedly less certain, more ambiguous, and more plural than the trope of certainty allows, the historical record likewise reveals a disconnect between tropes of uncertainty and social practices surrounding paternity. Put simply, paternity is more "certain" and "knowable" than the trope of uncertainty permits. This is so insofar as societies have always had clear, authoritative, and enduring social and legal rules for determining paternity. The presumption of marital legitimacy is of course one such rule—for, "fictitious" or not, it definitively and unambiguously identifies a father for a particular subgroup of children, those born of a married mother.

And even in the absence of marriage, in diverse societies, from medieval England to ancien régime France to early nineteenth-century Chile, paternity could be and was established, for social and legal purposes, through the sorts of empirical evidence that established myriad other questions of fact. Thus, local hearsay (the testimony of the priest, the servant, the neighbor), social acts of recognition on the part of the father (paying the midwife, a gift to the baby), social intimacy or cohabitation with the mother, or her own declaration about the identity of the father might all prove a man's paternity (Desan 2006; Fuchs 2008; Helmholz 1977; Milanich 2009). The notion of the essential, intrinsic, and inevitable unknowability of paternal identity obscures the extent to which, according to rules that varied cross-culturally and over time, filial relationships could be and were made perfectly legible by recourse to social facts. This was true for the purposes of familial and community knowledge, as it was true for legal procedure. One French jurist, writing in the years before the Revolution, articulated the social logic of paternal identification, observing: "Each [child] needs a father. . . . We are initiated enough into the mysteries of nature to know that it [paternity] belongs exclusively to one person." He then went on to cite "the interest of both the public and the child" in identifying "a father who will take care of his upbringing" in his defense of judicial methods for doing so (Desan 2006, 183).

Of course, not all socio-legal orders permitted such methods of paternal verification. Some very deliberately prohibited it—and, in so doing, again revealed the social and legal ordering of "uncertainty" as well as its historical reinventions. The obvious example is postrevolutionary France under the Napoleonic Code, which categorically prohibited the judicial investigation of fathers' identities in cases of extramarital children. If ancien régime jurists believed fatherhood was a verifiable relationship, postrevolutionary ones asserted just the opposite, that "paternity is as mysterious as the source of the Nile" (Fuchs 2008, 2). This natural fact in turn justified prohibiting its legal investigation. The Napoleonic Code's abolition of paternity suits, a measure that was adopted in countries across Europe and Latin America that modeled their civil law on the French code, signaled a profound transformation in the history of paternity, sexuality, and family. Although the meanings and consequences of this legal reform varied across societies, everywhere it heralded tectonic shifts in the relationship between privacy and the public good; the individual and the community; men's, women's, and children's rights; and the state and society (Desan 2006; Fuchs 2008; Hull 1997; Milanich 2009).

Accepting jurists' own rationale for this prohibition—that paternity could not be proven because it was naturally unknowable—obscures the extent to which legal ordering made it so. In fact, the notion of paternal uncertainty reflected a distinctly teleological logic. Circumstantial evidence such as witness testimony, which was deemed unproblematic and admissible in other kinds of disputes, was barred from paternity investigations because paternal identity was declared a priori unknowable. As Chilean jurists noted, paternity was a "mystery of nature" that "cannot be proven through the inductive facts that the judicial method generates," in contrast to maternity, which "involves a material fact, visible, subject to the domination of anyone's sense . . . that is, the birth" (Milanich 2009, 54). The reasoning that placed paternity outside of the law was thus circular: normal legal procedures for verifying disputed empirical facts were inadmissible because paternity was deemed unknowable, and paternity was unknowable because legal procedures could not be brought to bear in its proof.

In short, the trope of paternal uncertainty was less the reflection of a biological truth than a normative standpoint regarding the law's posture toward transgressive sexual relationships. "Will the law penetrate into the shadows of these clandestine connections and confer on them the right to constitute . . . the presumption of paternity, which is the privilege of matrimony?" asked the author of the Chilean Civil Code of 1855 (Milanich 2009, 64). He concluded that although paternity investigations had long been a routine procedure in Chilean law, they should now be prohibited. Meanwhile, even as certain legal regimes placed paternity outside of law's purview, they often actively sought to bring unwed maternity under public scrutiny. Laws criminalizing "hidden pregnancy," in which unwed mothers were required to reveal their condition lest they later be suspected of infanticide, are a case in point. Here, maternity was knowable not least because law required that it be made known.[7]

Finally, it bears emphasis that the alleged unknowability of paternity is strategically functional in certain social orders. In societies with strong norms of racial and class endogamy but widespread practices of exogamous coupling, such as many Latin American societies historically, the obfuscation of legal paternity protected patriarchal prerogatives as well as patrimonial interests. Meanwhile, as Isabel Hull (1997) has provocatively argued with regard to German jurisdictions that adopted the French civil code's prohibition of paternity investigation, the discourse of "uncertainty" was actually a stand-in for privacy. In deeming paternity unknowable, Hull argues, civil law carved out a new sphere of (male) privacy.

Yet another example of the functionality of unknowability is embodied in *partus sequitur ventrem*, the organizing principle of property and personhood in Atlantic slave societies. The principle, which holds that the child's status as free or enslaved follows that of the mother, renders moot the question of the paternal identity of the children of slave mothers. The quiet "obscurity" of slave children's paternity was, of course, a strategic fiction of slave-holding households. The oft-quoted Mary Chesnut, who kept a diary in South Carolina during the Civil War, observed, "This is only what I see: like the patriarchs of old, our men live all in one house with their wives & their concubines, and the Mulattos one sees in every family exactly resemble the white children—and every lady tells you who is the father of all the Mulatto children in everybody's household, but those in her own, she seems to think drop from the clouds or pretends so to think" (quoted in Edwards 2000, 62).

Such anecdotal evidence demonstrates how the idea of paternal uncertainty is historical in the sense that it changes over time. It further suggests how this idea is bound up not only with "private" relations of gender and generation, family and sexuality, but also, simultaneously, with class and racial orders. Indeed, in modern societies notions of paternal uncertainty help to construct the changing contours of what constitutes "public" and "private" in the first place.

One might justifiably conclude that in diverse sociocultural and juridical traditions, filiation is an arena in which law is never quite aligned with the natural facts. Through powerful sleights of social and legal alchemy, biological relationships are effaced and fictive ones take on legal incontrovertibility. Thus, the presumption of marital paternity makes possibly unrelated children the progeny of the father, while the erasure of illegitimate paternity makes biological offspring into *filius nullius*, the "children of nobody." Meanwhile, the trope of maternal certainty treats biological and socio-legal status of the mother as unambiguous and coterminous, when in fact they may be neither. We might add to this list of "legal fictions" certain forms of adoption and surrogacy, which make biological "strangers" into social and legal kin even as they "de-kin" biological mothers from their offspring.[8]

And yet the very notion of legal fictions implies the existence of corresponding, and opposing, natural truths; it implies that law normally reflects, or should reflect, natural orderings, and that the (presumably exceptional) cases when it does not are therefore "fictitious." It implies, in short, that there are natural relationships that exist ontologically prior to social and legal ordering, an idea that is itself deeply wedded to Euro-American constructs of kinship that follow a biogenetic logic.

SCIENCE IN THE TWENTIETH CENTURY: AMBIGUITIES RESOLVED OR REINSCRIBED?

The successive reinventions of maternity and paternity in the nineteenth century were made even more complex in the twentieth, as technoscientific developments created new ways of understanding relationships and identities. The history of biological parentage testing provides a perspective on these reinventions. Although DNA fingerprinting techniques, considered the first truly definitive method for identifying biological parentage, emerged only in the 1980s, the search for a hereditary marker of descent dates back to the first two decades of the twentieth century. Originating in hereditarian paradigms, race science, and research into techniques for establishing individual identity, the emerging science of parentage investigation sought to identify somatic or chemical traits passed from parent to child according to immutable and predictable laws of heredity. Though people had long been aware of the physical similarities between parents and children, the basic premise of parentage science was a novel one: that scientists might decipher the rules of inheritance governing specific physical features in order to unambiguously reveal the relationship between an individual and his or her progenitor(s). In their search for usable traits, scientists explored fingerprinting and biometrics; cataloged ear conformation and nose shape; studied eye, hair, and skin color; mapped dental structures; and scrutinized myriad other features of the body.

Ultimately, the most successful of these techniques was based on the analysis of blood types. The ABO blood groups were discovered in 1901, and a decade later, research revealed that blood types were passed from parents to children according to the laws of Mendelian genetics. Although knowledge of blood types did not make it possible to positively identify a progenitor, it was possible to predict which combinations of parental blood types could give rise to which types in the offspring and thus to exclude "impossible" combinations. Such techniques of parentage testing could be applied to both maternal and paternal identity, but in keeping with the idea that maternity was already certain and obvious, the social and legal uses of these tests usually involved the identification of fathers.

In a sense, scientific techniques made, or sought to make, paternity more like maternity, for whether based on blood or biometrics, biological testing rendered paternity an observable, physical condition. We are accustomed to thinking of maternity as an embodied identity, exemplified by mothers' gestating, birthing, lactating bodies. As paternity was mapped onto the physical body, it too became a bodily identity. To be sure, representations of the paternal body were very different; most obviously, they did not dwell on the body's reproductive organs or generative functions. Scientists instead pursued proof of paternity in the fingerprint, the skull, the earlobe, the soles of the feet. Where nineteenth-century jurists had once characterized birth, and by extension maternity, as "a material fact, visible, subject to the domination of . . . [the] senses" (Milanich 2009, 54), twentieth-century science pursued techniques that might make paternity an analogously "material, visible" fact. And whereas those jurists once referred to paternal identity as "veiled" or "shrouded," scientific tests quite literally stripped the male body of this protective mantle. In São Paulo, Brazil, beginning in the late 1920s, the first medico-legal institute in the Americas to perform biological paternity tests subjected putative fathers to full physiognomic and biometric examinations. In seeking proof of paternal identity, inspectors described more than a dozen characteristics of subjects' bodies and recorded scars, moles, and other unusual or distinguishing somatic traits.[9]

Scientists did not solve the "problem" of paternity in the first decades of the twentieth century, but the promising pace of developments in those years suggested that, in the not too distant future, they would. "Deep down in those minute eddies of the human blood, Nature has placed the hallmark of every man's heredity. In his blood cells is bound up the unmistakable record of his fatherhood," remarked the *Atlanta Constitution* (1921). "'Blood will tell' becomes an axiomatic truth of science along with the propositions of Euclid."[10]

During this period, the idea that science might identify biological paternity with the axiomatic precision of Euclidean geometry gained increasing credence not just among scientists but also among jurists as well as the lay public in diverse societies in Europe, Latin America, and North America. By the mid-1920s, courts in Germany, Austria, and Brazil began accepting scientific evidence, particularly blood group analysis, in cases of disputed paternity. By the 1930s, parentage testing found widening, if uneven and often controversial, application in U.S. courts. Meanwhile, it gained a growing presence in popular imaginaries, as global publics became acquainted with the new scientific techniques through avid reporting in the press.[11]

For observers, science promised to deliver paternity from the vexing obscurity in which nature had enveloped it and to reveal, for the first time in human history, the incontrovertible truth of filial relationships, identity, and descent. "One might well believe, without being guilty of excessive optimism, that the solution to a problem that seemed swathed in impenetrable shadows has today been achieved," noted an Uruguayan jurist. "Legal medicine has in effect erased the sentence 'pater semper incertus,' which, from Roman law forward, weighed on justice like a dogma of nature" (Carnelli 1938, 18). In a sequence that will be familiar to ART observers, these developments in turn raised the prospect—at once wondrous and disturbing—that in remaking the fundamental natural facts of reproduction, these powerful new scientific technologies would herald a transformation of social and sexual relations. "With . . . a scientifically accurate determination of paternity," observed the *Baltimore Sun* (1922), "a world of misery, suspicion, lies and faithlessness would be abolished from the earth."

But whose misery? Whose suspicion and lies? Whose rights and interests, in other words, would these developments serve—those of men or women? How would the ability to know paternal identity affect sexual morality and marriage? Would it strengthen the family or weaken it? And what about the impact on children's well-being? These were questions scientists, jurists, and laypeople would contemplate in the half century before DNA. The answers depended on when, and especially where, they were contemplated.

But if the consequences of paternity testing varied widely, one consistent pattern emerges across contexts: even as scientists continued to develop ever more powerful techniques for discerning parentage, "Euclidean certainty" would prove elusive indeed. This was due not to the shortcomings of science itself (although it was not until the DNA revolution of the 1980s that scientists could claim to have reached such precision in fixing identity). Rather, the enduring ambiguities and tensions surrounding definitions of paternity reflected the fact that the "problem" of paternity was not, as first jurists and later scientists contended, the problem of biological veracity at all. "Uncertainty" instead stemmed from the existence of competing and historically changing social, legal, and biological definitions of paternity.

Indeed, scientific testing arguably created new kinds of ambiguity in definitions of parentage. For one, even as paternity was mapped onto the body in an effort to make it a "visible, material fact," for lay observers, such techniques also made it more opaque. This was because the new techniques of identity—whether biometric measurement, fingerprint examination, or chemical analysis—were legible only to experts. They also competed with alternative modes of assessment. Once upon a time, physical resemblance had been the layperson's paternity test. In many societies, the vernacular assessment of paternity, and of parentage generally, was considered the special ken of older female relatives and community members who were charged with ascertaining physical resemblance and thereby kinship (Thomas 2003, 130; Shabana 2012).

Other modes of discerning parentage included maternal "feeling" or "hunch." In a notorious hospital baby-swapping case in Chicago in 1930, public health officials assembled a phalanx of eleven scientific experts to examine the infants for clues as to their identities. But neither the parents nor the public were entirely convinced by the experts' conclusions (which, in any event, contradicted one another). One newspaper invoked "the oldest and, as some say, the surest of knowledge, namely instinct. Though it has [as] yet received no scientific test, it has been stated often that 'a mother will unerringly know her own child,' that the call of blood is irresistible between a woman and the infant she has brought into the world" (*New York Herald Tribune* 1930). Or, as the exasperated father of one of the babies declared, "I'm sick of this science business. . . . My wife knows it's our baby and I guess a mother's instinct is as good as the experts" (*Chicago Tribune* 1930).

Beyond female vernacular knowledge or maternal instinct, other kinds of expert knowledge likewise competed with scientific assessments. In American and British courts in the first two decades of the twentieth century, sculptors and other artists were occasionally called upon in paternity suits to assess the physical resemblance between progeny and alleged progenitor (Newboldt 1923–24, 39).[12] Scientific modes of defining maternity and paternity did not, then, immediately displace alternative techniques; diverse ways of ascertaining identity coexisted, often uncomfortably, beside one another. Only gradually and unevenly would methods and experts deemed scientific gain authority as the exclusive arbiters of what counted as biological parenthood.

In part this was because scientific analysis had to compete with alternative methods and sources of authority. But it was also because science itself remained unclear about its object of investigation. The emergence of scientific methods of parentage testing did not herald a clear or categorical distinction between the natural and the social; indeed, scientific modes only made more obvious the persistent slippage between biological and socio-juridical constructions of filial relationships. In his celebrated *Commentaries on the Laws of England*, William Blackstone (1765–69, book 1, chap. 16) referred to "the most universal relations in nature . . . being that between parent and child," before continuing, "children are of two sorts; legitimate and spurious." The implication is that these two "sorts" of progeny, legitimate and illegitimate, are as "universal" and "natural" as the fact of reproduction itself.

That an eighteenth-century jurist might equate juridical and natural categories is not surprising. More surprising are the twentieth-century scientific treatises on parentage testing that routinely reproduced the same kind of slippage, invoking social and legal categories as shorthand for biological relationships. Explanations of the hereditary rules of blood type, for example, expressed this information not just in terms of scientifically compatible/incompatible types or biologically possible/impossible combinations of parents and progeny but also in terms of the natal status that these combinations implied. Typical is a chart in a 1931 Brazilian medical treatise that summarized ABO inheritance. The chart is entitled "Legitimate and Illegitimate Filiation" (Torres 1931, 212). That is, biological relationships were expressed through a socio-juridical vocabulary—significantly, not just by jurists but by scientists as well, a pattern that continued at least into the late 1940s.

Ultimately, scientific testing produced no immediate consensus about what paternity or parentage was or how to establish them. Scientific techniques, definitions, and authorities were hardly undisputed arbiters of kinship and identity, and scientists themselves continued to use socio-juridical referents to express biological concepts. By introducing new ways of understanding paternity, parentage science destabilized older social and legal constructions but did not entirely displace them. The advent of DNA testing made this truer than ever; even as it ostensibly solved the "problem" of paternal uncertainty, it simultaneously created new moral, ethical, and legal ambiguities. This is perhaps because, rather than simply conferring a method to reveal preexisting identities, paternity testing, like ARTs, ultimately defined identity in new ways. In other words, rather than heralding a watershed moment of ambiguity resolved, truth revealed, and certainty conferred, as is frequently asserted, the emergence of biological parentage testing in the twentieth century can be seen as the latest chapter in a much longer historical narrative.

CONCLUSION

Ultimately, the point here is not that we must reverse the signs by asserting that maternity is actually uncertain and paternity certain. Rather, it is that invoking the contrasting status of certainty in male and female procreation through recourse to natural facts obscures the decisive social and legal—indeed ideological and political—work at stake in these characterizations. It obfuscates the ways in which parentage and identity are deliberately rendered knowable or unknowable and how in particular contexts (un)knowability may serve partisan interests—those of mothers or fathers; those of children or adults; those of biological, adoptive, or surrogate parents; as well as those of specific groups within particular class or racial orders.

The naturalization of (un)knowability forecloses the critical historical question of when and under what circumstances paternity or maternity are said to be certain or uncertain, knowable or unknowable, biological or social, and the consequences of these assertions in particular social contexts. It obscures profound historical transformations, such as the redefinition of paternity, family, sexuality, and society as a result of legal reforms in the nineteenth century and scientific developments in the twentieth. In short, it forecloses an appreciation for the successive historical reinventions of maternity and paternity, filiation and parentage, descent and identity, of which paternity testing and ARTs are merely the latest examples.

NOTES

1. Indeed, these ideas may resonate in other, "non-Western" cultural and historical contexts as well, although this essay does not take up this question.
2. This quote is from a nineteenth-century French lawyer; jurists from Germany to Chile made similar observations, for reasons we will see here.
3. The literature on abandonment, particularly for Europe, is enormous. Representative works include Boswell (1998), Fuchs (1984), Kertzer (1994), MacClure (1981), and Sherwood (1988). For Latin America, see, among others, Marcílio (1998) and Venâncio (1999). Diverse forms of child circulation also have been ubiquitous in Latin America (see, for example, Fonseca 1995; Milanich 2004).
4. Examples of children coercively removed from their (usually unmarried) mothers or whose identities were deliberately erased by foundling home authorities may be found in Italy, Chile, and likely elsewhere (Kertzer 1994; Milanich 2009).
5. *Filius nullius* was a principle of Roman law later absorbed into English common law as well as into civil legal traditions.
6. The four seas principle was perhaps most recently quoted by a California court, in 1989 (Meyer 2006).
7. Laws criminalizing the concealment of either pregnancy or birth and requiring either mothers or midwives to reveal an expectant mother's condition operated at

various times in Germany, France, parts of Italy, England, Scotland, and no doubt elsewhere.

8. On adoption, see Fonseca (2011) and Bos (present volume).

9. Examples may be found in the medico-legal examinations performed by the Instituto Oscar Freire of the Universidade de São Paulo. Records of such exams are found in bound volumes housed at the institute, *Examenes e pareceres* (1920s–1950s). By the 1960s, corporal examinations had mostly ceased, and paternity tests primarily consisted of blood group analysis.

10. Also published in the *San Francisco Chronicle*, May 1, 1921: SM6.

11. This discussion is derived from my book (in progress), *Family Matters: Testing Paternity in the Twentieth Century* (Cambridge, MA: Harvard University Press, 2018).

12. See also "Evidence of Paternity," *The Lancet*, October 13, 1923: 840; "Likeness Not Proof of Paternity, Says Artist," *San Francisco Chronicle*, June 11, 1921: 4; "Art and Science to Fix Parentage of Boy in Court," *San Francisco Chronicle*, May 21, 1921: 6.

REFERENCES

Allen, Ann Taylor. 1999. "Feminism, Social Science, and the Meanings of Modernity: The Debate on the Origin of the Family in Europe and the United States, 1860–1914." *American Historical Review* 104, no. 4: 1085–113.

Atlanta Constitution. 1921 (April 24). "How the Blood Tests Made Love Test": G4.

Baltimore Sun. 1922 (October 29). "Has Science Found Answer to Question of Parentage?": 68.

Blackstone, William. 1765–69. *Commentaries on the Laws of England.* http://avalon.law.yale.edu/subject_menus/blackstone.asp#intro.

Boswell, John. 1998. *The Kindness of Strangers: The Abandonment of Children in Western Europe from Late Antiquity to the Renaissance.* Chicago: University of Chicago Press.

Carnelli, Lorenzo. 1938. *Investigación técnica de la paternidad.* Buenos Aires: Antologia Jurídica.

Chicago Tribune. 1930 (July 25). "Bamberger Flees with 'Watkins' Baby": 1, 8.

Coward, Rosalind. 1983. *Patriarchal Precedents: Sexuality and Social Relations.* London: Routledge & Kegan Paul.

Delaney, Carol. 1986. "The Meaning of Paternity and the Virgin Birth Debate." *Man* 21: 494–513.

de Parseval, Geneviève Delaisi, and Chantal Collard. 2007. "La gestation pour autrui: Un bricolage des représentations de la paternité et de la maternité euro-américaines. *L'Homme* 183: 25–53.

Desan, Suzanne. 2006. *The Family on Trial in Revolutionary France.* Berkeley: University of California Press.

Edwards, Laura. 2000. *Scarlett Doesn't Live Here Anymore: Southern Women in the Civil War Era.* Urbana: University of Illinois Press.

Fonseca, Claudia. 1995. *Caminhos da adoção.* São Paulo: Cortez Editora.

——. "The De-Kinning of Birthmothers: Reflections on Maternity and Being Human." *Vibrant* 8, no. 2: 307–38.

——. 2002. "Inequality Near and Far: Adoption as Seen from the Brazilian Favelas." *Law & Society Review* 36, no. 2: 397–432.

Fuchs, Rachel G. 1984. *Abandoned Children: Foundlings and Child Welfare in Nineteenth-Century France.* Albany: State University of New York Press.

——. 2008. *Contested Paternity: Constructing Families in Modern France.* Baltimore: Johns Hopkins University Press.

Gager, Kristin Elizabeth. 1996. Blood Ties and Fictive Ties: Adoption and Family Life in Early Modern France. Princeton, NJ: Princeton University Press.

Ginsburg, Faye D., and Rayna Rapp. 1995. *Conceiving the New World Order: The Global Politics of Reproduction.* Berkeley: University of California Press

Helmholz, Richard. 1977. "Support Orders, Church Courts, and the Rule of Filius Nullius: A Reassessment of the Common Law." *Virginia Law Review* 63: 431–48.

Hull, Isabel V. 1997. *Sexuality, State, and Civil Society in Germany, 1700–1815.* Ithaca, NY: Cornell University Press.

Inhorn, Marcia C., and Daphna Birenbaum-Carmeli. 2008. "Assisted Reproductive Technologies and Culture Change." *Annual Review of Anthropology* 37, no. 1: 177–96.

Kertzer, David I. 1994. *Sacrificed for Honor: Italian Infant Abandonment and the Politics of Reproductive Control.* Boston: Beacon Press.

MacClure, Ruth K. 1981. *Coram's Children: The London Foundling Hospital in the Eighteenth Century.* New Haven, CT: Yale University Press.

Marcílio, Maria Luiza. 1998. *História social da criança abandonada.* São Paulo: Hucitec.

Meyer, David D. 2006. "Parenthood in a Time of Transition: Tensions Between Legal, Biological, and Social Conceptions of Parenthood." *American Journal of Comparative Law* 54: 125–44.

Milanich, Nara. 2004. "The Casa de Huérfanos and Child Circulation in Late-Nineteenth-Century Chile." *Journal of Social History* 38, no. 2: 311–40.

——. 2009. *Children of Fate: Childhood, Class, and the State in Chile, 1850–1930.* Durham, NC: Duke University Press.

Newboldt, Sir Frances. 1923–24. "Evidence of Resemblance in Paternity Cases." *Transactions of the Medico-Legal Society* 18, no. 31: 31–44.

New York Herald Tribune. 1930 (August 17). "Science May Turn to 'Mother Instinct' in Puzzle to Establish Parentage in Baffling Cases": C2.

O'Brien, Mary. 1981. *The Politics of Reproduction.* London: Routledge & Kegan Paul.

Sá, Isabel dos Guimarães. 1995. *A circulação de crianças na Europa do Sul: O caso dos expostos do Porto no século XVIII.* Lisbon: Fundação Calouste Gulbenkian.

Satz, Debra. 2007. "Remaking Families: A Review Essay." *Signs: Journal of Women in Culture and Society* 32, no. 2: 523–38.

Schneider, David Murray. 1984. *A Critique of the Study of Kinship.* Ann Arbor: University of Michigan Press.

Shabana, Ayman. 2012. "Paternity Between Law and Biology: The Reconstruction of the Islamic Law of Paternity in the Wake of DNA Testing." *Zygon* 47, no. 1: 214–39.

Shapiro, E. Donald, Stewart Reifler, and Claudia L. Psome. 1992. "DNA Paternity Test: Legislating the Future Paternity Action." *Journal of Law and Health* 7, no. 1: 1–47.

Shaw, M. W. 1983. "Paternity Determination: 1921 to 1983 and Beyond." *Journal of the American Medical Association* 250: 2536–37.

Sherwood, Joan. 1988. *Poverty in Eighteenth-Century Spain: The Women and Children of the Inclusa*. Toronto: University of Toronto Press.

Shore, Cris, R. G. Abrahams, Jane F. Collier, Carol Delaney, Robin Fox, Ronald Frankenberg, Helen S. Lambert et al. 1992. "Virgin Births and Sterile Debates: Anthropology and the New Reproductive Technologies." *Current Anthropology* 33, no. 3: 295–314.

Stolzenberg, Nomi Maya. 2007. "Anti-Anxiety Law: Winnicott and the Legal Fiction of Paternity." *American Imago* 64, no. 3: 339–79.

Strathern, Marilyn. 1992. *After Nature: English Kinship in the Late Twentieth Century*. New York: Cambridge University Press.

Stumpf, Andrea E. 1986. "Redefining Mother: A Legal Matrix for New Reproductive Technologies." *Yale Law Journal* 96: 187–208.

Sussman, George D. 1982. *Selling Mother's Milk: The Wet-Nursing Business in France, 1715–1914*. Urbana: University of Illinois Press.

Thomas, Lynn M. 2003. *Politics of the Womb: Women, Reproduction, and the State in Kenya*. Berkeley: University of California Press.

Thompson, Charis. 2005. *Making Parents: The Ontological Choreography of Reproductive Technologies*. Cambridge, MA: MIT Press.

Torres, Octavio. 1931. "Estudo geral sobre os grupos sanguineos." *Archivos Brasileiros de Medicina* 21: 189–214.

Venâncio, Renato Pinto. 1999. Famílias abandonadas: Assistência à criança de camadas populares no Rio de Janeiro e em Salvador, séculos XVIII e XIX. Campinas: Papirus Editora.

2

ASSISTED REPRODUCTIVE TECHNOLOGIES AND THE BIOLOGICAL BOTTOM LINE

LINDA G. KAHN AND WENDY CHAVKIN

Once upon a time, the ability to have a child was limited by biology: the ability of aspiring parents to produce viable gametes and to effectively combine those gametes to conceive an embryo, and of the intended mother to carry a fetus to term. With the emergence of increasingly sophisticated assisted reproductive technologies (ARTs) over the past century, the ability to have a child is now limited only by the availability of financial, medical, and human resources necessary to assemble all of the requisite parts: maternal DNA, paternal DNA, egg, and incubating maternal body. Nowadays, producing a child can involve half a dozen people or more—commissioning parents, egg and sperm providers, surrogate, and even a cytoplasm donor, not to mention medical personnel and agents for the various parts that may be needed to complete the act. The situation is replete with contradictions, as the facts of human biology are simultaneously heralded and dismissed by those who avail themselves of ARTs. For example, would-be parents select gamete donors based on qualities that may or may not be heritable, yet they bargain-shop for surrogates abroad, when we now know that the "gestational environment" can be as determinative of a child's future health as his or her genes.

In this chapter, we will discuss the convergence of social and demographic trends that have contributed to a growing demand for ARTs, along with improvements in travel, communications, and scientific know-how that have increased the supply of both raw materials and medical expertise needed to meet that demand. We will explore how these dynamics have played out in a globalized marketplace characterized by discordant regulatory and legal systems and disparities of wealth, race, and gender. Finally, we will highlight the medical and public health consequences—known and unknown—of this radical reconception of the biology of conception.

A BRIEF HISTORY OF ASSISTED REPRODUCTIVE TECHNOLOGIES

Although many date the beginning of ART to the birth of the first "test-tube baby," Louise Brown, in England in 1978 (Steptoe and Edwards 1978), the earliest documented case of medically assisted reproduction occurred nearly a century prior. In 1884, a wealthy Quaker couple unable to conceive a child sought the advice of the respected Philadelphia doctor William Pancoast, who discovered, upon examination, that the wife was healthy but the husband's ejaculate contained no sperm. Without telling the couple, under the pretense of a follow-up visit, he chloroformed the woman and injected her uterus with a syringe full of fresh semen that had been provided by one of the medical students observing the procedure. After the woman was confirmed to be pregnant, the husband was told; overjoyed, he agreed to keep the secret from his wife, who delivered a healthy baby boy (Hard 1909).

Dr. Pancoast's successful experiment was not revealed until a quarter century later (Hard 1909). In the decades that followed, third-party insemination using fresh semen provided by doctors and medical students became an increasingly common, if still clandestine, means of treating male-factor infertility of married couples (Guttmacher 1962). Meanwhile, as the dairy cattle industry pressed for innovation in the freezing of bovine semen, because shipping a frozen sample across the country was far less costly than shipping a stud bull, researchers began to experiment with human samples as well (Polge, Smith, and Parkes 1949; Sherman 1964). In 1953, the first successful human pregnancies were achieved using frozen semen (Bunge and Sherman 1954). The establishment of semen banks soon followed and the secrecy and stigma around artificial insemination using third-party semen gradually lifted, aided in the United States by the 1973 Uniform Parentage Act, which conferred legitimate paternity on the non-sperm-providing husbands of women who gave birth via third-party insemination (National Conference of Commissioners on Uniform State Laws 2000).

While third-party semen provided a work-around solution for male-factor infertility, it was not until the development of in vitro fertilization (IVF) in 1978 that any help was available to couples suffering female-factor infertility. Via IVF, women with certain tubal or ovarian problems or advanced age could be helped to conceive. In IVF, the woman has her ovaries stimulated to produce multiple eggs in a given cycle, which are then extracted through a surgical procedure and combined with semen in a petri dish, where conception occurs. Because the embryo is grown in a laboratory for several days prior to implantation in the woman's uterus, IVF provides an opportunity to perform pre-implantation genetic diagnosis (PGD), which is useful when a couple is at high risk of passing on a genetic disease. By 2012, five million babies had been born worldwide using IVF (ESHRE 2012).

Meanwhile, in 1992, a technique called intracytoplasmic sperm injection (ICSI) was developed that provided a means for men with low sperm count or poor semen quality to father genetically related offspring (Palermo et al. 1992). In ICSI, which is always combined with IVF, a single sperm, sperm head, or nucleus, retrieved either from the man's semen or surgically if he is unable to ejaculate, is inserted directly into the cytoplasm of a mature egg. ICSI has been widely adopted among groups that prohibit the use of third-party semen, such as Sunni Muslims (Inhorn 2014).

For IVF to successfully enable a woman to give birth to a genetically related child, she needs to be able to produce viable eggs and carry a pregnancy to term, neither of which is always possible, especially in cases of advanced maternal age. Because oocyte quality declines with maternal age, a third-party egg business has sprung up. A supplier ("egg donor" in common parlance) has her ovaries stimulated in sync with the commissioning woman so that her eggs may be retrieved, fertilized, grown into embryos, and then implanted into the recipient in a carefully choreographed operation. Embryos also may be frozen for transport or stored for future use. In cases where a woman cannot carry a fetus to term, either because of advanced age, hysterectomy, or some other medical problem, a surrogate may be commissioned to receive fresh or frozen embryos conceived either with the intended mother's eggs or those of a third-party supplier. Surrogates and egg providers also may be hired by gay couples or single men seeking biologically related children.

In the popular press, women are now being encouraged to harvest their eggs during their reproductive prime and store them for future use (Slaughter 2012; Richards 2012). Although no longer considered experimental, egg freezing is not recommended by the medical establishment to circumvent reproductive aging (ASRM 2013a).

THE DEMAND FOR ASSISTED REPRODUCTIVE TECHNOLOGIES

The increase in technological interventions in reproduction has been fueled by an increase in demand resulting from momentous social and demographic transformations. Over the past two centuries, a historic shift has occurred in the heretofore relatively predictable pattern of human population growth. Beginning in nineteenth-century Europe, improvements in nutrition, sanitation, and medicine increased life expectancy and reduced child mortality, causing a spurt in population growth. Subsequently, however, a confluence of social, scientific, and economic forces led to improved educational and occupational opportunities for women, the development of effective family planning methods (including oral contraceptives, intrauterine devices, and legal abortion), and delayed marriage and childbearing, all of which resulted in a sudden and dramatic decline in fertility. Between 1960 and 2011 (the most recent data available), the total fertility rate, or average number of children a woman will bear in her lifetime, has dropped to near or below the "replacement" level at which births replace deaths, defined as approximately 2.1 births per woman, in every region of the world except sub-Saharan Africa (Searchinger et al. 2013).

One consequence of the delay in marriage and the increase in a woman's age at first birth is a shortened biological window in which to bear children prior to menopause. Advanced maternal age also is associated with a heightened incidence of miscarriage and chromosomal abnormalities as well as increased frequency of pregnancy complications, which put both the mother's and the baby's health at risk. Many women who find they have waited too long to try to conceive have turned to ARTs to help them achieve their reproductive goals. Single people and same-sex couples desiring parenthood also have contributed to the demand for ARTs.

CROSSING BORDERS TO MAKE BABIES

The availability of ART services and supplies varies across countries due to differences in pricing, medical norms, legal and regulatory decisions, and religious strictures. This has led to a robust international industry in "reproductive tourism." According to a 2010 study by the European Society of Human Reproduction and Embryology, an estimated 24,000 to 30,000 cycles of "cross-border reproductive care"—including IVF as well as artificial insemination—take place annually within Europe alone (Shenfield et al. 2010). Those seeking ARTs abroad report diverse motivations: restrictions on availability of products or services in their home country, limitations on who can gain access to available technologies, high cost, long wait times, desire for anonymous or identifiable gamete providers (commonly referred to as "donors," although in most cases the suppliers/providers are compensated; hence, the more accurate term would be "sellers"), shortage of gametes (particularly eggs), desire for PGD for sex or trait selection, and the perception that other countries provide higher-quality and/or more culturally sensitive care (Culley et al. 2011).

Laws dealing with gamete provision or purchase also vary widely across countries, creating trade and travel surpluses and deficits. In the United States, for example, rules governing the provision of sperm and oocytes are quite loose. Suppliers are allowed to remain anonymous and may be compensated—in the case of egg providers, quite liberally—ensuring a steady supply. Consequently, the United States is the world's largest supplier of semen, fulfilling the domestic demand and exporting to more than sixty other countries (Newton-Small 2012). By contrast, in many European countries and in Canada, suppliers are permitted minimal compensation, if any, and anonymity is prohibited, so future children may learn the identity of their genetic parents upon reaching the age of eighteen, a prospect that apparently deters many potential providers (Shukla et al. 2013). Seekers who face a gamete shortage at home, who want to avoid open-identity donation, or who come from places that prohibit gamete donation entirely, such as Sunni Muslim countries (Inhorn 2006) and Italy, or prohibit egg donation, such as Austria and Germany (see Palumbo, present volume), may travel to countries with looser restrictions to purchase gametes and/or receive treatment. Restrictions on who may obtain gametes also motivate consumers to cross borders. In France, for example, only infertile heterosexual couples married for at least two years can avail themselves of ARTs, and egg donation is strictly prohibited, so lesbian couples and single women typically cross the border into Belgium for artificial insemination, while heterosexual couples seeking third-party eggs travel to Greece or Spain (Pennings 2010; Rozée Gomez and de La Rochebrochard 2013).

In the case of surrogacy, which is restricted or completely outlawed in many nations, couples contract with women who may live hundreds or thousands of miles away to bear their children. Georgia, India, Russia, and Ukraine permit both altruistic and commercial surrogacy (in the former type, a surrogate may only be recompensed for reasonable expenses), whereas all forms of surrogacy are illegal in China, France, Germany, Hong Kong, Iceland, Italy, Japan, Saudi Arabia, and Serbia (Armour 2012). In Australia, Canada, and the United States, laws differ by state. In countries such as the United Kingdom, where altruistic surrogacy is legal but commercial surrogacy is not, there is a shortage of available surrogates; thus, couples seek surrogates in countries where commercial surrogacy is permitted, including the United States and countries in Eastern Europe (Gamble 2009). Since it legalized state-controlled surrogacy in 1996, Israel has permitted heterosexual couples to hire widowed or divorced women to become surrogates as long as they are of the same religion as, but not related to, the commissioning couple (Benshushan and Schenker 1997). Same-sex couples are excluded.

For years, India was a go-to destination for gay couples from Australia, Israel, and the United States (Rudrappa 2014). At its peak, surrogacy was estimated as a $400 million to $500 million annual business there (Stark 2012). Following the proposal of the Assisted Reproductive Technology (Regulation) Bill, 2014 (yet to be passed, as of this writing), which states that India will limit surrogacy to heterosexual commissioning parents who have been married for at least two years and have proof of the female partner's inability to carry a child, and which bans surrogacy for foreigners except for Indian nationals living overseas (Library of Congress 2015a), Thailand emerged as a new destination for single and gay parents, as it lacked laws specifically governing surrogacy (Library of Congress 2015b). Scandals involving dozens of gay Israeli couples whose children were rendered temporarily stateless while Thailand and Israel negotiated an agreement to allow Thai surrogates to relinquish their maternal rights (Lior 2014) and the widely publicized case of "Baby Gammy," a boy born to a Thai surrogate, whose parents refused to claim him because he had Down syndrome and instead took only his healthy twin sister, led Thailand to ban commercial surrogacy for foreigners. The market then shifted to Nepal, where surrogacy was unregulated until, following an exposé of the industry in which twenty-six babies commissioned by gay Israeli couples had to be airlifted out of the country following the devastating earthquake of 2015 (U.S. Embassy in Nepal 2017), it was deemed legal only for Nepali married couples.

Even if gamete donation, IVF, or surrogacy is legal in a particular jurisdiction, it may not be affordable for some would-be parents. In 2006, the cost of a cycle of IVF in the United States was more than double that in the United Kingdom or Australia, more than triple that in Japan, and nearly quadruple that in several Northern European countries (Connolly, Hoorens, and Chambers 2010). Currently, transnational surrogacy in India runs approximately $20,000, including travel and medical expenses, brokers' fees, and $6,000 compensation for the surrogate, compared with $80,000 to $100,000 in the United States (Vora 2013). In spite of potentially complicated issues around parentage and citizenship, it is still much cheaper to seek reproductive services abroad.

WHOSE RISK? WHOSE REWARD?

There has been much debate over whether the discrepancy in socioeconomic status and, frequently, race between consumers and purveyors of reproductive body parts represents an opportunity for economic advancement or exploitation. Many have written about the commodification of reproductive relationships and body parts and how inequities of power and need play out in the world of international gestational surrogacy. We add a review of the proven and potential medical and public health risks associated with the use of IVF, third-party gametes, and surrogates, issues too often ignored in the frenzy to make money and make babies.

IVF has been the best documented of the reproductive technologies, thanks to the availability of large national databases that include information on the frequency of different types of procedures and of perinatal outcomes. Thus, it has been known for a while that IVF is associated with increased rates of multiple gestation, preterm birth, congenital birth defects, and imprinting disorders as well as increased hospitalization costs. More recent studies have investigated the prevalence of autism, mental retardation, obesity, and cancer among IVF children, as we will discuss.

Twins and higher-order multiples are common outcomes of IVF, with the attendant risks of cesarean section, prematurity, low birth weight, infant death, mental retardation, cerebral palsy, and hearing and vision impairments. These problems strain both the parents of the affected children and society as a whole, psychologically as well as financially (Price 1988). From early on, physicians performing IVF have been encouraged to implant fewer embryos—ideally only a single embryo per cycle (ESHRE 2008)—but in the United States, market forces have perpetuated the practice of multiple implantations. Implanting more embryos increases clinics' rates of live births per cycle, a major marketing tool in the highly competitive world of fertility medicine.

In many countries where ARTs are publicly funded, policies have now been enacted that mandate single-embryo transfer for younger women but permit repeated cycles. Within the first eighteen months of adopting such regulations, Turkey experienced a statistically significant decrease in the incidence of multiples, prematurity, low birth weight, and a variety of neonatal morbidities (Guzoglu et al. 2012). In the United States, however, where ART is not always covered by health insurance, patients paying out of pocket want to minimize the number of costly IVF cycles they need to undergo, so doctors tend to implant multiple embryos. Even in women under age thirty-five, with a good prognosis, an average of two embryos were implanted per cycle in 2010, according to the most recent data from the U.S. Centers for Disease Control and Prevention. As a result, 43.4 percent of ART babies were twins, compared to only 3.3 percent of all newborns (Sunderam et al. 2013).

Even among singletons, adverse perinatal outcomes, including placenta previa, preterm birth, low birth weight, neonatal death, and congenital abnormalities, are more common among IVF babies than among those naturally conceived, although it is still not clear whether the increased risk of birth defects is due to the procedure or to the underlying infertility that necessitated it (Hansen et al. 2005). Beckwith-Wiedemann syndrome and Angelman syndrome, both imprinting disorders in which either the maternal or the paternal copy of a gene is mistakenly and irrevocably turned on or off from conception, leading to abnormal growth and development, are more prevalent among IVF children than among the general population (Manipalviratn, DeCherney, and Segars 2009). Although the increase in these rare diseases does not pose a public health risk, it indicates that IVF may be altering the epigenome—the complex of molecules that surrounds DNA, activating and inactivating genes—in ways that are still not fully understood. A population-based cohort study of all births in Western Australia from 1993 to 2008 found that ART singletons were three times more likely than their non-IVF counterparts to die within the first month of birth and were twice as likely to be born preterm or to have low birth weight. They also were more likely to be readmitted to the hospital in each of the first five years of life, resulting in 64 percent higher hospital costs over the first five years. Among multiples, the costs are "magnitudes" higher (Chambers et al. 2013).

Recently, researchers have turned their focus to the potential effect of IVF on long-term child health outcomes, including cardiometabolic indicators, cancer, and neurodevelopment. A series of follow-up studies comparing IVF-conceived children with age- and gender-matched children spontaneously conceived by subfertile parents found that from the age of eight to eighteen the IVF children had a higher percentage of body fat (Ceelen et al. 2007), higher systolic and diastolic blood pressure levels, and higher fasting glucose levels, putting them at risk for insulin resistance (Ceelen et al. 2008). Another study suggests that maternal ovarian hyperstimulation, part of the IVF protocol, may be causally associated with children's elevated blood pressure at age four (Seggers et al. 2014).

A record-linkage study of all children born in Britain between 1992 and 2008 found no increased risk of leukemia or malignant tumors of the brain and spinal cord, nerve tissue, eyes, kidneys, ovaries, or testicles over an average of 6.6 years of follow-up. Children conceived via IVF were at significantly elevated risk of cancer of the liver and muscle, but because these are rare, the number of excess cancer cases attributable to IVF was small (Williams et al. 2013).

A study linking all live births in Sweden from 1982 to 2007 to diagnoses in the National Patient Register of either autism spectrum disorder or mental retardation through 2009 found no increased risk of autism and a slightly elevated risk of mental retardation, though the latter disappeared when the analysis was restricted to singletons. Children conceived via fresh embryo IVF/ICSI, however, were 4.6 times as likely to have autism and 2.4 times as likely to be mentally retarded than children conceived via fresh embryo IVF without ICSI (Sandin et al. 2013).

In addition to being linked to autism and mental retardation, ICSI has been associated with an increased rate of major birth defects. This may be because ICSI requires stripping away the cumulus cells that normally surround the outer membrane of the egg and bind to the acrosome (the head of the sperm). These cumulus cells are believed to be nature's "quality control" mechanism, preventing weak or abnormal sperm from fertilizing an egg. In a study comparing five-year-old children conceived via IVF/ICSI with both non-IVF/ICSI children and naturally conceived children, congenital malformations, especially of the urogenital system, were more common among the ICSI children, particularly among boys (Bonduelle et al. 2005). Chromosomal abnormalities, especially of the sex chromosomes, and the genetic mutation associated with cystic fibrosis are increased in ICSI. These genetic defects are commonly found in infertile men, and bypassing natural selection through ICSI may put these men's children at risk of various disorders that otherwise would not have been passed to the next generation (ASRM 2008).

One way to avoid transmitting genes for devastating diseases such as cystic fibrosis is through PGD of the IVF embryo prior to implantation. In the most common technique, one or two cells are removed from the embryo after the third division, usually on the third day after conception, when there are at least six cells, and their genetic material is analyzed. The doctor can then select the most desirable embryo or embryos to implant (Sermon, Van Steirteghem, and Liebaers 2004). Although PGD has been in use for a quarter of a century, there have been no large studies to assess its long-term effects on children's health and development. One small randomized controlled trial of IVF children with and without PGD found an increased risk of adverse neurologic outcomes for those with PGD at birth and age two, but only in twins at age four (Middelburg et al. 2010; Middelburg et al. 2011; Schendelaar et al. 2013).

One of the newest frontiers in ART is cytoplasmic or mitochondrial transfer. Women with aberrant cytoplasmic structures that cause them to produce abnormal embryos (Fauser et al. 2014) or who have mutations in the DNA of their mitochondria that could cause devastating disease in their offspring may be candidates. In this procedure, a woman is stimulated to produce eggs alongside a "donor." Nuclei containing all of the genetic material from each of the donor's eggs are suctioned out and replaced with nuclei from the woman's eggs. These hybrid eggs are then fertilized via ICSI. The United Kingdom has legalized use of this technique, while the National Academy of Medicine has recommended that, at present, only carefully overseen clinical research be conducted in the United States (Vogel 2015; National Academies 2016).

Children are not the only ones who face potential adverse health outcomes from IVF. Women also face risks. In IVF as well as in egg or cytoplasm "donation," women must take medications to stimulate their ovaries to overproduce eggs, which normally are produced only one per month. A cohort study in the Netherlands, comparing more than nineteen thousand women who received IVF between 1983 and 1995 to more than six thousand subfertile women who did not, found that the treated women were more than twice as likely to be diagnosed with ovarian malignancies over the ensuing fifteen years (van Leeuwen et al. 2011). IVF also puts women at increased risk of blood clots during the third trimester and the first six weeks postpartum, one of the leading causes of maternal mortality (Hansen et al. 2014). Women who use third-party eggs or embryos have an increased chance of developing gestational hypertension and preeclampsia, conditions that can lead to emergency cesarean and preterm birth (Klatsky et al. 2010). Carrying multiples also puts women at high risk of pregnancy complications.

The use of third-party semen poses additional potential health risks to women and their children. In the United States, sperm provision is regulated when it is brokered by a licensed sperm bank, which must ensure that suppliers are screened for communicable diseases via medical history interview and physical exam and are tested for a number of infectious diseases (U.S. Food and Drug Administration 2009). The European Union's tissue directive mandates similar screening procedures to those required by the Food and Drug Administration (Commission of the European Communities 2006). Psychological screening and blood tests for common genetic diseases and for diseases prevalent among a supplier's ethnic group are recommended by the American Society for Reproductive Medicine (ASRM 2013b), but clusters of rare genetic diseases have occurred among "sperm donor siblings" (Grady 2006; Mroz 2012). With increasing frequency, women are bypassing sperm banks altogether and making direct contact with free semen donors via the Internet, putting themselves at risk of sexually transmitted diseases and their children at risk of heritable disorders.

Of all of the participants in the complex drama of ART, gestational surrogates may be putting their health at the greatest risk for the least reward. Like women undergoing IVF, they must take drugs to permit implantation. Because the embryo is not the product of their own egg, they have an increased likelihood of gestational hypertension and preeclampsia. Often, they are impregnated with multiple embryos, and if multiples ensue, they are not permitted the option of a therapeutic reduction to decrease their chance of complications. Nor are they permitted to protest when the commissioning parents decide to terminate the pregnancy after abnormal prenatal diagnosis; they have sold the right to make decisions about their own bodies. Indian surrogates carrying babies for foreigners are usually delivered by scheduled cesarean section to accommodate the commissioning parents, putting the surrogates at risk of complications from surgery (Rudrappa 2012). Surrogates also may experience negative psychological effects, especially upon relinquishing the baby or babies (European Centre for Law and Justice 2012; Palattiyil et al. 2010).

CONCLUSION

The recurring theme in the story of ARTs is the development and marketing of new scientific advances before they have been proven safe. Regulatory agencies must then play catch-up but often cannot outrun the determined consumers and purveyors of ARTs, who take advantage of discrepant laws between countries to obtain what they want through reproductive tourism. In the haste to make money or babies, the biological and relational dimensions of pregnancy are dismissed. There is a lack of scientific underpinning in the ascription of specified characteristics to the gamete, in the absence of caution about the wide use of new ARTs before we know what the long-term consequences might be, and in reductive medical approaches that isolate body parts from physiological and psychological processes. We need to continue to monitor the consequences through rigorous observational studies as we cautiously introduce technologies into populations, reminding ourselves of all that we have yet to learn about the complexity of reproduction.

GLOSSARY OF TERMS

CYTOPLASM: the jellylike substance that fills cells and contains the organelles

EMBRYO: an organism in its earliest stages of development; during in vitro fertilization, embryos are usually transferred into the woman's uterus three to five days after fertilization

GAMETE: a sex cell; i.e., a sperm or oocyte

MITOCHONDRIA: energy-producing organelles that are exclusively inherited from the mother

OOCYTE: an immature egg

ORGANELLE: a structure that carries out a particular function within a cell

REFERENCES

American Society for Reproductive Medicine (ASRM). 2008. "Genetic Considerations Related to Intracytoplasmic Sperm Injection (ICSI)." *Fertility and Sterility* 90, suppl. 3: S182–84.

———. 2013a. "Mature Oocyte Cryopreservation: A Guideline." *Fertility and Sterility* 99, no. 1: 37–43.

———. 2013b. "Recommendations for Gamete and Embryo Donation: A Committee Opinion." *Fertility and Sterility* 99, no. 1: 47–62.

Armour, K. L. 2012. "An Overview of Surrogacy Around the World." *Nursing for Women's Health* 16, no. 3: 231–36.

Benshushan, A., and J. G. Schenker. 1997. "Legitimizing Surrogacy in Israel." *Human Reproduction* 12, no. 8: 1832–34.

Bonduelle, M., U.-B. Wennerholm, A. Loft, B. C. Tarlatzis, C. Peters, S. Henriet, C. Mau et al. 2005. "A Multi-Centre Cohort Study of the Physical Health of 5-Year-Old Children Conceived after Intracytoplasmic Sperm Injection, in Vitro Fertilization and Natural Conception." *Human Reproduction* 20, no. 2: 413–19.

Bunge, R. G. and J. K. Sherman. 1954. "Clinical Use of Frozen Semen: Report of Four Cases." *Fertility and Sterility* 5, no. 6: 520–29.

Ceelen, M., M. M. van Weissenbruch, J. C. Roos, J. P. Vermeiden, F. E. van Leeuwen, and H. A. Delmarre-van de Waal. 2007. "Body Composition in Children and Adolescents Born after in Vitro Fertilization or Spontaneous Conception." *Journal of Clinical Endocrinology and Metabolism* 92, no. 9: 3417–23.

Ceelen, M., M. M. van Weissenbruch, J. P. Vermeiden, F. E. van Leeuwan, and H. A. Delemarre-van de Waal. 2008. "Cardiometabolic Differences in Children Born after in Vitro Fertilization: Follow-up Study." *Journal of Clinical Endocrinology and Metabolism* 93, no. 5: 1682–88.

Chambers, G. M., E. Lee, V. P. Hoang, M. Hansen, C. Bower, and E. A. Sullivan. 2013. "Hospital Utilization, Costs and Mortality Rates During the First 5 Years of Life: A Population Study of ART and Non-ART Singletons." *Human Reproduction* 29, no. 3: 601–10.

Commission of the European Communities. 2006. "Commission Directive 2006/17/EC." *Official Journal of the European Union* 38: 40–52.

Connolly, M. P., S. Hoorens, and G. M. Chambers. 2010. "The Costs and Consequences of Assisted Reproductive Technology: An Economic Perspective." *Human Reproduction Update* 16, no. 6: 603–13.

Culley, L., N. Hudson, F. Rapport, E. Blyth, W. Norton, and A. A. Pacey. 2011. "Crossing Borders for Fertility Treatment: Motiviations, Destinations and Outcomes of UK Fertility Travelers." *Human Reproduction* 26, no. 9: 2373–81.

European Society of Human Reproduction and Embryology (ESHRE). 2008. "Good Clinical Treatment in Assisted Reproduction—An ESHRE Position Paper." https://www.eshre.eu /Guidelines-and-Legal/ESHRE-Position-Papers.aspx.

European Society of Human Reproduction and Embryology (ESHRE). 2012. "The World's Number of IVF and ICSI Babies Has Now Reached a Calculated Total of 5 Million." http:// www.eshre.eu/Press-Room/Press-releases/Press-releases-ESHRE-2012/5-million-babies .aspx.

European Centre for Law and Justice. 2012. "Surrogate Motherhood: A Violation of Human Rights." Report presented at the Council of Europe, Strasbourg, April 26. http://www.ieb -eib.org/en/pdf/surrogacy-motherhood-icjl.pdf.

Fauser, B. C. J. M., P. Devroey, K. Diedrich, B. Balaban, M. Bonduelle, H. A. Delemarre-van de Waal, C. Estella et al. 2014. "Health Outcomes of Children Born after IVF/ICSI: A

Review of Current Expert Opinion and Literature." *Reproductive BioMedicine Online* 28: 162–82.

Gamble, N. 2009. "Crossing the Line: The Legal and Ethical Problems of Foreign Surrogacy." *Reproductive BioMedicine Online* 19, no. 2: 151–52.

Grady, D. 2006. "Sperm Donor Seen as Source of Disease in 5 Children." *New York Times*. May 19. http://www.nytimes.com/2006/05/19/health/19donor.html.

Guttmacher, A. F. 1962. "Artificial Insemination." *The Cervix* 97: 623–31.

Guzoglu, N., H. G. Kanmaz, D. Dilli, N. Uras, O. Erdeve, and U. Dilmen. 2012. "The Impact of the New Turkish Regulation, Imposing Single Embryo Transfer after Assisted Reproduction Technology, on Neonatal Intensive Care Unit Utilization: A Single Center Experience." *Human Reproduction* 27, no. 8: 2384–88.

Hansen, A. T., U. S. Kesmodel, S. Juul, and A. M. Hvas. 2014. "Increased Venous Thrombosis Incidence in Pregnancies After in Vitro Fertilization." *Human Reproduction* 29 no. 3: 611–17.

Hansen, M., C. Bower, E. Milne, N. de Klerk, and J. J. Kurinczuk. 2005. "Assisted Reproductive Technologies and the Risk of Birth Defects—a Systematic Review." *Human Reproduction* 20, no. 2: 328–38.

Hard, A. D. 1909. "Artificial Impregnation." *The Medical World* 27: 163–64.

Inhorn, Marcia C. 2006. "Making Muslim Babies: IVF and Gamete Donation in Sunni Versus Shi'a Islam." *Culture, Medicine and Psychiatry* 30, no. 4: 427–50.

——. 2014. "New Arab Fatherhood: Emergent Masculinities and Assisted Reproduction." In *Globalized Fatherhood*, ed. Marcia M. Inhorn, Wendy Chavkin, and José-Alberto Navarro, 243–63. New York: Berghahn Books.

Klatsky, P. C., S. S. Delaney, A. B. Caughey, N. D. Tran, G. L. Schattman, and Z. Rosenwaks. 2010. "The Role of Embryonic Origin in Preeclampsia: A Comparison of Autologous in Vitro Fertilization and Ovum Donor Pregnancies." *Obstetrics and Gynecology* 116, no. 6: 387–92.

Library of Congress. 2015a. "India: Draft Legislation Regulating Assisted Reproductive Technology Published." *Global Legal Monitor*. November 2. http://www.loc.gov/law/foreign -news/article/india-draft-legislation-regulating-assisted-reproductive-technology -published.

——. 2015b. "Thailand: New Surrogacy Law." *Global Legal Monitor*. April 6. http://www.loc .gov/law/foreign-news/article/thailand-new-surrogacy-law.

Lior, Ilan. 2014. "Deal Taking Shape in Thai-Israeli Surrogacy Crisis." *Haaretz*, January 23.

Manipalviratn, S., A. DeCherney, and J. Segars. 2009. "Imprinting Disorders and Assisted Reproductive Technology." *Fertility and Sterility* 91: 305–15.

Middelburg, K. J., M. J. Heineman, M. L. Haadsma, A. F. Bos, J. H. Kok, and M. Hadders-Algra. 2010. "Neurological Condition of Infants Born after in Vitro Fertilization with Preimplantation Genetic Screening." *Pediatric Research* 67, no. 4: 430–34.

Middelburg, K. J., M. van der Heide, B. Houtzager, M. Jongbloed-Pereboom, V. Fidler, A. F. Bos, J. H. Kok, and M. Hadders-Algra. 2011. "Mental, Psychomotor, Neurologic, and Behavioral Outcomes of 2-Year-Old Children Born after Preimplantation Genetic Screening: Follow-up of a Randomized Controlled Trial." *Fertility and Sterility* 96, no. 1: 165–69.

Mroz, Jacqueline. 2012. "In Choosing a Sperm Donor, a Roll of the Genetic Dice." *New York Times*. May 15. http://www.nytimes.com/2012/05/15/health/in-sperm-banks-a-matrix-of -untested-genetic-diseases.html?_r=1&pagewanted=all.

National Academies of Sciences, Engineering, and Medicine. 2016. *Mitochondrial Replacement Techniques: Ethical, Social, and Policy Considerations*. Washington, DC: National Academies Press.

National Conference of Commissioners on Uniform State Laws. 2000. "Uniform Parentage Act." http://www.law.upenn.edu/bll/archives/ulc/upa/final2002.htm.

Newton-Small, Jay. 2012. "Frozen Assets." *Time*. April 5. http://www.time.com/time/magazine /article/0,9171,2111234,00.html.

Palattiyil, G., E. Blyth, D. Sidhva, and G. Balakrishnan. 2010. "Globalization and Cross-Border Reproductive Services: Ethical Implications of Surrogacy in India for Social Work." *International Social Work* 53, no. 5: 686–700.

Palermo, G., H. Joris, P. Devroey and A. C. Van Steirteghem. 1992. "Pregnancies After Intracytoplasmic Injection of a Single Spermatozoon into an Oocyte." *The Lancet* 340: 17–19.

Pennings, Guido. 2010. "The Rough Guide to Insemination: Cross-Border Travelling for Donor Semen Due to Different Regulations." *Facts, Views, and Vision in Obstetrics and Gynaecology*, monograph: 55–60.

Polge, C., A. U. Smith, and A. S. Parkes. 1949. "Revival of Spermatozoa after Vitrification and Dehydration at Low Temperatures." *Nature* 164: 666–69.

Price, F. V. 1988. "The Risk of High Multiparity with IVF/ET." *Birth* 15, no. 3: 157–63.

Richards, S. E. 2012. "We Need to Talk About Our Eggs." *New York Times*, October 22.

Rozée Gomez, Virginie, and Elise de La Rochebrochard. 2013. "Cross-Border Reproductive Care Among French Patients: Experiences in Greece, Spain and Belgium." *Human Reproduction* 28, no. 11: 3103–10.

Rudrappa, Sharmila. 2012. "India's Reproductive Assembly Line." *Contexts* 11, no. 2: 22–27.

——. 2014. "Conceiving Fatherhood: Gay Dads and Indian Surrogates." In *Globalized Fatherhood*, ed. Marcia M. Inhorn, Wendy Chavkin, and José-Alberto Navarro, 291–311. New York: Berghahn Books.

Sandin, S., K.-G. Nygren, A. Iliadou, C. M. Hultman, and A. Reichenberg. 2013. "Autism and Mental Retardation Among Offspring Born after in Vitro Fertilization." *JAMA* 310, no. 1: 75–84.

Schendelaar, P., K. J. Middelburg, A. F. Bos, M. J. Heineman, J. H. Kok, S. La Bastide-Van Gemert, J. Seggers, E. R.Van den Heuvel, and M. Hadders-Algra. 2013. "The Effect of Preimplantation Genetic Screening on Neurological, Cognitive and Behavioural Development in 4-Year-Old Children: Follow-up of a RCT." *Human Reproduction* 28, no. 6: 1508–18.

Searchinger, Tim, Craig Hanson, Janet Ranganathan, Brian Lipinski, Richard Waite, Robert Winterbottom, Ayesha Dinshaw, and Ralph Heimlich. 2013. *Creating a Sustainable Food Future: Interim Findings*. Washington, DC: World Resources Institute.

Seggers, Jorien, Maaike L. Haadsma, Sacha LaBastide-Van Gemert, Mas Jan Heineman, Karin J. Middelburg, Tessa J. Roseboom, Pamela Schndelaar, Edwin R. Van den Heuvel, and Mijna Hadders-Algra. 2014. "Is Ovarian Hyperstimulation Associated with Higher

Blood Pressure in 4-Year-Old IVF Offspring? Part I: Multivariable Regression Analysis." *Human Reproduction* 29, no. 3: 502–9.

Sermon, K., A. Van Steirteghem, and I. Liebaers. 2004. "Preimplantation Genetic Diagnosis." *The Lancet* 363: 1633–41.

Shenfield, F., J deMouzon, G. Pennings, A. P. Ferraretti, A. N. Andersen, G. de Wert, and V. Goossens. 2010. "Cross Border Reproductive Care in Six European Countries." *Human Reproduction* 25, no. 6: 1361–68.

Sherman, J. K. 1964. "Low Temperature Research on Spermatozoa and Eggs." *Cryobiology* 1, no. 2: 103–29.

Shukla, U., B. Deval, M. Jansa Perez, H. Hamoda, M. Savvas, and N. Narvekar. 2013. "Sperm Donor Recruitment, Attitudes and Provider Practices—5 Years After the Removal of Donor Anonymity." *Human Reproduction* 28, no. 3: 676–82.

Slaughter, Anne-Marie. 2012. "Why Women Still Can't Have It All." *The Atlantic*, June 13.

Stark, B. 2012. "Transnational Surrogacy and International Human Rights Law." *ILSA Journal of International & Comparative Law* 18, no. 2: 1–18.

Steptoe, P. C., and R. G. Edwards. 1978. "Birth after the Reimplantation of a Human Embryo." *The Lancet* 2, no. 8085: 366.

Sunderam, S., D. M. Kissin, S. Crawford, J. E. Anderson, S. G. Folger, D. J. Jamieson, and W. D. Barfield. 2013. "Assisted Reproductive Technology Surveillance—United States, 2010." *MMWR Surveillance Summaries* 62, no. 9.

U.S. Embassy in Nepal. 2017. "Surrogacy Services Are Banned in Nepal." https://np.usembassy .gov/u-s-citizen-services/local-resources-of-u-s-citizens/surrogacy-in-nepal.

U.S. Food and Drug Administration. 2009. "Donor Eligibility Final Rule and Guidance Questions and Answers." *Vaccines, Bloods & Biologics*. http://www.fda.gov/Biologics BloodVaccines/TissueTissueProducts/QuestionsaboutTissues/ucm102842.htm.

van Leeuwen, F. E, H. Klip, T. M. Mooij, A. M. G. van de Swaluw, C. B. Lambalk, M. Kortman, J. S. E. Laven et al. 2011. "Risk of Borderline and Invasive Ovarian Tumours After Ovarian Stimulation for in Vitro Fertilization in a Large Dutch Cohort." *Human Reproduction* 26, no. 12: 3456–65.

Vogel, G. 2015. "Mitochondrial Gene Therapy Passes Final U.K. Vote." *Science*. February 24. http://www.sciencemag.org/news/2015/02/mitochondrial-gene-therapy-passes-final-uk -vote.

Vora, K. 2013. "Potential, Risk, and Return in Transnational Indian Gestational Surrogacy." *Current Anthropology* 54, no. S7: S97–106.

Williams, C. L., K. J. Bunch, C. A. Stiller, M. F. G. Murphy, B. J. Botting, W. H. Wallace, M. Davies, and A. G. Sutcliffe. 2013. "Cancer Risk Among Children Born after Assisted Conception." *New England Journal of Medicine* 369: 1819–27.

3

MULTIPLE "MOTHERS," MANY REQUIREMENTS FOR PROTECTION

Children's Rights and the Status of Mothers in the Context of
International Commercial Surrogacy

CLAIRE ACHMAD

International commercial surrogacy (ICS) is inherently complex, a method of having a child that is largely made possible through a combination of technological advances, market forces, and changing attitudes toward family structures and human reproduction. ICS raises a raft of profound, intersecting issues relating to, among other things, bioethics, commodification of human life, globalization, and migration. ICS operates in a generally unregulated manner across international borders. People from disparate corners of the world are drawn together in a relationship with its roots in the supply and demand of commercial human reproduction.[1] In this respect, ICS is different from other international commercial transactions, given that a child is the intended outcome. Work is currently under way internationally to assess whether an international regulatory framework for international surrogacy is viable.[2] Yet global consensus remains elusive, given the range of state views and approaches to ICS, the lack of domestic legislative and policy alignment and, in some instances, the polarity of these positions.[3]

ICS functions with the express aim of producing a child. Such children are often much wanted and longed for by the people seeking them.[4] However, sometimes minimal thought is given to how the eventual child's rights will be upheld and protected. This is despite a core principle of the United Nations Convention on the Rights of the Child: "In all actions concerning children . . . the best interests of the child shall be a primary consideration" (OHCHR 1989, article 3.1).

This chapter proceeds from an international human rights law perspective. The centrality of the child to ICS, and the child's inherent vulnerability, require that his or her best interests be held paramount. But such interests must also be balanced with the rights of other people involved, including those of the multiple women who may have claims to being recognized as a "mother."

UNDERSTANDING INTERNATIONAL COMMERCIAL SURROGACY AS A DISTINGUISHABLE PHENOMENON

In ICS, commissioning "parents" pay to have children through surrogacy in a state other than that in which they live. While the practice of surrogacy grew from the mid-1970s and through the 1980s (predominantly in the United States),[5] ICS has emerged forcefully over the past decade. International surrogacy markets have developed, particularly, in Global South states such as Thailand and India, with demand flowing predominantly from the Global North.[6] The supply of ICS from Global South states is dynamic in nature, adapting to demand and in reaction to changing social attitudes and political pressures (see Kahn and Chavkin, present volume). Notably, in early 2015, the Thai parliament passed a legislative ban on all commercial surrogacy services for non-Thai nationals (unless a person has been married to a Thai national for at least three years), with criminal penalties for commissioning parents and surrogate mothers who contravene the law (BBC News 2015). But the supply of ICS services is not limited to the Global South; Global North jurisdictions (such as the state of California) attract a significant part of the market.[7] Northern states offer certainty regarding legal parentage through the possibility of prebirth orders, while Global South states compete in part by providing ICS at lower cost and sometimes by offering surrogacy-related procedures unavailable in Global North states, such as multiple embryo transfer to increase the likelihood of pregnancy, selective fetal reduction, and mandatory cesarean deliveries.

Following the birth of a child through an ICS arrangement, the woman acting as the surrogate is expected to relinquish the child to the commissioning parents who intend to raise him or her. It will be the commissioning parents' choice whether to maintain contact with the surrogate; sometimes, surrogates act anonymously in ICS. Arrangements in which the surrogate provides the ovum are termed "traditional surrogacy" or "complete surrogacy" (Shanley 2001).[8] But in "gestational surrogacy"—which is the norm in ICS—embryos formed by the commissioning parents' gametes or by gametes obtained from third parties, or embryos made from gametes of a commissioning parent and a donor are implanted in the surrogate, sometimes after being shipped across borders for use. Therefore, the child may or may not be genetically related to one or both commissioning parents, to gamete donors, or to a mix of these.

Payments for ICS arrangements may flow in multiple directions. For example, fees may be paid to surrogacy clinics carrying out the associated medical procedures, and surrogacy brokers or third parties often are involved, arranging the surrogacy on a fee-for-service basis (Hague Conference on Private International Law 2011). The surrogate herself may be paid, either directly or through the clinic or other third party.[9] Contractual documents sometimes govern ICS arrangements, but not always.[10] The exact nature of each ICS arrangement differs in all these aspects, often making it difficult to fully map the people, places, and transactions involved.

THE CENTRAL FEATURE OF "MOTHER" IS CHILD

In ICS the rights (and obligations) of "motherhood" may apply to several women. The defining and universal feature of "mother" is "child." It is the existence of a child who is cared for or in some way related to a woman that leads to her being understood as a mother—legally and socially. Traditional understandings of whom and what constitutes a mother at law align with this definition. In many jurisdictions, the woman who gives birth is automatically considered the mother of a child, in accordance with the maxim "mater semper certa est."[11]

Although adoption and parentage laws have broadened the notion of a legal mother or parent, ICS poses a new set of questions. In ICS arrangements, as many as three different women can be identified as "mother" in relation to a particular child: the surrogate, the ovum donor, and the woman who (either alone or with a partner) commissions the child.[12] Who is considered the (or "a") mother affects not only that particular woman's rights but also those of the other women involved, as well as those of the child who is born.

MULTIPLE MOTHERS: THE MANY FACES OF "MOTHER" IN INTERNATIONAL COMMERCIAL SURROGACY

SURROGATE

As the woman who gives birth in ICS, the surrogate performs the role closest to the traditional notion of mother. In many ICS demand jurisdictions (the states in which commissioning mothers or parents originate from or reside in), under domestic legislation a woman who gives birth as a surrogate is held to be the legal mother of the child.[13] However, the surrogate's role in relation to the child is intended from the outset of an ICS arrangement to be time-limited to the gestation period and birth.[14] She is expected to relinquish the child at birth. But numerous legal cases and anthropological studies have shown that the surrogate's intentions and expectations may change over the course of her pregnancy; independently of whether she actually transfers the child to its commissioning parents, she may feel an enduring connection.

Where the law views the surrogate as the child's legal mother, this creates an obstacle to the smooth implementation of the ICS arrangement and contractual agreement (if there is one). In such cases, the position of the surrogate as a legal mother persists until her relationship with the child is severed at law, such as through the establishment of a legal parent–child relationship between the commissioning mother (or parents) and the child through adoption. But adoption is dependent on the consent of the woman who gave birth (following birth), such that the transfer of parental rights is not guaranteed. Moreover, in many jurisdictions, when a child is born through ICS, the surrogate is listed as "mother" on the child's birth certificate. India constitutes an exception to this rule: current guidelines stipulate that birth certificates in ICS will be issued in the names of the genetic or commissioning parents; therefore, the surrogate does not have formal "mother" status under Indian law (Indian Council of Medical Research 2005, clause 3.12.1).[15]

Thus, in many ICS situations, the surrogate is physically, socially, and legally viewed as the child's mother, despite having agreed to provide the child to the commissioning mother following birth. The possibility of the surrogate's intentions changing throughout ICS cannot be ruled out, however. Even in jurisdictions where ICS contracts are enforceable, situations may arise where the surrogate mother contravenes the agreement, and it may be extremely difficult to enforce contractual performance.

Surrogates have variously been described as "outsourced wombs" (Warner 2008), "cheap or rentable wombs" (Chu 2006), "human incubators" (Harari 2008), "gestational carriers" (Pande 2009), and "biological mothers" (van den Akker 2010). This range of terminology—which avoids reference to the term "mother"—arguably highlights the surrogate's vulnerability to marginalization and exploitation. Pande (2014, 64–65) observes the dual imperative under which surrogates in India are expected to carry out their roles, to simultaneously see themselves as workers and not mothers ("worker-producers") and as mothers and not workers ("mother-reproducers"); she describes this as "manufacturing the perfect mother-worker." The surrogate "is expected to be a disciplined contract worker who gives up the baby at the termination of the contract, [and] is simultaneously urged to be a nurturing mother for the baby, and a selfless mother who will not negotiate the payment received." Furthermore, an integral aspect of the conflict inherent in the surrogate's role in ICS is summarized in Pande's statement that "when one's identity as a mother is regulated and terminated by a contract, being a good mother often conflicts with being a good worker."

GENETIC

Other than in ICS arrangements in which the genetic mother is also the surrogate or commissioning mother, the genetic mother fulfills her obligations by providing her ovum. Although gestation entails biological processes that have an enduring effect on the child, only the genetic mother has a genetic connection to him or her. In ICS, should she therefore be considered a "mother"? A genetic relationship with a child cannot be severed at law or otherwise altered, and it can be proven through DNA testing. Yet a genetic mother may not be recognized as being a legal mother in ICS or other surrogacy situations, given that legal motherhood is generally reserved for the birth mother and, in some exceptions, the commissioning mother.

In ICS, the involvement of the genetic mother with the child may go no further than the provision of ova. The willingness of the commissioning parents to have the genetic "mother" involved in the child's life is the likeliest factor immediately determining the extent of any social relationship with the child.[16] In arrangements where the genetic mother acts anonymously, this will likely prove impossible.[17] Finally, it is important to note that the genetic mother often will be referred to as the "egg donor" (Smerdon 2008–09). The effect of this is to remove any reference to this woman as a mother in relation to the child, reducing her role to a purely transactional one, without recognition of her enduring genetic connection to the child.

COMMISSIONING

Although it is the genetic and surrogate "mothers" who physically enable a child's birth through ICS, most ICS arrangements begin with the desire of the commissioning mother (or the commissioning parents or the commissioning father) to have a child. However, in many ICS arrangements the commissioning mother is not the mother genetically connected to the child, and in all ICS arrangements she is not the woman who gives birth. Therefore, in ICS the woman who seeks to mother the child in a social sense is the mother with the most problematic link to the child and to the legal parental status of mother. Indeed, the law often does not recognize the commissioning mother as a mother at all. In jurisdictions where this is the case (and surrogacy is legal), the commissioning mother must either adopt the child or utilize other procedures to assert her legal parentage.[18]

This woman's status as mother in ICS situations is, at its crudest, borne of a transaction. However, to reduce her role to such a restricted reading ignores the fact that it is often only due to her deep desire to have a child to care for and to mother that the child has come into being. Her role as mother to the child, if she goes on to care for the child, is that of a mother in the social sense. The question is when—and how—across the many jurisdictions that may come into play in ICS, this desire can be coupled with legal recognition of her as "mother." In ICS cases where the commissioning "mother" is also the genetic "mother," it is arguable that her status is bolstered, given her enduring link to the child in terms of DNA. However, in practice, the feature most importantly distinguishing the commissioning mother from the other two potential mothers is that without her there would be no child, as she is the mother initiating the ICS process and is (usually) the only person intending to raise the child as her own.

Despite the surrogate mother's likely contractual obligation to transfer the child to the commissioning mother upon or shortly after birth, the commissioning mother remains highly vulnerable. Contracts governing ICS arrangements are often difficult to enforce and, as previously noted, the surrogate's intentions and decisions may change during her pregnancy or following the child's birth. Requiring specific performance of such contracts would be contrary to the child's rights under international human rights law, as specific performance would explicitly render children the product of such contracts and therefore commodify them. Requiring specific performance of such contracts also would be contrary to the surrogate's rights, as she may well have a valid claim to a legal mother–child relationship with regard to the child she brings to term and births. Requiring specific performance of ICS contracts would therefore ignore the reality of the surrogate mother's role in ICS arrangements.[19] Moreover, the commissioning mother's rights may be affected through a lack of clarity over her legal status as a "mother" in relation to the child.[20]

Therefore, although the commissioning mother is the "mother" intending to care for and raise the child as her own at all points throughout the course of an ICS arrangement (unless she changes her mind), she is the mother facing the most difficulty establishing a mother relationship in ICS.

ABSENCE OF "MOTHER" IN INTERNATIONAL COMMERCIAL SURROGACY

Despite multiple women being able to stake a claim as mothers, children born of ICS arrangements may be left "motherless." An absence of a mother can occur due to human and legal factors. The first situation where the absence of a mother to care for and raise the child is possible is when the commissioning mother decides she does not want to perform this role.[21] Such a decision undermines the ICS arrangement and means the child's vulnerability is further heightened.[22] This outcome can never be completely ruled out in ICS, given that, ultimately, such arrangements are based on a good faith understanding that all parties will follow through on the actions to which they commit. If the commissioning mother rejects the child, the surrogate or genetic mother might be willing to mother the child on an ongoing basis.

However, when none of the three mothers wants to do so, and if the partner of the commissioning mother (in instances where a partner exists who is legally recognizable as a parent) also reneges on the arrangement, it may fall to the state to assume care and protection of the child, if the state is unsuccessful in attempts to enforce maternal obligations where commissioning mothers have been deemed legal mothers. In such situations, the state will arguably be obliged to assume care, under articles 20.1 and 20.2 of the Convention on the Rights of the Child (OHCHR 1989). This raises further complex questions around which state should or is best positioned to take responsibility for the child when ICS arrangements go awry in this way. Arguably, in situations where demand flows from commissioning parents in the Global North to have a child through a surrogate in the Global South, international development burden-sharing theory can be applied by analogy.[23]

The second factor that may lead to a child being motherless or without parents committed to caring for him or her in ICS is the law, when national legislation and policy does not make provision for or actively prohibits ICS. The inadequacies of national frameworks, the conflicts among them, and the absence of international regulation interact, undermining the certainty that children born through ICS will have a legally recognized mother or parent(s). Where legal parentage cannot be established, the child may not have access to other entitlements, further negatively affecting his or her rights.[24]

Such situations occur when neither the commissioning mother nor the father can demonstrate a connection to the child meeting state requirements for legal parentage, such as when the state of origin of the commissioning mother—or parent generally—requires proof of a specific kind of connection (for example, genetic) to recognize parentage and, hence, citizenship.[25] Ireland is an example: under the Irish guidelines, the government will not consider a child for a travel document or citizenship unless DNA evidence of a genetic link to the commissioning father is provided by a "suitably qualified independent third party" (Government of Ireland, n.d., 6), although the guidelines also specify that a genetic link does not automatically create legal parentage.

This raises severe implications in situations where donor sperm has been used in ICS and no genetic link exists between commissioning father and child, or in instances where there is no commissioning father but only a commissioning mother or mothers. In such situations, the position of the children and protection of their rights remains highly uncertain. Whether the child's status is regularized by state exercise of exception-based discretionary decision making must surely be viewed as a remote possibility. State-level guidance has been established in the United Kingdom, requiring a genetic link to at least one commissioning parent for entry of the child into the United Kingdom. Proof must be gained via DNA testing through an accredited company (UK Border Agency 2009). This is a slightly less restrictive approach than that of Ireland, given the wider scope of the proof of a commissioning mother's or father's connection to the child.

In some other jurisdictions, where such formal guidelines and requirements do not exist, courts are sometimes taking into consideration evidence that proves some sort of link—usually genetic—between the commissioning mother and/or father before exercising discretionary powers to establish a legal parent–child relationship.[26] But where courts cannot establish such a link and government regulations prohibit establishing a legal relationship between the commissioning mother and the child, the commissioning mother is prevented from caring for the child in her home country.[27] In such situations, the commissioning mother still wants to mother the child. However, where neither surrogate nor genetic mother wants to mother the child in lieu of the commissioning mother, and if the commissioning mother cannot stay in the country where the child is born, the child may be abandoned there, without a legally recognized parent. Again, this undermines the child's rights to citizenship and nationality as well as his or her right to an identity and to grow up in a family environment.

THE CONTESTABLE NOTION OF "MOTHER" IN INTERNATIONAL COMMERCIAL SURROGACY AND IMPLICATIONS FOR THE RIGHTS OF THE CHILD

The timeline of ICS arrangements leads to the three different women discussed in this chapter being involved at different points and for different lengths of time. The fact that the genetic mother's gametes contribute to the genetic makeup of a child born through ICS means her link with the child is inherently unseverable. Despite the significance of this link, unless the genetic mother is also the surrogate, she will rarely be recognized as the child's legal mother at any point in the ICS timeline. This can have implications for the child's rights to identity and health, particularly if the genetic mother acts anonymously. Despite the position the law may take, the genetic mother's link does not stop at any time. It is arguably in both the child's and the genetic mother's best interests that there is at least social recognition of the mother role played by the genetic mother in relation to the child.[28] India's national guidelines for ART clinics (Indian Council of Medical Research 2005, para. 3.3.6) appear to acknowledge this, to some extent, providing that information about donors (including their identity) be released by ART clinics only "after appropriate identification, only to the offspring and only if asked by him/her after he/she reaches the age of 18 years, or as and when specified for legal purposes, and never to the parents (excepting when directed by a court of law)."

In contrast to the genetic mother, the surrogate mother, if acting purely as a surrogate, does not have any ongoing relationship with the child in ICS unless that is agreed to with the commissioning parents, or if the child seeks her out later in life and the relevant information is made available. Again, this will be extremely difficult if the surrogate acts anonymously. In most instances of ICS, it seems likely that the surrogate's role in the child's life will be time-limited to the period of pregnancy and birth, with the surrogate not playing any social mother role. This is unfortunate and should be guarded against, given that (as was previously noted in relation to the genetic mother) her ongoing role in the child's life, or at the very least the child's knowledge of the surrogate mother, can aid in realization of the child's rights to identity, nationality, and health. The legal position of the surrogate may well be to the contrary, however, given that in many jurisdictions the surrogate mother is recognized as the child's legal mother, a position often only displaced through legal extinguishment of the parent–child relationship between surrogate and child by establishing a new legal parent–child relationship via adoption.

In practice, it is possible in ICS situations for the commissioning mother to assume the social mothering role as soon as the surrogate relinquishes the child, despite her not having any guarantee she will eventually be recognized as the legal mother. A gulf between fact and law may therefore persist for quite some time, until a legal relationship is established. If the parent–child relationship between surrogate mother and child is extinguished through law, any reinstatement of the surrogate's maternal role in relation to the child will be dependent on whether the commissioning mother or parents involve the surrogate in the child's life in any capacity.

Again, from a human rights perspective, the surrogate arguably should continue to be construed to some extent as a mother in relation to the child, given that she brought the child to term and gave birth to the child. These facts cannot be displaced except through a social reconstruction of the circumstances of a child's gestation and birth. That the surrogate mother is unlikely to have any ongoing relationship with a child born through ICS, following his or her birth, may well have implications for the surrogate as well as the child. The surrogate's mental or physical health (or both) may be affected, in the absence of any ongoing role or recognition of the role she played (Sama Resource Group for Women and Health 2012). From a child rights perspective, the child's realization of his or her identity and health rights may be negatively affected by not knowing about his or her surrogate mother, especially later in life.

A converse argument exists, that knowledge about the surrogate mother may cause a child born through ICS confusion and bewilderment with regard to his or her identity. Equally, the surrogate may not wish to have contact with the child, who she may view as purely the child of the commissioning mother (or parents). However, steps can be taken to ameliorate these risks, to support the child's understanding of his or her birth circumstances.

As with the question of when and whether genetic and surrogate mothers in ICS stop being mothers, it is necessary to consider when a commissioning mother *starts* being a mother, despite the fact that she is the one woman of the three possible mothers who, throughout an ICS arrangement (unless she changes her mind), wants to permanently mother the child and be legally and socially recognized as such. She is the woman whom it is most difficult to construe as mother to the child, given that in most ICS arrangements she is not genetically related and the law will not automatically recognize her as the child's mother. Therefore, the question of when a commissioning mother becomes a mother in ICS requires consideration from social and legal perspectives.

Unlike the genetic and surrogate mothers, the commissioning mother's status in relation to the child is entirely socially constructed, until she is able to establish a legal parental relationship with the child. Her relationship to the child is arguably based on four factors that may be present prior to the establishment of any legal status: that she desires to have the child and intends to raise the child as her own; that she has paid money relating to the ICS arrangement; that she may be party to a written or oral agreement about the arrangement; and that she is likely to assume responsibility as the child's "mother" once the surrogate mother relinquishes the child.

Arguably, the commissioning mother becomes a mother to the child in a meaningful social sense once she assumes care for the child, following the child's birth. It is from that point that the surrogate's substantive involvement with the child is usually expected to end and that the child and commissioning mother can begin to form an attachment in the form of a mother–child relationship. However, the surrogate mother may want to maintain a connection to the child, and in some ICS arrangements there will be a period of substantive overlap regarding the mothers' involvement and the attachment of the child to these two mothers. For example, this may occur if, at the request of a commissioning mother, a surrogate breastfeeds the child during the initial weeks of its life.

It is understandable, however, that many commissioning mothers view themselves as the child's mother from the child's conception onward, given that the child carried by the surrogate is intended for the commissioning mother (or parents). This view likely holds even if the commissioning mother is not genetically related to the child and lives in a different country than the surrogate. Surrogates themselves may or may not subscribe to this view of who is the child's mother in ICS arrangements, which is understandable, given the complex practical and emotional aspects of carrying a child for another person—a child who may or may not be genetically related to the surrogate herself. Therefore, identifying when a commissioning mother in ICS becomes a mother, from a social mothering perspective, is a blurry exercise. In reality, in addition to what relevant laws and regulations prescribe, it will be largely dependent on the personal attitudes and individual circumstances involved in specific ICS arrangements. Navigation of who is "mother," and when, may prove complicated and fraught.

Although some jurisdictions, such as Ukraine and California, maintain a competitive edge in the ICS market by securing recognition of the commissioning mother as the legal mother of a child born through ICS, in some ICS supply states it can take a long time for commissioning parents to attain legal status relating to a child born through ICS. This leads to great uncertainty in status for both the child and the commissioning mother. The child's rights, under the Convention on the Rights of the Child, to nationality and identity and to grow up in a family environment again may be undermined. In some jurisdictions, gaining legal status as mother to a child in ICS may not be possible under the relevant domestic legislation, with discretionary measures such as adoption orders providing the only method to establish a legal parent–child relationship. Consequently, the child may be in a vulnerable situation with regard to his or her right to grow up in a family environment, and potentially could be rendered stateless, affecting his or her wider rights.

In countries such as Australia, New Zealand, and the United Kingdom, judges are grappling with the fact that although domestic legislation construes the birth mother as the child's legal mother and, furthermore, prohibits commercial surrogacy domestically, they are faced with applications from commissioning mothers for parentage or adoption orders for children born through ICS. But, as Justice Hedley of the UK High Court states, the "difficulty is that it is almost impossible to imagine a set of circumstances in which by the time the case comes to court, the welfare of any child (particularly a foreign child) would not be gravely compromised (at the very least) by a refusal to make an order."[29] Chief Federal Magistrate Pascoe of the Federal Circuit Court of Australia has described this as the "fait accompli upon return" in international surrogacy cases before Australian family law courts (Pascoe 2014). However, unless ICS is recognized by law and acknowledged on birth certificates that the commissioning mother's state of origin is willing to accept, she will have to overcome the hurdle of establishing her legal status in relation to the child to gain full recognition as the child's mother.

CONCLUSION

Establishing the status of the various "mothers" in ICS is legally and socially complex. This is problematic for the various women involved, and ramifications for the realization of the rights of the child born through ICS can be wide ranging, generating long-term negative effects. The common denominator in all ICS arrangements is what the arrangement is driven toward providing: a child. In the absence of international agreements regulating the attribution of motherhood, and parentage rules generally, children born through ICS are in positions of heightened vulnerability. As Michael Freeman (1992, 29) has said, "There can be no doubt that children are amongst the most vulnerable and powerless members of our society today." The risk is that the current uncertainty surrounding the attribution of motherhood in ICS exacerbates such vulnerability.

The speed with which the technological and medical advances underpinning ICS have progressed has outstripped the development of the law to regulate and protect vulnerable parties in these arrangements.[30] It is necessary that national legislators and policy makers engage with developing responses to ICS, focusing on human rights protection, and it is crucial that the international community continues to consider options for international regulation.[31] A focus on the rights of the child in ICS in relation to the position of the child's potential "mothers" is particularly important, given the current absence of any international regulatory framework governing ICS. The child has rights with regard to his or her "mothers," and the child's "mothers" have rights and interests with regard to the child. However, as this chapter has demonstrated, ICS entails distinctions between genetic, social, and legal "mothers," which affects the child's rights and the mothers' own situations. The child is the ultimate factor leading to a woman being understood as a mother, and although all the "mothers" involved in ICS have human rights that may be vulnerable and must be protected,[32] the rights of children born through ICS require protection alongside and balanced in relation to the situations of their multiple "mothers."

NOTES

1. Not all international surrogacy is commercial. Some international surrogacy arrangements are altruistic, characterized by a "gift relationship" (van Zyl and Walker 2013, 374). However, because this chapter takes international commercial surrogacy (ICS) as its focus, altruistic arrangements fall out of scope.

2. See the Parentage Surrogacy Project at https://www.hcch.net/en/projects/legislative -projects/parentage-surrogacy. This project was preceded by work led by Professor Paul Beaumont and Dr. Katarina Trimmings of the School of Law at the University of Aberdeen. See also Trimmings and Beaumont (2013).

3. Some jurisdictions extraterritorially criminalize commercial surrogacy (see, for example, sections 8 and 11 of the New South Wales Surrogacy Act 2010), whereas others (such as India and Ukraine) allow its operation in a largely unregulated manner.

For a discussion of the conflicts that discordant legal frameworks may produce, see Ergas (2013a).

4. This is true in the majority of ICS cases. However, the possibility of people commissioning children through ICS for purposes of child abuse, exploitation, and/or trafficking cannot be ruled out. This has implications for the rights of the child: they may be born into situations whereby their rights under articles 19, 34, 35, 36, and 37 of the United Nations Convention on the Rights of the Child (Nov. 20, 1989, 1577 U.N.T.S. 3) are breached.

5. Field (1990) discusses two of the most well-known U.S. cases from this period, Stiver v. Parker, 975 F.2d 261 (6th cir. 1992), and In re Baby M, 537 A.2d 1227 (N.J. 1988).

6. For discussion of the concept of a market for international surrogacy, see chapter 3 of Spar (2006). Commissioning parents from the Global North do also seek ICS in countries such as Ukraine and the United States. See, for example, Re Application by BWS, NZLFR 621 (2011), and X & Y (Foreign Surrogacy), EWHC 3030 (Fam. 2008).

7. Although comprehensive data on the incidence of international commercial surrogacy in the United States is not available, survey data of all fertility treatment provided in the United States shows approximately six thousand cycles are delivered to people domiciled outside the United States, amounting to 4 percent (Ethics Committee of the American Society for Reproductive Medicine 2013). For an overview of commercial surrogacy laws in the various U.S. states, see Creative Family Connections (2016).

8. Ryznar (2010, 1010) defines "traditional surrogacy" as a surrogacy that "results in a surrogate's genetic child following her artificial insemination with the intended father's sperm." The "traditional" aspect derives from the fact that the surrogate gives birth to her "own" child in the sense that it is genetically related to her and not genetically related to the commissioning mother or to a third-party egg donor.

9. For a discussion of the risk of exploitation faced by surrogate mothers in India, see Centre for Social Research (2013) and Pande (2014).

10. For discussion of the various types of surrogacy arrangements, see the Indian Supreme Court's observations in Baby Manji Yamada v. Union of India & ANR, INSC 1656 (September 29, 2008), para. 5–12.

11. "The mother is always certain." For example, section 5 of New Zealand's Status of Children Act 1969 establishes the presumption that it is the woman to whom a child is born who is the mother of the child; section 17 governs motherhood in assisted reproduction situations, positing that the woman who becomes pregnant is the mother, even though the ovum is donated by another woman. Section 33 of the United Kingdom's Human Fertilisation and Embryology Act 2008 specifies that the surrogate is always the mother of a child born through surrogacy.

12. In situations where there are two "commissioning mothers" (as will be the case where a same-sex couple commissions a child through ICS), this may be expanded to four potential mothers in relation to one child. This situation is not considered in this chapter, which is confined to consideration of the possibility of three mothers in ICS situations. In situations where there are no commissioning mothers (i.e., there are

only commissioning fathers), there will only be two potential mothers, and where the surrogate is also the genetic mother, only one mother will potentially exist.

13. This is the case, for example, in Australia, Israel, New Zealand, South Africa, and the United Kingdom.

14. One exception is when the commissioning mother or parents choose to involve the surrogate in the child's life or upbringing.

15. The contrary legal position may be taken in the commissioning mother's home country.

16. One UK study of surrogacy examined parental disclosure decisions and the relationships between the surrogate mother and the child. Of the thirty-three situations studied, nineteen children were genetically related to their surrogate mother. At age ten, only eleven of these children had been informed that their surrogate mother was their genetic mother. Some commissioning parents who had not disclosed this fact to the child said they intended not to disclose this to the child in future (Jadva et al. 2012). However, it remains to be seen whether children born through ICS are motivated, as they grow older, to seek to establish the identity of their genetic mothers. Furthermore, it is possible that, in the future, ICS gamete donors might be motivated to establish a relationship with their genetic child.

17. Likewise, this could be the case when a genetic father anonymously donates sperm used in an ICS arrangement.

18. For example, for a commissioning mother from New Zealand to be recognized as an ICS child's legal mother in New Zealand, she must apply to adopt the child under the Adoption Act 1955. An adoption can only be granted if the court is satisfied that, along with other factors, "the welfare and interests of the child will be promoted by the adoption" (section 11b). In the United Kingdom, a commissioning mother must seek legal parentage under section 54 of the Human Fertilisation and Embryology Act 2008.

19. For further discussion of the case against specific performance of surrogacy contracts, see Wolf (1987). On the commodification of the child, see Ergas (present volume).

20. For instance, the commissioning mother may argue that she is entitled to maternity leave equal to that received by mothers who give birth. This issue has been the subject of two conflicting decisions of the European Court of Justice. In Z v. A Government Department and the Board of Management of a Community School, C-363/12 (September 26, 2013), the decision of the Irish Equality Tribunal to refuse a commissioning mother equal maternity leave was upheld. However, CD v. ST, C-167/12 (September 26, 2013) held that a commissioning mother was entitled to a portion of maternity leave amounting to at least two weeks, and that the remainder was to be apportioned between the surrogate and commissioning mothers.

21. This was the case in Baby Manji Yamada v. Union of India & ANR, INSC 1656 (September 29, 2008), when the commissioning mother reneged on the ICS arrangement. Another example has been reported by CBC News (2011).

22. In practice, this may lead to the child being abandoned and rendered stateless due to an inability to establish a legal parental relationship or a nationality, due to the

circumstances of the child's birth. The case of Jan Balaz v. Anand Municipality, LPA 2151/2009 (November 17, 2009) is an example of an international surrogacy arrangement that led to twins being rendered stateless for two years in India, having received neither Indian nor German nationality. Such situations jeopardize the child's rights under the Convention on the Rights of the Child to nationality (article 7) and to identity (article 8). The child's right to grow up in a family environment also may be threatened. The *Balaz* case was only resolved after the commissioning parents received permission to go through the intercountry adoption process. For a report on the resolution of the case, see Mahapatra (2010).

23. The theory of burden sharing is often discussed in the context of the cross-border movement and reception of refugees among states, in relation to associated risks and costs and the notion of the "collective good." However, this concept arguably sits uneasily with ICS, given the lack of global consensus on the phenomenon, whereas strong international consensus exists in relation to reception of refugees.

24. Such entitlements might include, for example, health, social services, and education entitlements, or travel documentation. An example of the latter was Israel's refusal, in 2013/2014, to issue passports to children born in Thailand to Thai surrogates and Israeli same-sex commissioning parents. See Goldman (2014).

25. Some states indicate that this is preferred and may count in favor of the commissioning mother or parents. For example, under New Zealand's nonbinding ministerial guidelines, a minister may consider whether there is a genetic link between the child and at least one of the commissioning parents.

26. As with earlier cases of international surrogacy in the UK Family Court Division, in Re C (A Child), EWHC 2408 (Fam. 2013), the court considered whether there was a genetic link to at least one of the commissioning parents seeking parentage orders. The courts have also expressed some concern in relation to a lack of genetic link or absence of ability to trace a genetic link. For example, in Re Application by BWS to Adopt a Child ([2011] New Zealand Family Law Reports 621 at para. 82), Judge Walker expressed concern that the child had been created using anonymously donated ovum.

27. For example, Re an Application by KR and DGR to Adopt a Female Child ([2010] New Zealand Family Law Reports 97), the New Zealand commissioning mother cared for the child in Thailand on a temporary visitor's visa.

28. In situations where the child is not provided with information about the genetic mother, his or her rights under article 8 of the Convention on the Rights of the Child to identity may not be upheld, with implications for both cultural identity and personal health history, therefore also potentially affecting their health rights under article 24.1 of the convention.

29. See X & Y (Foreign Surrogacy), EWHC 3030 (Fam. 2008) at para. 24.

30. This was observed by Justice Hedley in W. and B. v. H. (Child Abduction: Surrogacy), 1 FLR 1008 (2008) at para. 1.

31. The Permanent Bureau of the Hague Conference on Private International Law (2012, 30) acknowledges international surrogacy as a global phenomenon that ultimately

may demand a global solution. For consideration of whether an international surrogacy treaty could be consistent with peremptory norms of international human rights law, see Ergas (2013b, 432–35).

32.   For discussion of some of these, see Achmad (2012, 211–13).

REFERENCES

Achmad, Claire. 2012. "Contextualising a 21st Century Challenge. Part 2—Public International Law Human Rights Issues: Why Are the Rights and Interests of Women and Children at Stake in International Commercial Surrogacy Arrangements?" *New Zealand Family Law Journal* 7, part 8.

BBC News. 2015 (February 20). "Thailand Bans Commercial Surrogacy for Foreigners." http://www.bbc.com/news/world-asia-31546717.

CBC News. 2011 (September 14). "Surrogate Mother's Trouble Concern Lawyer." http://www.cbc.ca/news/canada/new-brunswick/story/2011/09/14/nb-reproductive-lawyer-surrogate-mother-945.html.

Centre for Social Research. 2013. *Surrogate Motherhood: Ethical or Commercial.* https://archive.nyu.edu/bitstream/2451/34217/2/Surrogacy-Motherhood-Ethical-or-Commercial-Delhi%26Mumbai.pdf.

Child, Youth and Family. 2011. *International Surrogacy Information Sheet.* http://www.cyf.govt.nz/documents/adoption/is-information-sheet-june2011.pdf.

Chu, Henry. 2006. "Wombs for Rent, Cheap." *Los Angeles Times*, April 19. http://articles.latimes.com/2006/apr/19/world/fg-surrogate19.

Creative Family Connections. 2016. "Gestational Surrogacy Laws Across the United States: State-by-State Interactive Map for Commercial Surrogacy." http://www.creativefamilyconnections.com/us-surrogacy-law-map.

Ergas, Yasmine. 2013a. "Babies Without Borders: Human Rights, Human Dignity and the Regulation of International Commercial Surrogacy." *Emory International Law Review* 27: 117–88.

——. 2013b. "Thinking 'Through' Human Rights: The Need for a Human Rights Perspective with Respect to the Regulation of Cross-Border Reproductive Surrogacy." In *International Surrogacy Arrangements*, ed. Katrina Trimmings and Paul Beaumont, 427–38. Oxford: Hart Publishing.

Ethics Committee of the American Society for Reproductive Medicine. 2013. "Cross-Border Reproductive Care: A Committee Opinion." *Fertility and Sterility* 100, no. 3: 645–50.

Field, Martha A. 1990. *Surrogate Motherhood: The Legal and Human Issues.* Cambridge, MA: Harvard University Press.

Freeman, Michael. 1992. "The Limits of Children's Rights." In *The Ideologies of Children's Rights*, ed. Michael Freeman and Philip Veerman, 29–46. Leiden: Brill.

Goldman, Yoel. 2014. "Babies Born Through Thai Surrogacy Begin Arriving in Israel." *Times of Israel*, January 31. http://www.timesofisrael.com/babies-born-through-thai-surrogacy-begin-arriving-in-israel.

Government of Ireland. n.d. *Citizenship, Parentage, Guardianship and Travel Document Issues in Relation to Children Born as a Result of Surrogacy Arrangements Entered into Outside the State.* https://www.dfa.ie/media/dfa/alldfawebsitemedia/passportcitizenship /Surrogacy-Guidelines.pdf.

Hague Conference on Private International Law. 2011. *Private International Law Issues Surrounding the Status of Children, Including Issues Arising From International Surrogacy Arrangements.* https://assets.hcch.net/docs/f5991e3e-0f8b-430c-b030-ca93c8ef1c0a.pdf.

——. 2012. *A Preliminary Report on the Issues Arising From International Surrogacy Arrangements.* https://assets.hcch.net/upload/wop/gap2012pd10en.pdf.

Harari, David Y. 2008. "Surrogacy: Human Incubators and a Defense of Contractual and Financial Agreements." *The Interdisciplinary Journal of Health, Ethics and Policy* 7, no. 2: 5–9.

Indian Council of Medical Research. 2005. *National Guidelines for Accreditation, Supervision and Regulation of ART Clinics in India.* New Delhi: Ministry of Health and Family Welfare, Government of India.

Jadva, V., L. Blake, P. Casey, and S. Golombok. 2012. "Surrogacy Families 10 Years On: Relationship with the Surrogate, Decisions over Disclosure and Children's Understanding of Their Surrogacy Origins," *Human Reproduction* 27, no. 10: 3008–14.

Mahapatra, Dhananjay. 2010. "German Surrogate Twins to Go Home." *Times of India*, May 27. http://articles.timesofindia.indiatimes.com/2010-05-27/india/28279835_1_stateless -citizens-balaz-surrogate-mother.

Office of the United Nations High Commissioner for Human Rights (OHCHR). 1989. *Convention on the Rights of the Child.* http://www.ohchr.org/en/professionalinterest/pages /crc.aspx.

Pande, Amrita. 2009. "It May Be Her Eggs but It's My Blood: Surrogates and Everyday Forms of Kinship in India." *Qualitative Sociology* 32, no. 4: 379–97.

——. 2014. *Wombs in Labor: Transnational Commercial Surrogacy in India.* New York: Columbia University Press.

Pascoe, John. 2014. "State of the Nation—Federal Circuit Court of Australia." *Federal Judicial Scholarship* 21, http://www.austlii.edu.au/au/journals/FedJSchol/2014/21.html.

Ryznar, Margaret. 2010. "International Commercial Surrogacy and Its Parties." *John Marshall Law Review* 43, no. 4: 1009–39.

Sama Resource Group for Women and Health. 2012. *Birthing a Market: A Study on Commercial Surrogacy.* New Dehli: Sama.

Shanley, Mary Lyndon. 2001. *Making Babies, Making Families: What Matters Most in an Age of Reproductive Technologies, Surrogacy, Adoption and Same-Sex and Unwed Parents.* Boston: Beacon Press.

Smerdon, Usha Rengachary. 2008–09. "Crossing Bodies, Crossing Borders: International Surrogacy Between the United States and India." *Cumberland Law Review* 39, no. 1: 15–85.

Spar, Debora L. 2006. *The Baby Business: How Money, Science and Politics Drive the Commerce of Conception.* Boston: Harvard Business School Press.

Trimmings, Katarina, and Paul Beaumont (eds). 2013. *International Surrogacy Arrangements: Legal Regulation at the International Level.* Oxford: Hart Publishing.

UK Border Agency. 2009. *Inter-Country Surrogacy and the Immigration Rules*. http://www
.ukba.homeoffice.gov.uk/sitecontent/documents/residency/Intercountry-surrogacy
-leaflet.

van den Akker, Olga V. A. 2010. "Surrogate Mothers." In *Parenthood and Mental Health: A
Bridge Between Infant and Adult Psychiatry*, ed. Sam Tyano, Miri Keren, Helen Herrman,
and John Cox, 39–50. Chicester: John Wiley and Sons.

van Zyl, Liezl, and Ruth Walker. 2013. "Beyond Altruistic and Commercial Contract Motherhood: The Professional Model." *Bioethics* 27, no. 7: 373–81.

Warner, Judith. 2008. "Outsourced Wombs." *New York Times*, January 3. http://opinionator
.blogs.nytimes.com/2008/01/03/outsourced-wombs/?_php=true&_type=blogs&_r=0.

Wolf, Susan M. 1987. "Enforcing Surrogate Motherhood Agreements: The Trouble with
Specific Performance." *New York Law School Human Rights Annual* 4, no. 2: 375–412.

4

THE BORDERS OF LEGAL
MOTHERHOOD

Rethinking Access to Assisted Reproductive
Technologies in Europe

LETIZIA PALUMBO

Laws defining motherhood continue to focus predominantly on biology. Following the conventional principle "mater semper certa est" (the mother is always certain), the law equates the physical act of giving birth with maternity (Hague Conference on Private International Law 2012). But the normative force of the idea that there is an "obvious" and "natural" coincidence between biological reproduction and legal motherhood has been eroded by the advent of assisted reproductive technologies (ARTs), the emergence of reproductive surrogacy, and the globalization and formalization of adoption "markets." As a result, establishing legal certainty about the identity of a mother appears problematic, particularly in cases of surrogacy and oocyte donation.

ARTs have challenged the notion of natural reproduction, adding to physical reproduction a dimension some have perceived as "artificial," and fragmenting it (Gribaldo 2005). Blurring the borders between "natural" and "artificial" dimensions, and leading to a redefinition of what is thought to be natural and biological (Parolin and Perrotta 2012), ARTs have played a crucial role in transforming family ties and forms of parenthood and, accordingly, in changing the meaning and the shape of motherhood (Franklin and Ragoné 1998; Lombardi and De Zordo 2013).

The effects of ARTs can be contradictory. On one hand, they provide new ways to establish families, offering single individuals and same-sex couples the potential for parenthood, thus unseating traditional familial models. On the other hand, they can lead to the strengthening of "cultural motherhood mandates" for women (Inhorn and Birenbaum-Carmeli 2008, 180) or to the reinforcement of gender and social inequalities (Chavkin and Maher 2010). The liberating or restrictive potential of ARTs is determined by the interplay of economic, social, cultural, and normative factors within different countries.

National regulations on ARTs vary across Europe, ranging from liberal (as in Belgium, Finland, and Greece) to restrictive (as in Italy and Austria until recent years) (Piga 2013). Situated in specific cultural and social orders, legal rules on assisted reproduction can displace or confirm a conservative model of family relations, revealing tensions and inconsistencies in the context in which ARTs are inserted, and highlighting the ways in which women's bodies, which are the main targets of reproductive measures, are often reduced to a battlefield of different values and opposing rights (Zuffa 2005).

Women do not have equal access to ARTs; their access to motherhood is curtailed when they fail to fulfill the legal, social, and economic criteria embedded in national regulations. In Italy, for example, those who remain outside the borders of legal motherhood include single women, lesbians, and (until recently) women of fertile couples who carry genetic diseases and, wishing to have a healthy child, choose not to become pregnant. Also excluded are economically disadvantaged women who cannot afford to travel abroad for reproductive assistance (in particular, heterologous procreation techniques). Indeed, recourse to ARTs is allowed only for heterosexual married or cohabiting couples, as a support for reproductive problems arising from human sterility or infertility. Ovum and sperm donation was prohibited until May 2014, and healthy couples suffering from genetically inherited diseases were banned from accessing ARTs until May 2015.[1] The use of surrogate mothers is forbidden (Miranda 2010).

Who, then, may decide who may become a mother? Who specifically can determine access to ARTs that enable maternity, and on the basis of which principles? To explore these questions in the European context, this chapter focuses on two pivotal cases regarding gamete donation and genetic profiling of embryos prior to implantation, decided by the European Court of Human Rights: *S. H. and Others v. Austria* (Judgment of the Grand Chamber 57813/00, November 3, 2011) and *Costa and Pavan v.*

Italy (10th Sess., 54270/10, August 28, 2012). The chapter examines the legal meanings of motherhood these cases promote, the family models they enshrine, and the gendered norms that they incorporate. Ultimately, the essay concludes that, although restrictive regulations limiting access to ARTs further stratify motherhood, embedding new privileges and exclusions, legal challenges to such regulations on ARTs may result in a progressive expansion of the borders of legal motherhood.

ACCESS TO IN VITRO FERTILIZATION WITH DONOR GAMETES, OOCYTE DONATION, AND THE FEAR OF "SPLIT MOTHERHOOD": *S. H. AND OTHERS V. AUSTRIA*

In *S. H. and Others v. Austria*, the European Court of Human Rights (ECtHR) was, for the first time, called upon to assess the extent to which a national legal system can regulate access to in vitro fertilization (IVF) with donor oocyte and sperm.[2] It thus constitutes a significant moment in the court's case law on reproductive rights and offers an interesting perspective from which to examine and problematize the condition of (un)certainty that characterizes the legal definition of motherhood.

The case concerned two married couples, both resident in Austria, who, being infertile, wanted access to ARTs (in particular, to heterologous procreation techniques). The first couple needed to use IVF with donor sperm. The second couple needed to use IVF with oocyte donation. Both treatments were ruled out by the 1992 Austrian Artificial Protection Act. More specifically, until 2015, the act forbade the use of donor sperm for IVF and oocyte donation in general.[3] At the same time, it allowed IVF with egg or sperm from a couple themselves (if the couple is married or cohabiting) and permitted, in particular circumstances, in vivo fertilization with donor sperm. ART treatments for single women and surrogacy are still completely banned.

In 1998, both couples filed an application with the Austrian Constitutional Court for a review of the Artificial Protection Act provisions on heterologous procreation techniques. The court found that the decision of a couple to make use of medically assisted procreation techniques fell within the scope of article 8 of the European Convention on Human Rights (ECHR), which guarantees of respect for private and family life.[4] However, the court also found that the statute's interference was justified in view of the "well-being of the children thus conceived" and the ethical and moral implications that the procedures entailed (see *S. H. and Others* at § 17). It determined that the Austrian restrictions on ARTs were aimed at avoiding "the forming of unusual personal relations, such as a child having more than one biological mother (a genetic mother and one carrying the child)," and at avoiding the risk of exploitation of women. Thus, in the Constitutional Court's view, Austria had not exceeded the margin of appreciation—that is, the latitude that states may employ in interpreting their obligations under EU law.

In 2000, the couples appealed to the European Court of Human Rights. In its judgment of April 1, 2010 (*S. H. and Others*, ECtHR First Section 57813/00), the court found that the Austrian prohibitions on the use of donated gametes for IVF constituted a breach of the European Convention on Human Rights prohibition against discrimination, in conjunction with the respect for privacy and family life. In particular, the court argued that this prohibition produced discrimination among couples on the basis of fertility and that the Austrian government had not submitted "a reasonable and objective justification for the difference in treatment" between the applicants and a couple who wished access to ARTs without resorting to gamete donation.

The Austrian government appealed the decision before the court's Grand Chamber. In its judgment, the Grand Chamber, overruling the findings of the lower chamber, found that the Austrian prohibitions on the use of ARTs at issue did not constitute a violation of the ECHR's protections of privacy and family life. The Grand Chamber (57813/00, November 3, 2011 at § 84) clarified that it had to decide "whether these prohibitions were justified at the time they were considered by the Austrian Constitutional Court." However, it was not "prevented from having regard to subsequent developments in making its assessment."

The Grand Chamber observed that, where there is no shared approach among the member states of the Council of Europe, particularly in cases raising sensitive moral and ethical issues, the margin of appreciation will be broad. In this case, the chamber found that although there was a trend across Europe in favor of allowing sperm and oocyte donation for IVF, this emerging consensus was not based on settled legal principles "but rather reflect[ed] a stage of development within a particularly dynamic field of law and [did] not decisively narrow the margin of appreciation of the State" (§ 96). The Austrian legislation sought, among other things, to prevent the risk of exploitation of women and to avoid the possibility that "two persons could claim to be the biological mother of one and the same child (§ 104)," and thus to safeguard the civil law principle that the mother is always certain. In the Grand Chamber's view, Austria's legislation carefully addressed complex questions that gave rise to sensitive moral and ethical issues and did not prohibit individuals from going abroad to access ARTs. Therefore, the court held, Austria had not overstepped the margin of appreciation permitted to member states and, consequently, its law did not violate article 8 of the ECHR.

In the absence of a clear common ground, the Grand Chamber chose to "abdicate" in favor of the national legislature. However, this is not the only modus operandi of the court in determining the margin of appreciation of the states. In other cases—for example, in *Goodwin v. UK* (application 28957/95, July 11, 2002)—the court applied the doctrine of the margin of appreciation differently, giving less weight to the lack of a European consensus and engaging in a protection of individual rights instead.

As mentioned, the Grand Chamber confined its examination to the period of time in which the initial complaint was lodged (1999). However, it also specified that it was not prevented from considering current developments in making its assessment. But, as the joint dissenting judges argued (*S. H. and Others*, joint dissenting opinion at § 4), this specification remained "a dead letter in actual fact" as the Grand Chamber's decision did not take into consideration the development in medical science and current European consensus on heterologous IVF. This inconsistency deprived its judgment of "any real substance."

By not paying attention to advances in medical science and their legal implications, the Grand Chamber ended up privileging a questionable moral/ethical approach that does not take into account the issue of the health and well-being of couples and, especially, of women. In fact, it seemed to overlook the fact that infertility and sterility can cause psychological distress and social suffering (Vayena, Rowe, and Griffin 2002), which ARTs may remedy; access to ARTs may therefore promote individuals' right to health (Nardocci 2012).

This decision of the Grand Chamber underscores the crucial role that morals and ethics play in defining the margin of appreciation to be accorded to national authorities. Moreover, by stressing the central role of the state authorities, which are "in a better position than the international judge to give an opinion, not only on the 'exact content of the requirements of morals' in their country, but also on the necessity of a restriction intended to meet them" (*S. H. and Others* at § 94), this ruling reveals how the path toward a harmonization across Europe of the rights guaranteed by the ECHR is tortuous and full of obstacles (Nardocci 2012). At the same time, this decision highlights the concerns arising from oocyte donation, as this practice challenges the coincidence between legal motherhood and biological reproduction. The Grand Chamber observed that parent–child relationships not based on biological linkage were not new for the legal systems of the Council of Europe member states. In fact, adoption constituted a "satisfactory legal framework" (*S. H. and Others* at § 105) for these kinds of relations. But the Grand Chamber argued that the splitting of motherhood between two women (the oocyte donor and the birth mother) caused by oocyte donation "differs significantly from adoptive parent–child relations and has added a new aspect to this issue."

The Austrian government, in its argument to support the need for restrictions on access to heterologous IVF, pointed out that the donation of oocyte touches the issue of the production of unusual family forms; families "in which the social circumstances deviated from the biological ones, namely, the division of the motherhood into a biological [i.e., genetic] aspect and an aspect of 'carrying the child' and perhaps also a social aspect" (*S. H. and Others* at § 67). From this perspective, the Austrian ban on oocyte donation mainly aimed at maintaining and protecting the certainty of the identity of the mother.

Under the Austrian civil code (Allgemeines bürgerliches Gesetzbuch article 137b), the mother of a child is always she who has given birth to that child. The father of a child is the male person who has had sexual intercourse with the mother in the period of not more than three hundred days and not less than one hundred eighty days before the birth (article 163). Where ARTs with a sperm donor have been used, the father is the person who has given his consent to that treatment. A sperm donor is never recognized as the father of the child. Therefore, while the Austrian law provides a broad definition of "father" that does not rely only on biology, the definition of "mother" remains strongly rooted in biology and is dependent on childbirth.

From the Austrian government's argument it emerges that donation of oocytes, by splitting motherhood, produces a problematic situation of unmanageable uncertainty and destabilization. Similar concerns were also expressed by third-party interveners in the case. The German government pointed out that the split motherhood runs counter to the "principle of unambiguousness of motherhood which represented a fundamental and basic social consensus" (*S. H. and Others* at § 70). Split motherhood constitutes a serious threat to the child's welfare because "the resulting ambiguousness of the mother's identity might jeopardize the development of the child's personality and lead to considerable problems in his or her discovery of identity." More dramatically, the Austrian government stressed that "to call maternal filiation into question by splitting motherhood would lead to a weakening of the entire structure of society" (§ 73).

In contrast to these views, it can be argued that, as studies have highlighted, the uniqueness of the role of the parents does not depend on the biological link to the child; instead, it is based on the ability to nurture, protect, and love a child and to ensure the adequate environment for the child's well-being and development. All these factors, which are not dependent on biology, are extremely important for the welfare of the child (Brighouse and Swift 2006; D'Alton-Harrison 2014).

Here too, then, the Austrian government's argument reveals that its concern over unusual family relationships related only to cases involving distinct birth and donor "mothers." In fact, the Austrian authorities (like the ECtHR Grand Chamber) appeared unconcerned with the unusual family forms resulting from a split between the biological and the legal father. Split fatherhood seems not to produce uncertain and problematic situations—or, it may be better to say, it produces a situation the resolution of which appears straightforward. In the case in which ARTs with sperm donation have been used, the father is the person who has given his consent to the treatment. This is not regarded as negatively affecting the child's welfare. As Sanderson (2013, 38) has noted, in the Austrian government's argument "male reproduction (and the role of men as defined in law) is assumed to be simple and easily controlled while female reproduction (and the role of women as defined in law) is assumed to be complex and easily confused."

It is specifically oocyte donation that is perceived as a threat to the "natural unit" formed by the mother and her egg (and her child) (Melhuus 2005, 227). This unit is considered fundamental and, as such, inviolable; the mother and her oocyte go together. Oocytes belong to the body from which they come and thus can only move in the same body. From this perspective, oocyte donation, leading to the introduction of external eggs into the body of a woman, breaks what occurs in natural reproduction. Conversely, as Melhuus argues in relation to Norwegian law, which also permits sperm donation and not oocyte donation, "sperm donation is accepted because there is an intrinsic uncertainty about paternity as sperm 'comes from the outside' (in contrast to eggs which are on the inside) and does not create a situation different from natural reproduction." Aiming to protect the natural unity between the mother and her oocyte (and her child), Austrian law allowed no oocyte donation until 2014, even though it permitted sperm donation (in vivo fertilization with donor sperm). Biology *as represented by the ovum* constituted an essential element of motherhood.

For the Austrian government, oocyte donation does not raise only the issue of split motherhood. It also concerns the problem of the commodification of female body parts and the exploitation of women: oocyte donation depends "on the availability of oocyte and might lead to problematic developments such as the exploitation and humiliation of women, in particular those from an economically disadvantaged background" (*S. H. and Others* at § 66). Also, women may be pressured into providing more oocytes than is strictly necessary for their own treatment, in order to be able to afford the treatment itself.

Although there are cases in which oocyte donation constitutes a generous gift (Roberts 2009), oocytes are increasingly sold through commercial transactions (Almeling 2007; Chavkin and Maher 2010). This has led to "new forms of labor" among reproductive donors who experience risky hormonal treatment and egg-harvesting procedures (Inhorn and Birenbaum-Carmeli 2008, 183; see also Khan and Chavkin, present volume). Particular concerns have been raised about economically disadvantaged women who "donate" their eggs (sometimes traveling abroad in order to do so) in return for financial remuneration, which is often a small sum (Heng 2007; Chavkin and Maher 2010). The Austrian government's concern about the potential abuse of this body commodification (which was also expressed by the Grand Chamber) is therefore warranted.

However, the government focused exclusively on the risk of women's exploitation and humiliation in cases of oocyte donation, overlooking (or perhaps excluding) the risk of exploitation and humiliation of sperm donors. In other words, potential harm and dangers seemed to come into play only when oocyte donation is involved and, accordingly, women need to be protected. In contrast, men seem to have been assumed to be less susceptible to abuse and humiliation in the cases of sperm donation, and thus less in need of protection. Admittedly, oocytes constitute a scarce resource; their procurement requires risky interventions and women, especially those in economically disadvantaged conditions, often are unable to negotiate a fair bargain and ensure that they have adequate protections (Inhorn and Birenbaum-Carmeli 2008). However, problematic situations can also arise in the context of sperm donation. By ignoring this, the government's view implicitly reinforced gender-biased stereotypes, in particular with regard to women's particular vulnerability in the context of gamete donation.

The ban on oocyte donation, rather than leading to a decrease in this practice, in Austria as in other countries, has led to the development of cross-border reproductive care (Shalev and Werner-Felmayer 2012; Ferraretti et al. 2010), involving individuals going to another country in order to access ARTs. This is often associated with health risks, suffering, frustration (Ferraretti et al. 2010; Zanini 2011; Lombardi and De Zordo 2013), and disparities between those who can afford treatment in expensive and safe clinics and those who go to cheaper but often lower-quality clinics (Rodotà 2004; Ferraretti et al. 2010).

The issue of cross-border reproductive care was also touched on by the Grand Chamber, which pointed out that there is no prohibition under Austrian law against going abroad to access ARTs not allowed in Austria and that "in the event of a successful treatment the Civil Code contains clear rules on paternity and maternity that respect the wishes of the parents" (*S. H. and Others* at § 114). However, this argument is problematic for several reasons. First of all, the Grand Chamber did not take into account the emotional difficulties, economic burdens, and health risks that may be linked to traveling abroad to access ARTs. Moreover, as joint dissenting judges in the case argued (*S. H. and Others*, joint dissenting opinion at § 13), the Grand Chamber's concerns about the creation of atypical family relations and, specifically, the potential harm split motherhood might entail for the welfare of the child, seemed to disappear "as a result of crossing the border." The same can be said about the court's concerns about the exploitation and health of women.

Confirming and strengthening a biologically based conception of motherhood and family relationships, *S. H. and Others* marked a step backwards in the recognition and protection of the right to procreation for those people who need donor gametes. Nevertheless, the Grand Chamber concluded its judgment by noting that ARTs constitute an area of rapid development and, as a result, national legislations must be kept under review. The court thus recognized the need to align national legislations with changes in society, (possibly) allowing for further decisions in line with a general trend in favor of a permissive approach to ARTs.

It is in exactly this direction that Austria is moving. In particular, in December 2013, the Constitutional Court declared the statutory ban on donor insemination for lesbian couples to be a violation of human rights.[5] In 2015, distancing itself from the decision of the ECtHR in *S. H. and Others*, Austria amended its legislation on ARTs to permit egg donation, in vivo fertilization and IVF with donor sperm for lesbian couples, IVF with donor sperm for heterosexual couples, and pre-implantation diagnosis (PGD) in some cases. These important amendments, toward a more liberal approach to regulation of ARTs, have resulted in an expansion of the border of legal motherhood.

MOTHERS, EMBRYOS, GENETICS, AND GESTATION: *COSTA AND PAVAN V. ITALY*

In *Costa and Pavan v. Italy*, the European Court of Human Rights, for the first time, issued a judgment on the Italian Act on Assisted

Reproduction 40/2004 ("Norme in materia di procreazione medicalmente assistita"), and thus on the compatibility of this act with the fundamental rights protected by the ECHR. Since it entered into force, the Italian statute on ARTs has been challenged by a series of legal actions before the courts of first instance, the Constitutional Court and, recently, the European Court of Human Rights (see D'Amico and Liberali 2012; Penasa 2012; D'Amico 2015).[6] This process has led to a progressive dismantlement of the act, resulting in its reworking according to an approach that takes into account and balances the diverse rights and interests involved (D'Amico 2015). In *Costa*, the court examined the statute's (implicit) ban on pre-implantation genetic diagnoses.[7] This case offers a significant perspective to highlight how women's self-determination and right to health did not find a place in the Italian act on ARTs as originally approved.

Rosetta Costa and Walter Pavan were both healthy carriers of cystic fibrosis, a serious genetic disease that causes respiratory difficulties and can be fatal. In order to have a child while avoiding transmission of the disease, the applicants sought access to ARTs. They intended to use PGD to select an embryo that did not carry the disease. But the Italian statute on assisted reproduction limited access to ARTs to sterile and/or infertile married or cohabiting heterosexual couples. According to the guidelines on ARTs issued by the Italian Ministry of Health in 2008, access to ARTs was also allowed to couples in which the man is a carrier of sexually transmittable diseases, such as HIV/AIDS and hepatitis B or C infection, which de facto constitutes an obstacle for (sexual) procreation, "requiring precautions that necessarily result in infertility."[8] Healthy couples suffering from genetically inherited diseases were banned from accessing ARTs until May 2015; the ban continues for single women and same-sex couples. Moreover, donor-assisted reproduction was prohibited until May 2014, and, until April 2009, embryo freezing was banned, the number of embryos produced by each IVF cycle was limited to three, and all such embryos were required to be transferred to the uterus simultaneously.[9]

On September 20, 2010, Costa and Pavan petitioned the ECtHR, without previously referring the matter to the Italian courts.[10] They claimed that the Italian law preventing them from accessing ARTs and PGD violated their rights to privacy and respect for family life under the

European Convention for Human Rights (article 8). The only option available to them to have healthy babies, they argued, was to begin a pregnancy by natural means and to abort the fetus if it were affected with cystic fibrosis.[11] The couple also claimed that they were victims of discrimination as compared to couples who could access ARTs, including PGD.

The ECtHR found that the applicants' desire to access ARTs and PGD in order to conceive a child not affected with cystic fibrosis was "a form of expression of their private and family life." As such, it fell within the scope and protection provided by article 8 of the European Convention on Human Rights; the fact that Italian law did not allow them to access ARTs and PGD constituted an interference with their rights to respect for their private and family life.

But the European Convention's protection of privacy and family life is not absolute. Article 8 of the convention provides that interference by a public authority may be justified if it is "in accordance with the law and is necessary in a democratic society" in pursuit of recognized legitimate aims, including the protection of health, morals, and the rights and freedoms of others. The Italian government argued that the interference the court had found was aimed at protecting "the health of the child and the woman" ("the latter being susceptible to depression on account of ovarian stimulation and oocyte retrieval") and "the dignity and freedom of conscience of the medical professions," and at preventing the risk of eugenic selection (*Costa* at § 46).

In response, the ECtHR stressed that the notions of "embryo" and "child" are different and not to be confused. It argued that the government's emphasis on the couple's potential recourse to abortion if the fetus proved to be affected with cystic fibrosis was inherently contradictory, since abortion itself may be seen as provoking negative consequences for both the fetus and the parents, in particular for the health of the mother (*Costa* at § 62). In the court's view, by prohibiting PGD but authorizing the abortion of a fetus affected with the disease, the Italian legal framework showed itself to be incoherent (see Zagrebelsky 2012). This inconsistency left the applicants with only one painful choice: to start the pregnancy and terminate it through abortion in the event the prenatal test showed the fetus to be unhealthy. The court found that "the interference with the applicants' right to respect for their private and family life was disproportionate" and, accordingly, in breach of the European Convention on Human Rights (*Costa* at § 71). But it was not discriminatory: the court found that there was no violation of the principle of nondiscrimination, because the prohibition of PGD applied to all categories of people.[12]

Unlike the result it attained in *S. H. and Others*, in *Costa* the ECtHR held that the national legislation at issue exceeded the state's margin of appreciation. The court justified the change in the approach by highlighting the difference between the two cases. Although both heterologous insemination and access to PGD raise sensitive moral questions, in *S. H. and Others*, the court assessed the compatibility of the Austrian act on ARTs with article 8 of the European Convention; in *Costa* (§ 69), it verified the proportionality of the prohibition on PGD in light of the fact that Italian legislation authorizes abortion. Thus, in the *Costa* case, the court moved "towards a strict scrutiny [standard], which goes to verify the concrete content of the regulation, evaluating its effective proportionality and systematic coherence" (Penasa 2012, 177). The Italian government entered an appeal against this decision, which the Grand Chamber rejected.

The *Costa* case highlighted contradictions embedded in the Italian legal framework, which, while forbidding the use of PGD, authorized therapeutic abortion. This contradiction may be connected to the fact that, as many Italian feminist scholars and activists have argued, the statute on ARTs was intended to reimpose traditional values that were threatened by the legalization of abortion, by the emergence of new family forms, and by the expansion of women's freedom in the 1970s and 1980s (Bonsignori, Dominijanni, and Giorgi 2005). Dameno (2004) referred to the act as a "manifesto law" aimed at safeguarding a traditional idea of the family by emphasizing the link between family relationships and biological ties rather than attempting to support individuals wishing to access ARTs, thereby protecting their fundamental rights.[13]

Commentators have argued that, in Italy, people who do not have access to ARTs, such as single women and same-sex couples, often feel marginalized and stigmatized (Krause and De Zordo 2012). In her research on the politics of reproduction and migration in Italy, Marchesi (2012, 177) has pointed out that women who want access to ARTs often feel stigmatized as being "irrational" and "irresponsible" for "pushing the natural limits of reproduction by accessing fertility treatments." Many women decide to travel abroad to access ARTs and fulfill their desire for motherhood. Indeed, many commentators have noted that, feeling abandoned by their own national institutions, many people see the possibility of going abroad as the only way to claim their reproductive rights (Zanini 2011). But, as discussed in reference to *S. H. and Others*, cross-border reproductive care is often marked by suffering, health risks, discrimination, and frustration (Ferraretti et al. 2010).

As originally approved, the Italian statute on ARTs aimed to protect the embryo, overriding other interests and rights—most prominently, women's rights to self-determination and physical and psychological health. As Penasa (2012, 156) has stressed, embryo protection, and the attempt to support a traditional (i.e., heterosexual) and biologically based conception of the family, provided the "red thread" that linked the various provisions of the law (see also Marella and Virgilio 2004).

The first article of the statute describes its intention to guarantee "the rights of all subjects involved, including the *concepito* [the conceived]." Thus, it implicitly endows the concepito with rights that deserve legal protection. The term "concepito" appears only once, in article 1, while the rest of text refers to the "embryo," in the parts regarding the implementation of the technologies, and to the "unborn child" (*nascituro*). But the law never explicitly defines the rights of the concepito. Arguably, the statute refers to those rights that the concepito gains after birth but that are protected from the time of conception, such as rights regarding succession and property. If one looks at the letter of the law, the rights of embryo can be "deduced from the duties and prohibitions established" for the other subjects, the first of which is the woman (Boccia 2005, 70). For example, in its initial form, the act stipulated that no more than three embryos might be produced, and that all of them were to be simultaneously transferred to the mother's womb. Cryopreservation of embryos was not allowed, except in cases involving a serious danger to the woman's health. In these instances, the transfer of the embryos had to be realized as soon as possible.[14]

The act, as originally approved, seemed to rely on a conception of the embryo as a subject autonomous from the woman in whose uterus it will exist (Hanafin 2013) and to posit an interest in the protection that is superior to the protection of the rights of the pregnant woman. This eclipsed[15] the mother: she lost her sovereignty over reproduction and her body was reduced to the "status of incubator" (Fenton 2006, 104). From this perspective, the statute undermined the balance between the woman and embryo found in Italian law regarding abortion (Alesso 2013; Hanafin 2013). In particular, Italy's Constitutional Court held, in 1975, that the safeguarding of the embryo, "which is a person yet to be," does not prevail on a woman's right to life and health. Accordingly, the Italian Abortion Act of 1978 authorizes women to interrupt their pregnancy within a framework of permissible situations.

Feminist movements and other political groups have critiqued the statute on ARTs since its promulgation. In 2005, it was challenged through a referendum that sought its repeal, which ultimately proved unsuccessful. Moreover, as mentioned, it also has been challenged by a series of legal actions at the level of local courts, in the Italian Constitutional Court, and in the European Court of Human Rights, including in *Costa*. As a result of these judicial challenges, there has been a gradual redefinition of the normative content of the ART statute, which has led to a weakening of its ideological approach and its focus on the rights of the embryo (D'Amico 2015).

In particular, in 2009, the Constitutional Court (decision 151/2009) found unconstitutional the provisions imposing the transfer of all embryos in a single and simultaneous implantation and limiting to three the number of embryos that could be produced. It also struck down the provisions of the statute regarding the transfer of embryos, because these did not require that the woman's health should be safeguarded. The court found that these provisions overlooked the personal and medical conditions of the woman undergoing medically assisted reproduction, thereby depriving her physician of the possibility of deciding on the treatment to be followed, after evaluating her medical situation. Predetermining a unique procedure for the production of the embryos and their implantation entailed treating different cases in the same way. In the court's view, this breached the principle of substantive equality guaranteed by article 3 of the Italian constitution and the principle of reasonableness inferable from it. Moreover, it interfered with the right to health (article 32). The court thus quashed the provisions regarding the limitation on the number of embryos and their simultaneous transfer. It also relaxed the ban on the cryopreservation of embryos (article 14.1).

Highlighting that the protection of the embryo must not be considered absolute, the Italian Constitutional Court pointed out that the interests of all parties involved (and, in particular, the health of the woman) should be taken into account. In this regard, it expressly referred to its previous ruling on abortion, which stressed the priority of the rights of the woman to self-determination and health.[16] The court upheld the principle of the autonomy of the woman and of the autonomy and responsibility of physicians, allowing the latter to adapt ART treatment to concrete cases. It thus directly intervened in those parts of the statute in which there was a "manifest imbalance" in favor of the protection of the embryo at the expense of the woman's dignity, self-determination, and health (Alesso 2013, 107).

In continuity with the Italian Constitutional Court decision, the ECtHR, in *Costa*, considered the interests of all the parties involved, prioritizing the protection of the reproductive rights of the couple, including their right to health and, in particular, women's right to health. The *Costa* case has had a direct effect on the Italian legal system[17] and has significantly contributed to the progressive redefinition of the statute on ARTs, moving it toward a stronger protection of human rights. In 2014, this process led the Constitutional Court to declare unconstitutional those aspects of the statute that prohibited gamete donation for reproductive purposes. In this important ruling, the Constitutional Court (decision 162/2014) held that a ban on gamete donation conflicted with a couple's ability to choose to become parents and have a family, which is an expression of the fundamental freedom of self-determination. The court argued that the choice to resort to ARTs to become parents, which concerns the "most intimate and intangible sphere of the human person, must be free from constraint, provided that it does not violate other constitutional values." The court also highlighted that infertility and sterility are health issues and that the ban on gamete donation therefore violated the fundamental right to health, which includes the right to psychological health. In cases that involve illnesses that produce disabilities, the court argued, any decisions concerning the merits of therapeutic choices "cannot result from purely discretionary political assessments by the legislator" but must also take into account viewpoints based on medical science. In this perspective, the court affirmed, the basic rule must be the autonomy and responsibility of the physicians.

This approach takes into account the plurality of values and interests involved and recognizes as fundamental the principle of the autonomy and responsibility of couples and physicians. In May 2015, the Constitutional Court (decision 96/2015) declared unconstitutional the ban on PGD for healthy couples suffering from genetically inherited diseases that meet the criteria of seriousness established by the Italian statute on abortion for the interruption of pregnancy after ninety days of gestation. The court argued that the ban violated the principle of equality and the right to health. More specifically, in accordance with the arguments of the ECtHR in *Costa*, the court highlighted the unreasonableness of the ban, which was due to the fact that the Italian legal framework, with a "clear normative antinomy," allowed couples to resort to abortion in order to have a child unaffected by the genetically inherited disease. According to the court, the ban on PGD did not allow women to acquire information that would enable them to avoid making a decision (i.e., to abort) that is more damaging to their health. This entailed a violation of women's right to health: the limitation of this right was not counterbalanced by a need to protect the unborn child (nascituro), as he or she would in any case be "exposed to abortion." Therefore, the court held, the ban was the result of an "unreasonable balancing of the interests at stake" and it was also affected by irrationality in light of the statute on abortion.

CONCLUSIONS: CHALLENGING THE BORDERS OF MOTHERHOOD

Focusing on two key cases of the European Court of Human Rights, this chapter has examined the eligibility criteria for access to ARTs and, thus, to maternity in contemporary Europe, paying special attention to the legal meaning of motherhood, family models, and women's reproductive rights. It has highlighted how statutory law on ARTs can confirm and strengthen particular views of the family and of biologically based family relationships, often neglecting women's reproductive rights and placing many women, particularly single women, lesbians, and women of fertile couples with genetic diseases, outside the borders of legal motherhood. In Italy, one of the most restrictive regulations on ARTs has been repeatedly challenged through legal actions at the national and European levels. This process has resulted in a progressive redefinition of the ART statute and its attendant regulatory framework, moving it toward somewhat stronger recognition and protection of individuals'—and, in particular, of women's—rights to self-determination and health. In turn, this has undermined the biologically based conception of family on which the act seemed to rely. In July 2015, guidelines on ARTs were modified to reflect the legal changes. However, single women and same-sex couples are still banned from accessing ARTs.

In Austria, the model of the biological family also has been recently reframed through a more liberal reform of the statute on ARTs. Distancing itself from the stance enshrined in its earlier legislation, which was at issue in decision of the European Court of Human Rights in *S. H. and Others*, Austria seems to have overcome its concerns regarding the potential of oocyte donation to split motherhood between two women (the oocyte donor and the birth mother), opening up new family relationships that are not based on biological tie as an essential factor but rather on emotional and social bonds. Nevertheless, ART treatments for single women are still prohibited.

Restrictive regulations on assisted reproduction create inequalities and injustices and exacerbate tensions and suffering. They stratify motherhood (and parenthood), producing new privileges and exclusions and leading, as the European Court of Human Rights found in *Costa and Pavan v. Italy*, to violations of human rights. *S. H. and Others v. Austria* highlights the difficulties entailed in harmonizing standards of human rights with respect to such a sensitive issues. Nonetheless, as the experiences of Italy and Austria demonstrate, European countries seem to be moving toward the adoption of a permissive approach to ARTs. Rather than adopting a prohibitionist stance, regulation of ARTs should aim at ensuring that individuals can make their own decisions in relation to reproduction, in conditions of equality, adequate information, and accountability (Rodotà 2012). We can reasonably expect that, in the hope of satisfying their desire for reproduction, people will continue to challenge prohibitionist measures that currently limit access to ARTs, and thus seek to expand the borders of legal motherhood.

NOTES

1.   A recent ruling by the Italian Constitutional Court (162/2014) struck down the ban on gamete donation. The ban on access to assisted reproductive technologies (ARTs) by couples suffering from genetically inherited diseases was quashed in a recent decision by the Italian Constitutional Court (96/2015).

2.   Prior cases concerned access to ARTs generally, in particular, Evans v. UK, 6339/05 (March 7, 2006) and Dickson v. UK, 44362/04 (December 4, 2007).

3.   *Fortpflanzungsmedizingesetz*, Federal Law Gazette, 275/1992. In 2015, the act was amended to allow egg donation, insemination and in vitro fertilization (IVF) with donor sperm for lesbian couples, IVF with donor sperm for heterosexual couples, and pre-implantation diagnostics in some cases.

4.   The relevant parts of the text of article 8 of the European Convention on Human Rights provide: "1. Everyone has the right to respect for his private and family life . . . 2. There shall be no interference by a public authority with the exercise of this right except such as is in accordance with the law and is necessary in a democratic society in the interests of national security, public safety or the economic well-being of the country, for the prevention of disorder or crime, for the protection of health or morals, or for the protection of the rights and freedoms of others."

5.   This judgment by the Austrian Constitutional Court is the first in the world where a supreme court repealed the ban on donor insemination for lesbian couples as violating human rights. More specifically, by referring to the case Schalk and Kopf v. Austria (application 30141/04), decided by the European Court of Human Rights, the court highlighted that same-sex couples with children are a family. In this light, the insemination ban for lesbian couples cannot be justified by the need to protect the traditional "family," because same-sex couples do not replace or oppose marriage or heterosexual cohabitation but rather complement them in the definition of family. Therefore, the court stated that restricting access to ARTs on the basis of sexual orientation constituted an interference with the right to respect for private and family life as guaranteed by the European Convention on Human Rights, and a violation of the principle of equality guaranteed by the Austrian constitution.

6.   After Costa and Pavan v. Italy (10th Sess., 54270/10, August 28, 2012), the European Court of Human Rights pronounced on the Italian legal provisions on ARTs in Parrillo v. Italy (Judgment of the Grand Chamber 46470/11, August 27, 2015) regarding the ban, under the Italian statute on ARTs, on donating embryos obtained from IVF to scientific research. The Grand Chamber observed that there was no evidence that the applicant's deceased partner would have wished to give the embryos to scientific research and thus it held that the ban had been "necessary in a democratic society." As a consequence, there had been no violation of the right to respect for private and family life guaranteed by the European Convention on Human Rights. It is also worth mentioning that, at the moment, there is a case regarding surrogacy pending before the Grand Chamber (Paradiso and Campanelli v. Italy).

7. Pre-implantation genetic diagnosis (PGD) enables embryo selection on the basis of particular genetic characteristics. PGD is not clearly regulated by Act 40/2004. This has led to several (contrasting) judicial interpretations and, consequently, has created a condition of "legal uncertainty" (Penasa 2012). In Costa and Pavan v. Italy, the European Court of Human Rights adopted a strict interpretation of Act 40/2004, an interpretation suggested by both the applicants and the Italian government. Thus, the court read the lack of a clear provision on PGD as meaning that Italian law prohibits access to PGD. Nevertheless, it must be underscored that in the past ten years there has been a significant evolution within Italian case law toward the admissibility of PGD. See Tribunal of Cagliari, September 24, 2007; Tribunal of Florence, December 17, 2007; Tribunal of Salerno, January 2010. Also see, generally, Penasa (2012).

8. Ministry of Health Decree 31639 (April 11, 2008). According to the new guidelines adopted in July 2015, access to ARTs also is allowed when the woman of the couple is a carrier of sexual transmittable diseases.

9. See Italian Constitutional Court decision 96/2015; decision 162/2014; and decision 151/2009.

10. The European Court argued that the absence of an effective and available remedy within the Italian legal system legitimated Costa and Pavan to directly petition the European Court of Human Rights. Indeed, according to the court, the only relevant judicial decision regarding a similar case (Tribunal of Salerno, January 13, 2010) was an isolated ruling and was not confirmed by the following case law (Costa at § 38).

11. The Italian Abortion Act of 1978 ("Norme per la tutela sociale della maternità e sull'interruzione volontaria della gravidanza") permits women to interrupt a pregnancy during the first ninety days of gestation, when the pregnancy, childbirth, or motherhood entail a serious danger to the physical or psychological health of the woman, taking into account her state of health; her economic, social, or family situation; the circumstances under which conception occurred; or the probability that the child will be born with anomalies and malformations; and, after ninety days of gestation, when the pregnancy or childbirth entails a serious danger to the woman's life or when pathological processes constituting a serious danger to the physical and psychological health of the mother, such as those associated to malformations or pathologies of the fetus, have been diagnosed.

12. For a critical analysis of this point of the court's decision, see Penasa (2012).

13. Article 12 of the act provides administrative and criminal sanctions for the violation of the law.

14. This provision, as will be seen, has been revised by Constitutional Court decision 151/2009.

15. This verb recalls the expression "eclipse of the mother," which Boccia and Zuffa (1998) use to point out that discourse on assisted reproduction (whether for or against ARTs) eclipses the mother.

16. The court mentioned, in particular, decision 27/1975.

17. See, for example, the Tribunal of Cagliari (November 9, 2012) and Constitutional Court decision 96/2015, to be discussed.

REFERENCES

Alesso, Ileana. 2013. "Le questioni sottoposte al controllo di legittimità della Corte costituzionale." In *La procreazione medicalmente assistita e le sue sfide. Generi, tecnologie e disuguaglianze*, ed. Lia Lombardi and Silvia De Zordo, 105–10. Milan: Franco Angeli.

Almeling, Rene. 2007. "Selling Genes, Selling Gender: Egg Agencies, Sperm Banks, and the Medical Market in Genetic Material." *American Sociological Review* 72, no. 3: 319–40.

Boccia, Maria Luisa. 2005. "L'embrione sovrano." In *Si può. Procreazione assistita. Norme, soggetti, poste in gioco*, ed. Simona Bonsignori, Ida Dominijanni, and Stefania Giorgi, 69–78. Rome: Il Manifesto-manifestolibri.

Boccia, Maria Luisa, and Grazia Zuffa. 1998. *L'eclissi della madre. Fecondazione artificiale, tecniche, fantasie e norme*. Milan: Nuova Pratiche Editrice.

Bonsignori, Simona, Ida Dominijanni, and Stefania Giorgi, eds. 2005. *Si può. Procreazione assistita. Norme, soggetti, poste in gioco*. Roma: Il Manifesto-manifestolibri.

Brighouse, Harry, and Adam Swift. 2006. "Parents Rights and the Value of Family." *Ethics* 117, no. 1: 80–108.

Chavkin, Wendy, and Jane Maree Maher, eds. 2010. *The Globalization of Motherhood*. London: Routledge.

D'Alton-Harrison, Rita. 2014. "Mater Semper Incertus Est: Who's Your Mummy?" *Medical Law Review* 22, no. 3: 357–83.

D'Amico, Marilisa. 2015. "Opportunità e limiti del diritto giurisprudenziale in relazione alle problematiche dell'inizio della vita (i casi della procreazione medicalmente assistita e dell' interruzione volontaria di gravidanza)." *Forum di quaderni costituzionali*. http://www.forumcostituzionale.it/wordpress/wp-content/uploads/2015/07/damico.pdf.

D'Amico, Marilisa, and Benedetta Liberali, eds. 2012. *La legge n. 40 del 2004 ancora a giudizio*. Milan: Franco Angeli.

Dameno, Roberta. 2004. "La legge sulla procreazione medicalmente assistita: Una legge manifesto." In *Un'appropriazione Indebita: L'uso del corpo della donna nella nuova legge sulla procreazionne assistita*, ed. A. A. and V. V., 87–96. Milan: Baldini Castoldi Dalai.

Fenton, Rachel Anne. 2006. "Catholic Doctrine Versus Women's Rights: The New Italian Law on Assisted Reproduction." *Medical Law Review* 14, no. 1: 73–107.

Ferraretti, Anna Pia, Guido Pennings, Luca Gianaroli, Francesca Natali, and M. Cristina Magli. 2010. "Cross-Border Reproductive Care: A Phenomenon Expressing the Controversial Aspects of Reproductive Technologies." *Reproductive Biomedicine Online* 20, no. 2: 261–66.

Franklin, Sarah, and Helena Ragoné, eds. 1998. *Reproducing Reproduction: Kinship, Power, and Technological Innovation*. Philadelphia: University of Pennsylvania Press.

Gribaldo, Alessandra. 2005. *La natura scomposta. Riproduzione assistita, genere e parentela*. Rome: Luca Sossella Editore.

Hague Conference on Private International Law. 2012. *A Preliminary Report on the Issues Arising from International Surrogacy Arrangements*. http://www.hcch.net/upload/wop/gap2012pd10en.pdf.

Hanafin, Patrick. 2013. "Law, Biopolitics and Reproductive Citizenship: The Case of Assisted Reproduction in Italy." *Tecnoscienza* 4, no. 1: 45–67.

Heng, Boon Chin. 2007. "Regulatory Safeguards Needed for the Travelling Foreign Egg Donor." *Human Reproduction* 22, no. 23: 2350–52.

Inhorn, Marcia C., and Daphna Birenbaum-Carmeli. 2008. "Assisted Reproductive Technologies and Culture Change." *Annual Review of Anthropology* 37: 177–96.

Krause, Elizabeth L., and Silvia De Zordo. 2012. "Introduction. Ethnography and Biopolitics: Tracing 'Rationalities' of Reproduction across the North-South Divide." *Anthropology and Medicine* 19, no. 2: 137–51.

Lombardi, Lia, and Silvia De Zordo, eds. 2013. *La procreazione medicalmente assistita e le sue sfide. Generi, tecnologie e disuguaglianze*. Milan: Franco Angeli.

Marchesi, Milena. 2012. "Reproducing Italians: Contested Biopolitics in the Age of 'Replacement Anxiety.'" *Anthropology and Medicine* 19, no. 2: 171–88.

Marella, Maria Rosaria, and Maria Virgilio. 2004. "Una cattiva legge cattiva." In *Un'appropriazione Indebita: L'uso del corpo della donna nella nuova legge sulla procreazionne assistita*, ed. A. A. and V. V., 171–87. Milan: Baldini Castoldi Dalai.

Melhuus, Marit. 2005. "Better Safe than Sorry: Legislating Assisted Conception in Norway." In *State Formation: Anthropological Perspectives*, ed. Christian Krohn-Hansen and Knut Nustad, 212–33. London: Pluto.

Miranda, Antonello. 2010. "Maternity for Another—Italy." *The Cardozo Electronic Law Bulletin*, 16, no. 1.

Nardocci, Costanza. 2012. "La centralità dei Parlamenti nazionali e un giudice europeo lontano dal ruolo di garante dei diritti fondamentali. A commento della sentenza della grande Camera S.H. e altri vs Austria." In *La legge n. 40 del 2004 ancora a giudizio*, ed. Marilisa D'Amico and Benedetta Liberali, 129–52. Milan: Franco Angeli.

Parolin, Laura Lucia, and Manuela Perrotta. 2012. "On the Fringe of Parenthood: Othering and Otherness in the Italian Assisted Kinship." *About Gender* 1, no. 2: 100–31.

Penasa, Simone. 2012. "The Italian Law on Assisted Reproductive Technologies Facing the European Court of Human Rights: The Case of Costa and Pavan v. Italy." *Revista de Derecho y Genoma Humano* 37, 155–78.

Piga, Antonella. 2013. "Leggi e Norme sulla PMA: Il panorama legislativo europeo." In *La procreazione medicalmente assistita e le sue sfide. Generi, tecnologie e disuguaglianze*, ed. Lia Lombardi and Silvia De Zordo, 11–28. Milan: Franco Angeli.

Roberts, Elizabeth. 2009. "The Traffic Between Women: Female Alliance and Familial Egg Donation in Ecuador." In *Assisting Reproduction, Testing Genes, Global Encounters with New Biotechnologies*, ed. Daphna Birenbaum-Carmeli and Marcia C. Inhorn, 113–43. New York: Berghahn Books.

Rodotà, Stefano. 2004. Preface to *La fecondazione proibita*, ed. Chiara Valentini, 7–18. Milano: Feltrinelli.

———. 2012. *Il diritto di avere diritti*. Bari: Editorti Laterza.

Sanderson, Mike. 2013. "A New Approach to Sex-Based Classifications in the Context of Procreative Rights: *S. H. & Others v. Austria* in Context." *European Journal of Health Law* 20, no. 1: 21–40.

Shalev, Carmel, and Gabriele Werner-Felmayer. 2012. "Patterns of Globalized Reproduction: Egg Cells Regulation in Israel and Austria." *Israel Journal of Health Policy Research* 15, no. 1: 1–12.

Vayena, Effy, Patrick J. Rowe, and P. David Griffin, eds. 2002. *Current Practices and Controversies in Assisted Reproduction*. Geneva: World Health Organization.

Zagrebelsky, Vladimiro. 2012. "La irragionevolezza della legge italiana sulla procreazione assistita nel giudizio della Corte europea dei diritti umani." *Diritti umani e diritto internazionale* 6, no. 3: 669–71.

Zanini, Giulia. 2011. "Abandoned by the State, Betrayed by the Church: Italian Experiences of Cross-Border Reproductive Care." *Reproductive Biomedicine Online* 23, no. 5: 565–72.

Zuffa, Grazia. 2005. "Senza la madre, la tentazione dei diavoli. "In *Si può. Procreazione assistita. Norme, soggetti, poste in gioco*, ed. Simona Bonsignori, Ida Dominijanni, and Stefania Giorgi, 59–67. Rome: Il Manifesto-manifestolibri.

5

PREGNANT BODIES AND
THE SUBJECTS OF RIGHTS

The Surrogacy–Abortion Nexus

YASMINE ERGAS

Commercial reproductive surrogacy is often seen as an expansion of reproductive freedom. In particular, women's ability to engage in contractual gestation and thus the ability of men and (other) women to purchase their services appear seamlessly connected to the women's right to terminate their pregnancies; both are cast as variants of reproductive "choice." This chapter argues the contrary case: rather than existing along a continuum of reproductive autonomy, abortion rights and the rights implicated in commercial surrogacy in fact reflect very different understandings of women and their pregnancies. When these understandings are taken into account, it is far from evident that commercial surrogacy represents an expansion of the reproductive "choice" embedded in abortion rights. To the contrary, current theories of commercial surrogacy rest on a view of pregnancy as a "service" and of the embryo and fetus as always already the property and "child" of the commissioning parents. Severing the pregnant woman from the fetus itself, such a view of commercial reproductive surrogacy thereby jeopardizes the theories of a pregnant woman's embodiment and personhood on which abortion rights rest.

Women's abortion rights are not grounded in "choice" in and of itself. Rather, that "choice" is based in the essential unity of women's personhood and embodiment and in the inherent enmeshment of the evolving embryo and fetus with the pregnant woman's body.

It is sometimes suggested that the embryo and fetus embody other people as well—at the very least, the sperm provider and, in gestational surrogacy, the ovum provider.[1] This, of course, is true; but for the sperm, there would be no embryo, no fetus, no child. The same applies to the ovum. But the sperm and the ovum merge in the embryo, and the embryo merges into the body of the pregnant woman. There is no good analogy for the transformations undergone following the implantation within a woman of an embryo that has been produced externally to her, but one might invoke transplanted organs: they become elements of the person into whose body they have been incorporated, even as they reconfigure and profoundly alter that person's physiology. Analogously, the embryo becomes part of the pregnant woman's body, that is, of her "self."

Gestation is not simply encasement; if it were, a petri dish would suffice to change gametes into children. Instead, gestation entails a complex, transformative merging of the embryo into the mother's other organs, reconstituting her as a corporeal being. This is what, in the jurisprudence of the United States, authorizes a woman to choose whether to have an abortion; it is why the state may not delegate to any private individual a veto power over a pregnant woman's right to choose; and it is why, no matter how strong the state's interest may be in seeing that pregnancies are carried to term, the state's "interest in protecting potential life is not grounded in the Constitution. It is, instead, an indirect interest supported by both humanitarian and pragmatic concerns. . . . In counterpoise is the woman's constitutional interest in liberty. One aspect of this liberty is a right to bodily integrity, a right to control one's person" (*Planned Parenthood of Southeastern Pennsylvania v. Casey*, 505 U.S. 833 [1992], Stevens, J., concurring and dissenting opinion, para. 2).[2]

Indeed, under the jurisprudence of the U.S. Supreme Court, at viability, the state's interest in ensuring that a pregnancy is carried to term may be so strong as to legitimate the imposition of significant regulatory constraints on a woman's right to abort. Nonetheless, that moment marks only an accentuation of the state's interests (and correlative regulatory rights) in a *potential* human life; it neither endows the fetus with personhood nor transforms it into an object, external to the gestating woman. In line with that jurisprudence, neither parental rights nor property rights can be assigned to third parties over fetuses, for that would amount to assigning rights in a woman's body, and, hence, in her person.

Yet, in the United States as elsewhere, courts, legislators, and advocates have sought to ground the legality of commercial reproductive surrogacy in precisely such assignments of rights. Viewing the commissioning parents as always already the owners and then the parents of the gametes/embryo/fetus/evolving child has served at least three interrelated purposes. First, it has obviated the charge that commercial reproductive surrogacy constitutes a form of the market in babies, a prohibited exchange of children for compensation. Second, and relatedly, it has grounded legal certainty regarding the parentage of the child in contract—assigning it to the commissioning parents while simultaneously negating any claims that either "external" gamete providers (that is, external to the commissioning parents) or the woman who gives birth might have. Finally, it has appeared to promote a gender equality agenda.

If gestation can be purchased, as can ova and sperm, then the major element that differentiates the reproductive capacities of men and women becomes a subject of contract.[3] Unlike ova or sperm, however, which are sold as property (albeit of a particular kind), a pregnant woman who sells the result of her gestation is selling a child. Only if one posits that the implanted embryo, the evolving fetus, and the resulting child were never "of" the pregnant woman but merely "in" her, and that the relevant property and/or parental rights always pertained to the commissioning parents, can this conclusion be avoided. While this ensures certainty of the commissioners' parentage displacing traditional legal rules that allocated maternity to the woman who gave birth, it also implies disjoining the implanted embryo and fetus from the pregnant woman. The biology of reproduction that underwrites abortion jurisprudence is recast: rather than part of the pregnant woman, the embryo and fetus assume a quasi-autonomous status; they are housed within, not integral to, her body.[4] Legalized under this set of assumptions, commercial surrogacy is on a collision course with women's right to abortion. Perhaps it is best to take a step back and ask what alternative frameworks might be available. To do this, however, it is necessary to understand the arguments being put forth now.

GENES, EQUALITY, AND THE REDEFINITION
OF BIOLOGY

"So she *was* actually the mother!" Brian Lehrer, a well-known New York talk show host, exclaimed on television, in November 2014. Lehrer was referring to Mary Beth Whitehead, the protagonist of the Baby M case, a 1988 legal battle over who could claim parental, and hence custodial, rights to a child Whitehead had borne on behalf of a commissioning couple (*In re Baby M*, 537 A.2d 1227, 109 N.J. 396 [1988]).

"She was the traditional surrogate," came the firm response of Lehrer's interlocutor, Nathan Schaefer, the executive director of the Empire State Pride Agenda. "And that's very different from what is commonly practiced now, which is gestational surrogacy." As a traditional surrogate, Schaefer explained, Whitehead had provided "her egg, and so she had a biological connection to the baby that she was having . . . for this family from Manhattan." But in gestational surrogacy, "you identify an egg donor and then a separate gestational carrier who, in turn, has *no biological connection to the child*" (Lehrer 2014).[5] It is a surprising understanding of pregnancy and/or biology: the ovum is biological, but pregnancy and childbirth are not.

The segment of Lehrer's show on which Schaefer appeared focused on the campaign to liberalize New York State's surrogacy law. Approved in 1993 in a climate marked by the Baby M case to which Schaefer referred, New York law prohibits contracts that entail compensating a woman to carry a pregnancy and give birth to a child on behalf of third parties (New York Code, Domestic Relations, article 8, § 121–24). Criminal penalties may be imposed in such cases, although donor—that is, unremunerated—arrangements are permitted.[6] More than two decades after passage of the New York statute, as Schaefer argued for a bill before the state legislature that would strongly favor the commissioning parents, he insisted on the distinction between the processes entailed in traditional and gestational surrogacy. A new technology, he contended, demanded a new legal approach.[7] The advent of gestational surrogacy has indeed seemed to calm the polemic surrounding surrogacy itself, at least in the United States (Scott 2009). A legislative laggard, New York State, Schaefer maintained, was "los[ing] an opportunity" to allow third-party reproduction.

Yet the issue was not just one of technological modernity. That would not have elicited Schaefer's astonishing negation of the biology of pregnancy and childbirth. Rather, his words resonate with the high-stakes re-visioning of maternity that is under way today. "Mother" is a legal status; it carries rights to child custody and companionship, to support and, at times, to citizenship, as well as obligations. It is legally difficult to shed and difficult to negate—although, as Dorothy Roberts's essay in the present volume demonstrates, the law itself may be applied discriminatorily, thus eroding the right of disadvantaged women to their status as mothers. Generally, as a legal matter, maternity cannot be exclusively determined by agreement among private parties; states are centrally involved (Ergas 2013). Thus, legal definitions of motherhood cast a long shadow over surrogacy arrangements; they determine the framework within which any particular bargain occurs.

The traditional legal rule attributes maternity to a woman who gives birth. That childbirth makes the mother is a principle that has been largely underwritten in both common and civil law systems (Hague Conference on Private International Law 2014).[8] But paternity has been circumscribed by institutional relationships. William Blackstone (1765–69, book 1, chap. 16) cited the Roman maxim "Pater est quem nuptiae demonstrant" (the father is he whom marriage indicates) in his *Commentaries on the Laws of England*.[9] Conventionally, then, maternity is grounded in bodily facticity, paternity in the relationship between a man and a specific woman—the one who gave birth. In this view, the converse does not hold; the mother is such because of her direct, physical connection to the child to whom she gives birth, not because of her relationship to any particular man.

Although other pathways to parenthood, including adoption, have long been recognized in many countries, these traditional presumptions still generally apply. Recent surveys show that, in most instances, "by operation of law" (Hague Conference 2014, 9), the mother is she who has given birth and "pater est quem nuptiae demonstrant." Nonetheless, as other contributors to the present volume note, sociological trends and technological factors in recent decades have converged to cast doubt on traditional definitions of parenthood. In numerous states today, biological, sociological, and institutional factors may now be considered in adjudicating claims to fatherhood. DNA testing may be used to rebut and, at times, to prove paternity. Likewise, paternity may be proven by conduct, such as when a man "openly hold[s] the child out as his natural child," voluntary acknowledges parenthood (following legally prescribed procedures), or fails to contest judicial or administrative proceedings (Hague Conference 2014, 11).

Moreover, assisted reproductive technologies have allowed the separation of the various elements of the corporeal nexus between mother and child that once appeared indissoluble. The provision of ova, on one side, and the functions of gestation and childbirth, on the other, can now be delinked—as occurs, Schaefer rightly noted in talking with Brian Lehrer, in gestational surrogacy. The question that arises then is whether all, some, or none of the elements of corporeality involved in pregnancy and childbirth can support a claim to motherhood. In substantiating such a claim, is having provided an ovum (or a part thereof, as one would have with a mitochondrial transfer) the same as having gestated?[10] Can a contract override either, neither, or both?

In the past decade, some courts have insisted on the primacy of gestation as a *biological* determinant of motherhood (as in, for example, *Judgment of April 6, 2011*, Cassation Civile 1re. Arrêt n. 370 [10-19.053]).[11] This stance resonates with the view enshrined in the 1993 "Adoption Convention" (Hague Conference on Private International Law 1993). Although the convention never specifically defines "mother," it consistently distinguishes between the "mother" (or the "father") and the "prospective adoptive parents." The default rule for the Adoption Convention, then, is that the mother is she who gives birth. Implicitly establishing an analogy between adoption and surrogacy, Whitehead's contract in the *Baby M* case required her to renounce her right to being a mother so as to enable the commissioning mother to adopt the child. (The identity of the father was not an issue). But, backed by key judicial decisions, many surrogacy advocates eschew this approach, for it entails accepting the basic premise of adoption law—that the birth mother is, in the first instance, the mother of the child, and that just as she may choose to renounce her maternity, she may also choose not to do so. Even where the prospective adoptive parents have paid her "reasonable expenses," a woman who gives birth cannot be compelled to give up her child.

In contrast to adoption's reliance on gestation and delivery as the determinants of maternity at birth, the claim that only genetics provides a biological link between a child and its parents negates the biologically based claim that a gestational surrogate may have to motherhood. At the same time, it places male and female claims to parenthood on par with each other. The physiological processes of reproduction may be divided into several moments—the provision of sperm, the provision of ova, fertilization and the formation of an embryo, the implantation of the embryo, gestation, and childbirth—each associated with a specific actor. A woman provides the ovum, a man provides the sperm; the ovum is fertilized either by the man and woman acting together (generally through sexual relations) or through assisted reproductive technologies. Transfer is effected into the body of a woman and it either does or does not result in implantation and pregnancy. If it does so, and there is no miscarriage or abortion, childbirth marks the termination of the process. At present, only a person who is physiologically female can give birth.

As table 5.1 illustrates, female and male roles parallel each other only at the very beginning of the process, and only in reference to the provision of reproductive cells. Fertilization can take place within the woman who will carry the pregnancy or separately from both the man and any woman (whether ovum provider or gestator) involved in the reproductive process. In either case, it is entirely situated outside the male body

TABLE 5.1 Phases in the Process of Reproduction

Phase	Male	Female*	External to Either
Gametes	+	+	
Fertilization		+	(++)
Transfer		+	
Implantation and pregnancy		+	
Childbirth		+	

*In gestational surrogacy, two women are involved: the provider of the ovum and the woman who is implanted with the embryo, becomes pregnant, and ultimately gives birth.

(++) In gestational surrogacy, fertilization occurs outside the body of either woman involved in the reproductive process.

and no longer entails the sperm provider's direct physical engagement. To suggest that the provider of the ovum is the only woman who is biologically implicated in the various stages that lead from the provision of egg and sperm to a child is, then, to attribute the status of "biology" only to those aspects of the reproductive process for which a direct parallel between male and female roles can be established.

In the genetic view of parenthood, sexual difference disappears. As if to correct the misalignment of women's claims to motherhood and men's to fatherhood inherent in conventional rules that ground motherhood in the physiological attachment of mother and child and fatherhood in the institutional relationship of the father to the mother, this re-visioning of reproductive biology coheres with an antiessentialist deracination of maternity and maternal qualities from the female body and with a formally gender-egalitarian stance. Here, mothers and fathers share the same corporeal nexus to the child. And if the corporeal nexus on which only the identity of the mother could once be grounded no longer differentiates her from the father—for he has the same biological connection to the child as she does—either "biology" grounds both their parental claims or it grounds neither. Moreover, because, in an egalitarian perspective, men and women are equal, a father need no longer be institutionally (or otherwise) connected to the mother to assert his paternal claims.

In 1993, in a pivotal case regarding the legality and enforceability of surrogacy contracts, which ensured that California would become a national and international center for reproductive surrogacy, the Supreme Court of California adopted such an "egalitarian" perspective. *Johnson v. Calvert* (5 Cal. 4th 84, 1993) pitted Crispina and Mark Calvert, commissioning parents who had supplied their personal gametes, against Anna Johnson, the surrogate mother who had borne the child, who each side now claimed as its own.[12] Anna Johnson based her claim to motherhood on childbirth; Crispina Calvert based hers on the fact that she had provided the ova and on the contract that obligated Anna to give up her parental status.

The court first considered the competing biologically based claims of the two women. In the court's reading, childbirth, while the only marker of motherhood explicitly recognized by the California civil code, was nonetheless only one among several possibilities. That interpretation was supported by the code, which allowed genetic testing to be used to disclaim paternity and also declared "that, insofar as practicable, *provisions applicable to the father and child relationship apply in an action to determine the existence or nonexistence of a mother–child relationship.*" Hence, "*by parity of reasoning,*" blood tests could also be "dispositive of the question of maternity" (*Johnson v. Calvert*, 92).[13]

Although the law that the court invoked allowed a genetic test to disprove paternity, in its application to the facts at hand it served, rather, as an element of proof of maternity. Genetics, in the court's analysis, enabled Crispina Calvert to assert a viable claim to motherhood. "Both women have thus adduced evidence of a mother and child relationship as contemplated [by California law]" (*Johnson v. Calvert*, discussion 1c). Applying the genetic rule of paternity to maternity, and extrapolating from it, the court found that Crispina Calvert met California's requirements for motherhood—there was no evidence of a "clear legislative preference . . . as between blood testing and having given birth" (92). But the law allowed for only one mother, a rule the court did not see fit to disturb. As a result, "because two women each have presented acceptable proof of maternity, we do not believe this case can be decided without enquiring into the parents' intentions as manifested in the surrogacy agreement" (93).

Biology did not suffice to establish maternity, for, as functional equivalents, genetics and gestation canceled each other out. Citing scholarship that advocated an intent-based approach to determinations of parentage, the court turned to the contract to resolve the contest between Crispina Calvert and Anna Johnson. And since the intent of the contract had been to ensure that the Calverts would be the parents of the child once it was born—as would be the case with any surrogacy contract—the court definitively concluded that Anna had no parental rights to the child.[14] Anna, in other words, having *only* biology in her favor, had no claim to maternity.

That view resonates today in popular discussions of surrogacy. "*Actually, there is no biological mother,*" Melanie Thernstrom (2010) took to saying, in reference to her children. Born less than a week apart to two separate surrogate mothers, the children posed a conundrum to well-meaning strangers: neither twins nor adopted, how could children born so few—yet so many—days one from the other be siblings? And so Thernstrom coined a new term: they were "twiblings," she declared.

"You see, both the donor and the carrier contributed biologically to each child, so the term cannot encompass this situation." And, reflecting on the hard-to-name relationship between her children and the carriers' children, she noted, "Third-party reproduction creates all kinds of relationships for which there are not yet terms." But for one term there still seemed to be certainty. " 'I'm the only mother,' I'd correct people brightly, again and again" (Thernstrom 2010). The twiblings may have had female biological progenitors but, while there was no name for them in Thernstrom's lexicon, they were definitely not "mothers." Like the Supreme Court of California in *Johnson v. Calvert*, Thernstrom de facto limited maternity in the context of surrogacy to the woman who had commissioned the children who would be borne.

Because anyone can become party to a contract—independently of their sex—the adoption of intent-based approaches to maternity may be portrayed as a triumph for gender egalitarianism and its corollary transformation of notions associated with "mothering" and "fathering" into the all-encompassing concept of "parenting." That transformation has undoubtedly promoted greater equality among mothers and fathers, enabled the recognition of the parenting capacity of same-sex couples, and served to discredit the idea that two parents (of opposite sexes, contributing different capacities) are required for good parenting to occur. But when an egalitarian framework is mechanistically applied to the biology of human reproduction, the physiological capacities required for gestation that are uniquely associated with female bodies disappear. The asymmetry that is actually inscribed in reproduction becomes legally—as well as "biologically"—irrelevant. The implications of this erasure directly undermine women's reproductive rights, in particular with respect to abortion.

"THE BABY," "ITS" "MOTHER," AND THE NATURE OF THE EXCHANGE

"I tell them, 'You will take care of the baby for nine months and then give it to its mother. And for that you will be paid,'" a supervisor of gestational surrogates in an Indian clinic recounted to anthropologist Amrita Pande (2014, 70). The Supreme Court of California could not have asked for a better representation of its position. The Calverts' contract had required Anna Johnson's renunciation of her parental rights. Characterizing Anna's obligation as one of renunciation, however, raised the problem of illegally commercializing children and placed the Calverts in the position of having violated the laws regulating adoption, which prohibited compensation for the transfer of children. Under the Penal Code of California, quoted at length by the court in *Johnson v. Calvert* (n. 11):

> Every person who . . . assumes or attempts to assume, right of ownership over any person, or who sells or attempts to sell, any person to another, or receives money or anything of value, in consideration of placing any person in the custody, or under the power or control of another, or who buys or attempts to buy, any person, or pays money, or delivers anything of value, to another, in consideration of having any person placed in his custody, or under his power or control, or who knowingly aids or assists in any manner any one thus offending, is punishable by imprisonment in the state prison for two, three or four years.

This is not an issue only under California law. Similar prohibitions against selling children (among others) have been widely adopted throughout the United States and abroad. The Convention on the Rights of the Child—ratified by every state other than the United States and Somalia—explicitly obligates state parties to the convention to "take all appropriate national, bilateral and multilateral measures to prevent . . . the sale of . . . children *for any purpose in any form*" (Convention on the Rights of the Child 1990, article 35). And the Adoption Convention, which allows only for "reasonable expenses" to be paid, aimed to eliminate the exchange of children for compensation.[15]

Some have called for an explicit recognition of the market for children, and the development of regulation built upon that acknowledgment. In the words of Debora Spar (2006, xix), "It is far better to concede the commerce [of the sale of children] . . . than to insist it does not exist." But, whatever the merits of this stance as a political and regulatory matter, at the time of *Johnson v. Calvert* it was legally untenable and largely remains so today.

In *Johnson v. Calvert*, the court solved the conundrum of commercialization by determining that Anna Johnson had never had any parental claims at all. Never having been the child's mother, she could not have relinquished her rights to the child, she could not have sold the child to the Calverts, and they, therefore, could not have bought him. In the court's words: "At the time when Anna entered into the contract . . . she was not vulnerable to financial inducements to part with her own expected offspring. . . . Anna was not the genetic mother of the child. The payments to Anna under contract were meant to compensate her for her service in gestating the fetus and undergoing labor, rather than for giving up 'parental' rights to the child" (*Johnson v. Calvert*, 96, para. 4). Anna, in sum, was a hired service provider.

The same perspective reverberates in the words of the Indian supervisor quoted by Pande as she inserts a radical disjuncture between the "you" being addressed—that is, the gestational carrier—and "*its* [the child's] *mother*," to whom "you" will give the child (Pande 2014, 70). Throughout the process of gestation, Pande tells us, the clinic insists to the gestators that they are not mothers but service workers—providers of a service that consists in gestation.[16]

This framework rests on two closely related premises. The first is that the surrogate is engaged solely to provide a service of gestation that culminates in childbirth. The second is that the embryo, the fetus, and thus the child who issues from the gestator have never been "*of*" the gestator but merely "*in*" the gestator. From conception to birth, the commissioning parents have had distinct and exclusive proprietary and/or parental rights relating to that embryo, fetus, and (ultimately) child. This, in turn, entails the idea that the evolving being has been the "subject" of a set of rights that are distinctly its own and that relate it to the intending parents rather than to the woman who gives birth—the right, for example, to become the child of its commissioning parents and thus to be counted as a potential child of *these* parents for inheritance purposes (and, at the moment of birth, for such purposes as protection from abandonment, except in specified circumstances, and legal recognition of parentage).[17] Can these premises survive scrutiny?

Imagine a scenario in which gestation per se *is* the object of a service contract. That scenario might look like this: a group bound by ethnic ties believes that its well-being requires ensuring that as many children sharing its ethnicity are born as possible. The group therefore procures gametes that satisfy its criteria for membership, engages a woman who also meets its criteria, and establishes a gestational service agreement with that woman. She is implanted with an embryo formed by the ethnically suitable gametes, carries the pregnancy to term, and ultimately gives birth to a child. She has performed her obligations under the gestational service contract; there is now one more member of that ethnic group in the world. And here our story ends. A service contract to gestate is performed through gestation.

But, as the supervisor of Pande's (2014, 70) account so clearly instructs her trainees in the phrase quoted above, this is not how surrogacy works. "And for *that* you will be paid," she says, referring to a "that" with two components. First: "You will take care of the baby for nine months." Second: "*And* then give it to its mother." Without the second part—the giving of the child to "its mother"—the surrogacy contract is meaningless. The interest of the commissioning parents is not simply in bringing one more child into the world; it is in having a child of their own. From their perspective, the contract they have entered into is not fulfilled until the child has been handed over to them. This is not simply a contract for a gestational service but a contract for the gestation and *delivery of a child into a specific set of hands.* The exchange of a child for compensation, in other words, is an essential part of the bargain. How can such an exchange *not* qualify as a form of human commerce?

The *Calvert* court's solution to this conundrum was to find that the baby had been that of the commissioning parents from its very conception. Inter alia, the court grounded its analysis in but-for causation, finding that "the child would not have come into being *but for* the efforts of the intending parents" (94). But, as dissenting Judge Kennard forcefully pointed out, it is hard to imagine the child coming into being but for Anna's gestation, so that such causation—canceling itself out as an argument that could be validly sustained by the opposing parties—could not be dispositive. The court also based its decision on the notion that the "mental concept of the child is a controlling factor in its creation, and the originators of the concept deserve full credit as conceivers." This idea's vagueness and potential overreach as a test of parenthood are breathtaking (one need only think of how many grandparents have initiated the mental concepts of subsequent children), but it highlights the analogy that the court implicitly drew between ownership and parenthood. As Judge Kennard notes, "the 'originators of the concept' rationale seems comfortingly familiar. . . . [It] is frequently advanced as justifying the law's protection of intellectual property." However, "the problem with this argument, of course, is that children are not property" (*Johnson v. Calvert*, Kennard, J., dissenting, 114, § 7).[18]

In response, the *Calvert* court might have argued that the owners of the "genetic material" are parents from the start. From this perspective, although children are not property, gametes (and embryos) are, and a straight line leads from the property rights they embody to the parental rights associated with children. As we shall see, this argument would support legislation and jurisprudence that regard the commissioning parties' ownership of the gametes as sufficient to make them parents of the child, thus bolstering theories that lie in direct contradiction to abortion rights.

FROM OWNERSHIP TO PARENTHOOD: THE "STRAIGHT-LINE" HYPOTHESIS AND WOMEN'S RIGHT TO ABORTION

According to the "straight-line" hypothesis, if the parents are the owners of the gametes and the embryo from which it is formed, they become the parents of the child. But no analogous transformation affects the status of the woman as she goes through the various phases that lead from pre-implantation to impregnation, gestation, and childbirth. Skipping over the transformation of matter that is external to the nonpregnant woman into matter that is internal to, and part of, her pregnant body, this argument resonates with the view that gestation is biologically irrelevant and suggests that it also is legally irrelevant. The woman begins as a vessel (waiting to be filled) and ends as a vessel (whose contents have been removed).

From this perspective, the embryo and fetus can never be seen as an inherent part of the gestating woman's body. The gradualist scheme based on the progressive evolution of an embryo into a nonviable and then into a viable fetus, which is enshrined in so much reproductive rights jurisprudence, is jettisoned, along with that which ties reproductive rights to a woman's liberty rights, physiological security and, generally, her habeas corpus protections. An extensive analysis of the relevant legislation and jurisprudence in an international and comparative perspective is beyond the scope of this essay, but a brief discussion focused on a few major U.S. cases can highlight the issues entailed.

In *Roe v. Wade* (410 U.S. 959 [1973], 153), the landmark decision sanctioning abortion rights, the U.S. Supreme Court held that the "right of privacy, whether it be founded in the Fourteenth Amendment's concept of personal liberty and restrictions upon state action, *as we feel it is*, or, as the district court determined, in the Ninth Amendment's reservation of rights to the people, is broad enough to encompass a woman's decision whether or not to terminate her pregnancy." With these words, the court declined to ground the right to privacy conclusively in either the Fourteenth or the Ninth amendment to the U.S. Constitution. But, echoing its previously held view that "if the right of privacy means anything, it is the right of the individual, married or single, to be free from unwarranted governmental intrusion into matters so fundamentally affecting a person as the decision whether *to bear* or beget a child" (*Eisenstadt v. Baird*, 405 U.S. 438 ([1972]), it also expressed a clear preference for the Fourteenth Amendment and the linkage of abortion rights to personal liberty. Almost two decades later, in *Planned Parenthood of Southeastern Pennsylvania v. Casey* (844) a plurality of the Supreme Court confirmed this view: "Constitutional protection of the woman's right to terminate her pregnancy derives from the . . . Fourteenth Amendment. . . . The controlling word in the case before us is 'liberty.'" Moreover, *Roe* "may be seen . . . as a rule . . . of personal autonomy and bodily integrity" (857).[19] Despite the fact that *Planned Parenthood v. Casey* imposed significant limitations on the court's previous abortion-related jurisprudence, including *Roe*, the right of a woman who has "begotten" a child to decide whether to "bear" it (i.e., her right to have an abortion) remained—and remains—inextricably bound to her personhood and its attendant liberties.

For the *Roe* court, it followed from this basic premise that, although a "woman cannot be isolated in her privacy," the state's right to interfere cannot amount to "unwarranted governmental intrusion" (as specified in *Eisenstadt v. Baird*); to the contrary, it must be informed by a "compelling" interest (*Roe v. Wade*, 163).[20] *Roe* devised a trimester framework, situating the first "compelling point" at the end of the first trimester and the second at the beginning of the third trimester. During the initial three months of pregnancy, the woman's personal liberty interest (and that of her physician) ensured that the decision whether or not to abort was unfettered.[21] At the end of this period, the first "compelling point" authorized regulation. But such regulation was not linked to the state's interest in the fetus. Rather, it turned on "the preservation and protection of maternal health." Abortion could therefore be regulated from the third to the sixth month *not* because the fetus was distinct from the woman's body but because, *as a part of her body*, it needed to be removed in such a way as to safeguard her health. Only at the second "compelling point," identified as "viability," could the state's "important and legitimate interest in potential life" per se justify intervention.[22]

Legitimating subsequent jurisprudence that has weakened abortion rights, the plurality that decided *Planned Parenthood v. Casey* (886) rejected *Roe*'s trimester framework. It emphasized, instead, that the state's interest in the "potential life" embodied in the fetus (sometimes referred to as "fetal life") extends throughout a pregnancy and, on that basis, authorized regulatory measures before viability "even if those measures do not further a health interest." Nonetheless, the opinion retained several fundamental elements of *Roe*'s holding. First, the fetus is a part of the pregnant woman and any protective regulation must be balanced against her liberty interests and right to bodily integrity. Second, the interest that justifies regulation is specifically that of the state.[23] Concern for—or even an interest in—"potential life" does not entitle any person or entity other than the state to restrict a woman's right to terminate a pregnancy; it grants no one else a claim over her body or over the evolving fetus within it.[24] Third, viability remains a significant legal turning point with respect to the balancing of women's rights and those of the state's interest but does not indicate that a fetus has legal personhood. Parenthood, in consequence, cannot begin before birth,[25] nor can property rights be asserted by third parties over a woman's body. Taken together, these three elements undermine the straight-line hypothesis, which separates the fetus from the pregnant woman and directly connects the property rights that inhere in gametes to the parental rights that are associated with children. Conversely, accepting the straight-line hypothesis—precisely because it is based on the separation of the pregnant woman from the embryo/fetus and on the attribution of rights to the embryo/fetus and consequent child to third parties—subverts those abortion rights that *Roe* established and *Planned Parenthood v. Casey* reaffirmed.

While noting that "a husband has a 'deep and proper concern and interest . . . in his wife's pregnancy and in the growth and development of the fetus she is carrying'" (*Planned Parenthood v. Casey*, 895) the court explicitly rejected the suggestion that such an interest was sufficient to justify regulation mandating that a woman notify the future father of the child she was gestating of her intention to abort. A mother might reasonably be required to notify the father of a "living child raised by both" of a decision regarding that child, for under such circumstances—that is, of a living child, raised jointly—"as a general matter . . . the father's interest in the welfare of the child and the mother's interest are equal" (896). But "*before birth* . . . the issue takes on a very different cast. It is an inescapable biological fact that state regulation with respect to the child a woman is carrying will have a far greater impact on the mother's liberty than on the father's." Moreover, "the husband's interest in the life of the child his wife is carrying does not permit the State to empower him with this troubling degree of authority over his wife" (898). Recognizing the husband's potential claim to be informed, then, would amount to a grant of "authority over" his wife and over her body. Indeed, the court noted, with some irony, that "if the husband's interest in the fetus' safety is a sufficient predicate for state regulation . . . perhaps married women should notify their husbands before using contraceptives or before undergoing any type of surgery that may have complications affecting the husband's interest in his wife's reproductive organs."[26] As the analogy illustrates, for the court, the fetus is not separable from the body (and, thus, the person) of the woman of which it is a part. Consequently, the attribution of rights with respect to the fetus to *any* other party necessarily implicates (and curtails) her constitutionally protected rights in her own physical integrity and personal liberty.

In counterposition to the pregnant woman's constitutionally protected interests, the state may seek to further its own interests in potential human life. Such interests, as Justice Stevens noted, are generally not detailed in the legislation of abortion. He surmised that they could entail a concern to minimize social conflict over abortion itself, or an interest in demographic growth that might produce geniuses like "the occasional Mozart or Curie" (*Planned Parenthood v. Casey*, 915). But these are "indirect," supported by "humanitarian and pragmatic" considerations, and not of a constitutional nature. The different weight of these two sets of interests can only be explained by reference to the status of the fetus: the fetus is not a "person" entitled to constitutional protections, and hence the state's interests in it cannot be of a constitutional nature.[27] Indeed, as Justice Stevens stressed, *Planned Parenthood v. Casey* did not disturb *Roe*'s recognition of only "narrowly defined" rights to the unborn or its parents, and it related these rights directly to live birth.[28] U.S. states' subsequently enacted legislation (and attendant jurisprudence) has ridden roughshod over this limit, but the Supreme Court's jurisprudence does not support the position that fetuses are persons and hence neither recognizes their own entitlement to the protections of such rights nor provides support for whatever derivative rights other parties may claim (Paltrow and Flavin 2013). By necessary implication, the would-be parents of a potential child cannot claim the rights attributable to the actual parents of an actual child.

BEYOND CALVERT: FROM VESSEL TO MOTHER (AGAIN?)

Unsurprisingly, the *Calvert* court denied the validity of the federal and state constitutional arguments that Johnson put forth relating to privacy and reproductive rights. Referring to a brief filed by the American Civil Liberties Union, *Johnson v. Calvert* (100) noted:

Amicus curiae fails to articulate persuasively how Anna's claim falls within even the broad parameters of the state right of privacy. Amicus curiae appears to assume that the choice to gestate and deliver a baby for its genetic parents pursuant to a surrogacy agreement is the equivalent, in constitutional weight, of the decision to bear a child of one's own. We disagree. *A woman who enters into a gestational surrogacy agreement is not exercising her own right to make procreative choices; she is agreeing to provide a necessary and profoundly important service without (by definition) any expectation that she will raise the resulting child as her own.*

And, eliding the specific issues that would be raised were *Roe v. Wade* (or other, related constitutional decisions) taken into account, the court specified: "We note that although at one point the contract purports to give Mark and Crispina the sole right to determine whether to abort the pregnancy," at another point it acknowledges that "all parties understand that a pregnant woman has the absolute right to abort or not abort any fetus she is carrying. Any promise to the contrary is unenforceable" (96). That the acknowledged unenforceability of the clause granting the Calverts the ability to determine an abortion might be related to the nature of pregnancy termination rights was simply excluded from consideration.

Perhaps seeking to inure its ruling against further challenge, the court thus unmoored from its constitutional grounding Anna's right to abort: Anna does not have rights of "equivalent constitutional weight" to those of the genetic parents because she is "is not exercising her own right to make procreative choices" (100). Johnson instead appears to be an element of the "novel medical procedures" through which the Calverts can "exercise *their* right to procreate in order to form a family of their own" (99). Why, then, should she have a right to abort (or to refuse to do so), thereby endangering the rights of the Calverts?[29]

The simple answer is that if the *Calvert* court's analysis is followed to its logical conclusion, she should not. In the court's view, the Calverts always had parental rights over the implanted embryo and developing fetus, that is, over that part of Anna's body that under *Roe* would have been not only *in* her but *of* her, an indistinguishable aspect of her personhood. The corollary of this view is either that it is possible to have rights to other people's bodies (and, hence, selves) or that those parts to which others can have rights are not actually parts of the first person's body at all (and can thus be the object of other people's rights). From this perspective, the clause of the Calverts' contract that assigned them exclusive rights to determine an abortion is logically correct. To avoid this conclusion, the assumption of the status of the woman who is pregnant and gives birth—the conventional "mother"—needs to be reconsidered.

One possible way forward is simply to prohibit commercial reproductive surrogacy. Another, however, might be based on affording the woman who gives birth the protections that are currently embedded in adoption law. This would require significant legislative creativity;

surrogacy is not adoption. Adoption law recognizes that a woman who gives birth may renounce her parental rights. But, in the first instance, she is the mother of the child. Understandably, surrogacy advocates dislike this view. It creates moral hazards. Commissioning parents may be held hostage to further payments, suffer the imposition of vexatious conditions on their family life, or even risk not being given the child they have expected. Moreover, it embeds surrogacy in a family law context rather than in that proper to contract law.

Surrogacy skeptics also dislike this view. It sanctions the commodification of human beings (specifically, of both the mothers and the children they bear), imports contract law into the regulation of family matters, and continues a trade in which surrogates may be exploited. But the market in baby making is a reality; illegality has not expunged it, nor is it likely to do so. Moreover, as has been demonstrated in a plethora of cases, courts faced with actually existing children often find that considering the best interests of the child—the internationally mandated standard applicable in all legal and administrative matters regarding children—requires recognizing the parentage of the commissioning parents, even when the child was born of locally prohibited commercial surrogacy arrangements (*Mennesson v. France*, App. no. 65192/1 Eur. Ct. H.R. [2014]; *Labassee v. France*, App. no. 65941/11 Eur. Ct. H.R. [2014]; *Paradiso and Campanelli v. Italy*, App no. 25358/12 Eur. Ct. H.R. [2015]).[30] Such ex post facto legalization resonates with humanitarian concerns. But precisely because judicial deliberation must be guided by the best interests of the child, attention is funneled to the status of the child; other considerations are inevitably elided. Among those considerations are the implications of different approaches to surrogacy for women's reproductive rights, which are based on the principle that a fetus is an evolving part of a woman's body, of her self, and not extraneous to it. It is time to put these rights back on the agenda. Legal imagination will be required to craft solutions simultaneously capable of recognizing that women are not vessels, that fetuses are not children, and that children are now being born of a new commingling of contractual and familial relationships. That is a challenge worth accepting.

NOTES

1. As Claire Achmad discusses in the present volume, reproductive surrogacy has evolved from its "traditional" (or "complete") form, in which one woman provided the ovum and the womb, to its "gestational" form, in which separate women provide the ovum and the womb. Further splitting of the ovum is now also possible.

2. Arguably, under Roe v. Wade (410 U.S. 959 [1973]), the woman's physician shares in her decision-making ability. But read in the context of the rest of the Supreme Court's opinion, the relevant passages may be interpreted as assigning the physician a role with regard to the feasibility and modalities of the performance of the abortion rather than a more substantial veto power over the woman's choice per se. As discussed in this essay, subsequent Supreme Court jurisprudence makes it very clear that the abortion decision is that of the pregnant woman or of the state, not that of any private party.

3. I use the terms "man" and "woman" here and throughout this essay to denote physiologically male and female individuals, recognizing that the issue of identifying the characteristics that define a person as belonging to either category (or situating them on a spectrum of possibilities) is highly complex and subject to historical and cultural re-visioning.

4. For an analysis of visual representations that similarly separate the pregnant woman from the fetus, see Anne Higonnet, present volume.

5. Here and throughout this essay, emphasis in quotations has been added unless explicitly noted.

6. Under this framework, certain expenses related to gestation and childbirth may be payable, but compensation for the transfer of the child itself is prohibited.

7. For the proposed revision of New York State's surrogacy law, see Child–Parent Security Act, S02765, New York Senate (2016).

8. As Nara Milanich shows in the present volume, other definitions of maternity also could prevail. Despite the fact that the French civil code requires women to acknowledge their maternity in order for a relationship with the child to be established, the Cour de Cassation (2011) remarked that "in effect, it is a matter of principle in French law, that the mother of the child is she who gives birth."

9. Biological impossibility could also serve to disprove paternity, such as, for example, in the case of a husband's absence or death.

10. Mitochondrial transfers, recently approved in the United Kingdom for use in mitochondrial DNA replacement therapy, further segment the process of conception, adding another woman with a corporeal nexus to the embryo/fetus/child (Vogel and Stokstad 2015).

11. In U.S. jurisprudence, the role of biology as a determinant of motherhood is intensely disputed. For two decisions espousing different views, see In the Matter of the Parentage of a Child by T.J.S. and A.L.S., 419 N.J. 46 (2011); and Bani Chatterjee v. Taya King, 2012-NMSC-019 (2012). Many courts, both in the United States and elsewhere, have

also found nonbiological determinants of motherhood in adoption procedures, de facto parenting arrangements, and surrogacy contracts.

12. The Calverts had originally sued for a declaration of legal parentage, prior to the birth of the child; by the time the case reached the Supreme Court of California, the child was already born.

13. The court stressed the point, noting, "Further, there is a rebuttable presumption of paternity (hence, maternity as well) on the finding of certain genetic markers" (Johnson v. Calvert 5 Cal. 4th 84 [1993], 92).

14. In the court's words, when both "genetic consanguinity and giving birth . . . do not coincide in one woman, she who intended to procreate the child—that is, she who intended to bring about the birth of a child that she intended to raise as her own—is the natural mother" (Johnson v. Calvert, 93). The court asserted that only one distinction among "mothers" could be valid under California law—that between "natural" and "adoptive" mothers. That distinction had been enshrined by California's adoption of the Uniform Parentage Act in 1975, a time at which—as the court recognized—the biological fragmentation produced by assisted reproductive technologies was far from lawmakers' contemplation. Changes in the technologies of reproduction, the court noted, need not motivate changes in statutory interpretation and, in this case, there was no cause for doing so.

15. The Adoption Convention (Hague Conference on Private International Law 1993) specifically prohibits "improper gain." Despite debates over the definition of "reasonable expenses"—which the convention is generally understood as allowing—and the limits of propriety, the convention's *travaux preparatoires* demonstrate the intent to eliminate commercialization as a factor in adoption (Parra-Aranguren 1993, 3).

16. Interestingly, as Pande (2014) points out, at the same time that the gestators are being instructed to think of themselves as workers whose work consists in providing "wombs," they also are being required to exhibit "maternal" characteristics—specifically, by not endangering the pregnancy and not negotiating for additional compensation.

17. If at birth the child is automatically the child of the commissioning parents, then the commissioning parents must be automatically the parents of the born child. If this were not the case, the parents could refuse to recognize the child as "theirs" upon birth, but the woman who gives birth could also do so (since she is viewed as never having had any parental rights to the child), thus leaving the child at risk of being parentless.

18. Judge Kennard also discussed the two remaining rationales upon which the majority in Johnson v. Calvert based its decision: the primacy of the bargained-for expectations embodied in the contract, and the best interest of the child. With respect to the predominant weight to be assigned to the primacy of contractual obligations, Kennard noted that U.S. courts do not usually compel specific performance of contractual obligations and that the "unsuitability" of applying that concept is particularly evident in reference to a child because "children are not the intellectual property of their parents,

nor are they the personal property of anyone, and their delivery cannot be ordered as a contract remedy on the same terms that a court would, for example, order a breaching party to deliver a truckload of nuts and bolts" (Johnson v. Calvert, 28). Kennard further argued that automatically identifying the best interests of the child with that of the commissioning parents suppressed the very inquiry to which it purported to respond: *Which* "mother" did the best interest indicate?

19. Enumerating possible approaches to the doctrinal interpretation of *Roe*, the court noted that "the destiny of the woman must be shaped to a large extent on her own conception of her spiritual imperatives and her place in society. . . . It was this dimension of personal liberty that *Roe* sought to protect" (Planned Parenthood of Southeastern Pennsylvania v. Casey, 505 U.S. 833 [U.S. 1992], 853).

20. In Planned Parenthood of Southeastern Pennsylvania v. Casey, a plurality of the court weakened the standard of review applicable to states' regulation of abortion, exchanging the more exacting "strict scrutiny" standard with a prohibition against regulations that entail an "undue burden" on a woman's right to terminate her pregnancy. The court characterized the "undue burden" standard as "a shorthand for the conclusion that a state regulation has the purpose or effect of placing a substantial obstacle in the path of a woman seeking an abortion of a nonviable fetus" (877). Even so, the court explicitly noted, "Before viability, the State's interests are not strong enough to support a prohibition of abortion or the imposition of a substantial obstacle to the woman's effective right to the elective procedure" (846).

21. "This means . . . that, for the period of pregnancy prior to this 'compelling' point, the attending physician, in consultation with his patient, is free to determine, without regulation by the State, that, in his medical judgment, the patient's pregnancy should be terminated. If that decision is reached, the judgment may be effectuated by an abortion free of interference by the State" (Roe v. Wade, 163).

22. And "We conclude that the line [demarcating 'the woman's liberty to determine whether to carry the pregnancy to full term'] should be drawn at viability, so that before that time the woman has a right to choose to terminate her pregnancy" (Planned Parenthood v. Casey, 870).

23. "The State has legitimate interests from the outset of the pregnancy in protecting the health of the woman and the life of the fetus that may become a child" (Planned Parenthood v. Casey, 932).

24. The court upheld a parental notification requirement for minors but distinguished their situation from that of adult women. As has been repeatedly stressed, the parental notification requirement imposes substantial burdens on minors. But the relevant point here is that no third party can limit an adult woman's decision about whether to terminate her pregnancy, not even her husband (or, by extension, an unmarried, putative father).

25. The Uniform Parentage Act, for example, allows a proceeding to determine parentage to be commenced before the birth of the child but precludes it from being concluded until after the birth of the child (National Conference of Commissioners on Uniform State Laws 2000).

26. In a paragraph remarkable for its tone, the court (Planned Parenthood v. Casey 1992, 898) explicated its views on the predicates for state regulation:

> A husband has no enforceable right to require a wife to advise him before she exercises her personal choices. If a husband's interest in the potential life of the child outweighs a wife's liberty, the State could require a married woman to notify her husband before she uses a post-fertilization contraceptive. Perhaps next in line would be a statute requiring pregnant married women to notify their husbands before engaging in conduct causing risks to the fetus. After all, if the husband's interest in the fetus' safety is a sufficient predicate for state regulation, the State could reasonably conclude that pregnant wives should notify their husbands before drinking alcohol or smoking. Perhaps married women should notify their husbands before using contraceptives or before undergoing any type of surgery that may have complications affecting the husband's interest in his wife's reproductive organs. And if a husband's interest justifies notice in any of these cases, one might reasonably argue that it justifies exactly what the Danforth Court held it did not justify—a requirement of the husband's consent as well. A State may not give to a man the kind of dominion over his wife that parents exercise over their children.

27. Justice Stevens dissented in part and concurred in part. Underlining his concurrence with the plurality opinion of the court on the issue of fetal personhood, Stevens noted:

> I also accept what is implicit in the Court's analysis, namely, a reaffirmation of *Roe*'s explanation of *why* the State's obligation to protect the life or health of the mother must take precedence over any duty to the unborn. The Court in *Roe* carefully considered, and rejected, the State's argument "that the fetus is a 'person' within the language and meaning of the Fourteenth Amendment." . . . After analyzing the usage of "person" in the Constitution, the Court concluded that that word "has application only postnatally." . . . Commenting on the contingent property interests of the unborn that are generally represented by guardians ad litem, the Court noted: "Perfection of the interests involved, again, has generally been contingent upon live birth. In short, the unborn have never been recognized in the law as persons in the whole sense." . . . Accordingly, an abortion is not "the termination of life entitled to Fourteenth Amendment protection." . . . From this holding, there was no dissent, see id., at 173; indeed, no member of the Court has ever questioned this fundamental proposition. Thus, as a matter of federal constitutional law, a developing organism that is not yet a "person" does not have what is sometimes described as a "right to life." This has been and, by the Court's holding today, remains a fundamental premise of our constitutional law governing reproductive autonomy. (Planned Parenthood v. Casey, internal references omitted)

28. The court explicitly limited personhood to live birth: "The Constitution does not define 'person' in so many words. . . . The use of the word is such that it only has application post-natally" (Planned Parenthood v. Casey). A child—being, undeniably, a person—is not therefore such prenatally.

29. Paradoxically, the court reaffirms Anna's right over the abortion decision (which, it should be noted, was moot by the time the case was heard, because the child had already been born), despite finding that she cannot raise a constitutional argument regarding her right to the companionship of the child (an issue rendered salient, not moot, by the birth of the child) because that "would necessarily detract from or impair the parental bond enjoyed by Mark and Crispina" (Johnson v. Calvert, 100).

30. See also the judgment of Justice Hedley in X & Y (Foreign Surrogacy), EWHC 3030 (Fam. 2008).

REFERENCES

Blackstone, William. 1765–69. *Commentaries on the Laws of England*. http://avalon.law.yale .edu/subject_menus/blackstone.asp#intro.

Cour de Cassation. 2011. Communiqué de la Première Présidence, April 6. http://www .courdecassation.fr/IMG/File/communiquePP_avril_2011.pdf.

Ergas, Yasmine. 2013. "Babies Without Borders: Human Rights, Human Dignity, and the Regulation of International Commercial Surrogacy." *Emory International Law Review* 27: 117–88.

Hague Conference on Private International Law. 1993. *Convention of 29 May 1993 on Protection of Children and Co-operation in Respect of Intercountry Adoption*. http://www.hcch .net/index_en.php?act=conventions.text&cid=69.

——. 2014. *A Study of Legal Parentage and the Issues Arising from International Surrogacy Arrangements*. https://assets.hcch.net/upload/wop/gap2014pd03c_en.pdf.

Lehrer, Brian. 2014 (November 10). *Zero Tax Game*. New York: CUNY Television. http://www .cuny.tv/show/brianlehrer/PR2003628.

National Conference of Commissioners on Uniform State Laws. 2000. *Uniform Parentage Act (Last Amended or Revised in 2002)*. http://www.uniformlaws.org/shared/docs/parentage /upa_final_2002.pdf.

Paltrow, Lynn M., and Jeanne Flavin. 2013. "Arrests and Forced Interventions on Pregnant Women in the United States, 1973–2005: Implications for Women's Legal Status and Public Health." *Journal of Health Politics, Policy and Law* 38, no. 2: 299–343.

Pande, Amrita. 2014. *Wombs in Labor: Transnational Commercial Surrogacy in India*. New York: Columbia University Press.

Parra-Aranguren, Gonzalo. 1993. *Explanatory Report on the Convention on Protection of Children and Co-operation in Respect of Intercountry Adoption*. https://assets.hcch.net /upload/expl33e.pdf.

Scott, Elizabeth S. 2009. "Surrogacy and the Politics of Commodification." *Law and Contemporary Problems* 72, no. 3: 109–46.

Spar, Debora L. 2006. *The Baby Business: How Money, Science, and Politics Drive the Commerce of Conception.* Boston: Harvard Business Press.

Thernstrom, Melanie. 2010. "Meet the Twiblings." *New York Times Magazine*, December 29. http://www.nytimes.com/2011/01/02/magazine/02babymaking-t.html?_r=0.

Vogel, Gretchen, and Erik Stokstad. 2015. "U.K. Parliament Approves Controversial Three-Parent Mitochondrial Gene Therapy." *Science*, February 3. http://www.sciencemag.org/news/2015/02/uk-parliament-approves-controversial-three-parent-mitochondrial-gene-therapy.

6

THE MOTHERLESS FETUS

Ultrasound Pictures and Their Magic

Disappearing Trick

ANNE HIGONNET

When does life begin? Religion, philosophy, and law have all given different answers to this fundamental question. In 2017, the most popular answer is given by fetal ultrasound pictures. Life begins when we see a person in a fetal ultrasound. Yet ultrasound pictures do as much to conceal life as to reveal it. They eliminate the body on which the life of the fetus depends. No more mother.

Our own voluntary use of fetal ultrasound pictures has achieved what law and politics could not command. This triumph of the ordinary picture is all the more remarkable because, for two decades, law and politics included an attempt to control ultrasounds. On June 15, 2015, a chapter in the history of abortion rights seemed to have ended. The Supreme Court effectively overturned a North Carolina state law forcing women who sought abortions to look at an ultrasound image of the fetus inside them and to listen to a description of the image. Similar laws in twenty-two other states are unlikely to survive the North Carolina decision. Already, however, the power of ultrasound images to decide the fundamental legal issue at stake—the issue of when life begins—was beyond the control of law.

Ultrasound images of the fetus exist, of course, regardless of abortion debates. The technology predates its mandated use, doctors suggest ultrasounds for many reasons, and women voluntarily seek ultrasounds, more often out of curiosity or sentiment than for medical reasons. Most importantly, countless people around the world keep the printed or electronic traces of ultrasounds for reasons that have nothing to do with abortions. Once ultrasound technology became widely available, it was inevitable that it would be used and that it would alter the history of childhood.

Nonetheless, the stakes of what ultrasound imagery has accomplished can only be measured by considering a generation of debate over whether ultrasound images are legally binding proof of when autonomous life begins. Or rather, we have to look back at what that debate left out. In a Pyrrhic victory of major cultural proportions, the mandatory viewing of ultrasound pictures has been defeated without addressing what it is about the pictures that caused the laws in the first place. Ultrasound imagery now does the work that mandatory viewing laws hoped for, more powerfully than ever.

The 2011 North Carolina law is roughly typical of the laws that began to govern twenty-three out of fifty American states since the mid-1990s.[1] And so is the debate around it, which was a major one. The law was passed by a legislature over the veto of the state's governor. The legislature was dominated by Republicans, while the governor, Beverly Perdue, was a Democrat, and a woman (Jenkins 2014). The law was overturned by U.S. District Judge Catherine Eagles in January 2014 (O'Dell 2014), and the following December her ruling was upheld by the Fourth U.S. Circuit Court of Appeals, in an opinion written by Judge J. Harvie Wilkinson III.

I quote the North Carolina appeals decision at length to emphasize that the argument says nothing about what actually appears in the ultrasound image. Wilkinson's decision, like the rest of the debate, concentrated on the conditions in which the ultrasound was taken and, secondarily, on whether those conditions were medically justified.

Informed consent frequently consists of a fully-clothed conversation between the patient and physician, often in the physician's office. It is driven by the "patient's particular needs and circumstances" . . . so that the patient receives the information he or she wants in a setting that promotes an informed and thoughtful choice. This provision, however, finds the patient half-naked or disrobed on her back on an examination table, with an ultrasound probe either on her belly or inserted into her vagina. . . . Informed consent has not generally been thought to require a patient to view images from his or her own body much less in a setting in which personal judgment may be altered or impaired. Yet this provision requires that she do so or "avert her eyes." Rather than engaging in a conversation calculated to inform, the physician must continue talking regardless of whether the patient is listening. . . . The information is provided irrespective of the needs or wants of the patient, in direct contravention of medical ethics and the principle of patient autonomy. Forcing this experience on a patient over her objections in this manner interferes with the decision of a patient not to receive information that could make an indescribably difficult decision even more traumatic and could "actually cause harm to the patient." . . . And it is intended to convey not the risks and benefits of the medical procedure to the patient's own health, but rather the full weight of the state's moral condemnation. (Quoted in Lithwick 2014)

The argument is logical, and echoes a string of public and academic arguments for the privacy of the maternal body. One scholar has even memorably argued that mandatory ultrasounds turn the uterus into a "public square" (McCulloch 2012, 1).[2] Once a woman can no longer control her interior body-space and the fetus becomes a citizen in its own right, then the state exercises its power to regulate its citizens or to protect some of its citizens from others—to protect the fetal citizen from its maternal citizen. The North Carolina decision, upheld by two federal courts, also recognizes that no proof has ever been found for a principal counterargument: that ultrasound images promote bonding between a mother and a fetus, let alone that an ultrasound is medically necessary for an abortion (Taylor 2008; Hopkins, Zeedyk, and Raitt 2005; Roberts 2012; Sasson and Law 2009). In a strictly legal sense, the decision was made on the basis of the right of doctors to free speech.

Yet the fundamental argument made by proponents of mandatory ultrasounds rests on what appears in the ultrasound image. Because something, anything, appears on the ultrasound screen, opponents of abortion claim it represents a person. More to the point, they claim it reveals a soul. However ideological this argument, however tied in its political manifestations to religion, and however it has been bypassed in recent legal decisions, it taps into a pervasive cultural belief. Though advocates of reproductive rights have made a successful case against mandatory ultrasounds on logical and sustainable grounds, they too have left in place the most fundamental basis on which mandatory ultrasounds were demanded. That basis has become an unspoken and unexamined assumption of our world visual culture. Left and right, religious and secular, we now see in ultrasound images the first pictures of a baby, the beginning of childhood, the origin of ourselves.

"You see, but you do not observe," Sherlock Holmes famously said to his friend Watson. We see ultrasound imagery, but we do not observe what exactly we see. Most importantly, we do not observe what we do *not* see. And so we do not reckon what is at stake in ultrasound imagery. We do not feel ourselves remaking the history of childhood and the history of women.

A primarily visual attention to images is usually the province of art historians or art critics, people whose professional experience is premised on an integration of formal analysis into the study of visual content or context. Art experts, however, especially the ones who believe the most in pure form, usually study art. And yet, I believe, the political debate around ultrasound images is much in need of some formal analysis of the art-historical sort.

First things first. A fetal ultrasound, even while it is moving on the screen, is fundamentally a *representation*. At the risk of stating the obvious (but then, why is it not stated more often?), an ultrasound image is not a fetus. What appears on the screen is not a uterus. It is a picture mediated by an image technology, which can be preserved by being printed on a piece of paper (figure 6.1). It's worth going back to the most basic issues of representation as a way to start considering the use of fetal imaging, because it is at the most basic level that our understanding of ultrasound images has gone astray. A picture is not what it represents. It is always an artificially created transformation of what it represents into a medium, which an audience then interprets. Over and over, across history, we have lulled ourselves into believing in the truth of one medium after another and one interpretation after another. Caring about the pictures we make has been a favorite human occupation for at least thirty-nine thousand years, from the date of the earliest surviving and dateable cave paintings.

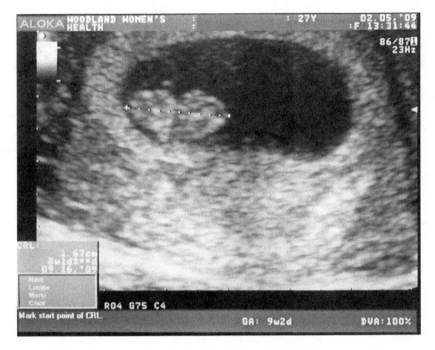

FIGURE 6.1 Eight-week fetal ultrasound picture. Courtesy of Sage Ross/Wikimedia.

Putting aside whatever makes us care about a fetal ultrasound image, let us try to look at a typical two-month example objectively. I propose the eight-week image because "89–92% of all abortions happen during the first trimester, prior to the 13th week of gestation" (Abort73 2017).[3] Inside strips of flat black and gray with white words and numbers, a white on black image appears. The image is so indistinct that it looks almost abstract. A kind of cone occupies most of the image, with a dark oval at its top, and within the oval, a light peanut shape. That's really all there is.

We need to have learned to read and count to recognize the letters and numbers; we need to have learned the gestation process to recognize something in the center of the image. We also need to use what we already have learned about internal anatomy to imaginatively project color and three dimensions onto the white marks on a black background (although some very recent ultrasound technology has introduced color

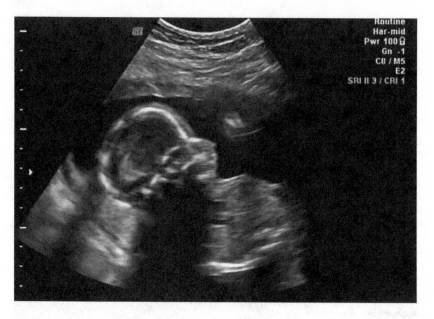

Routine
Har-mid
Pwr 100 0
Gn -1
C0 / M5
E2
SRI II 3 / CRI 1

FIGURE 6.2 Four-month fetal ultrasound picture. Personal collection.

into its imagery). Then we have to extrapolate backward from what we know about later stages of gestation to see a human being in the two-month ultrasound, because no living human being has ever looked like such an abstract white blob.

A human shape is easier to recognize in a four-month-stage ultrasound image (figure 6.2). At this point, the shapes in the center of the image still do not look like any living human beings, but they are one major step closer to images that do. Something like a head and a torso can be discerned, but no limbs. The image is fan-shaped, against a flat black background. More than half of the ultrasound is white alphabetic and numerical information written on black.

In both the eight-week image and the four-month image, size is a crucial issue. Like all photographs, fetal ultrasound images are potentially scale free. They can be projected or printed at any size. A two-month fetus is 2.5 centimeters long. The ultrasound technician interpreting the image would have to peer closely if it were projected at 2.5 centimeters on the screen. Certainly, a pregnant woman obliged to look at the fetal

image could hardly see it from the bed on which she lies, if it were projected life-size on the screen. The printed image of the ultrasound could
be life-size, but it might not be. We are so accustomed to looking at—and
unconsciously accepting—changed sizes in printed photographs that we
might never think about how much larger than reality the image of the
fetus could be. When, for instance, the Life Matters website *At the Center*
illustrated its article "Effective Life-Saving Ultrasound Legislation"
(Glessner 2012) with a stock online image of a human hand holding an
ultrasound (figure 6.3), it displayed a justified confidence in our scale
amnesia. The hand reveals the fetus to be so small it could not possibly
survive outside the mother, yet this was apparently of no concern to the
site's authors. They correctly assumed that their audience would not
notice, nor wonder whether the ultrasound had been enlarged before it
was photographed.

Our digital ability to resize images on our computer screens has made
the relationship between the real size of things and their represented

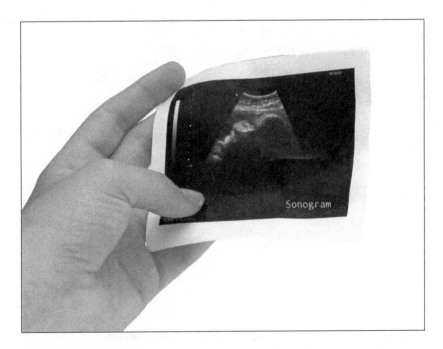

FIGURE 6.3 Hand holding a fetal ultrasound picture. iStock Photos/© Anita Patterson-
Peppers.

appearance even harder to remember. Yet the enlargement of the fetus by its projection makes it seem so much closer to the size of a baby that could be or has been born. In other words, the very enlargement of the fetus on a screen or on a piece of paper suggests a viability that is not actually possible.

Ironically, handmade anatomical illustrations can now be more truthful than ultrasounds. Take, for example, the work of Peg Gerrity, among the most easily accessible illustrations of pregnancy online today. A number of websites allow viewers to study the development of the fetus week by week. Let's go back again to the eight-week mark (figure 6.4), to be within the time zone in which most abortions occur.

To show pregnancy at eight weeks, the illustration provides a cross section of reproductive organs within an image of the exterior of a female torso. The illustrator shows us (part of) the pregnant female body, and demonstrates the actual size of the fetus in relation to that body. Precisely because the fetus is so small at the eight-week stage, the illustrator

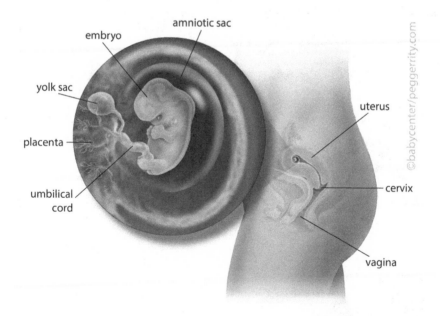

FIGURE 6.4 *Fetal Development at Eight Weeks.* Drawing by Peg Gerrity, ca. 2012. Courtesy of Peg Gerrity.

uses the device of a dramatic enlargement that projects out from the pregnant body. An inorganic, perfectly geometric purple oval makes it clear that the enlarged fetus is an artificial graphic device, though the fetus is nonetheless still represented in relation to the immediate parts of the pregnant body on which its life depends: an amniotic sac and a maternal placenta.

When the website BabyCenter (2016) used this illustration, however, it added a black-and-white, ultrasound-like picture of an eight-week fetus. Framed by a rectangle, it projected the enlarged fetus the way the illustration's enlarged fetus was projected from the pregnant torso. Though the size difference was subtle, the ultrasound fetus was larger than the illustration's enlarged fetus. Moreover, the ultrasound-like zoom, like ultrasounds themselves, did not include an amniotic sac or a placenta, let alone a torso. Presumably, the ultrasound-like fetus was added to Gerrity's illustration so viewers could see what would look more "real" to them. The impulse was correct. Despite an ultrasound's elimination of vital information, and no matter what misleading scale we see it on, it now looks more real to us than an illustration that in many ways is actually more accurate.[4]

Ultrasounds lie by omission. In a typical rectangular ultrasound picture, the shape of the fetus appears next to an area of white marks that cannot be identified as anything, usually because the area is demarcated by sharp boundaries between a sweeping fan shape and black outer zones. Unlike the illustration, which draws and labels an umbilical cord, an amniotic sac, a placenta, and a uterus, the ultrasound image is designed to allow the identification of one thing: the fetus. The abstract fan shape and the empty black of the image's outer zones visually enhance the illusion that the fetus exists on its own.

Flat bars, letters, and numbers turn the sides of the image into abstract spaces—the opposite of the visceral interior of the body within which the fetus actually exists. People with technical ultrasound training read the actual size and medical condition of the fetus in those letters and numbers. Most people cannot. The technical information doesn't even matter to them, because they only look at the picture in the center of the ultrasound. Often when ultrasounds are used after they are made, as much technical information as possible is removed (as in figures 6.6 and

6.7 presented later in this chapter). In a remarkable act of selective seeing, we focus only on one part of the total ultrasound.

Yet, in reality, at eight weeks the fetus not only is surrounded by a woman's body but also is utterly and totally dependent on that body to exist. The formal design of the ultrasound image allows us to ignore the biological reality of fetal life. Art historians call this "cropping." Cropping defines where an artist decides the image ends, or, in other words, how to frame the work. The device has always been a key decision an artist makes to define his or her subject. In many works of art, the artist decides to crop an image so that the viewer will be forced to reconstruct some aspects of the subject in his or her mind, often in order to urge the viewer to become conscious of where the image situates the viewer in relation to the subject. In the case of ultrasound images, the effect is the opposite. The effect is to urge a viewer to ignore where the fetus is situated, or where the viewer is situated in reality in relation to the subject. The impersonal, scientific, clinical look of the ultrasound image creates a powerful effect on the viewer by appearing not to make any subjective (that is, artistic) decisions about its visual messages.

Yet decisions have been made. No ultrasound machine, no scientific facts, no technology can take the blame for human decisions about how to use machines, facts, and technology.

Ultrasound images encourage us to ignore the bodies of pregnant women, not to mention women's financial and social circumstances. Under what real conditions will the woman carrying the fetus conclude her pregnancy, give birth, and raise a child? The form of ultrasound images convinces us these issues are irrelevant.[5] A 2014 layout in a *New York Times* article played on this irony when, as an illustration for a "Your Money" column on insurance coverage for reproductive technologies, it showed an isolated fetus in an oval in the space usually reserved for a portrait on a U.S. dollar bill (Bernard 2014).

While mandatory ultrasound viewing laws were still a judicial possibility, their proponents lobbied legislators with a live version of context elimination. In at least one instance, a typical ultrasound picture was projected on a screen for legislators to see—live, but many times larger than life (figure 6.5). Meanwhile, the pregnant woman whose uterus was being imaged lay on a gurney behind a partition, hidden from legislators. At an Idaho legislative session, a clever photographer captured the ironies of the

FIGURE 6.5 Antiabortion activist Brandi Swindell narrates for the audience as volunteers from Stanton Healthcare, a Boise crisis pregnancy center, conduct a live ultrasound demonstration with a woman who is eleven weeks pregnant with her sixth child, in an Idaho State Capitol hearing room. Courtesy of AP Photo/*Idaho Press-Tribune*/Charlie Lichtfield.

situation by taking a picture that caught both the projected ultrasound, in the background, and the actual mother, in the foreground.

Far from being a fact, or a reality, the ultrasound image is an extreme example of social imagination. Printed ultrasound pictures have become integral parts of our child-picture culture during the past two decades, a new starting point for the visual life stories we construct with our mobile phone applications, our photo albums, and our displays of framed photographs all around our homes and offices. The question is no longer whether to host an ultrasound picture party. It is now whether the party "overshares" (ABC News 2013).

Products abound. For $14.95 you can "Give grandpa a first glimpse of his little one with this elegant frame. This white 5" x 7" frame features a die cut window for that precious ultrasound photo and features the poem 'Grandpa's Heart'" (BabySakes.com; see figure 6.6).

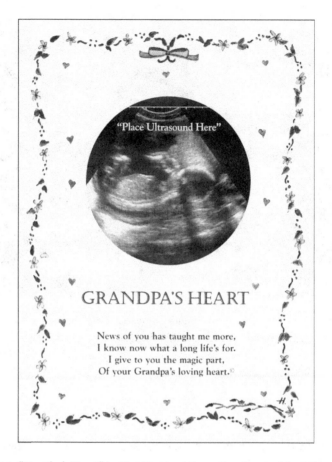

FIGURE 6.6 "Grandpa's Heart," by Teri Harrison. Framed and matted fetal ultrasound. Courtesy of Teri Harrison.

Despite its seeming banality, an item like this serves several important and exemplary cultural purposes. The window in the mat creates a visual context for the ultrasound picture. Where the original ultrasound eliminates the pregnant body, the mat replaces it. Where the original ultrasound provided letters and numbers incomprehensible to anyone without ultrasound technology training, the mat provides an easily understood semantic field of flowers combined with part of a poem by Teri Harrison.[6] The very title of the poem transfers the biological information from a uterus into a metaphoric organ, the grandfather's heart.

The poem projects across time, forward and backwards from the moment the ultrasound was taken; an older man plans for a child's future as the culmination of his long experience. It is all about how adults imagine an ideal life through a loving fantasy about childhood. Every generation is involved, because although the poem is written in the grandfather's voice, the whole item is intended to be a gift from parents to grandparents in honor of children.

Among the ideal grandfather's plans are "take lots of photographs." We live in a society that constructs ideal childhood largely through photographs. Now that digital technology and social media have infinitely expanded the number of photographs to which we expose one another, there is no point trying to count how many. No one escapes pictures of healthy, happy infants, of adorable chubby toddlers, of smiling tykes on vacation, of cute kids doing charming imitations of adults. They are all so persuasive, such positive aspects of our society's aspirations. We invoke each and every one when we look at the grainy white marks on empty black of ultrasounds. We do not see what is actually in the ultrasound image. We imagine, by association, a multitude of other pictures, none of which is a reality either, but which promise us emotional relationships and social ideals we long to see. The life we see in fetal ultrasound images is not the autonomous biological life of the fetus. It is the collective imaginary life of childhood we construct with pictures.

The lines in "Grandfather's Heart" that precede "I'd take lots of photographs" are "I'd play games of make-believe / Pull magic tricks from up my sleeve." Indeed. In May 2015, shortly before the Supreme Court shut down mandatory ultrasound laws, Wisconsin governor and Republican presidential candidate Scott Walker did play the ultrasound game of make-believe. He said:

> I'll give you an example. I'm pro-life, I've passed pro-life legislation. We defunded Planned Parenthood, we signed a law that requires an ultrasound. Which, the thing about that, the media tried to make that sound like that was a crazy idea. Most people I talk to, whether they're pro-life or not, I find people all the time who'll get out their iPhone and show me a picture of their grandkids' ultrasound and how excited they are, so that's a lovely thing. I think about my sons are 19 and 20, you know we still have their first ultrasound picture. It's just a cool thing out there.

We just knew if we signed that law, if we provided the information, that more people if they saw that unborn child would, would make a decision to protect and keep the life of that unborn child. (Williams 2015)

Unfortunately for Walker, whose high-profile remarks aroused brisk debate, the Supreme Court action on the North Carolina mandatory ultrasound law came only a few weeks later. It certainly discouraged the legal part of Walker's agenda. Yet, in a larger sense, Walker is right. He even has the time frame right. Over the past twenty years, ultrasound images of the fetus have become "just a cool thing out there." We take them for granted, because they have become an axiom of our mind-set.

With increasing frequency, since about 2013, the logic of the ultrasound picture has been extended to 3-D or even "4-D" ultrasound pictures (the fourth D is time). Using technology developed since the 1970s (Stephenson 2005), ultrasound pictures can now represent the skin surface of a fetus, not just its skeleton and organs. Typically, these pictures are even more closely cropped around the fetal body than 2-D ultrasounds. There is almost no medical purpose for 3-D or 4-D ultrasounds, and commercial websites promise none. If anything, the prolonged exposure needed for 4-D pictures could harm a fetus (Mackenzie-Morris 2015).

One typical commercial website, A Tiny Perspective, advertises: "We feel that realistic surface images provide a connection between parents and child that can be beneficial to the whole family. Something special happens to parents when the 3D & 4D images are seen compared to the 2D image because the picture of the baby is far more realistic." The website landing page includes two photographs taken from outside the bodies of noticeably pregnant women, one of whom looks at a 3-D ultrasound projected on a screen (figure 6.7). To capture attention, several 3-D ultrasounds, framed by lines, flash in succession in the upper-right corner of the layout.

The layout with several kinds of pictures allows the 3-D ultrasound picture to appear many times larger than fetal life; using their scale, the complete fetus would be far larger even than the entire bellies pictured in the same layout. Moreover, demonstrating the crucial importance of visual argument by association, the layout includes three pictures of

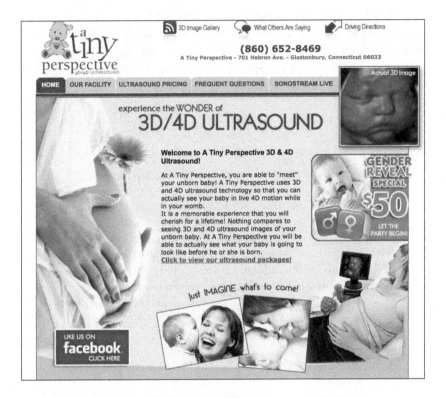

FIGURE 6.7 Web page from A Tiny Perspective, 2016.

babies several months after birth, including two with happy mothers, to situate the ultrasound pictures in a narrative arc of ideal infancy. Both textually and visually, websites like this promote the conviction that, although pregnancy can certainly be pictured as a pregnant woman's body from the outside, when it comes to "actually" seeing "your baby," you look at a picture from which any sign of the pregnant body has vanished.

People can be "freaked out" by how a 3-D or 4-D ultrasound appears. An article on BuzzFeed, "A Couple Decided Not to Get A 4D Ultrasound After Seeing This Picture," included debate over the merits of 3-D and 4-D pictures (McNeal 2015). Some argue that 3-D ultrasounds can be "cute," while others find them "alien." But no one wonders what happened to the body of the mother.

The more "real" the picture of the fetus feels to us, the more thoroughly we can forget the body of which it is a part. When someone says metaphorically that something is "out of the picture," they mean it is irrelevant. Literally and metaphorically, the mother has become out of the fetal picture.

NOTES

1.   For information about variations in rights, see Guttmacher Institute (2017):

> Since the mid-1990s, several states have moved to make ultrasound part of abortion service provision. Some laws and policies require that a woman seeking an abortion receive information on accessing ultrasound services, while others require that a woman undergo an ultrasound before an abortion. Since routine ultrasound is not considered medically necessary as a component of first-trimester abortion, the requirements appear to be a veiled attempt to personify the fetus and dissuade a woman from obtaining an abortion. Moreover, an ultrasound can add significantly to the cost of the procedure.
>
> Highlights:
>
> - 12 states require verbal counseling or written materials to include information on accessing ultrasound services.
> - 23 states regulate the provision of ultrasound by abortion providers.
> - 3 states mandate that an abortion provider perform an ultrasound on each woman seeking an abortion and requires the provider to show and describe the image.
> - 10 states mandate that an abortion provider perform an ultrasound on each woman seeking an abortion, and require the provider to offer the woman the opportunity to view the image.
> - 9 states require that a woman be provided with the opportunity to view an ultrasound image if her provider performs the procedure as part of the preparation for an abortion.
> - 5 states require that a woman be provided with the opportunity to view an ultrasound image.

See also Henry J. Kaiser Family Foundation (2016), which reports that "9 states require that a woman be provided with the opportunity to view an ultrasound image if her provider performs the procedure as part of the preparation for an abortion" and "5 states require that a woman be provided with the opportunity to view an ultrasound image." On the legal and policy implications of mandatory ultrasounds, see Sanger (2008). On the problem of the severance of the woman from the fetus and its recasting as a "child" from the earliest stages of pregnancy, see Ergas and Chavkin and Kahn in the present volume.

2. "The inside of a woman's body, in particular her uterus or womb, has become a public space, perhaps even a public square, populated—when she is pregnant—by a 'person.' Fetal heartbeats, 2-D, 3-D, and 4-D ultrasound imaging (now in colour!) have opened up her interior spaces to public gaze. . . . For making her interior a public space has also made it a space to be kept under surveillance and, ultimately, controlled" (McCulloch 2012, 1).

3. Abort73 is a U.S. organization that opposes abortion rights.

4. This is not the first time photographic imagery has been used to create politically influential but mendacious arguments about abortion. In 1984, obstetrician Bernard Nathanson released his famous film *Silent Scream*, which purported to document fetal pain during abortions, using photographic images that turned out to have been edited and altered.

5. Already, in 1987, before ultrasounds were required by law, Rosalind Pollack Petchesky (1987, 69) called for public policies that take into account whole women:

> First, we have to restore women to a central place in the pregnancy scene. To do this, we must create new images that recontextualize the fetus, that place it back into the uterus, and the uterus back into the woman's body, and her body back into its social space. Contexts do not neatly condense into symbols; they must be told through stories that give them mass and dimension. For example, a brief prepared from thousands of letters received in an abortion rights campaign, and presented to the Supreme Court in its most recent abortion case, translates women's abortion stories into a legal text. Boldly filing a procession of real women before the court's eyes, it materializes them in not only their bodies but also their jobs, families, school work, health problems, young age, poverty, race/ethnic identity, and dreams of a better life.

6. News of you has taught me more,
I know now what a long life's for.
I've found through you my magic heart,
The kinder, gentler, patient part.
While I waited those months for you,
I reflected on the things we'd do.
I would be your special friend,
Have secrets to share and pennies to spend.
I would tell you of the past,
Leave you memories that would always last.
I would grant your every wish,
Like bigger scoops in your ice cream dish.
I would be your biggest fan,
The one cheering loudest from the stands.

I'd play games of make-believe,
Pull magic tricks from up my sleeve.
I'd take lots of photographs,
And be generous with smiles and laughs.
The first time you were in my arms,
I felt the miracle of your charms.
I placed your newborn hand in mine,
And understood the gift of time.
Tender feelings are hard to express,
Grandchild, it is me you've blessed.
Your life gives me another chance—
A youthful heart and eyes that dance.
News of you has taught me more,
I know now what a long life's for.
I give to you the magic part,
Of your Grandpa's loving heart.

(Teri Harrison, "Grandpa's Heart," quoted at Modern Mommy Boutique)

REFERENCES

ABC News. 2013. "Over-Sharing at Ultrasound Party?" *ABC News* video, 2:09. January 8. http://abcnews.go.com/GMA/video/ultrasound-party-parents-share-sonogram-images -18160314.

Abort73. 2017. "U.S. Abortion Statistics." Accessed February 14, 2016. http://www.abort73 .com/abortion_facts/us_abortion_statistics.

A Tiny Perspective. n.d. "Experience the Wonder of 3D/4D Ultrasound." Accessed July 27, 2016. http://www.atinyperspective.com.

BabyCenter. 2016. "What Your Baby Looks Like at 8 Weeks." Accessed February 14, 2016. http://www.babycenter.com/fetal-development-images-8-weeks.

BabySakes.com. n.d. Grandpa's Heart Ultrasound Frame. Accessed February 14, 2016. http:// www.babysakes.com/grandpa-s-heart-ultrasound-frame?utm_source=google_shopping &gclid=CMii0MDXtMQCFehj7Aod1j0AZQ.

Bernard, Tara Siegel. 2014. "Insurance Coverage for Fertility Treatments Varies Widely." *New York Times*, July 25. http://www.nytimes.com/2014/07/26/your-money/health-insurance /insurance-coverage-for-fertility-treatments-varies-widely.html?_r=0.

Glessner, Thomas. 2010. "Effective Life-Saving Ultrasound Legislation." At the Center. http:// www.atcmag.com/Issues/ID/408/Effective-Life-Saving-Ultrasound-Legislation.

Guttmacher Institute. 2017. "Requirements for Ultrasound." January 1. https://www.gutt macher.org/state-policy/explore/requirements-ultrasound.

Henry J. Kaiser Family Foundation. 2016. "State Ultrasound Requirements in Abortion Procedure." September 1. http://kff.org/womens-health-policy/state-indicator/ultrasound -requirements/?currentTimeframe=0.

Hopkins, Nick, Suzanne Zeedyk, and Fiona Raitt. 2005. "Visualising Abortion: Emotion Discourse and Fetal Imagery in a Contemporary Abortion Debate." *Social Science and Medicine* 61, no. 2: 393–403.

Jenkins, Colleen. 2014. "U.S. Court Strikes Down North Carolina Ultrasound Abortion Law." Reuters, December 22. http://www.reuters.com/article/2014/12/22/us-usa-north-carolina -abortion-idUSKBN0K01M920141222.

Lithwick, Dahlia. 2014. "North Carolina's Outrageous Abortion Requirement Is Struck Down." *Slate*, December 22. http://www.slate.com/articles/news_and_politics/jurispru dence/2014/12/north_carolina_abortion_ultrasound_decision_quotes_from_judge _wilkinson.html.

Mackenzie-Morris, Kim. 2015. "What Are 3D and 4D Ultrasound Scans?" Babycentre. http:// www.babycentre.co.uk/x557299/what-are-3d-and-4d-ultrasound-scans.

McCulloch, Alison. 2012. "The Rise of the Fetal Citizen." *Women's Studies Journal* 26, no. 2: 17–25.

McNeal, Stephanie. 2015. "A Couple Decided Not to Get a 4D Ultrasound After Seeing This Picture." BuzzFeed, August 13. www.buzzfeed.com/stephaniemcneal/ultrasound-terror.

Modern Mommy Boutique. n.d. "Grandpa's Heart" poem. Accessed February 14, 2016. http:// www.modernmommyboutique.com/Grandpas-Heart-Poem_p_489.html.

O'Dell, Larry. 2014. "4th Circuit Strikes Down NC's Abortion Ultrasound Law." *Daily Record*, December 22. http://thedailyrecord.com/2014/12/22/4th-circuit-strikes-down-ncs-abortion -ultrasound-law.

Petchesky, Rosalind Pollack. 1987. "Fetal Images: The Power of Visual Culture in the Politics of Reproduction." *Feminist Studies* 13, no. 2: 263–92.

Roberts, Julie. 2012. *The Visualised Foetus: A Cultural and Political Analysis of Ultrasound Imagery*. Farnham: Ashgate.

Sanger, Carol. 2008. "Seeing and Believing: Mandatory Ultrasound and the Path to a Protected Choice." *UCLA Law Review* 56: 351–408.

Sasson, Vanessa R., and Jane Marie Law. 2009. *Imagining the Fetus: The Unborn in Myth, Religion, and Culture*. Oxford: Oxford University Press.

Stephenson, Susan Raatz. 2005. "3D and 4D Sonography History and Theory." *Journal of Diagnostic Medical Sonography* 21, no. 5: 392–99.

Taylor, Janelle S. 2008. *The Public Life of the Fetal Sonogram*. New Brunswick, NJ: Rutgers University Press.

Williams, Thomas D. 2015. "Planned Parenthood Lies About Scott Walker Ultrasound Quote." Breitbart, May 28. http://www.breitbart.com/big-government/2015/05/28/planned -parenthood-lies-about-scott-walker-ultrasound-quote.

7

CONTRACTING FOR MOTHERHOOD

Postadoption Visitation Agreements

CAROL SANGER

C ontracts have long been used in family formation. In thinking about the contractual acquisition of relatives, the most familiar example is probably marriage. Historically, marriages commonly resulted from bargaining between families or ministers of state, particularly when diplomatic or dynastic concerns were at stake. Over time, men and women began to contract with each other individually. Indeed, by the nineteenth century, couples were regarded as contractually bound by virtue of their engagement alone; thus the lively cause of action for breach of the promise to marry (Lettmaier 2009). There also were less congenial examples of the contractual acquisition (and deacquistion) of spouses. Both in England and in the colonies, husbands could sell their wives, and some did (Dayton 1995).

Of course, things have changed over the past few centuries. Consent of the parties is now regarded as a desirable social practice as well as a legal prerequisite. Yet aspects of private contracting still sometimes structure a marriage, even if contract no longer creates it. Consider prenuptial agreements. The assurance of a background regime of enforceable contracts is understood to bring about marriages that might otherwise not have been entered. In 1990, the Pennsylvania Supreme Court upheld a prenuptial agreement between an unemployed nurse and a neurosurgeon, observing that parties "might not have entered their marriages, if they did not expect their agreements to be strictly enforced" (*Simeone v.*

Simeone, 581 A.2d 162, 166 [PA 1990] at 401). In 2010, the Supreme Court of the United Kingdom similarly recognized that an important factor in the enforceability of prenuptial agreements is "whether the marriage would have gone ahead without an agreement, or without the terms which had been agreed" (*Radmacher v. Granatino* [2010] U.K.S.C. 42, All. E.R.[D] 186 [Oct.] at 72).

This chapter focuses on the use of contract not to acquire a spouse but to obtain a child. As with wives, children were also acquired contractually in the past. In the United States, enslaved children were sold outright; during the colonial period, free children were often indentured or "placed out" by their parents as apprentices. These arrangements were highly contractual; actions for breach of contract were brought by apprentices against masters for failing to teach them the promised craft, and by masters against parents for harboring runaway apprentices (Bremner 1970, 103; Demos 1970, 71). Masters may have agreed to certain parent-like obligations, such as feeding and housing. But they understood themselves to be acquiring not a relation but an employee or, more generally, a worker (with indenture) or a trainee (with apprenticeship).

In this chapter, I consider the modern use of contract to transfer the custody of children not for educational or training purposes but to create the legal relationship of parent and child. The use of contract to create children is increasingly familiar, as gestational services and genetic material are legally bought and sold in much of the United States. But not all contracting for children involves reproductive technology. Foster parents, for example, contract with the state to raise children, a form of temporary parenting. I investigate only the use of contracts for permanent parenting. My focus is a new category of contract, the post-adoption visitation agreement.

ADOPTION TRANSFORMED

To understand how contract has made its way into adoption, it helps to understand how adoption practices in the United States have evolved, in the past few decades, from a regime of closed and confidential proceedings into the more transparent process of open adoption. In traditional closed adoption, birth mothers surrendered their parental rights to the state or to a licensed private adoption agency (Hollinger 1997). The agency then selected an appropriate married couple from its applicant pool to become the infant's new parents. Following a satisfactory home study, the family or probate court then issued an order declaring the adoption to be in the baby's best interest. The childless couple had become legal parents with a baby of their very own.

In the Connecticut General Statutes (2011, § 45-61b, § 45-64a), the combination of the termination of the birth mother's parental rights ("the complete severance of the legal relationship") and the final adoption decree ("all rights, duties and other legal consequences of the genetic relation of parent and child shall hereafter exist between the adopted person and the adopting parent") created a new legal family and obliterated the old. The birth mother had no idea who the adoptive parents were, and they knew very little about her. The baby's original birth certificate was sealed and replaced by a new one with the adoptive parents' names. Under prevailing mid-twentieth-century ideology, this process was understood as a domestic trifecta: the birth mother was now free from the stigma of unwed motherhood; the adoptive parents could proceed, secure in their parental status; and the child could be raised by parents whose dominion over him was as complete as that of any natural parent.

Beginning in the 1970s, the logic of this system of secrecy began to unravel. Adult adoptees challenged the view that they were better off not knowing anything about their birth families. They were supported by research findings identifying "genealogical bewilderment" and "identity lacunae" in adopted children (Baran and Pannor 1993, 119–20).[1] The widespread popularity of Alex Haley's novel *Roots* also sparked great interest in the pursuit of one's origins (Modell 2002). Best-selling confessional books such as Betty Jean Lifton's (1975) *Twice Born: Memoirs of an Adopted Daughter* contributed further to a cultural rethinking of closed adoption (Carp 2000). The early adoptee rights campaigns were rarely successful in court; claims that confidentiality violated a fundamental right to personhood were largely rejected.[2] Nonetheless, state legislatures began to authorize the collection of nonidentifying information about birth parents—such as ethnicity and medical histories—which adult adoptees might access.

At about the same time, women who had placed children for adoption in the past also began to step forward and to identify themselves. As a category of motherhood, birth mothers were fairly invisible. As birth mother Jan Waldron (1995, xvii) observed, "There are millions of birth mothers in this country, yet most people will tell you they've never met one." In the pre-Internet days of the 1980s, birth mothers who wanted to talk about their feelings—whether loss or guilt, regret or relief—began to meet in living rooms and church basements. And although they too rarely prevailed in court in efforts to open sealed adoption records, some states created official registries where birth parents and adult children could inquire about one another and, if both agreed, raised the possibility of reunion.[3]

These early forms of adoption activism took place against a perfect demographic storm regarding the availability of "desirable" (read: white) newborns. The decriminalization of abortion, the advent of the contraceptive pill, and the greater acceptability of unwed motherhood resulted in a significant decrease in the number of infants placed for adoption. As the National Committee for Adoption stated in 1989, "More than a million couples are chasing the 30,000 white infants available in the country each year" (quoted in Crossen 1989, A1). In consequence, the market power of birth mothers increased and adoption agencies began to pay attention to what it would take to get them to surrender their newborns (Carp 2000).

The answer was greater control by birth mothers over the adoption process. This control manifested itself in two ways. First, the selection of the adoptive parents moved from agency social workers to birth mothers themselves. Agencies began to act more as brokers, presenting information about their childless clients to pregnant women and girls considering adoption (Caplan 1990). As birth mothers increasingly knew the identity of the adoptive parents, the confidentiality of adoption records became a relic of a collapsing regime. Second, contractual practices began to envisage ongoing communication between birth mothers and adoptive families.

EARLY POSTADOPTION AGREEMENTS

With the help of agency social workers, birth mothers and adoptive families began to negotiate postadoption contact: the promise of photographs or progress reports, and even scheduled visits between birth mother and adopted child. The question of the legal status of such agreements arose most often when the adoptive parents discontinued visitation. In such cases, the birth mother typically sued to have the agreement enforced, and typically lost. Courts held that because adoption is a status created by statute, parties could not by agreement add to or detract from whatever rights and duties the state had fixed. As the Oregon Supreme Court explained in the early 1950s, "When the adoption took place, old ties were severed and it was off with the old and on with the new, so to speak" (*Whetmore v. Fratello*, 252 P.2d 1083 [Or. 1953] at 397).

Yet, in the 1980s, courts began to reassess the nonenforceability of visitation agreements. Most of the cases involved mothers who had existing relationships with their children; the adopted children were not newborns but children who had lived with their birth mothers for some time. In 1988, the Connecticut Supreme Court upheld a visitation agreement between a birth mother and the adoptive parents of her four-year-old son. The court found that the agreement had been "openly and lovingly negotiated, in good faith, in order to promote the best interest of the child" and that the child thought the agreement between her mother and her soon-to-be adoptive parents would be "the best world that she could imagine" (*Michaud v. Wawruck*, 551 A.2d 738 [CT 1988] at 742). Such decisions took a broader view of the changing nature of American families. The Connecticut court observed that it was "not prepared to assume that the welfare of children is best served by a narrow definition of those whom we permit to continue to manifest their deep concern for the child's growth and development." As with prenuptial agreements, courts acknowledged a possible relationship between postadoption visitation and a birth mother's decision to place her child in the first place: visitation agreements "will not ordinarily impede adoptions, but might even foster them in cases where . . . the natural parent is reluctant to yield all contact with his or her child" (*Weinschel v. Strople*, 466 A.2d 1301 [Md. Ct. Spec. App. 1983] at 262).

POSTADOPTION VISITATION STATUTES

By 2009, twenty-four states had enacted laws providing for some form of enforceable agreement between birth parents and adoptive parents.[4]

While the statutes differ in interesting ways, each provides that post-adoption visitation agreements are legal as long as the agreement is in writing and is approved by the court, most often by being incorporated into the final order of adoption. The statutes also clarify who may seek visitation with an adopted child. All include the birth parents, but several also include adult siblings and grandparents, aunts, and uncles; Minnesota permits visitation by foster parents. When the adopted child is an Indian child, three states (California, Minnesota, and Oklahoma) provide that members of the child's tribe may seek visitation. Although most statutes apply to *any* adopted child, Connecticut and Nebraska permit visitation only for the birth parents of children adopted from foster care, and Indiana limits coverage to foster children who are age two and older. Anticipating that postadoption visitation may not always go smoothly, a number of statutes require the parties to participate in mediation before they may seek specific performance (getting the contract enforced) in court. Importantly, at the time enforcement is sought, the court must determine whether visitation is in the child's best interests.[5]

The enactment of these statutes and the developing case law make clear that open adoption is now part of adoption practice and culture. It is the subject of workshops and continuing legal education programs, and it is a ubiquitous feature on adoption agency websites. Indeed, most adoptions in the United States are now open to some degree. Details from a set of actual agreements give the individualized flavor of the bargains: "The Adopting Parents . . . shall provide the Maternal Aunt . . . with a 'letter of update' two times each year describing the minor's adjustment, developmental progress and any significant achievements"; the parties "shall utilize 'skype' as a method of contact every other month for the first seven (7) years of the Child's life"; "Birth Mother agrees to not put any photos, now or forever . . . on Facebook or other public website without the express written permission of the Adoptive Parents" (Sanger 2012–13, 321).

Postadoption visitation agreements appear to secure the preferences of birth mothers who recognize that the demands of motherhood are too much at this stage in their life. Adoption presents itself as a sensible, satisfying alternative to motherhood (or to abortion). Doing what is best for the baby is both maternal and altruistic. Even so, "giving away one's baby" may still be unsettling. Open adoption is meant to soften the situation. With a postadoption visitation agreement in place, the birth mother may no longer be the child's legal mother, but neither is she a stranger at law. She is able to provide her child with able parents while preserving a bond for herself. Nonetheless, as one birth mother testimonial on the American Adoptions (2017) website states, "Even though it was the right choice, it was the hardest decision I have ever had to make, but through the grace of God and this amazing couple we have all found a new sense of hope."

In this regard, open adoption provides the adoptive parents with a keen understanding of the birth mother's sacrifice. After watching the birth mother of his adoptive son "crumple into a ball sobbing" when adoptive father Dan Savage and his partner left the hospital with their new son, Savage (2000, 215) explains "the logic of open adoption, its absolute necessity":

> In a closed adoption, we wouldn't have witnessed the moment our son's mother gave him up. . . . Because of open adoption, we'll be able to sit him down and . . . be able to describe the moment Melissa gave him to us, and how hard it was for her. We won't have to guess at what it was like or tell him that we're sure his mother loved him. We know she loved him; we saw it.

Open adoption supplemented by postadoption visitation agreements seems both to create new and to preserve existing parent–child relationships. Indeed, the preservation appears to make the creation possible. One might say that these agreements are to adoption what prenuptial agreements are to marriage: a species of contract that facilitates the primary relationship—whether wedlock or parenthood—and that makes the acquisition of relatives, whether spouses or children, possible. If the adoptive parents renege, the birth mother can seek specific performance, unless of course the court finds that visitation is not in the child's best interest. This all sounds very good and very promising.

Yet things are seldom exactly what they seem. That is because it turns out that unwed pregnant girls not quite ready for motherhood are not the only women who enter into postadoption visitation agreements. This is where the story becomes more complicated and my celebration of contract as the special glue that law can provide becomes somewhat messier.

THE SIGNIFICANCE OF VOLUNTARY AND
INVOLUNTARY RELINQUISHMENT

The imagined poster girl for open adoption may be the white, unwed, college-bound student who struggles with her decision but ultimately does the right thing by her baby. Yet many of the cases seeking enforcement of postadoption visitation agreements are brought by women with a very different profile. These are women who never wanted to relinquish their children in the first place but whose children have been removed by the state on account of abuse or neglect. These are women whose parental rights the state seeks to involuntarily terminate.

And here a shadow set of legal rules comes into play. The first and crucial rule is this: involuntary termination permanently and comprehensively severs the legal parent–child relationship. However, if the mother agrees to terminate her parental rights voluntarily, then she too can bargain for contact under the postadoption visitation statutes. Indeed, many mothers facing involuntary termination are advised by their social workers or attorneys to do exactly that.

In her study of parental termination cases over a ten-year period in St. Joseph County, Indiana, Hilary Baldwin (2002, 274) concluded that "knowing that a termination petition is imminent, and feeling as if they probably will not win," many parents decide to give up their children for adoption rather than have them taken away. "Voluntary termination gives the parent his only chance to work out a postadoption visitation agreement. If the termination proceeds involuntarily, the parent risks never seeing the child again." In Baldwin's study, the parent retained his or her child in only three of 303 involuntary termination cases decided in court. Baldwin observes, "If statistically a parent's chance is less than one percent . . . word will get around." I will return later to the matter of why so few mothers prevail in their attempts to keep their children.

As might be expected, in some cases, adoptive parents have cut off or suspended visitation when birth mother visitation has not gone as planned. Their reasons for doing so have included ongoing maternal drug problems,[6] missed visitation,[7] or simply their own belief that visitation is no longer in the child's best interests. The remedy these disappointed birth mothers tend to seek, however, is not specific enforcement of the visitation agreement. Instead, they seek to revoke their consent to the entire adoption and to have their own parental rights restored. Their argument is that their agreement to terminate was expressly conditioned on ongoing visitation, and once that is cut off, the arrangement has failed and everyone should return to Go. This argument is put clearly in a 2005 California case, *In Re Joe C v. Mary Ann S* (No. F047570, 2005 WL 2008461 [Cal. Ct. App. 2005] at 2). The birth mother "claims she is entitled to reversal of the order terminating parental rights because she did not get what she bargained for, namely [an enforceable] postadoption contact agreement." As the birth mother explained, she had "forfeited her right to a contested hearing as to whether the court should terminate her parental rights in return for a valid and enforceable postadoption contact agreement."

Here the key is the process of the formation of the postadoption visitation agreement, the exact circumstances under which it was entered. The general rule under state adoption law is that once an adoption is final, the only grounds for the revocation of parental consent are the traditional equitable defenses of fraud, mistake, undue influence, or misrepresentation. Though these defenses are seldom successful, the outcome seems to depend in part on just what kind of mother is seeking to overturn the adoption. We see this in a comparison of two Texas cases, the first involving a "good girl gone temporarily wrong" and the second involving a mother who failed to protect her baby from abuse.

In *Vela v. Marywood* (17 S.W.3d 750 [Tex. App. 2000]), nineteen-year-old, unmarried Corina sought to rescind her consent to the surrender of her infant. While pregnant, Corina had gone to Marywood, a licensed adoption agency, to learn about adoption. Her Marywood "maternity counselor" explained that, in an open adoption, Corina would "always be the child's birth mother"; that she would "always have a relationship with her [child]"; that the baby would have "two mothers"; and that that the birth family would be "like the child's extended family" (755). Corina testified that these representations were "the only reason" she signed the relinquishment. The court held that Marywood's "statements and omissions to Corina constituted misrepresentation, fraud, or overreaching" (763). Marywood's statements were fraudulent in part because Marywood's close counseling relationship with Corina created a fiduciary relationship between them. This meant that Marywood was bound "in equity and good conscience" to fully disclose that the so-called shared parenting plan had no legal effect at all. This they had clearly failed to do. In addition, it is worth noting that, throughout the decision, the court radiates sympathy for Corina and her family. She is described as "an exemplary young woman who made a mistake," and the decision details her record of community service and testimony characterizing Corina as "the envy of all the mothers in the neighborhood" (753).[8]

But not all birth mothers are so warmly regarded. Let us then examine another Texas case, from 2009, *In the Interest of DEH, a Minor Child* (301 S.W.3d 825 [Tex. App. 2009]). DEH was six months old when she was removed from her unmarried parents on grounds of abuse: the baby had been beaten by her father and suffered two fractures to each femur, multiple rib fractures, a liver contusion, and a spleen laceration. DEH was placed in foster care, and the Texas Department of Family and Protective Services moved to terminate the parental rights of the father and of the mother, EL. The father's rights were involuntarily terminated, but following mediation with her attorney and the baby's preadoptive foster parents, EL agreed to voluntarily relinquish her parental rights and enter into a post-termination agreement with the foster parents. A month later, EL sought to have her consent withdrawn on the grounds of fraud, duress, and coercion. Her claim was that she had been told that if the termination case against her went to trial, "the likely outcome was that she would never see [her child] again" and that her only other option was to sign the affidavit of relinquishment and enter into an agreement for limited visitation. EL stated that she had "no way out" (830–31).

After reviewing the evidence, the court concluded that EL "failed to demonstrate by a preponderance of the evidence that signing the affidavit in exchange for an allegedly legally unenforceable promise resulted from fraud, duress, or coercion" (*In the Interest of DEH* at 832). Coercion, the court explained, "occurs if someone is compelled to perform an act by threat or force"; duress occurs when "a person is incapable of exercising her free will"; fraud has five elements, which the court then listed. But the court found that EL had legal counsel, took advice from her family, and had been told that the visitation agreement was not "a contract that we could take to court."

The affidavit of relinquishment, printed in all capital letters, had been translated and read to EL at least twice before she signed it. It stated:

> I realize that I should not sign this affidavit of relinquishment if there is any thought in my mind that I might someday seek to change my mind ... Because I realize how important this decision is for the future of my child, I have put my initials beside every line of this paragraph so that it will always be understood that I have read this affidavit of relinquishment, understand it, and desire to sign it. (*In the Interest of DEH* at 831)

Although witnesses testified as to EL's anguish and fear at the possibility of losing all contact with her child, EL's own attorney testified that the pressure on her was not "undue"; it was "just a very emotional time" (830). Other attempts in other cases to prove duress, fraud, misrepresentation, or coercion have been similarly unsuccessful.[9]

Yet a closer look at the facts of some of the cases suggests why a birth mother might well have plausible expectations about the bargain she has entered into and may not have understood technical requirements, such as the obligation to file the final agreement with the court. In *Carla M v. Susan E* (No. H035781, 2011 WL 2739649 [Cal. Ct. App. 2011]), Carla contacted the adoptive mother Susan only after she had read Susan's "Dear Birth Mother" letter at the adoption agency. The letter stated, "We admire your courage and love in considering open adoption. If you choose to do this, you will ... become part of our lives forever" (§ 2, para. 2). The parties then met, developed a close friendship, were in nearly daily contact, and were even filmed for a program on open adoption for the Discovery Health Channel. At the same time, however, Susan notified the adoption agency that she and her husband would not sign any visitation agreement that was legally binding and would not go through with the adoption if they were required to do this. The agency's adoption counselor told Susan that if they signed a preliminary agreement, they would not have to file the official form. It is not hard to imagine that Carla might have misunderstood the importance of the formal filing, especially against the background of the encouraging promise in Susan's Dear Birth Mother letter.

A 2002 Nevada case similarly turned on the issue of filing (*Birth Mother v. Adoptive Parents*, 59 P.3d 1233 [NV 2002]).[10] Here, too, the birth mother relinquished her parental rights, having entered into a "communication agreement" with the adoptive parents, which had been drafted by their adoption agency. When the birth mother sought to overturn the adoption, the adoptive parents denied all contact. The birth mother then sued for specific performance. The district court granted the adoptive parents' motion to dismiss on the grounds that unless the agreement is incorporated into the final adoption decree (this one was not), "a natural parent has no rights to the child" (1235). Yet, while holding that the birth mother had no basis for relief, the court paused to note that:

> This decision leads to an unsatisfactory result in that natural parents may consent to an adoption because, pursuant to an agreement, they believe they have a right to postadoption contact with the child. However, what they natural parents fail to realize is that, if the agreement is not incorporated in the adoption decree, their rights as to the child are terminated upon adoption and any contact with the child may be had only upon the adoptive parents' permission, regardless of the agreement.

The dissent put the case even more forcefully. Declaring the result to be "patently unfair," Judge Rose observed, "The enforcement of the adoption agreement without also recognizing the contract provision leaves the biological parent with an adoption she or he never would have agreed to otherwise. We should not permit birth parents to be so misled" (1236).

Some of the problem of mothers not grasping the significance of the incorporation of their agreement into the final adoption decree may stem from the confusing structure of the entire arrangement. Open adoption is not one transaction but several, each with distinct significance. There is the relinquishment of the natural mother's parental rights to the state or licensed agency; there is the agreement between the natural mother and the adoptive parents; there is final decree issued by the court, and into which the private agreement must be folded. The first two of these are often executed at or around the same time, though each has its own requirements and protocols. For example, the relinquishment must contain clear and conspicuous language of its irrevocability, often to be separately acknowledged by the mother through her initials or signature.

Yet it is not hard to understand how a birth mother might think that the irrevocability that has been so pointedly brought to her attention applies to the obligations undertaken by *all* parties. She has foresworn her parental rights forever, and the adoptive parents have made what sounds like a binding promise. Yet, in agreeing to terminate her parental rights, the birth mother may not have understood that her consent to termination is really the only thing that will stick.

A DIFFERENT ANALOGY

In light of all this, I want to make a substitution in my earlier analogy. I suggested that postadoption visitation agreements were like prenuptial agreements. Both contracts make the desired, underlying endeavor of marriage or parenthood possible by settling terms of particular importance to the parties. Having looked more closely at the case law and sketched out how this all works in practice, I now think that the more accurate analogy, at least in cases involving mothers facing termination of parental rights, is not between postadoption visitation agreements and prenuptial agreements but rather between postadoption visitation agreements and plea bargains.

Like plea bargains, voluntary relinquishments are hard decisions made under hard circumstances. As one mother facing involuntary termination testified in her unsuccessful attempt to rescind her consent:

> I thought I was . . . actually, I don't know exactly what I was doing. All I know is that I wanted to see [AY], and that I'm continuing to see . . . I was told if I . . . if I didn't sign them and [the trial court] took my rights, I would never see her, and if I did sign them I could. This . . . I wasn't really . . . I don't know. I wasn't thinking right. I just wanted her to be happy, and I wanted her to be with me. (*Youngblood v. Jefferson County Division of Family and Children*, 838 N.E.2d 1164 [Ind. App. 2006] at 1167)

Like prisoners rolling the dice with regard to their liberty, mothers who are about to lose their children have a very small range in which to operate. Recall Baldwin's (2002) study of St. Joseph County, where only three of 303 mothers prevailed in hearings to prevent the involuntary termination of their parental rights. Mothers know they will either lose all contact with their children, forever, under an involuntary termination, or they can negotiate some form of contact under a voluntary relinquishment.

Plea bargaining and voluntary relinquishment share another crucial feature: each implicates due process concerns. In the criminal context, the defendant agrees to waive his right to a jury trial in exchange for the prosecutor's promise of a sentencing recommendation to the court.[11] In the termination context, the mother agrees to waive the hearing that is required if the state wants to terminate her parental rights involuntarily.[12]

Our concern here is the process by which the waiver is obtained, a concern raised by the dissent in the Texas *DEH* case. Recall that unlike the sympathetic Corina, the very unsympathetic EL could not unwind her relinquishment. But, as dissenting Justice Terrie Livingston stated, the involuntary termination of parental rights is a decision of constitutional significance. The evidence regarding the knowing and voluntary nature of the consent should therefore be "clear and convincing." Justice Livingston noted that, in *DEH*, EL's Spanish-speaking therapist testified that EL "signed the agreement because she thought it was irrevocable and that it would ensure her lifetime visitation" (*In the Interest of DEH* at 835).

Attempting to rescind the relinquishment of one's parental rights is akin to attempts to withdraw a plea bargain after the deal is done. Such cases are rarely successful. For example, in *Allen v. State* (509 A.2d 87 [Del 1986]), a defendant sought to withdraw his guilty plea because both the public defender and the judge had misinformed him about the range of punishment he should expect if convicted at trial (they told him three to thirty years when the range was three to fifteen years).[13] Nonetheless, the Delaware Supreme Court held that the defendant had "not suffered prejudice amounting to manifest injustice" (89). So, too, with parental relinquishment. In only a few cases has a court acknowledged the constitutional dimension of postadoption visitation. In one such case, *TB v. Indiana Department of Child Services* (921 N.E.2d 494 [Ind. 2009]), the state moved for termination of the mother's visitation on grounds of the children's best interests, but the mother did not receive notice of the hearing. The court held that this amounted to a denial of her due process rights and remanded the case for a hearing on the merits.

There is one final structural piece to consider in all of this, and that is the role of expert opinion. Expert opinion plays an important role in creating the background conditions against which relinquishment decisions are made. Recall that the reason mothers agree to relinquish their children is that their chances of succeeding at a termination hearing are worse than dismal. Why is this? Part of the answer concerns judicial reliance on the expert opinion of social workers or, more precisely, on the opinions of court appointed guardians ad litem (GALs) or court appointed special advocates. But as Baldwin (2002) and others have pointed out, these guardians and advocates are often community volunteers with little or no training in child development.[14] Their job is to represent the interests of the child, but as Baldwin shows, their assessments are often based on personal opinion or prejudice.

Moreover, studies have shown that many GALs do not even meet with the children whose interests they purport to represent. A 2000 study of Colorado GALs indicated that, in 41 percent of cases, the GAL did not meet with the child; a 2007 study of Ohio GALs showed that although 90 percent of attorneys indicated that they nearly always met with the children face-to-face, only 63 percent of them documented these meetings (Fines 2008, 428). Even fewer attorneys observed the child interacting with his or her parents: 82 percent reported they did so, but only 41 percent documented these observations.

In addition, because the court appointed special advocates are regarded as neutral evaluators rather than as witnesses for the state, they are not subject to cross-examination by the mother's counsel, and their views are most often accepted by judges as the final word on what is best for any particular child (Lidman and Hollingsworth 1998). Thus, the recommendations of layfolk, well intentioned as they may be, set the statistical stage for the one percent success rate reported by Baldwin (2002), which makes voluntary relinquishment by mothers facing termination something less than a foolhardy choice.

CONCLUSION

My focus has been on the circumstances under which postadoption visitation agreements are entered into and the circumstances under which they are enforced. Whether an analogy to plea bargains or to prenuptial agreements is more apt may be a matter of maternal circumstances. In cases where adoption is actively, if reluctantly, sought by a woman represented as the heroic birth mother doing the best for everyone, the logic of open adoption is clear. In cases where a mother's children have already been removed and termination looms, open adoption and the promise of visitation look quite different indeed.

Although every case does not fall neatly into one pile or the other, it seems clear that there are important differences in how postadoption visitation agreements are used, depending on where in the tricky constellation of motherhood the birth mother finds herself. The bargains look one way when sought by birth mothers who have considered their options and are satisfied with the slice of relational association that visitation or progress reports provide. They look quite another way for mothers for whom open adoption is simply the least-bad choice.

NOTES

1. Carp (2000, 219) expresses skepticism, noting that "both open and closed adoption advocates marshaled pseudoscience to advance their positions."
2. See, e.g., In re Roger B, 418 N.E.2d 751 (Ill. 1981).
3. See, e.g., In re Christine, 397 A.2d 511, 513 (R.I. 1979); State of New Jersey (2007).
4. For an overview, see Child Welfare Information Gateway (2011).
5. See, e.g., In the Interest of CS, 49 So.3d 38 (La. App. 2010); In the Matter of Heidi E, 889 N.Y.S.2d 762 (N.Y. App. Div. 2009).
6. In re Judicial Surrender of Daijuanna Priscilla M, 290 A.D.2d 298 (N.Y. App. Div. 2002).
7. In re Mya VP, 79 A.D.3d 1794 (N.Y. App. Div. 2010).
8. See also Jones v. Texas Dept. of Protective and Regulatory Services, 85 S.W.3d 483 (Tex. App. 2002).
9. See, for example, In re Daijvanna Priscilla (2002); In re Termination of Parent–Child Relationship of KV v. IDCS, 946 N.E.2d 655 (Ind. App. 2011).
10. See also Fast v. Moore, 135 P.3d 387 (Or. App. 2006).
11. For an expanded contractual analysis, see Scott and Stuntz (1992).
12. See Stanley v. Illinois, 405 U.S. 645, 65 (1972), and MLB v. SLJ, 519 US 102 (1996), stating that "parental status termination is irretrievably destructive of the most fundamental family relationship."
13. On plea bargaining as contracts, see Scott and Stuntz (1992).
14. See also Russ (1998, 308): "In most jurisdictions these individuals are typically not attorneys, they do not have adequate training, and they often do not have any idea what children are all about or how to deal with them." Peterson (2006, 1083) states,

"Many guardians ad litem have very little training or education in children and families, receive little compensation for their work, and often are reported to provide substandard representation to their child clients."

REFERENCES

American Adoptions. 2017. "Jenny's Adoption Experience." Accessed March 21, 2017. http://www.americanadoptions.com/pregnant/article_view/article_id/4219?cId=138.

Baldwin, Hilary. 2002. "Termination of Parental Rights: Statistical Study and Proposed Solutions." *Journal of Legislation* 28, no. 2: 239–323.

Baran, Annette, and Reuben Pannor. 1993. "Perspectives on Open Adoption." *Future of Children* 3, no. 1: 119–24.

Bremner, Robert H, ed. 1970. *Children and Youth in America: A Documentary History.* Vol. 1, *1600–1865.* Cambridge, MA: Harvard University Press.

Caplan, Lincoln. 1990. *An Open Adoption.* Boston: Houghton Mifflin.

Carp, Wayne. 2000. *Family Matters: Secrecy and Disclosure in the History of Adoption.* Cambridge, MA: Harvard University Press.

Child Welfare Information Gateway. 2011. "Postadoption Contact Agreements Between Birth and Adoptive Families." www.childwelfare.gov/systemwide/laws_policies/statutes/cooperative.cfm.

Crossen, Cynthia. 1989. "In Today's Adoptions, the Biological Parents are Calling the Shots." *Wall Street Journal,* September 12: A1.

Dayton, Cornelia H. 1995. "Divorce: The Limits of a Puritan Remedy." In *Women Before the Bar: Gender, Law, and Society in Connecticut,* ed. Cornelia Hayes Dayton, 104–56. Chapel Hill: University of North Carolina Press.

Demos, John. 1970. *A Little Commonwealth: Family Life in Plymouth Colony.* Oxford: Oxford University Press.

Fines, Barbara Glesner. 2008. "Pressures Toward Mediocrity in the Representation of Children." *Capital University Law Review* 37, no. 2: 411–48.

Hollinger, Joan H. 1997. *Adoption Law and Practice.* New York: Matthew Bender.

Lettmaier, Saskia. 2009. *Broken Engagements: The Action for Breach of Promise of Marriage and the Feminine Ideal, 1800–1940.* Oxford: Oxford University Press.

Lidman, Raven C., and Betsy R. Hollingsworth. 1998. "The Guardian ad Litem in Child Custody Cases: The Contours of Our Judicial System Stretched Beyond Recognition." *George Mason Law Review* 6, no. 2: 255–306.

Lifton, Betty Jean. 1975. *Twice Born: Memoirs of an Adopted Daughter.* New York: McGraw Hill.

Modell, Judith. 2002. *A Sealed and Secret Kinship: The Culture of Policies and Practices in American Adoption.* New York: Berghahn Books.

Peterson, Hollis R. 2006. "In Search of the Best Interests of the Child: The Efficacy of the Court Appointed Special Advocate Model of Guardian ad Litem Representation." *George Mason Law Review* 13, no. 5: 1083–114.

Russ, George H. 1998. "The Child's Right to Be Heard." *Georgetown Journal on Fighting Poverty* 5, no. 2: 305–11.

Sanger, Carol. 2012–13 "Bargaining for Motherhood: Postadoption Visitation Agreements." *Hofstra Law Review* 4: 309–39.

Savage, Dan. 2000. *The Kid: What Happened After My Boyfriend and I Decided to Go Get Pregnant*. New York: Plume.

Scott, Robert E., and William J. Stuntz. 1992. "Plea Bargaining as Contract." *Yale Law Journal* 101, no. 8: 1909–68.

State of New Jersey. 2007. "Adoption Registry." Department of Children and Families. Accessed February 1, 2017. www.nj.gov/njfosteradopt/adoption/registry.

Waldron, Jan L. 1995. *Giving Away Simone*. New York: Times Books.

8

RELINQUISHMENT AND ADOPTION
IN TAMIL SOCIETY

Mothers' Experiences with De-Kinning

PIEN BOS

Every year, thousands of children flow from their Indian birth origins to be welcomed by adoptive parents in India or abroad. Usually a happy event for the adoptive parents, it generally occurs after a wrenching decision has been made on the "supply side," by the mothers[1] and their families, who relinquish children for adoption. Precious little is known about these mothers—their deepest feelings, thoughts, and experiences. I had an opportunity to examine their narratives during and after two years of fieldwork in Tamil Nadu, South India.

From the outset, the notion of "relinquishment" points to its legal implications. Relinquishment means that at a certain stage a mother's parental rights are legally withdrawn, paving the way for outsiders to adopt the now "parentless" child. Beyond the field of adoption, withdrawing parental rights is commonly intended as a child protection measure, and those involved (officials as well as parents) search for opportunities to maintain some form of relationship between birth parents and children. In case of transnational adoption, however, legal disconnection is definitive, and the ties between a mother and her child are irreversibly severed.

As a consequence, relinquishment and adoption transform kinship constructions. But kinship is not merely a legal construction. As a cultural anthropologist, I prefer to approach kinship—motherhood in particular— as a notion with a cultural meaning. As a social and cultural construct, kinship has puzzled anthropologists for centuries. Kinship is a complex notion, determined by many factors, such as history, culture, and religion. Thus, the meaning of kinship and kinship constructions is not unequivocal. This is especially true in intercontinental relinquishment and adoption, because this process may involve people from different cultures.

The kinship patterns and kinship terminology of Tamils have developed over millennia, merging pre-Hindu meanings with Hindu influences and modern ideas (Dumont 1986; Busby 1997; Carsten 2004). The deeply anchored truths of Tamilian kinship have shaped contemporary adoption practices and their meanings as they have been legally constructed and experienced since intercontinental adoption became common, in the 1970s.

In her study of adoptive kinship, anthropologist Signe Howell (2006, 8) has introduced the notion of "kinning," by which she means "the process by which a foetus or newborn child is brought into a significant and permanent relationship with a group of people." Often, kinship is taken for granted and is regarded as an automatic relation. However, kinship is not automatic when adoption is concerned. Howell (2004) emphasizes the hard work required for adoptive parents to develop and maintain kinship with their adoptees. Apparently, the absence of consanguinity challenges the self-evident bond of a mother with her child and requires transformation of a noun (*kin*) into a verb (*to kin*).

By contrast, when relinquishment is concerned, it is that very self-evident bond of a mother with her child that is supposed to be dissolved by means of a legal document. This becomes especially challenging in Tamil culture, because the affiliation of a mother and her child is considered to be a particular form of kinship. Tamils believe that a mother and her child share the same blood. What are the consequences of a legal document for mothers who are embedded within a culture where consanguinity—especially the mother–child bond—is extremely meaningful? Inspired by Howell's notion of kinning, I focus on the other side of the process as a form of "de-kinning," or at least as an attempt to de-kin. Better than "relinquishment," the notion of de-kinning captures the complexity of severing mother–child bonds, because it not only embraces its legal or biological dimensions but also gives expression to its social and emotional effect (Fonseca 2011; Mookherjee 2007).

Figure 8.1 portrays the "adoption triad." The three angles represent the mother, the adoptive parents, and the relinquished child. Noticeably,

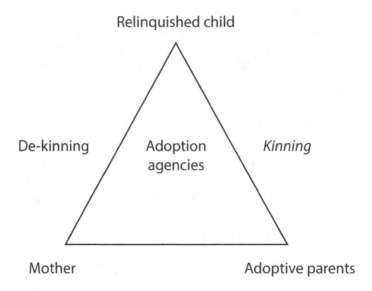

FIGURE 8.1 The adoption triad.

the line between the mother and the adoptive parents is unmarked. In India, open adoptions are uncommon and are usually obstructed (Bos 2008). Hence, to a Tamilian mother, the adoptive parents are usually strangers; they have neither names nor faces. As an abstraction, the adoptive parents gain respect, because they are willing to care for the child of a stranger, but—as elaborated here—the relationship does not fit within the mother's framework of descent or kinship alliances.

At the top of the triad is the relinquished child. Usually, the child is mentioned as the "adoptive" child. From the perspective of a mother, however, the child is *relinquished*, not adopted. In this chapter, the mothers' perspective is center stage, and from a mother's perspective relinquishment is not an intervention to be overlooked, because it is irrevocable and therefore consequential for her as well as for her child.

FIELDWORK

This article is based upon data collected during 2002 and 2003 across the state of Tamil Nadu. In these two years of fieldwork, I found that women were willing to share their lives in elaborate and intimate ways, and I was privileged to be able to meet with thirty-six pregnant women or mothers who ultimately relinquished their children.[2] These women usually stayed in short-stay homes (run by nongovernmental organizations) that were affiliated with agencies licensed to place children into adoptive families in India or abroad. Many of the pregnant women or mothers were unmarried. (I elaborate on their backgrounds in the next section.) Occasionally, I also observed and spoke to these women's significant family members.

In addition to conducting formal interviews, I also interacted with many mothers on an informal basis, spending hours chatting in the corridors, the baby room, or the maternity room. Observing mothers taking care of their newborn babies during their decision-making process before, and even after, relinquishment provided deep insight into their lives, feelings, and considerations. I also collected data from counselors, social workers, nurses, doctors, police, officials, and policy makers in counseling centers, family planning units, and maternity wards of government and private hospitals, offices, and private residences—wherever was preferred by the people involved.

THE INDIAN CONTEXT OF RELINQUISHMENT AND ADOPTION

In contemporary India, professionals perceive adoption as a better way to rehabilitate orphaned and/or relinquished children than raising them in institutions. Yet adoption debates among social workers and other professionals working in the field of adoption are in flux, and the family of origin, specifically that of the mother, is gradually gaining priority. For instance, twenty years ago, poverty and financial problems were perceived as legitimate reasons for relinquishing children born in wedlock. Just two decades ago, many professionals regarded adoption as an acceptable intervention to increase the opportunities for the education and health care of a child from a poor background. Nowadays, adoption professionals generally express the view that mothers of *legitimate* children should be offered alternative forms of support to enable them to raise their own children. With regard to these (once-) married mothers, it is commonly believed that the mother and child belong together. Growing up in an adoptive family is perceived as "second best," but still preferable to raising children in institutions.

Discourses concerning *unmarried* mothers are different. Most professionals believe that a mother's unmarried status legitimizes relinquishment without a thorough search for alternatives. They assume that children from "culturally awkward" circumstances are better off with adoptive parents who can financially and morally afford to raise them, and that unmarried mothers will be better off continuing their lives without their illegitimate children (Bos 2008).[3]

Legal procedures and guidelines for relinquishment are clear about the rules and formalities, giving fathers priority in cases of legitimate children but no voice in cases of illegitimacy. A child's father and, in the case of his death or disqualification, the child's mother are legally allowed to relinquish a child. If both parents are absent, the child's guardian is allowed, with permission of the court, to relinquish a child for adoption. In the case of a child born out of wedlock, the law grants "the mother herself and none else" the right to surrender the child (see Indian Council for Child Welfare–Tamil Nadu 1998, 144; Indian Ministry of Welfare 1995, 25).

Once a child is adopted, contact between mothers and their relinquished children is generally discouraged and information regarding both identities is legally withheld. Confidentiality is the norm and secrecy the rule. "Confidential adoptions are characterized by 'a severing of relationship between the child and his or her biological parents.' . . . All adoptions in India are confidential. . . . The Supreme Court of India had ruling [sic] that 'it was absolutely essential that biological parents should not have an opportunity of knowing who are the adoptive parents taking their child in adoption' " (Indian Council for Child Welfare 2001, 83). Likewise, information about the mother—for instance, her name and address—is kept from a child seeking to learn about his origins (Dohle 2008). All adoption records, including the original birth certificate of the child, are sealed by court order (Indian Council for Child Welfare 2001). Thus, adoptive children are obstructed in their efforts to trace their mothers, and mothers do not have access to information regarding the adoptive family of their children (Indian Council for Child Welfare 1998).

How does such policy affect the mothers themselves? In the Indian context, the child belongs to a family; a child is culturally embedded in an extended family and the wider community and is significantly related to his or her family members. In this same context, the relationship between a mother and her child is recognized as particularly meaning-ful. "Water is water and blood is blood" was a saying repeated by a social worker whose daily business was to match adoptive parents with relin-quished children. "Adoption is just a paperwork construction" is another one-liner shared with me by Ramachandran,[4] an older Tamilian Brah-min father, who went on to explain.

> RAMACHANDRAN: Your own child is your blood. But if you buy a child, you are buying only the body, not the soul. An adoptive mother does not love. . . . I mean in India, in our system, if you are sleeping and your child, the child that is born to you, cries in the night, you wake up immediately without anybody waking you. But in this case [adop-tion], someone has to wake you up to enable you to help the child.
> BOS: You mean that feelings for a biological child and for an adopted child differ significantly?
> R: Definitely.
> B: What makes the difference?
> R: A mother has feelings for her child from the state of conception onwards. She does not only feel her blood, she enjoys the child for nine months for the full one hundred percent. She will talk with her child and her child will share in the mother's thoughts and feelings. . . . As far as adoption is concerned, the child will always be her guest and will not become her child.

Ramachandran was expressing the widely held belief that the rela-tionship between a mother and her child reaches beyond conscious con-fines. While emphasizing the intuitive and spiritual aspects of parental relationships in general and of motherhood in particular, he also shared his personal experience of these aspects as a father of his own children.

Indian mythology is a significant source of inspiration for Ramachan-dran; he finds his conviction reconfirmed in ancient holy stories. The significance of parental relationships is embodied by and anchored in old mythological examples. Human beings cannot change or manipulate these sacred truths and also, according to this Brahmin man, *should not* challenge them. Whereas Ramachandran specifically emphasized the spiritual aspects of a relinquished child, others regularly stressed the genetic inheritance. A child born to an unmarried mother—and thus to an immoral and irresponsible woman—will subsequently be affected by this problematic background, as is expressed in the saying "How can a wild tree bear good fruit?" (Godbole 1986, 88).

Within Tamil culture, according to Karin Kapadia (1995, 30), " 'blood' is probably *the* dominant metaphor of 'connectedness.' " Consanguinity is a notion with an evident cultural meaning and, especially for non-Brahmin Tamils, a blood bond stands for relatedness, attachment, and affection (*pācam*). Kapadia (1995) records the dominant idea that a child has more of the mother's blood than the father's because a baby grows in a mother's womb. After conception, the mother's uterine blood nurtures a child; thus, a baby shares the mother's blood. Sharing blood implies attachment, and the blood bond between a mother and her child is considered to be the strongest, because a mother's blood runs through her child's veins. This blood-relatedness stands for unique affection between both of them (Uberoi 2002; Van Hollen 2003).

For Tamils, mother's milk and breastfeeding constitute another biological matter with a significant cultural meaning. Mother's milk is a rich transmitter, not merely in a biological sense. Once, when a mother started shedding tears during an interview, my assistant Cecilia advised her to control her sadness. Cecilia explained that a mother's uncontrolled sadness would affect the baby through the blood, if the woman is pregnant, or through milk, if a baby is being breastfed. Blood and mother's milk emerge as transmitters of a mother's emotions, including her love. According to Margaret Trawick (1992), Tamils believe that a baby who is ten months old needs to be weaned to prevent transmission of too much love, resulting in a fat and proud child who would even beat his or her own mother.

LIVED EXPERIENCES

The bond of a mother with her child is extremely meaningful; nevertheless, to date, Tamilian mothers do relinquish children. In this section,

I discuss mothers' life histories and experiences. By signing a legal document, these mothers give up their children for adoption. The formal procedure is juridical but the significance of the act reaches far beyond legalities. What makes a mother decide to relinquish her child, and what are her expectations after doing so?

The mothers who participated in this research shared the predominant cultural meanings of important notions such as consanguinity and mother's milk. Nevertheless, the differences in their personal circumstances and situations were also important. For that reason, I prefer to introduce individuals rather than "categories" of women. I will focus on one woman, Sundari, and then discuss several others whose experiences also reveal elements of the attempt to de-kin.

Sundari was an unmarried pregnant woman when I met her. For nine months, from the discovery of her pregnancy until she relinquished her child, she was hiding in an institution that was licensed to arrange adoptions. An intelligent woman, she was well able to reflect upon her situation and expressed complex mixed feelings and conflicting interests. During her long stay in the institution, she participated in three formal interviews—two during her pregnancy and one after giving birth to her daughter, before leaving the institution. I also regularly chatted with her informally and observed her while she interacted with others and, after she gave birth, in the presence of her baby. The dilemmas that Sundari revealed and the aspects of her situation that were crucial in her narratives appeared, in different ways, in interviews with other women.

When I first met Sundari, I saw a young woman in her early twenties. Her family belonged to the Christian Nadar community from the deep south of Tamil Nadu. At the time, they were living in Chennai, in the northern part of Tamil Nadu, but most of her kin remained in the southern part of the state. Sundari's parents' marriage had not worked out well. After too many quarrels, her father left Chennai for his native place and now only joined his wife, three daughters, and son occasionally, during festivals. Formally, he was the head of his family, yet he was not much in charge when it came to family decisions. Sundari's mother was the informal leader of the family and managed it according to her standards. Her husband's approval of her decisions was merely a formality; he "rubber-stamped" whatever she decided.

At school, Sundari had been a bright pupil, but after she completed high school her mother started searching for an appropriate marriage alliance and learned about a suitable groom. Sundari's mother was pleased with this specific alliance. The man, a Christian Nadar, came from the "right" community, and had a "good family background." Meanwhile, Sundari found herself a job as a tailor in an export company at the outskirts of Chennai. Here, she met a twenty-five-year-old mechanic. They worked closely together—closer than was considered appropriate in Tamil custom, where boys and girls, men and women, are usually segregated in schools, on public transport, while waiting in lines, and elsewhere. But export companies do not observe these culturally determined rules and restrictions. Spending working hours together, Sundari and the mechanic started chatting. With time, they became more intimate. For a year, they were romantically involved and had sex on a regular basis.

The couple discussed marriage and dreamed about a future together. His family did not raise any objections concerning his choice; according to Sundari, his parents knew about his love for her and approved of the marriage. In Sundari's family, however, the situation was more complicated, and she was aware that she was in trouble. The man she was in love with would never be acceptable to her mother because he belonged to a scheduled caste community. As Sundari explained, "All my family members marry within our caste. People from my caste are very particular about that. Throughout, we have married within the caste. Besides, he is a low-caste boy."

As time passed, Sundari realized that she had missed her periods. She became anxious, and thoughts about being pregnant ran through her mind. This idea distressed her, and Sundari revealed her worries to her elder sister—the secret of her love affair and her delayed menstruation. Her sister immediately informed their mother and, from this moment onward, Sundari's life turned into chaos.

Her mother was extremely upset. She shouted, cried, and physically abused her daughter. After her first emotional outbursts were spent, she inquired about the father of the child. Sundari described his merits and tried to present an acceptable background for her lover, but her mother was far from impressed. She instantly rejected Sundari's requests and arguments to arrange a marriage with him and instead decided to continue negotiations with the groom she had selected. She informed this family that she needed some more time to arrange money for a dowry by selling some land. The groom's family accepted her excuse, and wedding arrangements were postponed.

To execute her plan, Sundari's mother opted for an abortion. She immediately packed a bag and took Sundari to visit the government hospital in their native area, in the southern part of the state. But the visit was disappointing. Two doctors confirmed that it was too late for Sundari to have a legal abortion. In addition, both reacted angrily to the delay and blamed Sundari's mother for raising an immoral daughter: "Look what kind of daughter you have given birth to!"

Sundari's mother then remembered a nongovernmental organization that provided shelter for unwed mothers in an area where the family had once resided. That same night, her mother admitted Sundari to this institution. Sundari described the intake procedure as an exchange between her mother and the counselor. Sundari listened to her life story as represented by her mother. Her mother requested that the institution hide Sundari for two weeks after delivery of the child. The counselor advised Sundari's mother to relinquish the child for adoption, and Sundari's mother grasped this as an appropriate solution, because time was running out and the groom was waiting.

A couple of weeks after her admission, I had my first interview with Sundari. In the first hour of this interview, I could see that she was trying very hard to accept her mother's decision to relinquish the child. However, the character of the interview, as well as Sundari's attitude, changed remarkably when I offered her an opportunity to ask me some questions. She visibly perked up and reversed our roles. From that moment on, she became the person who was asking the questions.

She started by inquiring about formalities regarding relinquishing and adoption procedures. Her first question was about her baby: "Will they raise my child here, or will it go to any other place?" I told her that the baby would stay in the institution for at least two months, because this was the time available to her as a mother to reclaim her child.

"How long will my baby stay here before it will be given to adoptive parents? What will happen if I reclaim my child? Do I need to pay to get my child back? Can I visit my child if it is placed for adoption?" She was asking many questions, but the thread running through all of them was her fear that her child would be neglected: "Sometimes people who should give care to somebody else's children do not care for the children properly. They may ill-treat my baby. That is the reason that I prefer to see my child and to keep in touch with my child."

Because the baby rooms were near the section where she was residing, Sundari had observed how babies were taken care of. Clearly, she was not happy with the idea of handing over her baby. She was convinced that there was a difference between the quality of her personal care as a mother and that of the paid caregivers. She also was worried about her child in the long term, after placement in an adoptive family. Adoptive care did not fit in her frame of reference regarding motherhood. From her perspective as a mother, she preferred to control the care of and the policy regarding her relinquished child.

In answer to her questions, I provided her with the official guidelines and explained that she had a right to retain her child, because she had not yet signed any legal document. I also told her that she had a right to reclaim her child within sixty days of signing a legal document. As Sundari listened to my answers, I could see that something was happening in her mind. Apparently, she was confused by what I had told her, and I observed that her submissive and obedient attitude was vanishing. But it was only in the second interview that I became aware of my role in her decision-making process: in light of the information that I provided, she was starting to consider different scenarios.

The second interview took place only a few weeks later. Sundari still had not given birth and her belly had grown. The conversation started spontaneously, and Sundari explicitly stated that she was of two minds about the decision to relinquish her child.

SUNDARI: Sometimes I feel like keeping the child with me. But at other moments, I think it is better to leave it here and continue my life without the baby. . . . If they keep the child here for six months, I have a chance to ask [for] my child back. . . . In case my family members start quarrelling with me, I am at risk of being thrown out. Then I can come back here, take my child back, and stay alone with my child . . . I can go back to the export company. The company has a crèche for children. I can leave my child there in daytime and work. . . .

BOS: Do you know any other woman who is having a child without having been married?

s: There is a woman living next door to our house. She has given birth to a child before she got married. She looks after it herself.... Her baby is two years old. She is leaving her child in the crèche and goes for her job in the export company. She has rented a house and stays alone. Nobody speaks badly about her....

b: If this is really what you prefer to do, what makes you listen to your mother?

s: It will embarrass my mother if I take my child. My mother has told the people in our neighborhood that I went back to our village. If I come back with a child, everybody will talk badly about us. But even if I go home without my child, there are chances that problems will come up in my house. If the fights start, I will come back [to this institution]. I will collect my child and stay somewhere else, in a different area of Chennai, where people do not know about me....

Sundari had developed an alternative scenario. If her family expelled her, she would reclaim her baby. Similarly, if the marriage arrangements with the man her mother had selected for her continued and she was expelled from her marital home, she would return for the baby. Her major concern in this latter scenario was time. I had told her that, legally, she had two months to reclaim her baby, but she thought that six months would be more appropriate for her. She would need all that time to reconsider, after leaving the institution, and time was putting pressure on her. She just hoped that the child would remain in the institution long enough for her life to become stabilized, either in her mother's place or in the household of her husband-to-be.

But the child had not been born yet. When Sundari elaborated her plans in this second interview, she was still pregnant; her baby was still an abstraction, not a child of flesh and blood. How would she look upon her situation after giving birth? She predicted that the delivery would bring her to a different state of mind. Presently, she felt stigmatized as an immoral unwed pregnant girl, because her pregnancy was associated with her uncontrolled sexuality.[5] But after her delivery she would be the mother of a child.

"For my mother and the other people in my family, it will not make any difference. For myself, however, I predict that the gossips and bad talking of people will hurt me less with my baby in my arms." Sundari believed that motherhood would provide her with strength to face society. She considered the possibility of being expelled by her mother, and with this scenario in mind, she made calculations and hoped to get back in time to reclaim her child. She would then opt for the alternative scenario: a life as a single mother.

Sundari gave birth to a baby girl through a quick delivery. On the day she returned to the institution from the hospital, I dropped in. She was lying on her mat with her back toward the wall, resting her head on one hand. Next to her, under the sheet, I noticed a small and uneven bundle of clothes moving slightly. She was staring at it. She looked tired; the sparkling appearance that had characterized her during pregnancy had vanished. She offered me a pale smile as I settled myself on the floor next to her mat. Immediately, she turned her baby over to show her to me. The girl was extremely tiny, around four pounds in weight, with slightly yellowish skin. She looked vulnerable, and I could see that Sundari was worried too.

Two weeks after the delivery, Sundari's mother showed up. Again she locked herself in with the counselor, who advised her to take some more time and be transparent about Sundari's past when it came to making wedding arrangements. Finally, Sundari's mother was convinced. She decided to inform the family Sundari was to marry into that she was withdrawing. Sundari felt incredibly relieved by this action and grateful to the counselor and to her mother for sparing her this awkward marriage.

It was after her mother's visit that I observed Sundari becoming ambivalent toward her child. She was keeping more distance from her baby, who was no longer sleeping with her on one mat and had been removed to the baby room. During the third interview, soon after her mother's visit, I told her about my observations, and Sundari explained, "I am willing to relinquish the baby. I have informed them [the institution authorities] about this and asked them to place the baby for adoption." This time, Sundari was short in her answers. I noticed her irritation with my questions. Obviously, she was tired of being of two minds. She had just delivered a child and this was not a moment to resist authority.

SUNDARI: Before delivery, I was in two minds. Only after delivery I decided to relinquish the baby and to marry the person my mother tells me to marry.

BOS: What kind of thoughts ran through your mind after delivery? What made you decide to relinquish?

S: First I thought I can keep the baby with me. But when I sat down and thought of the baby's future, I decided to give it up. Also, here they advised me, "How can you stay alone and survive? Your people will not allow you, and your neighbors will ask questions. The baby will get a good future when she is adopted."

Nobody in this institutional surrounding supported Sundari's initial plans to reclaim the child. Moreover, her future scenario had changed since her mother cancelled the wedding. She was more confident about her rehabilitation within her family. But, most of all, she was too tired to resist firmly and decided to act according to the advice. Along with her surrender came her actions to distance herself from her baby.

BOS: As soon as you decided, did your relationship with your baby change?

SUNDARI: Yes. I stopped sitting with her in daytime. Only in the night I sit some time with her. . . . From the time my mother visited me, I stopped feeding her [by the breast]. . . . I am not happy with feeding the baby. My mother told me to stop feeding since my breast will be lowered. This will be discovered in future and may reveal my secret history. I personally do not want to feed the baby since it will depress me too much in leaving the child behind. Breastfeeding will attach me to my baby.

This decision had tremendous consequences. A few days after she stopped breastfeeding, the child suffered from diarrhea and was admitted in the hospital in a serious condition. The disease turned out to be septicemia, a life-threatening condition, especially because the baby was only three weeks old and weighed so little. I could see that Sundari was in great distress. When I met her in the corridors and inquired how she and the baby were, she again kept her answers short. She obviously felt worried and overwhelmed with guilt.

Sundari knew that her child's life was in danger, but the institution's authorities did not inform her about the details. Information about the baby's condition only leaked out to her incidentally; apparently Sundari was not in a position to inquire. The baby needed to stay in the hospital for weeks, but even after she returned, her condition was not good. She was still extremely tiny and listless.

Three months after giving birth, Sundari was packing her bag to leave the institution. Formalities had been completed, the surrender deed had been signed, and the festival season was driving her family together. On that day, I saw her getting into an auto rickshaw with her mother. The strain had left its marks on her face. Her initial worries about handing her baby over to the care of strangers had become well grounded: for the second time, her baby had been admitted to a hospital in critical condition with septicemia. But this was not her business anymore; she had lost her child in any case.[6]

GENDER, MONEY, AND KEEPING BABIES

Sundari did not elaborate upon the gender of her child. She did not stress the fact that her baby had turned out to be a girl, and this did not seem to influence her thinking. This was not the case for another mother in the institution, Amuda. Twenty years old, Amuda came from a very poor family that struggled daily to make ends meet with farming. She was in the last term of her pregnancy when we met.

Initially, she seemed to accept the idea of relinquishment. However, during the second interview, after she had given birth to her son, it became apparent that her state of mind had changed. At first, she repeated what she had mentioned during the first interview: that she could not raise her child because people would "talk bad" about an unmarried mother. This time, however, she also stressed how difficult it was for her. She deliberately described her physical pains during delivery and emphasized how she had suffered to give birth to her son.[7] She was breastfeeding him and caring for him wholeheartedly.

AMUDA: It will never be like before.
BOS: What will not be like before?
A: Before, I was free. From now onwards, I will always have this sorrow in my heart. A woman can never forget the baby she had.

B: During pregnancy, you explained that you were sure about relinquishing your baby. How do you feel now about this?

A: I promised [the institution staff] to give the child [to them]. I will not
go back on my word. . . . Leaving the child here does not mean forget-
ting the child; the mothers will be burning within their hearts. . . . It
is all gone. At least hereafter I will lead a decent life. I don't think I
can attach myself to any worldly thing.

In spite of deep sorrow, Amuda seemed to continuously hear the echo of
the dominant conviction that retaining the child was impossible. For
some unmarried mothers, however, their thinking changed after giving
birth to a boy.

Chellam, another unmarried mother of a male baby, also came from a
very poor family. In the first interview, during her pregnancy, she
stressed the shame for her family and having to answer to her child after
it grew up. But the child turned out to be a boy, and this was of great
importance for Chellam (see Srinivasan 2006).

CHELLAM: My baby is a beautiful and lucky boy. In my old age, he will
look after me. But not if I give him up. If I see him now, I feel very sad
about losing him.

BOS: If the baby had been a girl, what would you do?

C: I would leave her behind. No second thought. But since it is a boy and
since his skin is fair, I want to bring him up.

B: What makes the difference between a boy and a girl?

C: A girl is like me. She needs to be taken care of. There are too many
expenses. For a boy, there is not much expense. He is an asset. If we
bring him up, he will look after us in old age. I think my mother will
also change her mind once she sees the child because he is very
beautiful. . . . I am least worried about my family. If they [the institution staff] give the child to me I will take him and stay separately.
Eventually, I will bring him up alone by doing domestic work. For six
months I can feed him and keep him with me. After that I can leave
him with somebody to take care of him and go for work. I can bring
him up, but I am upset for having signed the papers. . . . Everybody
here is saying, "Why would you leave such a beautiful baby?" If they
allow me to take the child, I will take him. He has six toes on his

right feet. It seems that this means that he will be rich in the future. I
have written down his birth day and time to check [his horoscope].

B: Who said to you that you should leave the child here behind?

C: All the caregivers who are looking after the babies said so. But what
can I do? I have signed the papers that I will relinquish the baby after
delivery. If I want the baby, I have to pay lots of money, they say.

Chellam was clear in her wish to keep the child, but in practice it did
not work out. On the day that her mother, aunt, and stepfather arrived
(I was also inside the institution and able to observe the process), she lost
control of the situation. She was not invited to participate in discussions
and was in no position to take the floor on her own initiative. The formalities were arranged between the authorities of the institution and
Chellam's mother and aunt. Chellam listened submissively to what the
authorities had decided. The surrender document, including the possibility of reclaiming the child within two months, was read for her. Orally,
she was told that—according to the institution policy—if she aimed to
reclaim her child, she would have to bring her husband with her. In this
way, the authorities communicated another implicit message: raising her
child as a single mother was unacceptable.

After Chellam had signed the surrender document, her aunt and
mother were offered a chance to see the baby—an opportunity, I have
noticed, that is rarely offered. Chellam's mother rejected this opportunity and waited outside the building, but her aunt accepted the offer
and had a glimpse of the baby. She was moved by the appearance of the
child and had tears in her eyes when she came out. But the case was
closed. Without talking, Chellam and her family left the institution,
walking behind one another. Chellam was the last in line. Her hanging
head contrasted with the bright colors of her sari, expressing her sorrow
about leaving behind the son she so eagerly wanted to take home.

Sometimes the child's gender had an effect on decision-making processes, but more often it was the financial issues that appeared to be
influential. Mothers who reside in the institutions are aware of the connection between their babies and the flow of money. During interviews,
mothers shared observations or rumors that the babies were usually
"bought by rich people." Mothers perceive themselves as a financial
investment for the organization, and in many interviews mothers stated

that they had heard that a substantial amount would be required if they decided to reclaim their babies. Most women I met were not in a position to comply with such a financial claim. Whether in reality or merely in their perception, the bill that a mother has to pay in order to reclaim her baby pushed further away the idea of keeping it.

In addition to the financial arguments, moral judgments also pressed mothers to accept the fact that they must relinquish their children. For some women, these arguments underscored their own wish. Many expressed anxious feelings, like Chitrapathi: "Every night I am staring at my child and cry about losing her. I want to keep my child with me but how is it possible? How can I bring her up? Where can I leave her when I go for work?"

The management of the nongovernmental organizations used breast-feeding policy to direct mothers' decision making. Depending upon a mother's interest and the health of her baby, mothers were instructed to breastfeed their own babies, and were sometimes requested to breast-feed somebody else's. Despite feelings of resistance, one woman explained that she was not in a position to refuse. "The milk is there, so why to waste it?" she loyally glossed the staff's request. Nevertheless, if a mother was too obviously motivated to breastfeed her child, she risked provoking an end to her feeding. A mother who is expected to relinquish her baby is not supposed to develop too much interest in or attachment to her child: "Then *we* have a problem," one nurse explained. She meant by this that she did not appreciate having to have discussions or arguments with mothers who were expected to relinquish. One mother expressed that she felt uncomfortable, irritated, and judged by the counselors: "If I keep too much distance from my baby, I will be judged as a bad mother, and if I show too much affection toward my child, I get punished for getting too much attached."

CONCLUSION

In the lived experiences of mothers who eventually relinquish, delivery becomes a milestone. With a baby in her life, a mother's circumstances are significantly changed. In Tamil culture, motherhood is perceived as sacred, enabling a woman to develop specific, powerful feelings expressed as "pure love." This same love, however, forms the basis of her capacity to suffer and sacrifice for the sake of her children. The fact that a mother shares her blood with her child is believed to result in a strong relatedness between mothers and children. Mother love, in its divine cultural meaning, can only come from a biological mother, who is regarded as a unique and irreplaceable person for her child. The intimate attachment inherent in this blood relationship is enforced by breastfeeding. The separation of mother and child therefore results in deeply rooted pain.

An examination of how relinquishing mothers perceive the mother–child relationship gives insight into how mothers experience relinquishment and what they expect afterward with regard to their children's relationship with their adoptive mothers. They do not perceive caring, suffering, and sacrificing for the sake of somebody else's child to be inherent in human nature. Thus, while relinquishing mothers may respect and value adoptive mothering, they also consider themselves a threat to the adoptive parents, because they believe that adoptive motherhood is not true motherhood.

In dominant discourse, Tamils perceive adoptive motherhood as a connection that lacks this specific attachment and affection. Motherhood is everlasting; the tie cannot be broken with a legal document. Relinquishing a child for adoption by signing a document is considered an artificial construction that does not reflect the complexity of breaking the fundamental bond between mother and child. One of my informants labeled adoption as merely a "paperwork construction," since from his point of view it does not represent what it pretends, namely parenthood. Similarly, the legal act of relinquishment may be considered a paperwork construction too.

Mothers experience motherhood even after relinquishment. Hence, they expressed personal and social reasons for a reunion even before they had actually signed a surrender document. They regularly revealed that being socially embedded in webs of significance, with their relational aspects—such as being the daughter of parents, sister of brothers, or niece of aunts—conflicted with their individual aims. Different and contradictory individual emotions, such as love, feelings of responsibility and worry for the child, and enthusiasm and pride about the newly acquired status as mother, were mixed with feelings such as shame, responsibility for the family's reputation, and stigmatization. Depending on where a mother positions herself, and taking into account her changing priorities and perceptions over time, mothers were able to express their usually deepest wish to meet the relinquished child.

Because biological mothers recognize themselves as the only true mother, they are consequently supposed to be a threat to the adoptive relationship. In practice, surrendering mothers assumed that the institutions were on the side of adoptive parents. For this reason, they seldom considered reunions to be real possibilities. Paradoxically, these same institutions defended their policy of preventing reunions by claiming that they wanted to protect the mothers, but at the same time they argued that mothers should not be allowed to disturb their children's lives. Reunions are not a priority for people working in the adoption field, and they nip many in the bud without consulting either the mothers or the adoptees who are directly involved.

Women who were known to have relinquished children were generally presumed by their community to have received money for this transaction. This supposed commercial aspect consequently resulted in ridicule and in their stigmatization as bad mothers. Mothers who have relinquished a child are disdained. Good mothers will not give children away and, especially where (once-) married mothers are concerned, it is generally assumed that money is the motivation for the mother's actions.

If you have sold something, you have truly lost it. But in legal adoption procedures, mothers do not receive substantial amounts of money for their children. If mothers received cash at all, it was to cover an allowance and travel expenses. For the mothers, the fact that they had not received money for their children corroborated their idea that they were still the actual mothers.

An unmarried mother is regarded as being sexually immoral, but her reputation as a mother is stained as well. "Which mother can give her child away?" many Tamils asked rhetorically while discussing the subject of my research. "Not even a dog will give her puppies away," others commented. Apparently, relinquishment is overloaded with negative connotations, and in situations where relinquishment initially appears to be a solution, it turns out to be an extra stigma preventing a mother's rehabilitation as a moral person.

In today's practice in Tamil Nadu, significant kin who are involved in decision-making processes usually maintain a physical and emotional distance from the involved mother and her child, either by choice or as directed by institutional policy. Apart from some occasional visits, the pregnant woman or mother lives in temporary isolation. Physical and emotional distance between the true decision makers and the people who actually live the decision—the mothers—comes with socially disruptive mechanisms, because the people who are responsible for the decision do not directly experience the implications and consequences of their decision.

The dominant theme that emerged from my research was that mothers of relinquished children eventually experience an irreplaceable and unbreakable connection with their child, if not at the moment of relinquishment then in the months or years to come. Therefore, many mothers believe, expect, and for different reasons hope that their children will return. Implicitly, mothers made it clear that they have merely relinquished the *care* of their children, not the children themselves. But adoption is not about merely giving care; it is a legal claim of parenthood (Ergas 2013).

Signing a surrender deed is an irrevocable intervention for reversible adversities, and the Indian mothers in this research demonstrated that blood relationship has a meaning far beyond the two dimensions of a legal document. Subsequently, relinquishment creates legal ex-mothers and paves the way for adoptive parents to "own" a child. But legal adoption procedures do not make sense to mothers because it does not match their experienced truths about kinship in general and motherhood in particular. Hence, de-kinning a mother and her child may be an aim of policy makers, social workers, adoptive parents, and even of the mothers themselves at a certain period in their lives, but de-kinning eventually turns out to be an idée fixe, and relinquishment aggravates problems instead of solving them.

This chapter has looked at relinquishment in a particular cultural context. Yet it seems that child relinquishment must often, if not always, be painful for women in *all* cultures, even if their cultural values are not exactly the same as those of the Tamils. In one way or another, most cultures honor the mother–child bond, making relinquishment seem anomalous. Although Tamilian values surrounding motherhood are unique in some ways, in other ways they appear similar to those in other cultures (Briggs 2012). This raises the question of whether attempts at de-kinning occur in other cultures as well, and this is something scholars may consider when analyzing relinquishment and adoption in other settings.

NOTES

1. In studies on adoption, these mothers are referred to as birth mothers, natural mothers, biological mothers, real mothers, and so forth. These labels have connotations that mothers experience as instrumental and stigmatizing. I aim to avoid this consequence by using the notion of "mother" (see Nandy 2015). This chapter focuses on mothers who relinquish a child. Naturally, these children have another parent and more kin. However, I confine myself to this one perspective. Mothers with planned pregnancies (surrogates) were excluded from the study.
2. For details with regard to sampling, see Bos (2008).
3. Personally, I feel uncomfortable using the term "illegitimate" for a child, because it has a negative connotation and I believe that a human being, a child in particular, cannot be illegitimate. However, this is the term most often used in the Indian adoption field when pointing to the reason for relinquishment.
4. All names have been changed.
5. For married Tamil women, too, pregnancies become associated with sexuality. Anandi (2005) corroborates in her narratives that, after their wives conceived, husbands regularly made obscene comments about their pregnant wives' sexuality—for instance, by aggressively denying their fatherhood.
6. Soon after Sundari went home, her baby passed away.
7. Steenbeek (1995, 160–64) elaborates on the purifying effects of suffering from labor pains.

REFERENCES

Anandi, S. 2005. *Women, Work and Abortion Practices in Kancheepuram District, Tamil Nadu*. Chennai: Madras Institute of Development Studies.

Bos, Pien. 2008. *Once a Mother: Relinquishment and Adoption from the Perspective of Unmarried Mothers in South India*. Nijmegen: Radboud University.

Briggs, Laura. 2012. "Feminism and Transnational Adoption: Poverty, Precarity, and the Politics of Raising (Other People's?) Children." *Feminist Theory* 13, no. 1: 81–100.

Busby, Cecilia. 1997. "Of Marriage and Marriageability: Gender and Dravidian Kinship." *Journal of the Royal Anthropological Institute* 3, no. 1: 21–42.

Carsten, Janet. 2004. *After Kinship*. Cambridge: Cambridge University Press.

Dohle, Arun. 2008. "Inside Story of an Adoption Scandal." *Cumberland Law Review* 39: 131–86.

Dumont, Louis. 1986. *A South Indian Subcaste: Social Organization and Religion of the Pramalai Kallar.* Oxford: Oxford University Press.

Ergas, Yasmine. 2013. "Babies Without Borders: Human Rights, Human Dignity, and the Regulation of International Commercial Surrogacy." *Emory International Law Review* 27, no. 1: 117–88.

Fonseca, Claudia. 2011. "The De-kinning of Birthmothers: Reflections on Maternity and Being Human." *Vibrant: Virtual Brazilian Anthropology* 8, no. 2: 307–39.

Godbole, Mangala. 1986. *Thinking of Adoption?* Pune: Rajhans Prakashan.

Howell, Signe. 2004. "The Backpackers That Come to Stay." In *Cross-Cultural Approaches to Adoption*, ed. Fiona Bowie, 227–41. New York: Routledge.

——. 2006. *The Kinning of Foreigners: Transnational Adoption in a Global Perspective.* Oxford: Berghahn Books.

Indian Council for Child Welfare–Tamil Nadu. 1998. *Handbook on Child Adoption in India: Laws, Procedures, Guidelines and International Conventions.* Chennai: Amrit Press.

——. 2001. *Child Adoption and Thereafter.* Chennai: Indian Council for Child Welfare.

Indian Ministry of Welfare. 1995. *Revised Guidelines for Adoption of Indian Children.* New Delhi: Indian Ministry of Welfare.

Kapadia, Karin. 1995. *Siva and Her Sisters: Gender, Caste and Class in Rural South India.* Boulder, CO: Westview Press.

Mookherjee, Nayanika. 2007. "Available Motherhood: Legal Technologies, 'State of Exception' and the De-kinning of 'War-babies' in Bangladesh." *Childhood* 14, no. 3: 339–54.

Nandy, Amrita. 2015. "Natural Mother = Real Mother? Choice and Agency Among Un/natural 'Mothers' in India." *Women's Studies International Forum* 53: 129–38.

Srinivasan, Sharada. 2006. *Development, Discrimination and Survival: Daughter Elimination in Tamil Nadu, India.* Maastricht: Shaker.

Steenbeek, Gerdien. 1995. *Vrouwen op de Drempel: Gender en Moraliteit in een Mexicaanse Provinciestad* [Women on the Threshold: Gender and Morality in a Mexican Provincial Town]. Amsterdam: Thela.

Trawick, Margaret. 1992. *Notes on Love in a Tamil Family.* Berkeley: University of California Press.

Uberoi, Patricia, ed. 2002. *Family, Kinship and Marriage in India.* New Delhi: Oxford University Press.

Van Hollen, Cecilia. 2003. *Birth on the Threshold: Childbirth and Modernity in South India.* Berkeley: University of California Press.

9

MARGINALIZED MOTHERS AND INTERSECTING SYSTEMS OF SURVEILLANCE

Prisons and Foster Care

DOROTHY ROBERTS

S ocial scientists, legal scholars, and policy makers have noticed the intersection of the foster care and prison systems in children's lives. Many have long sounded the warning that foster care leads to prison, with children who have been placed in foster care at increased risk for incarceration (Barth 1990). More recently, a literature has developed on the risk that children with incarcerated parents will end up in foster care (Phillips and Dettlaff 2009). The dominant framing of the intersection of foster care and prison tends either to blame incarcerated mothers for the systemic deprivations their children experience or to ignore these mothers altogether. But foster care is more than a precursor to prison and prison is more than a precursor to foster care for children.

This chapter develops the argument that punishing black mothers is pivotal to the massive buildup and operation of both prisons and foster care, and that black mothers suffer the brunt of the intersection of both systems in their lives. In addition, the prison and foster care systems work together to punish black mothers in particular ways, thereby preserving U.S. race, gender, and class inequality in a neoliberal age. The intersection of the foster care and prison systems is only one example of many forms of overpolicing that overlap and converge in the lives of poor women and women of color. Looking at this particular intersection of punitive systems exposes how state mechanisms of surveillance and punishment operate to penalize the most marginalized women in our society while blaming them for their own disadvantaged position. In this way, punishing black mothers in the prison and foster care systems naturalizes societal inequity and obscures the need for social change.

TWO OVERLAPPING SYSTEMS

The prison and foster care systems are marked by glaring race, gender, and class disparities: the populations in both systems are disproportionately poor and African American, and poor black mothers are overinvolved in both systems. In the 1990s, although about 12 percent of the U.S. population was African American, about one-third of children in foster care were black, and most had been removed from black mothers who were their primary caretakers (Needell and Barth 1998). Likewise, about one-third of women in prison are black and most are the primary caretakers of their children (Glaze and Maruschak 2008).

This statistical similarity is striking, but its significance is not self-evident. Some see the disproportionate number of black mothers involved in prison and foster care as the unfortunate result of their disadvantaged living conditions. Others argue that the statistical disparities in both systems reflect the appropriate response to black mothers' antisocial conduct, which puts their children and the larger society at risk of harm (Bartholet et al. 2011). Both of these views are wrong. In fact, the statistical overlap is evidence of a form of punitive governance that perpetuates social inequality.

Over the past several decades, the United States has embarked on a pervasive form of governance labeled "neoliberalism" that transfers services from the state to the private realm of family and market while promoting the free market conditions conducive to capital accumulation (Harvey 2007). At the same time that the government is dismantling the social safety net, it has intensified its coercive interventions in poor communities of color. The neoliberal regime does not entail a unidimensional shrinking of government. It equally depends on the brutal containment of the nation's most disenfranchised groups (Giroux 2004; Wacquant

2009). The welfare, prison, foster care, and deportation systems all have become extremely punitive mechanisms for regulating residents of the very neighborhoods most devastated by the evisceration of public resources. Yet the state's brutal aggression in black communities seems normal and justified, if not invisible, to many Americans.

INCARCERATED MOTHERS

A compelling body of social science research now details how the astronomical escalation of imprisonment inflicts devastating havoc on the neighborhoods where most incarcerated individuals come from and to which they return. Legal scholar Michelle Alexander (2010, 13) has demonstrated that black incarceration functions like a modern-day Jim Crow caste system because it "permanently locks a huge percentage of the African American community out of the mainstream society and economy," replicating the subjugated status of blacks that prevailed before the civil rights revolution (Butler 2009).

We can trace today's prison system all the way back to the enslavement of African people, through the convict lease system that took hold after the 1863 emancipation, in which police picked up black men from the streets on trumped-up charges and consigned them to work in mines and former plantations for some of the nation's biggest corporations until an early and miserable death (Blackmon 2009). It was after the civil rights movement of recent decades that the war on drugs—a war that disproportionately targeted black communities—escalated the prison population to proportions greater than anywhere else in the world and unheard of in the history of Western democracies (Alexander 2010). Mass imprisonment of blacks and Latinos is a way for the state to exert direct control over poorly educated, unskilled, and jobless people who have no place in the market economy because of racism and capitalism, while preserving a racial caste system that was supposed to be abolished by civil rights reforms (Gilmore 2007; Wacquant 2009).

While this account of the prison system's role in maintaining a racial caste system is important, it tends to neglect incarcerated women (Chesney-Lind 2002; Richie 2002). Women are the fastest-growing segment of the prison population, with an 828 percent increase in the number of black women behind bars for drug offenses, in the 1990s (Geer 2000). For most of these women, prison constitutes a culminating victimization (Richie 1996; Geer 2000; Glaze and Maruschak 2008; Alfred and Chlup 2009). U.S. law enforcement treats the health problem of drug addiction as a criminal offense, and black women who have inadequate access to drug treatment are most vulnerable to the punitive approach. Women who depend on public assistance to care for their children are increasingly treated as criminals (Gustafson 2011). Accusations of welfare fraud are brought as felony charges punished with prison sentences rather than as administrative violations garnering civil penalties. Thousands of black women in prison today, mostly for nonviolent offenses, need treatment for a substance abuse problem, support for their children, or safety from an abusive relationship, rather than criminal punishment.

Much of the injury that high incarceration rates inflict on black communities results from the system's effect on black mothers. Most incarcerated women are mothers. Mass incarceration strains the extended networks of kin and friends that have traditionally sustained poor African American families in difficult times, weakening communities' ability to withstand economic and social hardship (Braman 2002). This injury to social networks counterbalances the claim that removing criminal mothers benefits their children and extended family by relieving them of problems caused by the offenders' antisocial behavior (Hagan and Dinovitzer 1999).

The type of offender has changed as a result of sentencing reforms since the 1980s, which impose harsh prison terms for relatively minor drug offenses. Most incarcerated mothers were convicted of drug-related offenses or of property crimes that involved drug use, not for violent felonies (Ross, Khashu, and Wamsley 2004). Increasing incarceration of mothers who are first-time, nonviolent offenders, who have viable ties to their children, to other family members, and to neighbors, inflicts incalculable damage on communities by severing those ties.

Locking up black mothers and fathers is a powerful way of transferring racial disadvantage to the next generation. In 2007, there were 1.7 million children in America with a parent in prison; more than 70 percent of these were children of color. This was an 82 percent increase since 1991 (Mumola 2000; Schirmer, Nellis, and Marier 2009). One in fifteen black children had a parent in prison, making them eight times more likely than white children to have an incarcerated parent (Schirmer, Nellis, and Marier 2009). Over the course of a childhood, black children's risk of experiencing parental imprisonment is even greater than this point-in-time estimate suggests. By age fourteen, one in four black children born in 1990 had a parent imprisoned, compared to one in twenty-five white children (Wildeman 2009).

Mass incarceration deprives tens of thousands of children of important economic and social support from their parents, placing extra economic and emotional burdens on remaining family members (Hagan and Dinovitzer 1999). Not surprisingly, separation from imprisoned parents has serious psychological consequences for children, including depression, anxiety, feelings of rejection, shame, anger, and guilt, and problems in school (Johnston 1995; Bernstein 2005). Incarcerating mothers tends to upset family ties, because inmate mothers are usually the primary caretakers of their children before entering prison. Although judges used to show mothers some leniency, they are now more often compelled by mandatory sentencing laws to give mothers long prison terms (Daly 1994). As a result, the number of children with a mother in prison more than doubled between 1991 and 2007 (Glaze and Maruschak 2008).

MOTHERS WITH CHILDREN IN FOSTER CARE

If you go into dependency court in Chicago, New York, or Los Angeles without any preconceptions, you might conclude that the child welfare system is designed to monitor, regulate, and punish black mothers (Roberts 2002). Before the civil rights movement, black children were disproportionately excluded from openly segregated child welfare services, which catered mainly to white families (Billingsley and Giovannoni 1972). By 2000, however, black children made up the largest group of children in foster care (Administration for Children and Families 2001), and they are still grossly overrepresented in the U.S. child welfare system: even though they represent only 15 percent of the nation's children, they make up about 30 percent of the nation's foster care population (Administration for Children and Families 2011). In some cities and states, the disparity is much greater (Hill 2007).

It is often forgotten that most of these children have been forcibly removed from black mothers by state agents; these mothers are then intensely supervised by child welfare authorities as they comply with the agency requirements in order to be reunified with their children. This state intrusion is typically viewed as necessary to protect maltreated children from parental harm. But the need for this intervention is usually linked to poverty, racial injustice, and the state's approach to caregiving, which addresses family economic deprivation with child removal rather than with services and financial resources.

Little attention is paid to the political function of this massive removal of children from black mothers. How does child welfare policy in the United States, historically and today, both reflect and reinforce the disadvantaged political status of African American families? As I have shown elsewhere (Roberts 2002), the racial disparity in the child welfare system reflects a political choice to address the startling rates of child poverty by investigating mothers instead of tackling poverty's societal roots. Child welfare philosophy became increasingly punitive as black children made up a greater and greater share of the caseloads. Since the 1970s, the number of children receiving child welfare services in their homes has declined dramatically, while the foster care population has skyrocketed. As the child welfare system began to serve fewer white children and more minority children, state and federal governments spent more money on out-of-home care and less on in-home services.

The end to the welfare safety net coincided with the passage of the Adoption and Safe Families Act of 1997 (Public Law 105-89), which emphasized adoption as the solution to the rising foster care population. Both were neoliberal measures that shifted government support for children toward reliance on employment and adoptive parents to meet the needs of struggling families. This coincidence marked the first time the federal government mandated that states protect children from abuse and neglect without a corresponding mandate to provide basic economic support to poor families (Courtney 1998). Both systems responded to a growing black female clientele by reducing services to families while intensifying their punitive functions.

As such policies strip poor African American neighborhoods of needed services, poor and low-income black mothers must rely on a family support system that arrives only *after* they are charged with child mistreatment. An African American woman I interviewed in a black Chicago neighborhood poignantly captured this fundamental problem with our child welfare philosophy:

> The advertisement [for the child abuse hotline], it just says abuse. If you being abused, this is the number you call; this is the only way you gonna get help. It doesn't say if I'm in need of counseling, or if my children don't have shoes, if I just can't provide groceries even though I may have seven kids, but I only get a hundred-something dollars in food stamps. And my work check only goes to bills. I can't feed eight of us all off a hundred-something-dollar food stamps. . . . I don't want to lose my children, so I'm not going to call DCFS [Department of Children and Family Services] for help, because I only see them take away children. (Roberts 2008, 145)

She and other residents I interviewed challenged the disruptive formula of child protection that hinges family assistance on state custody of children. The child welfare system exacts an onerous price: it requires poor mothers to relinquish custody of their children in exchange for the state support needed to care for them (Roberts 2001).

The turn to a punitive foster care approach is justified by stereotypes of black maternal unfitness. In a qualitative study of Michigan's child welfare system, for example, the Center for the Study of Social Policy (2009) discovered that many social workers negatively characterized or labeled African American families, mothers, and youth and failed to fairly assess or appreciate their unique strengths and weaknesses. In case files, they frequently described African American parents with terms such as "hostile," "aggressive," "loud," and "cognitively delayed," without any justifications for these labels. They assumed that black parents had substance abuse problems, without making similar assumptions about white parents. The report concluded, "The belief that African American children are better off away from their families and communities was seen in explicit statements by key policy makers and service providers. It was also reflected in choices made by DHS [Department of Human Services]" (17).

One of these choices is for caseworkers to be more aggressive in their decision to remove black children from their homes rather than to provide services to their families. A study of the intersection of race, poverty, and risk in this decision concluded that the racial disparity occurred because the risk threshold for more intrusive case decisions is higher for white than for African American children (Rivaux et al. 2008). In other words, it takes more risk of maltreatment for caseworkers to place a white child in foster care than it does to remove a black child. This devaluation of the bonds between black children and their mothers discounts the harm inflicted on both parties when these children are removed from their homes.

The effect of state disruption and supervision of families is intensified when it is concentrated in inner-city neighborhoods, what I call the system's "racial geography" (Roberts 2005; Roberts 2008). In urban areas, most child protection cases occur in poor and low-income African American neighborhoods, and most African American families live in neighborhoods with the highest rates of child welfare agency involvement. Black children are thus at greater risk than whites of growing up in a neighborhood where child protection services are heavily involved, and black mothers are at greater risk of losing their children to the system. The spatial concentration of child welfare supervision creates an environment in which state custody of children is a realistic expectation, if not the norm. This degree of state supervision has damaging community-wide effects. As with the prison system, placing large numbers of children in state custody interferes with a community's ability to form healthy connections and to engage in collective action.

SYSTEM INTERSECTIONALITY

To this point, I have discussed how the prison and foster care systems operate in similar ways, based on the punishment of black mothers, which is often neglected in feminist and antiracist discourse (Crenshaw

1989). But prisons and foster care also function together to discipline and control poor and low-income black women by keeping them under intense state supervision and blaming them for the hardships their families face as a result of societal inequities.

As a result of the political choice to fund punitive instead of supportive programs, criminal justice and child welfare supervision of mothers is pervasive in poor black communities. The simultaneous explosion of foster care and prison populations reflects an alarming abandonment of black mothers. Instead of devoting adequate resources to support their families, the state increasingly shuffles family members into the punitive machinery of law enforcement and child protection. Child protection proceedings are more akin to criminal trials than most civil adjudications because they pit mothers accused of child maltreatment against the state and morally condemn them. The rejection of public aid to poor families in favor of private solutions to poverty—low-wage work, marriage, and child support—mirror the appeal to adoption to fix the public foster care system.

Stereotypes about black female criminality and irresponsibility legitimate the massive disruption that both systems inflict on black families and communities. A popular mythology promoted over centuries portrays black women as unfit to bear and raise children (Roberts 1997). The sexually licentious Jezebel, the family-demolishing matriarch, the devious welfare queen, the depraved pregnant crack addict, accompanied by her equally monstrous crack baby, all paint a picture of a dangerous motherhood that must be regulated and punished. Unmarried black mothers represent the epitome of irresponsibility: a woman who raises her children without the supervision of a man.

These stereotypes do not simply percolate in some disembodied "white psyche." They are reinforced and recreated by the foster care and prison systems, which leave the impression that black women are naturally prone to committing crimes and abusing their children. Stereotypes of maternal irresponsibility, created by the child welfare system's disproportionate supervision of black children, help to sustain mass incarceration, while stereotypes of black female criminality help to sustain foster care. As Angela Davis (1998) has observed, the prison-industrial complex "relies on racialized assumptions of criminality—such as *images of black welfare mothers reproducing criminal children*—and on racist practices in arrest, conviction, and sentencing patterns" (emphasis added).

The joint production of stereotypes in the child welfare and prison systems helps to explain why juvenile justice authorities send black delinquents to juvenile detention while referring white delinquents to informal alternatives for the same offenses. Many officials think that black children come from female-headed households that are ill equipped to handle a troubled child (Bishop and Frazier 1996). Because they perceive black single mothers as incapable of providing adequate supervision of their children, officials believe they are justified in placing these children under state control. "Inadequate family correlates with race and ethnicity. It makes sense to put delinquent kids from these circumstances in residential facilities," a Florida juvenile court judge told researchers Donna Bishop and Charles Frazier (1996, 409). "Detention decisions are decided on the basis of whether the home can control and supervise a child," explained a prosecutor. "So minorities don't go home because, unfortunately, their families are less able to control the kids." Another prosecutor's racial (and patriarchal) views were more blunt: "In black families who the dad is, is unknown, while in white families—even when divorced—dad is married or something else. The choices are limited because the black family is a multigenerational non-fathered family. You can't send the kid off to live with dad" (410).

A PECULIAR PUNISHMENT

The intersection of these punitive systems of child welfare and prison policies in the lives of black mothers makes it extremely difficult for incarcerated women to retain legal custody of their children. According to the U.S. Department of Justice, in 2004, 11 percent of mothers incarcerated in state prisons reported that their children were in the care of a foster home, agency, or institution, five times the rate reported by fathers (Halperin and Harris 2004; Glaze and Maruschak 2008).

Prisons degrade child-rearing by incarcerated women in multiple ways, starting with childbirth itself. The devaluation of incarcerated mothers is perhaps most vividly captured by the common practice of shackling pregnant inmates. In many states, when incarcerated women go into labor, they are routinely shackled to the hospital bed, their legs, wrists, and abdomens chained during the entire delivery of their babies (Amnesty International 2001; Doetzer 2008). In the vast majority of states, newborns are automatically placed in foster care immediately after delivery. Moreover, federal law governing child welfare practice encourages the termination of incarcerated mothers' parental rights, and local policies do too little to keep incarcerated mothers in contact with their children or to support their families after they are released from prison (Halperin and Harris 2004).

Incarcerated mothers are much more likely than incarcerated fathers to be living with their children when they are sent to prison. Moreover, about one-third of mothers in prison were living alone with their children when they were arrested, compared to only 4 percent of incarcerated fathers (Mumola 2000; Glaze and Maruschak 2008). Therefore, when mothers go to prison, their children's fathers often are not readily available to care for the children, increasing the chances of foster care placement.

Incarcerated mothers then find it difficult to hold on to legal custody of their children who have been placed in foster care. State-imposed obstacles to maintaining contact with them and meeting other requirements imposed by child protective services often lead to termination of parental rights. As Halperin and Harris (2004, 340) explain, "To avoid having their parental rights terminated, incarcerated women, like their counterparts in the community, must participate in case planning, remain involved in their children's lives, and demonstrate their commitment and ability to reform, typically by enrolling in corrective programs as set forth in the case plan." However, the conditions of incarceration, coupled with the policies of the prison and child welfare systems, make it "virtually impossible" to meet these requirements from behind bars. Moreover, authorities often impose onerous requirements that are unrelated to the family's needs and are not necessary to tell whether the mother is fit to care for her child but that end up creating further obstacles to her retaining custody.

A chief threat to reunification is the difficulty of visiting with children while in prison (Seymour 1998). Child welfare agencies may construe a parent's failure to visit and communicate with his or her child as abandonment and grounds for terminating parental rights (Ross, Khashu, and Wamsley 2004). Despite or perhaps because of being the primary caretaker of their children before arrest, incarcerated mothers are less likely than fathers to have family visits. When a father is imprisoned, the mother usually continues as the child's primary caretaker (Schirmer, Nellis, and Mauer 2009). She may maintain a relationship with the father while he is in jail and help him keep in touch with the child. When mothers are imprisoned, however, fathers seldom play that role, and children usually must leave home.

Most prisons are located in remote areas far away from the cities where inmates' families live. A 1995 study reported that the average female inmate in federal prison was 160 miles farther from her family than the average male inmate (Coughenour 1995). The cost of traveling long distances, including bus fare or gas, hotel, and time away from work, usually thwarts personal visits. Even telephone calls to prison, which typically are saddled with exorbitant fees and charges, may be too expensive for regular communication. Relative caregivers who fill in for incarcerated mothers receive inadequate government support, and most cannot meet the increased childcare expenses, let alone the cost of maintaining contact with incarcerated mothers. What is more, a felony conviction often disqualifies family members from becoming legal caregivers, making it more likely that the children will be placed in foster care with strangers, who may be less willing to keep in touch with mothers behind bars. Relatives and foster parents are further discouraged from arranging visitation by the complicated and time-consuming logistics that they must navigate. As a result of all these obstacles to visitation with their children, "more than half of all mothers in prison receive no visits at all from their children" (Halperin and Harris 2004).

Incarcerated mothers risk permanently losing custody of their children, because it is considered in a child's best interests not to wait for his or her mother's release to have a stable family life. Some states relieve child welfare agencies from the requirement to provide reunification services in the case of parents who are convicted of felonies (see, for example, Colorado Revised Statutes 2011, § 19-3-604[1][b][III]; California Welfare and Institutions Code 2012, § 366.26[c][1]). Incarceration itself constitutes statutory grounds for termination of parental rights in some states (see, for example, Iowa State Code 2012, § 232.116[j][2]).

The risk of termination was increased by the Adoption and Safe Families Act of 1997, which places foster children on a fast track to adoption as a strategy for curing the ills of the child welfare system, especially reducing the enormous foster care population. The act mandates that state agencies initiate termination proceedings if a child spends fifteen out of any twenty-two months in foster care. The swift federal timetable is often grounds for severing incarcerated mothers' ties to their children (Kennedy 2012).

Even when incarcerated mothers are able to keep legal custody of their children, the collateral penalties inflicted on them pose barriers to maintaining a relationship with their children once they are released from prison. A host of state and federal laws impose draconian obstacles to women's successful reentry into their struggling communities by denying drug offenders public benefits, housing, education, and job opportunities (Levy-Pounds 2006; Brown 2010; Lipsitz 2012). Formerly incarcerated women are barred from many occupations held predominantly by women, such as childcare worker, certified nurse's aide, or beautician. Under U.S. Code 21 (§ 862a), Denial of Assistance and Benefits for Certain Drug-Related Convictions, states have the option of denying food stamps to applicants with a felony drug conviction. With no job, public assistance, or stable housing, a mother released from prison will find it extremely difficult to meet the child welfare agency's requirements for reunification with her children and risks termination of her parental rights. Thus, the convergence of prison and foster care, for many incarcerated mothers, means losing custody of their children permanently. This is, for many women, the ultimate punishment the state can inflict.

CONCLUSION

An analysis of the intersection of prison and foster care in black women's lives shows how punishing black mothers is pivotal to the joint operation of systems that work together to maintain unjust social hierarchies in the United States. Black mothers are caught by the neoliberal agenda because state regulation of their bodies, already devalued by a long history of reproductive regulation and derogatory stereotypes of maternal irresponsibility, makes excessive policing through foster care and prison seem necessary to protect children and the public from harm.

This analysis suggests that there is a need for cross-movement strategies that can address multiple forms of systemic injustice to contest the overpolicing of women of color and expose how it props up an unjust social order (Roberts and Jesudason 2013).

REFERENCES

Administration for Children and Families. 2001. *Child Welfare Outcomes 2001: Annual Report.* Washington, DC: U.S. Department of Health and Human Services.

———. 2011. *The AFCARS Report: Preliminary FY 2010 Estimates as of June 2011.* Washington, DC: U.S. Department of Health and Human Services.

Alexander, Michelle. 2010. *The New Jim Crow: Mass Incarceration in the Age of Colorblindness.* New York: New Press.

Alfred, Mary V., and Dominique T. Chlup. 2009. "Neoliberalism, Illiteracy, and Poverty: Framing the Rise in Black Women's Incarceration." *Western Journal of Black Studies* 33, no. 4: 240.

Amnesty International. 2001. *Abuse of Women in Custody: Sexual Misconduct and Shackling of Pregnant Women.* New York: Amnesty International.

Barth, Richard P. 1990. "On Their Own: The Experiences of Youth After Foster Care." *Children and Adolescent Social Work Journal* 7, no. 5: 419–40.

Bartholet, Elizabeth, Fred Wulczyn, Richard P. Barth, and Cindy Lederman. 2011. "Race and Child Welfare." *Chapin Hall Issue Brief,* June. https://www.chapinhall.org/sites/default /files/publications/06_27_11_Issue%20Brief_F.pdf.

Bernstein, Nell. 2005. *All Alone in the World: Children of the Incarcerated.* New York: New Press.

Billingsley, Andrew, and Jeanne Giovannoni. 1972. *Children of the Storm: Black Children and American Child Welfare.* New York: Harcourt College Publications.

Bishop, Donna M., and Charles E. Frazier. 1996. "Race Effects in Juvenile Justice Decision-Making: Findings of a Statewide Analysis." *Journal of Criminal Law and Criminology* 86, no. 2: 392–414.

Blackmon, Douglas A. 2009. *Slavery by Another Name: The Re-Enslavement of Black Americans from the Civil War to World War II.* New York: Anchor.

Braman, Donald. 2004. *Doing Time on the Outside: Incarceration and Family Life in Urban America.* Ann Arbor: University of Michigan Press.

Brown, Geneva. 2010. *The Intersectionality of Race, Gender, and Reentry: Challenges for African-American Women.* American Constitution Society for Law and Policy Issue Brief. https://www.acslaw.org/files/Brown%20issue%20brief%20-%20Intersectionality .pdf.

Butler, Paul. 2009. *Let's Get Free: A Hip-Hop Theory of Justice.* New York: New Press.

Center for the Study of Social Policy. 2009. *Race Equity Review: Findings from a Qualitative Analysis of Racial Disproportionality and Disparity for African American Children and Families in Michigan's Child Welfare System.* http://www.cssp.org/publications/child -welfare/institutional-analysis/race-equity-review-findings-from-a-qualitative-analysis -of-racial-disproportionality-and-disparity-for-african-american-children-and-families -in-michigans-child-welfare-system.pdf.

Chesney-Lind, Meda. 2002. "Imprisoning Women: The Unintended Victims of Mass Impris- onment." In *Invisible Punishment: The Collateral Consequences of Mass Imprisonment,* ed. Marc Mauer and Meda Chesney-Lind, 79–94. New York: New Press.

Coughenour, John C. 1995. "Separate and Unequal: Women in the Federal Criminal Justice System." *Federal Sentencing Reporter* 8, no. 3: 142–44.

Courtney, Mark E. 1998. "The Costs of Child Protection: Implications for Welfare Reform?" *The Future of Children* 8, no. 1: 88–103.

Crenshaw, Kimberlé. 1989. "Demarginalizing the Intersection of Race and Sex: A Black Fem- inist Critique of Antidiscrimination Doctrine, Feminist Theory and Antiracist Politics." *University of Chicago Legal Forum* 140: 139–67.

Daly, Kathleen. 1994. *Gender, Crime, and Punishment.* New Haven, CT: Yale University Press.

Davis, Angela. 1998. "Masked Racism: Reflections on the Prison Industrial Complex." *Color- lines,* September 10. http://colorlines.com/archives/1998/09/masked_racism_reflections _on_the_prison_industrial_complex.html.

Doetzer, Geraldine. 2008. "Hard Labor: The Legal Implications of Shackling Female Inmates During Pregnancy and Childbirth." *William and Mary Journal of Women and the Law* 14, no. 2: 363–92.

Geer, Martin A. 2000. "Human Rights and Wrongs in Our Own Backyard: Incorporating International Human Rights Protections Under Domestic Civil Rights Law—A Case Study of Women in United States Prisons." *Harvard Human Rights Journal* 13: 71–140.

Gilmore, Ruth Wilson. 2007. *The Golden Gulag: Prisons, Surplus, Crisis, and Opposition in Globalizing California.* Berkeley: University of California Press.

Giroux, Henry A. 2004. *The Terror of Neoliberalism: Authoritarianism and the Eclipse of Democracy.* Boulder: Paradigm Publishers.

Glaze, Lauren E., and Laura M. Maruschak. 2008. *Parents in Prison and Their Minor Chil- dren.* Bureau of Justice Statistics Special Report. Washington, DC: U.S. Department of Justice. http://www.bjs.gov/content/pub/pdf/pptmc.pdf.

Gustafson, Kaaryn S. 2011. *Cheating Welfare: Public Assistance and the Criminalization of Poverty.* New York: New York University Press.

Hagan, John, and Ronit Dinovitzer. 1999. "Collateral Consequences of Imprisonment for Children, Communities, and Prisoners." In *Crime and Justice: A Review of Research.* Vol. 26, *Prisons,* ed. Michael Tonry and Joan Petersilia, 121–62. Chicago: University of Chicago Press.

Halperin, Ronnie, and Jennifer L. Harris. 2004. "Parental Rights of Incarcerated Mothers with Children in Foster Care: A Policy Vacuum." *Feminist Studies* 30, no. 2 (Summer): 339–52.

Harvey, David. 2007. *A Brief History of Neoliberalism.* New York: Oxford University Press.

Hill, Robert B. 2007. *An Analysis of Racial/Ethnic Disproportionality and Disparity at the National, State, and County Levels.* Washington, DC: Casey Family Programs.

Johnston, Denise. 1995. "Effects of Parental Incarceration." In *Children of Incarcerated Parents*, ed. Katherine Gabel and Denise Johnston, 59–88. New York: Lexington Books.

Kennedy, Deseriee A. 2012. "'The Good Mother': Mothering, Feminism, and Incarceration." *William and Mary Journal of Women and the Law* 18, no. 2: 161–200.

Levy-Pounds, Nekima. 2006. "Beaten by the System and Down for the Count: Why Women of Color and Children Don't Stand a Chance Against U.S. Drug Sentencing Policy." *University of St. Thomas Law Journal* 3, no. 3: 462–95.

Lipsitz, George. 2012. "In an Avalanche Every Snowflake Pleads Not Guilty: The Collateral Consequences of Mass Incarceration and Impediments to Women's Fair Housing Rights." *UCLA Law Review* 59: 1746–1809.

Mumola, Christopher J. 2000. *Incarcerated Parents and Their Children.* Bureau of Justice Statistics Special Report NCJ 182335. Washington, DC: U.S. Department of Justice. http://www.bjs.gov/content/pub/pdf/iptc.pdf.

Needell, Barbara, and Richard P. Barth. 1998. "Infants Entering Foster Care Compared to Other Infants Using Birth Status Indicators." *Child Abuse & Neglect* 22, no. 12: 1179–87.

Phillips, Susan D., and Alan J. Dettlaff. 2009. "More Than Parents in Prison: The Broader Overlap Between the Criminal Justice and Child Welfare Systems." *Journal of Public Child Welfare* 3, no. 1: 3–22.

Richie, Beth E. 1996. *Compelled To Crime: The Gender Entrapment of Battered Black Women.* New York: Routledge.

——. 2002. "The Social Impact of Mass Incarceration on Women." In *Invisible Punishment: The Collateral Consequences of Mass Imprisonment*, ed. Marc Mauer and Meda Chesney-Lind, 136–49. New York: New Press.

Rivaux, Stephanie L., Joyce James, Kim Wittenstrom, Donald Baumann, Janess Sheets, Judith Henry, and Victoria Jeffries. 2008. "The Intersection of Race, Poverty, and Risk: Understanding the Decision to Provide Services to Clients and to Remove Children." *Child Welfare* 87, no. 2: 151–68.

Roberts, Dorothy. 1997. *Killing the Black Body.* New York: Pantheon.

——. 2001. "Kinship Care and the Price of State Support for Children." *Chicago-Kent Law Review* 76: 1619–42.

——. 2002. *Shattered Bonds: The Color of Child Welfare.* New York: Basic Books.

——. 2005. "The Community Dimension of State Child Protection." *Hofstra Law Review* 34, no. 1: 23–37.

——. 2008. "The Racial Geography of Child Welfare: Toward a New Research Paradigm." *Child Welfare* 87, no. 2: 125–50.

Roberts, Dorothy, and Sujatha Jesudason. 2013. "Movement Intersectionality: The Case of Race, Gender, Disability, and Genetic Technologies." *Du Bois Review* 10, no. 2: 313–28.

Ross, Timothy, Ajay Khashu, and Mark Wamsley. 2004. *Hard Data on Hard Times: An Empirical Analysis of Maternal Incarceration, Foster Care, and Visitation.* New York: Vera Institute of Justice.

Schirmer, Sarah, Ashley Nellis, and Marc Mauer. 2009. *Incarcerated Parents and their Children: Trends 1991–2007.* Washington, DC: The Sentencing Project.

Seymour, Cynthia. 1998. "Children with Parents in Prison: Child Welfare Policy, Program, and Practice Issues." *Child Welfare* 77, no. 5: 469–93.

Wacquant, Loïc. 2009. *Punishing the Poor: The Neoliberal Government of Social Insecurity.* Durham, NC: Duke University Press.

Wildeman, Christopher. 2009. "Parental Imprisonment, the Prison Boom, and the Concentration of Childhood Disadvantage." *Demography* 46, no. 2: 265–80.

10

CARE AND GENDER

MARTHA ALBERTSON FINEMAN

During the 1970s and 1980s, feminist law reformers in the United States developed an agenda shaped by the belief that women, both inside and outside the family, were constrained by their assigned family roles, which reflected gendered norms of economic dependency, self-sacrifice, and subservience (Fineman 2008, 2009). Different expectations for women, as well as distinct rights and responsibilities, were built into the "complementary" roles of husband and wife, father and mother. In particular, the caretaking expectations placed on wives and mothers were seen by many to be an impediment to women's career opportunities and financial independence. Expectations associated with family roles were in conflict with and often displaced other aspirations, a process that had concrete implications for the opportunities available to women outside of the family, as norms governing the "private" (family) sphere restricted possibilities for women in the "public" (workplace) sphere.

Because the distinctions drawn between both the realms of public and private and the roles of men and women had disadvantaged women in the past, reformers urged passage of gender-neutral laws and classifications to govern actions and transactions in both the family and market. Moreover, because gender differences were seen as a source of inequality, establishment of a broad egalitarian family ideal required an assertion of sameness. The metaphor of "partnership" to replace the gendered and hierarchical common law model reflected the attempt to establish and inaugurate a gender-neutral and broadly egalitarian family law paradigm.

As a result of these reforms, the law now refers to "parents" and "spouses" instead of incorporating gendered notions associated with mother and father, wife and husband.[1] Such changes were more than mere linguistic manipulation; they were intended to operate as a form of social engineering. The goal was to encourage both husbands and wives to experience the complete range of responsibilities associated with marriage and parenthood, a transformation deemed necessary if opportunities outside of the family were also to be equalized (Fineman 2004).

Social engineering aside, the effect of the reforms on divorce cases was significant.[2] In the economic context, an egalitarian partnership model provided the rationale for the idea of "marital property," which recognized that the contributions of married partners to the acquisition of property could be equal in value, even if different in kind. This contribution rationale legitimated the transfer of money and property accumulated during a partnership (marriage) from the wage-earning partner (husband) to the domestic service–providing partner (wife) at the termination of the partnership (divorce). However, this spousal partnership model, with its norms of formal equality and shared responsibility, also operated to significantly alter expectations concerning provisions for the future economic well-being of the family. Both parents are now deemed equally responsible for the support of their children and individually responsible for providing for themselves. The idea of an economically dependent housewife and mother entitled to alimony as well as child support is incompatible with this new model of marriage.

These revisions in the understanding of the economics of marriage have been particularly significant for the postdivorce economic position of women and children (Fineman 1991). While the new norm of equal division of marital property at divorce bettered the position of some women, the virtual abolition of alimony or spousal maintenance denied custodial mothers access to ongoing support from husbands and forced them to rely on work and to earn their own wages. Arguments that a custodial mother needed to continue to have a share in her husband's postdivorce income, because her ongoing childcare responsibilities would inhibit her full participation in the workforce, were cast aside as antiquated and inappropriate for our new gender-neutral world.

Economically based arguments that child-rearing resulted in losses from lost opportunities and forgone income that should be equitably shared gained some traction in moving away from the formal gender equality model, but only in limited cases, where the stereotypical breadwinner/caretaker model was present in a long-term marriage. Arguments for more than half of the property or for ongoing spousal support were seen as a form of stigmatizing special pleading for women who also just happened to be mothers.

The expectation of equality also applied in custody decisions, with mixed or dubious benefits for many women.[3] The assertion of equality between parents resulted in adoption of an idealized notion of "shared parenting," which, in its extreme form, supported laws establishing a presumption of joint physical and legal custody over an award of custody to one parent with visitation for the other, or punitive custody awards to the "most generous parent" when joint custody was not feasible. What tended to get lost in the wake of this type of imposed formal equality between parents was the very unequal nature of the costs associated with raising and caring for children—costs related to the incompatibility of care and market work. Caring for children drains time and energy from the pursuit of career and human capital. When a parent assumes the role of primary caretaker, these losses are part of the bargain. Ironically, this type of unequal sacrifice is obscured in the shared-parenting paradigm. The appeal of an androgynous family law is so strong that some scholars, legislators, and judges even resist explicitly valuing primary caretaking in custody determinations because to do so would typically result in favoring mothers over fathers (Klaff 1982).

THE INADEQUACIES OF EGALITARIAN
FAMILY LAW REFORM

For decades I have argued that although the concepts of formal equality and gender neutrality are useful in defining some relations between adults, they are inadequate, even detrimental, in addressing the dynamics inherent in the family.[4] The gist of my argument was that the family, as our most gendered institution, was not susceptible to the imposition of a formal equality model. The way the family in society had been structured both produced and reinforced inequality. I identified three sites of entrenched inequality affecting most marriages. First was the wage and employment inequality, which disadvantaged women in terms of compensation and conditions of employment. Next was the inequality of bargaining power that persisted in family negotiations about whose individual interests should be sacrificed for the larger family welfare. This was a process that disadvantaged women, partly due to their lower earnings but also because of culturally imposed altruism (they were the ones who were supposed to be making sacrifices for others). Finally, there were inequalities in family burdens that would be carried forward into the future. These were the inequalities that arose postdivorce, with the responsibilities of custody overwhelmingly assigned to women. Maternal custody was further disadvantaging due to the difficulty of collecting even inadequate child support awards.

Although gender-neutral, equality-based reforms are now firmly in place in the statute books and have proven successful on a rhetorical level, structural family disadvantages associated with caretaking still typically burden women more than men, even after decades of feminist equality reform. My hope, twenty-some years ago, was that we might fashion a more substantive or result-sensitive version of equality in the family context. The law would allow unequal or different treatment of divorcing spouses, such as unequal distribution of family assets and obligations, in order to address the existing inequalities created or exacerbated by past and future family responsibilities. I argued that this more result-oriented version of equality was "just" and appropriate in that it would satisfy the need that arose because one spouse typically assumed primary responsibility for children both within and after marriage.

I have come to realize that any concern with gender equality must expand to consider social relations far beyond the roles of men and women within the family. The family is only one part of a more complex societal system that creates social identities and assigns expectations, norms, and values to those identities and the functions they serve. The problem was not—or not only—discrimination based on their sex, when it came to women's subordinate economic status. Rather, the problem was the devaluation of the social role and function women had been historically assigned. Women were constructed as caretakers, men as heads of households. Different social identities were imposed on the sexes, assigned through cultural, legal, and social norms defining gender differences. These identities structured how individuals would be located within societal relations: real women were to attend to men and children in the private family; real men were to compete and provide for that family in the public, economic, and political worlds.[5]

What the push for equality failed to take into account was the fact that there are very different functions associated with gendered roles—functions that are complementary and equally essential to the effective workings of the family as a unit. Mother embodies care and nurture; father, economic responsibility and support. Gender neutrality linguistically flattens out such differences in roles and assumes that an achievable reallocation or sharing of the gender-specific societal tasks between men and women is possible and desirable. It does not address or necessarily alter the differing values that have been placed on those tasks formerly gendered nor consider the degree to which other societal institutions would have to change if reforms were to be successful. What has resulted could be labeled a "care crisis," with care devalued or ignored in the name of achieving gender equality.

CONSTRUCTING MOTHER: STRUCTURING DEPENDENCY AND THE FAMILY

Historically, family law reform primarily focused on the relationship between husband and wife. It should have focused on dependency, directed by the needs of children and informed by experiences of caretaking. The relationship between the dependent child and the caretaker cannot be conceptualized as a relationship between equals, founded on principles such as partnership and contract that guided the recasting of the social identities of husband and wife. Indeed, childhood is mired in an inevitable inequality that is founded on the child's dependency. Children are inherently dependent on others to care for them, a reality that historically has shaped the social and legal meanings of family as well as of mother and father.[6] This type of dependency is developmental and biological in nature; it is also universally experienced. I have called this form of social relationality "inevitable dependency."[7]

There are other forms of need, such as economic and or emotional, that coincide with developmental dependency. These needs are part of the general obligations of caring for another. Those needs of the inevitable dependent are central to the norms associated with the social identity of caretakers, structuring a relationship I have labeled "derivative dependency." It also connotes a relationship of inequality, one resulting from an unequal assignment of responsibility and the assumption of burdens associated with caring for children. The concept of derivative dependency captures the very simple but often overlooked fact that those who care for inevitable dependents (such as mothers caring for children) are dependent on resources in order to successfully undertake that care. In contrast to inevitable dependency, derivative dependency is *not* universally experienced. Many in society avoid taking responsibility for caring for children, the elderly, or the ill. The role of being derivatively dependent is thus experienced by only some members of our society. Cultural, ideological, and legal structures define the caretaker role and assign it to those who are expected to assume the work of caring for those who cannot care for themselves (Fineman 2011).

In the United States, both types of dependency have been assigned to an ideal family, which historically was marital and heterosexual in form (Fineman 1995). This traditional family was also gendered and hierarchically organized, with a wage earner and a domestic laborer complementing each other in addressing dependency. Economic contributions are privileged in relation to care work, which is not assigned a market value but is compensated through a duty to support, placed on the wage earner. At least in its ideal form, this family was also expected to be self-sufficient and independent and to provide adequate economic and caretaking resources to manage both the inevitable and derivative dependencies of its members.

This image of the ideally self-sufficient family achieved through complementary family roles also has determined the appropriate relationship between that family and the state, as well as between the family and economic or market institutions. The self-sufficient family is separated from other institutions, being a private family. In fact, the family is positioned as the quintessential private institution, while the state represents the quintessential public sphere (Fineman 2004). The market and its institutions are more fluid; chameleonlike, they are seen as public vis-à-vis the family but private vis-à-vis the state. In the United States, the appropriate relationship between the public state and the private family (as well as between the state and market institutions) is that of nonintervention and noninterference.

The imagining of a gender-neutral, egalitarian family has not done away with either inevitable or derivative dependency. Children still need care, and caretakers still need economic and material resources to undertake that care successfully. The conceptualization of the role of the private family means that those resources must come from within the family itself. Although family law reforms have tried to mandate that the burdens and responsibilities associated with dependency be shared within the family by husbands and wives, economic realities and cultural patterns work against such sharing. Therefore, as long as dependency is cast as primarily the responsibility of the private family, gender equality will be difficult to accomplish. Women will continue to find themselves making sacrifices in the gendered roles of mother, wife, sister, daughter, and daughter-in-law in order to care for those who are dependent.

PENALIZING MOTHERING

Motherhood has measurable economic disadvantages. Recent economic and social science literature references something called a "motherhood penalty" (Correll, Benard, and Paik 2007). Interestingly, this literature begins with the insight that gender equality policies pursued by feminists decades ago have worked, at least in some contexts. In the workplace, the gender wage gap has just about disappeared—if we compare men only with childless women with equivalent qualifications and in similar jobs; in other words, if we drop from the equation women who are mothers. In fact, the gender pay gap has been reported now to be less than a few cents for women holding professional positions. Some studies indicate that childless women can even earn more than men in equivalent positions, in some instances.

However heartening such studies are, a recently discovered "parental pay gap" should give us pause before celebration. In hearings on gender pay equity before the United States Congress Joint Economic Committee, sociologist Michelle Budig testified that, while childless professional women earned 94 cents for every childless man's dollar, mothers in those positions earned 60 cents for every father's dollar. This latter difference she labeled a "wage penalty" for motherhood and, notably, *all* women experience reduced earnings for each child they have.[8]

There is some dispute about what causes this gap, with some commentators arguing that the difference is related to the fact that women who are mothers perceive the need to work fewer hours and thus may accept lower earnings to secure more family-friendly jobs (Christopher 2010). Interruptions in work life due to childbearing also have been blamed for the motherhood penalty. Significantly, such explanations focus on individual women's choices and minimize the significance of structural reasons for the motherhood wage gap. These reasons might even be used to argue that additional policy initiatives are unnecessary because the unbalanced wages are the result of choices, not of discrimination or bias.

Nevertheless, Professor Budig concluded that even if such choices accounted for some of the gap, the available research indicated that, after taking preferences into account and adjusting for differences, there would still be a roughly 3 percent wage penalty accruing to a mother for each child she has. In other words, the studies demonstrate that there is some residual gendered wage gap not explained by aggregate choices. Budig and others argue that this gap is due to discrimination against mothers by those (both men and women) who feel that, if they have children, women should not be working full time.

It is certainly true that fatherhood does not carry the same penalties and collateral consequences as motherhood. In fact, research finds that fatherhood has the effect of enhancing a man's wages. Fathers in all racial and ethnic groups received what Budig referred to in her testimony as a "fatherhood bonus" when compared with childless men. Once again, some of these fatherhood benefits or premiums were attributed to "gender-neutral" factors, such as the fact that men who were fathers were on average older than childless men and thus had more work experience or opportunities for advancement in a profession or position. However, a lack of discrimination is not the same thing as the existence of equality of opportunity or access, let alone equality of result. Together, the findings on motherhood and fatherhood indicate that parenthood exacerbates gender inequality in American workplaces. As a result of parenthood, mothers lose wages while fathers gain them.

Arguments that the motherhood penalty is due to some residual discrimination against women who are mothers should be understood in the contexts of equality law in the United States and of civil rights and employment law requirements that there be some impermissible discrimination before state remedial action is deemed appropriate.[9] Discrimination focuses legal inquiry on the specifics of an individual case (or a class of cases). It is based on intentional and knowing discriminatory actions by an individual or individuals that exclude or treat some person or persons differently based on select or "suspect" individual characteristics, such as race, gender, or ethnicity.[10]

Motherhood is not a suspect category entitled to special or strict scrutiny. Even if the argument was made that the motherhood penalty was a form of gender discrimination, each individual plaintiff would have to show that her personal penalty was the result of discrimination based on her status as a mother and not due to the limitations that status placed on her ability to do the same job as an unencumbered woman or man.

PENALIZING CARE

As interesting as a speculative inquiry into the extent of discrimination against mothers might be, I suggest that the real heart of the dilemma presented by what is called the motherhood penalty is not found in discrimination, at least as it is understood in equality jurisprudence. Rather, the penalty arises from and is rooted in cultural and social legacies arising from historically gendered patterns of family formation. Such legacies still shape expectations and aspirations of and for women who are mothers, on an individual level. Importantly, these cultural and social legacies are further exacerbated by institutional and structural arrangements. The assignment of primary responsibility for dependency to the family has meant that other societal institutions have not had to change to accommodate the needs of those who undertake care work, such as by offering flexibility in the time and place of work. Institutionally, regardless of who assumes the burdens of caretaking within the private family, unless there are such corresponding adjustments in the so-called public sphere, caretaking will result in disadvantages in the market and workplace.

The policy response most likely to be made when structural disadvantages are noted is to suggest that support should be forthcoming from the state. Such suggestions point to tax-subsidized initiatives, including child allowances, universal long-term job protection following birth or adoption of a child, and short-term paid maternity and paternity leaves. These provisions are often found in societies in which the government has historically been deemed to have some responsibility to help the family with the economic and structural costs associated with having and raising children (Budig, Misra, and Böckmann 2010). Data from countries with universal free early childhood education for preschool children, accompanied by high-quality day care for very young children, indicates that such employment supports are particularly effective in increasing mothers' employment rates. Further, such programs have a truly universal reach. In countries like Sweden and France, 80 to 95 percent of children three to five years old are in publicly supported day care. In contrast, only about 14 percent of U.S. children in the same age group have access to publicly subsidized childcare.

It seems indisputable that such measures would help the middle-class and professional American mother avoid some of the economic burdens associated with motherhood and might also lessen the wage penalty. Such measures might also help to reduce maternal poverty for single and low-wage-earning mothers (Christopher 2010). There are serious road-blocks to implementing such programs in the United States, however. Recently, the economic recession has served as an excuse and provided political cover for arguments to further dismantle what was an already weak commitment to social welfare programs. But the real hurdles are ideological, epitomized in the particularly distorted vision of what constitutes autonomy, independence, and individual responsibility that has overtaken political rhetoric and action in the United States.[11] In addition, the ideal of responsibility for reproducing society does not extend to the market, which remains largely self-regulated and self-referential with regard to the important social roles it performs.

THE NEED FOR A RESPONSIVE STATE

The approach to family well-being in the United States has largely excluded the role of the market and its institutions in situating the family within society. The responsibility of the state may be part of the discussion, but even if there were some miracle of mass conversion and policy makers supported mother-friendly state subsidies, we would still find a significant percentage of mothers clustered in or near poverty level, as well as only a slight decrease in the pressures experienced by wage-earning mothers. State provision of benefits, such as childcare or child allowances, although necessary, will not be sufficient to significantly alleviate maternal poverty or eliminate the motherhood penalty in the United States (Christopher 2010).

This assertion forces us back to consideration of the relationships among family, state, and market institutions. Even if we seek to significantly reform the family, and even if that is accompanied by state provision of services and subsidy, if the market and its institutions remain unreformed, then transformations in the family and, consequentially, in the gendered nature of the relationship between men and women will elude us (Fineman 2004). State provision of subsidy and services for the family must be complemented by market accommodations for caretakers and caretaking. The ways in which market institutions are currently structured means that family-friendly changes will probably not be voluntarily undertaken, at least not in regard to all or most workers.[12] Rather, they will realistically require state encouragement in the form of the establishment of systems of market incentives and regulations to make accommodation a new, generally applicable workplace norm. Consequently, the first category of responses by the state would address the structure of market institutions and their flexibility in accommodating caretaking.

But measures beyond accommodation are also necessary. The state must also act to ensure a more egalitarian workplace by fostering measures that will move evolving workplace practices and norms of compensation more toward equalization than have those that have evolved under a relatively unsupervised system of neoliberal capitalism. This second set of responses takes us well beyond a focus on just motherhood and the family to consider the position of families and individuals in relation to market institutions more broadly.

Taking equality of opportunity seriously requires consideration of structural arrangements and disadvantages that are produced by forces more ubiquitous than discrimination in the market (Fineman 2004). The fact that we talk about "work/family conflict" is in and of itself an indication or symptom of conceptual distortion, in which a distinction in policy and law is drawn between what is public and what is private. This line defines what is appropriate for state action in contemporary political and policy debates in the United States, but it does so without considering the basic conceptual incoherency upon which the distinction rests. Interests are organized into aggregates such as family and market in ways that suggest differences in regard to state involvement and positioning. The whole idea that the state is not implicated in, and can be an outsider to, the reconciliation of family and market must be called into question.[13]

In sharp contrast, a responsive state recognizes that true equality of opportunity is impossible without regulation and vigilance with regard to both family and market relations. Other modern governments have recognized this and have responded accordingly. Some states have actually promoted more economic democracy and mediated capitalism by evolving social democratic political parties that directly address workers' general needs across the full range of work/family situations. This means viewing the state in alliance with workers and the market in defining the terms of employment and responsibility. It means not abandoning workers or rendering them dependent upon the perceived self-defined needs of the market. Higher rates of unionization are supported through union-friendly laws that lead to more egalitarian wage structures and more universal access to pension plans (Noah 2010). In some societies, in order to more equally balance the power disparity between market institution and the individual worker, the government is even a partner to wage and workplace negotiations, something that would be unthinkable in the United States.

These kinds of state responses evident in other nations raise the issue of what is the appropriate nature and extent of state responsibility with regard to the organization and operation of the interaction between family (and individual family members) and the market and its institutions. My argument for greater state involvement has been based on my perception that the work that is done in the family—work that produces the citizen, the worker, the consumer, the soldier, the student, the teacher, and so on—is essential to the continuation and well-being not only of the state but also of the market and its institutions. As a result, it is incumbent upon the state to redistribute responsibility for dependency across societal institutions so that the burdens of caretaking, and not just the benefits, are more equitably shared and distributed.

One way to do this would be to ensure a more egalitarian workplace that does not disadvantage those who engage in caretaking. Beyond this, it is also necessary to monitor market activity more actively to ensure that it does not frustrate equality of opportunity through existing systems of compensation and privilege more generally (Fineman 2004). Importantly, such measures not only would alter market–state relations but also would transfer onto the market and away from the state some of the economic costs of family or individual failure to thrive under neocapitalism. It would not be the state supplying subsidies and support in the form of welfare to the family, job training to individuals, and so on; instead, the market would be mandated to provide what should be deemed a "living wage" and other positive goods, such as insurance to working individuals and families. It should not be the case—as it currently is in the United States—that someone who works full time can nonetheless live below the poverty level and have to rely on stigmatized state assistance.[14]

This wage inequity may be most extremely evident in the case of mothers and children, but this is not merely a product of gender discrimination—or even discrimination against mothers—at least not as it is narrowly understood. Rather, it is the result of a relatively unfettered market system operating under cover of an asserted mantle of meritocracy and neutrality (Fineman 2004). This system proceeds under simplistic and individualistic premises that value autonomy more than equality (Dube and Jacobs 2004). In such a system, inequality is bound to prevail for most participants who are isolated from structures of power and privilege, whether they are men or women, mothers or fathers (Fineman 2004).

In the United States, the system facilitates and continues existing entrenched privilege and disadvantage. Furthermore, while politicians mouth platitudes about equal access and opportunity, they have proposed severe cuts in education spending, child welfare benefits, and programs designed to lift the poor out of situations of severe deprivation, in order to address federal and state deficits (Fineman 2004). This rhetoric is presented without any sense of irony or shame for these politicians' participation in earlier spectacles of bailouts for financial institutions and the profiteers who caused the economic crisis and/or the extension of tax breaks for the very wealthiest Americans. The wealthy corporations and individuals have now "recovered" from the Great Recession, experiencing record profits and huge bonuses, while unemployment rates remain high if the number of "discouraged workers" are included, and the poverty rate continues to hover at around 15 percent (Noah 2010; Stiglitz 2013; Bureau of Labor Statistics 2017; UC Davis n.d.).

Our current constitutional jurisprudence offers little help to the disadvantaged. Although we talk about equal opportunity, there is no constitutional right to an education at all, let alone to an equal education.[15] We tolerate, even justify, widespread and gross instances of inequality not only in opportunity but also in the distribution of basic social goods—goods necessary for human survival, such as housing, food, and health care.

THE RHETORIC OF SHARED RESPONSIBILITY

Experience with an attempt to use gender-neutral and egalitarian family policies to increase the position and participation of women in the workplace in the United States suggests that it will fail unless there are also corresponding changes in other societal institutions. In other words, there are no separate spheres. There are only symbiotic, overlapping, and often simultaneously complementary and conflicting institutional relationships. It is important for those seeking changes within the family to realize that the structure and intricacies of both market and state profoundly affect the well-being of and possibilities for the family, making change difficult or impossible to accomplish. We can impose all the gender equality aspirations we want in the family, but if the state and the market continue to operate in ways that conform to old gendered patterns, gender equality will be close to impossible to achieve, particularly for women who are mothers.[16]

The types of systematic and comprehensive restructuring of the intertwined market–state–family relationships that must take place to provide meaningful equality of opportunity would necessitate a vastly more active, responsive, and responsible state than seems possible under prevalent contemporary ideology in the United States. In the first place, the equality narrative in the United States is based on an antidiscrimination model that valorizes sameness of treatment and is intentionally oblivious to individual differences in situation and circumstance. In addition, unlike many other industrialized democracies, we have a venerated ideology of a restrained state and a sacrosanct free market, and any form of regulation is violently resisted, as contemporary American political rhetoric clearly shows.[17] The result of this ideology is a system in which American women, men, and children experience significantly higher levels of economic hardship and less social mobility than their counterparts in other affluent Western nations (Noah 2010, 3).

Achieving a more equitable and just society requires challenging the terms of the contemporary discussion about "personal responsibility," as well as confronting and exposing the conceptual flaws inherent in the idea of a restrained state. There are two unifying threads between arguments for valuing caretaking and arguments for a right to a living wage that might aid in that endeavor. First, societal wealth is not the only measure of national or individual well-being. Second, wealth is the product of various, complementary, and often very different types of contributions, including care work and physical or intellectual labor.[18]

The second of these ideas recognizes that wealth does not only or even primarily arise from investment of capital. Recognition of the noncapital contributions to societal wealth and well-being should require a corresponding assessment of the costs associated with making those contributions. Such an analysis might lead to a reassessment of the current attempt to ideologically confine such costs only to the family and individual caretakers. It also might prompt public and political recognition that worker and caretaker contributions not only have been seriously undervalued but also accrue penalties in a system that privileges economic over physical, material, emotional, and intellectual contributions, a system that ignores the costs placed on labor as well as the benefits produced by non-entrepreneurial work, for both market and state institutions.

In a just system—one that recognizes that there are responsibilities that accrue when benefits are conferred—market institutions would not only better share benefits[19] but would also more equitably distribute responsibility for dependency, valuing the work of caretakers and accommodating or facilitating fulfillment of their role as partners in productivity and the generation of wealth. More specifically, the performance of market institutions should be based not only on the legal profits they amass for shareholders but also on the quality of their policies toward their workers and the contributions they make to a more egalitarian society. Tax policy could be one mechanism for recognizing institutional expressions of shared responsibility and actions or policies that reflect commitment to equality of opportunity and intergenerational equity (Bodie 2011).[20]

The economic rewards an institution accrues are made possible by a combination of contributions. Family and care work, labor productivity, and capital investment should not only be counted but also should be more equitably distributed. In asserting this vision for societal reformation, it is important not to unduly privilege the existing mechanisms and values of our current workplace and other public institutions. And, certainly, it will be important to make the domestic and care aspects of life much more central to our understanding of institutional responsibility than they were in earlier feminist, gender-neutral family law reforms.

At this point, I cannot resist the temptation to suggest that the many positive and care-affirming norms associated with archetypal notions of mothering be expanded and employed to define what is expected from institutions acting within the "private sphere." The experience and practice of motherhood, along with its demands and dilemmas, should inform our social policy and define our expectations for the state and all its institutions. If we were to adopt this perspective, dependency and vulnerability could no longer be ignored or made to seem incidental to defining state and societal responsibility. Politicians, pundits, economists, and legal and political theorists would not be permitted to ignore dependency and vulnerability, as they now do in spinning out their incomplete and incoherent visions for efficiency, justice, and equality.

VULNERABILITY AND THE HUMAN CONDITION

While I still believe in the justness of substantive gender equality, my vocabulary and arguments have changed to become more focused on institutions and relations of power than on identities or individual characteristics like gender.[21] The traditional situation of women as wives and mothers is not inevitably tied to the fact that they are women but to the reality that, historically, women have been assigned responsibility for dependency and care work. Indeed, the institutions built up around that reality are unaccommodating, even hostile, to their assigned roles. Thinking in terms of identities and characteristics suggests that the problems women face are the result of discrimination; the solution is therefore equality of treatment and correction of the discriminatory behavior. I now understand that, although discrimination does sometimes occur and should be addressed, the problems are systemic and structural in nature. The relevant issues in securing gender justice far exceed the reach of an antidiscrimination model. They also exceed the family as an institution and implicate the very basis on which the whole society is organized.

In my recent work, I have been developing a vulnerability thesis in which the autonomous individual subject of liberal theory is replaced with a construct that I call the "vulnerable subject." The use of this vulnerable subject as the basis for analysis would anchor our discussions of equality in the actual lived human condition rather than in some abstract construct built around the false assumptions that all citizens are fully functional, capabilities are equivalent across individuals, and capabilities remain constant throughout an individual's lifetime.[22] The analysis begins with the insight that vulnerability is inherent in the human condition and, further, that when our vulnerability is realized, we may become dependent—economically, socially, psychologically, and physically. Vulnerability comes partly from our materiality, our embodiment, and, as such, it is both universal and constant. Our bodily vulnerability is apparent at the beginning of life, when we are totally dependent on others for our survival. But vulnerability in the sense in which I am developing it accompanies us continuously throughout life, as we age, become ill, disabled, or need care from others, and, finally, die.

But a vulnerability analysis does not depend on the image of a dependent individual. Even fully realized and functioning adults remain vulnerable to external, "natural" forces, such as the environment or climate, which may inflict bodily harms. In addition, it is significant that a great deal of our vulnerability, whether of a physical, nature-related, or societal form, is beyond our control as individuals. Some vulnerabilities we cannot even anticipate, let alone protect against. Vulnerabilities also may be beyond the capacity of society and its institutions to eliminate completely.

Vulnerability, as I am theorizing it, extends beyond the body, with its interior weaknesses and fallibilities. Institutions play a central role in the analysis, and a significant part of the vulnerability conceptualization focuses on the fact that the state can and does create institutions, relationships, entitlements, and other methods or mechanisms whereby individuals can gain "resilience" in the face of vulnerability. The role of law in the creation, maintenance, and regulation of those institutions is central. Whether we discuss the family, the corporation, or the market more generally, law and legal institutions define the principles for and consequences of formation and dissolution, determining legitimacy and defining when coercion, subsidy, or regulation is appropriate. The point is that, as social animals, humans are vulnerable to the institutions and structures that define life's circumstances and opportunities. Because these institutions may themselves be vulnerable to corruption, decay, capture, or decline, the state has a corresponding responsibility to see that these institutions afford equal opportunity and access, that they do not unduly privilege some while tolerating the disadvantage of others or expose some to risk while protecting others from it.

My hope is that taking human vulnerability seriously, and placing it at the core of our understanding of state responsibility, will lead to an expansion of the way we think about regulation and market responsibility. The realities of our universal, constant, and inescapable vulnerabilities argue for a responsive state that ensures equality of opportunity and individuals' access to society's institutions. True access requires the state to take existing structural differences into account and to work to mitigate them, so that those who historically have been disadvantaged are uplifted to a more level playing field.

NOTES

1. I have further explored this phenomenon in Fineman (1995, 67–71).
2. See, generally, Fineman (1991).
3. This paragraph draws directly from Fineman (2004, 159–66).

4.   This section draws on Fineman (1991).

5.   For a rich exploration of the gendered, binary roles between men and women from a historical and economic perspective, see Carbone (2000, 3–8).

6.   I also argue that discussions of the family must include the concepts of dependency and caregiving (Fineman 2004, 186–87).

7.   It is inevitable because all human beings are dependent in this sense as infants and children, and many will be dependent as they age or become disabled or ill as adults (Fineman 2004, 162).

8.   See *New Evidence on the Gender Pay Gap for Women and Mothers in Management: Hearing Before the Joint Economic Committee*, 111th Congress, S. Hrg. 111-789, September 28, 2010 (statement of Dr. Michelle J. Budig, Associate Professor of Sociology, University of Massachusetts).

9.   See Title VII of the Equal Employment Act, 42 U.S.C. § 2000e-2 (2011).

10. See, e.g., International Brotherhood of Teamsters v. United States, 431 U.S. 324 (1977) at 335, which found that proof of discriminatory intent is critical for a discrimination action under Title VII of the Equal Employment Act.

11. I develop this argument fully in Fineman (2004).

12. For instance, the Family and Medical Leave Act (1993) covers only work environments with fifty or more employees. Some work environments offer childcare for highly valued workers, but it is not generally available throughout American society, nor are flexible hours, shared job positions, or other accommodations for caretakers.

13. I earlier noted that the market has the best of all worlds when it comes to the public/ private divide: being labeled public vis-à-vis the family but private vis-à-vis the state. A positioning as a public institution for some purposes allows the market to claim a privileged relationship when it comes to subsidy and positive state interventions, while its private alter ego, categorized in terms of noninterference, allows it to resist negative incursions by regulatory agencies and state administrators.

14. About one-third of U.S. women earn wages too low to free their families from poverty; many Walmart workers are on food stamps. Minimum wage is another state subsidy of business, and arguments that workers won't be hired and so forth should the minimum wage increase should not obscure this transfer of wealth from taxpayers to corporate profits (see Dube and Jacobs 2004, 4–8).

15. See, for example Plyler v. Doe, 457 U.S. 202 (1982) at 221, finding that education is not a fundamental right. See also Brown v. Board of Education, 74 S.Ct. 686 (1954) at 688, overruling the "separate but equal" doctrine of Plessy v. Ferguson, 16 S.Ct. 1138 (1896) at 1143. Despite the monumental dictum of *Brown*, the U.S. Supreme Court did not recognize education as a fundamental right under the U.S. Constitution.

16. Attempted changes in the structure or function of the family also affect other institutions and place pressure on both market and state. Such pressure creates tensions, ruptures, and demands for accommodation and supportive adjustment. These requisite changes in market and state do not always happen easily, successfully, or at all.

17. See, for example, Causes of Poverty, with a Focus on Out-of-Wedlock Births: Hearing Before the Subcommittee on Human Resources of the House Committee on Ways and

Means, 104th Congress, Serial 104-52, March 5, 1996 (statement of Representative Tim Hutchinson). During this hearing, Hutchinson stated, "Instead of lifting people out of poverty and despair, we have developed a cycle of dependency that is now entering its third generation. . . . Welfare reform legislation must also include strong work requirements. We must restore to individuals the dignity of work" (13, 16). In contrast, the United Kingdom recently passed the Equality Act, which requires public decision makers to have "due regard" for the need to advance equality of opportunity (Fredman 2010).

18. I am going to focus on the second insight, but it is important to note that it seems to be the distribution of wealth that is critical to "happiness," and inequality of wealth seems to be an indication of aggregate and individual unhappiness. In this regard, it is interesting that, despite its provisions against discrimination, the United States ranks just below Singapore as one of the most unequal countries among the rich industrialized nations. Social mobility is also limited. Data from the 1980s and 1990s shows that about 36 percent of children who are born into the bottom fifth of wealth distribution will remain in that class as adults. Studies of fathers' incomes when their sons were born, in comparison to their sons' incomes at age thirty, show that social mobility has declined rapidly since the 1980s. Research reported in *The Spirit Level* (Wilkinson and Pickett 2010, 17; 54–57; 159–61) suggest that greater inequality decreases levels of trust in a society, and less-trusting members of society are less willing to donate time and money to helping others.

19. See Noah (2010, 54), which illustrates the rise in productivity in the United States over the past decades but also the stagnation and decline in real wages.

20. One way to accomplish this would be by raising corporate and business taxes and giving tax credits for concrete programs that recognize the institution's shared responsibility. This way, Costco, which pays for health insurance and provides more of a living wage to its workers, would have tax advantages. These corporate tax advantages would be denied to Walmart, with its low wages, because this company, along with many others, refuses to provide for these fundamental needs of income and health care coverage, forcing its workers to resort to food stamps for groceries and Medicaid for health needs.

21. This concluding section is based on Fineman (2011).

22. For further exploration of how vulnerability analysis enables lawyers, advocates, policy makers, and scholars to rise above competing claims of identity discrimination, see Fineman (2012, 1726–27).

REFERENCES

Bodie, Matthew T. 2011. *Employees and the Boundaries of the Corporation.* Saint Louis University Legal Studies Research Paper no. 2011-03. Saint Louis: Saint Louis University School of Law.

Budig, Michelle J., Joya Misra, and Irene Böckmann. 2010. *The Wage Penalty for Motherhood in a Cross-National Perspective: Relationships with Work–Family Policies and Cultural Attitudes.* http://paa2010.princeton.edu/download.aspx?submissionId=101609.

Bureau of Labor Statistics. 2017. "Unemployment holds steady for much of 2016." *Monthly Labor Review* March: 1.

Carbone, June. 2000. *From Partners to Parents: The Second Revolution in Family Law.* New York: Columbia University Press.

Christopher, Karen. 2010. "Family-Friendly Europe: Decent Wages and Generous Social Supports to Reconcile Work and Parenting Add Up to a Family Policy That's Smarter Than Marriage Promotion." *American Prospect* 13, no. 7: 59.

Correll, Shelley J., Stephen Benard, and In Paik. 2007. "Getting a Job: Is There a Motherhood Penalty?" *American Journal of Sociology* 112, no. 5 (March): 1297–1338.

Dube, Arindrajit, and Ken Jacobs. 2004. *Hidden Cost of Wal-Mart Jobs: Use of Safety Net Programs by Wal-Mart Workers in California.* Berkeley, CA: UC Berkeley Labor Center Briefing Paper Series.

Fineman, Martha Albertson. 1991. *The Illusion of Equality: The Rhetoric and Reality of Divorce Reform.* Chicago: University of Chicago Press.

——. 1995. *The Neutered Mother, the Sexual Family, and Other Twentieth Century Tragedies.* New York: Routledge.

——. 2004. *The Autonomy Myth: A Theory of Dependency.* New York: The New Press.

——. 2008. "The Vulnerable Subject: Anchoring Equality in the Human Condition." *Yale Journal of Law & Feminism* 20, no. 1: 1–23.

——. 2009. "Equality: Still Illusive After All These Years." In *Gender Equality: Dimensions of Women's Equal Citizenship*, ed. Joanna Grossman and Linda McClain, 251–67. New York: Cambridge University Press.

——. 2011. "The Vulnerable Subject: Anchoring Equality in the Human Condition." In *Transcending Boundaries of Law: Generations of Feminism and Legal Theory*, ed. Martha Albertson Fineman, 161–75. New York: Routledge.

——. 2012. "Beyond Identities: The Limits of an Antidiscrimination Approach to Equality." *Boston University Law Review* 92, no. 6: 713–70.

Fredman, Sandra. 2010. "Positive Duties and Socio-Economic Disadvantage: Bringing Disadvantage onto the Equality Agenda." *European Human Rights Law Review* 3: 290.

Klaff, Ramsay Laing. 1982. "The Tender Years Doctrine: A Defense." *California Law Review* 70 no. 2: 335.

Noah, Timothy. 2010. "The United States of Inequality." *Slate*, September 16. http://www.slate.com/id/2266025/entry/2266026.

Stiglitz, Joseph. 2013. *The Price of Inequality: How Today's Divided Society Endangers Our Future.* New York: Norton.

University of California at Davis, Center for Poverty Research. N.d. "What is the current poverty rate in the United States?" https://poverty.ucdavis.edu/faq/what-current-poverty-rate-united-states.

Wilkinson, Richard, and Kate Pickett. 2010. *The Spirit Level: Why Greater Equality Makes Societies Stronger.* New York: Bloomsbury Press.

11

THE DOUBLE LIVES OF TRANSNATIONAL MOTHERS

SONYA MICHEL AND GABRIELLE OLIVEIRA

n late October 2012, New Yorkers and parents everywhere were distressed to learn about the stabbing murder of two Upper West Side children by their nanny, who also tried to kill herself. According to the *New York Times* (Rashbaum 2012), friends and relatives were shocked by the news, noting that the children's mother, Marina Krim, had treated the nanny, a migrant worker from the Dominican Republic, "as a member of their own family." A police official told the *Times* that the Krim family did not have problems with their employee, Yoselyn Ortega, and "seemed to live an idyllic life." Ms. Ortega, however, "had a different view." According to the official, "she had resentment toward the parents" and said they "were always telling her what to do."

Despite being intimately connected through the children, the Krims and their nanny inhabited separate universes. The Krims lived comfortably in a spacious apartment off of Central Park West, while Ortega, beset with financial problems, was forced to share a crowded apartment much farther uptown with her teenage son and other relatives. The Krims were apparently unaware of Ortega's difficulties even though, according to Marina Krim's blog, they had spent several days visiting Ortega and her family in her home country.

Most of the newspapers dismissed Ortega's claims that she was being mistreated and underpaid by her employers. It is not clear whether Ortega knew that the Krims were paying a monthly rental of $10,000 for their apartment, but she reportedly became angry when they refused her request for a raise. Instead, they offered her additional hours of work—cleaning, something she did not want to do (Gillman 2015).

This kind of employer obliviousness to the personal lives of individuals working in their households is not uncommon in the United States. Perhaps years of watching TV series like *Upstairs, Downstairs* or *Downton Abbey* have inured Americans to the lopsidedness of such relationships, naturalizing them, making them seem familiar, unavoidable, even amusing. Thus, a neighbor of the Krims could write in the *New York Times* (Dell'Antonia 2012), quite unselfconsciously:

> Part of the reality of living on the Upper West Side of Manhattan is that there are very few day cares. Some of us rely on nannies every day so that we can go to work and earn money for our families. Some of us rely on nannies so that we can have alone time with each child to make them feel special. Some of us rely on nannies so that we can take one of our children to swim class, or dance class, or go for a run in the park or dash to a crowded grocery store. It is a delicate and intimate relationship to leave your child with paid help, but many of us don't have family nearby, and we are fortunate enough to have the means to hire lovely women (and occasionally men) to help us. And we all know that we are lucky and blessed.

There is no indication here—or in any of the 169 responses to this column—that the writers were aware of, much less empathetic toward, Yoselyn Ortega and the conditions of her life.[1] Most focused on the anxieties they themselves experienced when leaving their children with "paid help." Some called for better screening and licensing procedures for nannies, others for more formal childcare provisions. Several attributed Ortega's actions to the assumption that she was mentally ill (as had been reported in the *Times*), but no one suggested that feelings of stress, conflict, anger, and resentment toward her well-heeled employers might well be a normal response by a low-paid domestic employee. Although faced with the challenges of raising her own son with only limited resources and opportunities, Ortega was somehow expected to maintain a cheerful, selfless demeanor as she witnessed, day after day, the Krims' privileged existence—not only witnessed it but also participated in and *enabled* it, by caring for two of the children so Marina Krim could lavish attention on the third (something Ortega did not have the luxury to do for her own son), or by taking the Krim children to the kinds of classes and events that her own son would never enjoy. Only a psychotic, in the view of the *Times* respondents, would act out so violently under such conditions.[2]

M(OTHER)HOOD DENIED

We do not wish to deny the horror of this event or to suggest that, because of their class privilege, the Krims deserved to lose two of their children so tragically. Nevertheless, we cannot help noticing the discrepancy between the outpouring of public sympathy for the Krims and the relative silence surrounding Yoselyn Ortega's situation. Although the *Times* reported a few sketchy details about her life, none of the comments that appeared in the paper acknowledged this information, and Marina Krim herself seemed to be unaware of it. In the contemporary United States, this lack of awareness about the life conditions of low-paid domestic employees is not unusual; rather, as the neighbor's post suggests, it is probably the norm. Employers tend to view nannies and other caregivers from the perspective of their own needs and those of their children and other loved ones, not from that of the nannies.

How can we understand such willful insouciance on the part of the hundreds of thousands of Americans who hire migrant workers to care for their children, elders, or family members with chronic illness or disability? What explains how employers who are themselves mothers can fail to inquire into the circumstances of other mothers working in their own households, intimately engaged in their daily lives? Is this, as we suggested somewhat blithely at the outset, the result of watching too much *Upstairs, Downstairs*? Or does it reflect a deeper strain in American life—a tendency to devalue the mothering of lower-class and minority women?

If we look at certain recent developments in American social policy, we can find that same tendency. Take, for example, welfare reform in the mid-1990s—the displacement of Aid to Families with Dependent

Children (otherwise known as "welfare") by Temporary Assistance for Needy Families. This shift signaled that Congress was no longer willing to support the mothering of poor women—something they had done through federal policy since the Great Depression, and at the state level since the Progressive Era (Mink 2002).[3] Instead, poor mothers were now mandated to find work—in some states, as early as six weeks after the birth of a child. To be sure, lawmakers' change of heart was partly driven by a general increase in female labor force participation since the 1960s and feminists' endorsement thereof. But it also had to do with the fact that welfare mothers were widely coded (however inaccurately) as minorities, and their parenting abilities generally devalued (Mink 2002; Hancock 2004; Roberts, present volume).

Similarly, the Family Medical Leave Act, signed into law by President Bill Clinton early in his first administration, offers only *unpaid* leave for childbirth or adoption or to care for a sick child or other relative. This means that minority mothers, who earn less on average than their white counterparts, are less able to take advantage of this policy (Michel 2014). Thus, federal law implicitly valorizes the mothering of middle-class, mainly white, women while dismissing that of their lower-income, mainly minority, counterparts.

A similar disregard prompts middle-class American employers to block out the personal mothering roles of their migrant nannies—and with them, the conflicting emotions presumably produced by the nannies' attachment to their own children. This allows employers to feel entitled to arrogate all the nannies' affections and direct them solely to the employers' children. Moreover, they expect the nannies to conduct this form of emotional abandonment of their own children without complaint, thereby engaging in a kind of continuous dissemblance (for historical examples, see Clark Hine 1989; Parkhurst 1938). For the nannies, employers' insistence that they are "like one of the family" ends up being a command to lead a double life. Thus, this type of employment, more than housecleaning or even caring for elders or the disabled, constitutes a particularly poignant appropriation of their affections—of their inner selves (see Zelizer 2005, chaps. 4–5; Hochschild 2013, chaps. 9–10).

Although the foregoing suggests that employers' willful ignorance of their employees' private lives is uniquely American, similar phenomena can be found in myriad settings around the contemporary globe—anywhere migrant workers from "emerging economies," as the Organisation for Economic Co-operation and Development euphemistically calls them, provide care for the citizens of the "rich" countries. For example, one Filipina mother told geographer Geraldine Pratt (2012) that when she first took a job as a nanny in Hong Kong, she missed her children terribly, but a coworker warned her to hide her feelings, because her employer would not want to have an "unhappy" nanny caring for her children.

Over the past few decades, aging populations and the shift of women into the labor force have reordered the gender division of labor worldwide. In nearly every country, these changes have created a massive demand for extrafamilial care work, including care for elders as well as children, but this demand is met differently in different places. Strong, well-developed welfare states, such as those in the Nordic countries, drawing on long traditions of public provision, offer high-quality public childcare by native-born workers. But in weaker welfare states, such as the United States, parts of Southern Europe, and newly rich countries such as Singapore and the United Arab Emirates, parents rely on the market for individual care workers. These patterns are reinforced by strong cultural preferences for providing care within the household—if not by family members, then by those who are considered to be "like one of the family" (Bettio, Villa, and Simonazzi 2006; Michel and Peng 2012).

In response to the demand, over the past decade or so, hundreds of thousands of women have been migrating annually from poorer to richer countries to take up jobs as care workers. Women now constitute roughly half of the world's labor migrants, and unlike female migrants in the past, who were mostly young, single, and childless, those who move now are somewhat older, often married, and often have children. Indeed, earning money for children's education and health care is women's prime motivation for seeking work abroad, and their remittances make up more than half of the money sent back to home countries (women tend to remit more than men, even though they generally earn less)—nearly $300 billion annually in 2010 (Le Goff 2016).

Because migrant women tend to cluster in caring occupations, often in private homes, sometimes as live-in employees, they are more likely to face difficult working conditions, with few protections when it comes to hours, wages, and accommodations (Boris and Klein 2006; Poo 2011). At the same time, immigration restrictions in most destination countries force women to leave children and other dependent relatives behind, creating "care deficits" in their home countries, for which the governments of those countries cannot compensate because they lack the financial resources to establish social services to substitute for lost maternal care (Badasu and Michel 2016). The result is a worldwide redistribution—or maldistribution—of motherhood.

Absent mothers go to great lengths to maintain relationships with their children via various forms of "transnational mothering"—letters, phone calls, e-mails, Skype, and a steady stream of gifts, as well as financial remittances—but the effects of such practices are not clear. Research to date has been spotty, and the findings of preliminary studies are inconclusive. Some scholars argue that migrants' remittances go so far in remedying the dire poverty of family members in home countries that they more than compensate for the emotional strains of maternal absence; receiving housing, adequate food, school fees, and other necessities offsets the pain of long-term separation. Others, however, claim that, despite women's efforts to provide "mothering across borders," extended mother–child separation leads to attenuated relationships, trauma, awkward visits, and difficulties in family reunification (Hondagneu-Sotelo and Avila 1997; Parreñas 2005; ILO/UNDP 2009; Francisco 2015).

Moreover, while remittances in foreign currencies go a long way in poorer countries, helping to launch families into the middle class, global economic inequalities make it difficult for families to sustain their newfound status without continuing influxes of cash. These same inequalities also affect domestic job markets in the sending countries, with the result that even children who, with the help of remittances, have managed to receive a decent education, perhaps including advanced degrees or professional training, may still be unable to find decently paying jobs commensurate with their skills and thus, like their parents, will go abroad to seek work. And so the cycle continues.

THE STORY OF HELENA,
A "TRANSNATIONAL MOTHER"

Understanding that transnational mothering is multisited, scholars have devised innovative methodologies to study the practical, financial, and emotional complexities of transnational mothering, which entails working with family members at both ends of the "global care chain."[4] This was the course pursued by Gabrielle Oliveira, coauthor of this chapter, in her interviews with Helena, a migrant mother from Mexico working as a nanny in New York City, and with Helena's relatives in both New York and Mexico.[5] Oliveira's research offers important insights into the lives of other migrant mothers working as nannies, such as Yoselyn Ortega, and the conflicts they experience. The following is Oliveira's first-person report.

When I met her, in 2012, Helena had lived in Sunset Park, Brooklyn, for almost eleven years. She had three daughters, one son, and two grandchildren. She had immigrated to the United States without documentation and as a result had not been home to Tlaxcala, Mexico, for more than a decade. Helena, like other mothers in this research, revealed that she had been in an abusive relationship in Mexico. Upon her departure from Tlaxcala, she left one son, Julio, who at that time was eight, and took with her a daughter, Lina, then seven. According to Helena, Julio remained in Mexico because he wanted to stay with his father. After Helena left with her daughter, her husband served her with court papers alleging that she had kidnapped Lina and left the country. This situation, Helena told me, also prevented her from ever getting formally divorced and remarried and from going back to Mexico for her son and extended family.

At the time of our interview, Helena lived in a two-bedroom apartment with her three daughters, her partner, her granddaughter, and her daughter's boyfriend (the father of her grandchild). At night, the living room became a third bedroom, where Helena slept with her partner, Armando. Upon arriving in New York, Helena and Lina lived on their own for almost two years until Helena met Armando and they decided to get together, or "*juntarse*." When she first arrived in New York City, it had taken Helena a bit of time to settle in and find a job that paid well. As soon as she could, however, she began sending Julio money every month, which supported his schooling. After one year with Armando, Helena had Mariana, and then Rosa (eight and seven years old, respectively, in 2012).

I met Helena when I was volunteering at a small organization based in Sunset Park that ran a cooperative for domestic workers. In this cooperative, a group of almost sixty women participated in workshops on cardiopulmonary resuscitation, the developmental psychology of babies, children's language learning, nutrition, and health. According to Helena, those workshops taught her how to be a "better" mother. I asked Helena what this meant for her, and she explained, "I was not a good mother to Lina when she was younger. I would get hysterical, and I have hit her before. . . . One day I slapped her in the face. I feel terrible about it. . . . I didn't know what I was doing. I regretted it. I would never do that with my younger daughters now . . . because I learned here in America, through my work at the cooperative."

RAISING BABY VICTORIA

Helena worked as a nanny for a young couple, both doctors, in Manhattan. She took care of their eleven-month-old baby, Victoria. Working eight to nine hours a day, she was able to earn more than $500 a week. The co-op in Sunset Park had helped her secure this job. Helena carried a picture of baby Victoria in her wallet. She proudly showed it to me, saying, "Look at her beautiful blue eyes and blond hair."

"The little baby cries when her mother holds her; she prefers being with me. . . . I probably take better care of her than I do my own children!" Helena told me at her kitchen table, as her two daughters watched her closely. I asked her, "Why do you think that happens?" She answered that she gives baby Victoria a lot of affection. "I hold her close, I kiss her and I tell her stories. . . . She feels safe with me." I asked Helena if Victoria's mother was not bothered by their close relationship, and she replied, "Mayara is a doctor, she is married, they live in a beautiful apartment, they travel, they have beautiful clothes. I think she doesn't care so much because her life is so good."

Helena was very dedicated to Victoria, making sure she kept the girl's daily routine interesting and different. She told me she was using all the baby development strategies she had learned at the co-op to "educate" Victoria. The baby's room was beautiful, decorated with her name on the wall and dozens of books in different languages. Helena arrived before seven each morning and sometimes did not leave until after nine in the evening. It was not just Helena who missed her children's nighttime routines; Mayara often came home after Victoria's bedtime.

Helena felt good when Mayara complimented the way in which she was caring for Victoria. As she explained, "It's very different, the idea of caring and raising. For example, if you have a baby and you ask me to come and 'watch' her and play with her for a few hours every day, I am caring for her and I am helping you. But in my case, I raise Victoria because I am with her all day and her parents miss everything. They missed when she first started sitting on her own at five months and seventeen days." Helena had been caring for Victoria since she was two weeks old, and she described her relationship with the child as "very close." When I asked her if she would miss caring for Victoria when the child was old enough to go to preschool, Helena replied, "I can't really think about it; I got really used to her."

A common feeling reported by immigrant mothers who are nannies is that caring for a baby or a child professionally allowed them to be someone different from who they were at home. Helena believed that she had made many mistakes with all her children—mistakes that in her opinion were hard to erase. With Victoria, she was using the knowledge she had learned at the co-op, and she felt empowered as a worker. "There is only love between Victoria and I. That's how I raise that little angel," Helena told me. "She doesn't hold anything against me. . . . There is nothing wrong with me in her eyes." (This was in contrast to her other children, whom she felt she had let down too many times.) The doctors, her bosses, had cameras in their home, but Helena did not mind. She felt very secure about the way she cared for Victoria.

CARING FOR HER OWN CHILDREN

At her house, Helena showed me the different charts she had learned to make at workshops and at the house where she worked. From the beginning, her boss, a pediatrician, wanted Helena to keep a detailed schedule of Victoria's feedings, playtime, what kind of food she ate, what books she read, and so forth. Helena had a similar schedule in her own house: a large, pink, thick piece of paper that featured a reward system with chores on the left, names on the top, and space for stars on the right. On her refrigerator door there was a smaller piece of paper with rules for how to behave at home and in school, copied by the girls themselves: "Respect the teacher"; "Respect mother"; "Do the homework"; "Study hard to be the best"; and finally, "Love school." Those sentences were also posted in the house where Helena worked.

Helena's daughters Mariana (second grade) and Rosa (third grade) were mostly meeting grade-level expectations in school; their report cards were filled with 2s and 3s (the range is 1 to 4, with 1 being the lowest). They both struggled in math and English, however, and their teachers sent comments with recommendations: "Please practice writing these words at home" or "Read more at home." At the same time, Helena was taking Victoria to the local library every day, reading to her in Spanish as she cuddled with her in a big pouf chair, and tenderly talking to her about the importance of reading and writing. Mariana and Rosa did not get that time with their mother.

Helena's other daughter, Lina, who at the time of our interview was the seventeen-year-old mother of four-month-old Graciela, had dropped out of school when she got pregnant but currently was studying for her General Educational Development test. Her report cards from high school were filled with 9s and 10s (on a ten-point scale), with teacher comments such as "Lina is one of our best students" and "We are always very impressed with her passion for learning." Helena told me she thought it was because she had raised Lina herself and had helped her with everything in school, as she was now doing for Victoria. When I asked her about Mariana and Rosa, Helena replied, "With Victoria, it's like I can be a different person. My boss Mayara respects me for my work, and for the first time in my life I feel like I know more than someone that is more educated than I am. Victoria is a princess, and when I'm there at her house, I feel like she is mine."

Helena continued to send remittances home to Mexico; in five years, she had regularly sent over $1,000 a month to her son, Julio, and to her mother. Julio had just finished high school (*la prepa*) and been accepted into university to study law. For Helena, as for most of the fifty other mothers I interviewed in New York City, providing a better education for her children was the principal motive for migration. As Helena put it,

> Do you know what a good mother does? A good mother teaches her children. A good mother is patient with her children and shows them that school is the best pathway. When I was in Mexico, I could not give my kids the best education. . . . I had to leave Mexico because my husband was not a good man. He was violent. And I lent money to the wrong people in the town and ended up owing more money than I will ever have. I needed to make money and a clean break. I was under a lot of stress, you know? I needed to *care* [emphasis added] for my children. . . . That is my role, a mother's role [is] to care. If I can't take care of them, I have nothing left. . . . With my son, Julio, I feel guilt. I left him. So I compensated [for] that by putting him through school and now college. I send him money religiously every week. . . . I pray to the Virgin and send him the money. He deserves everything.
>
> With Lina . . . *Ai!* [Tears start to come down her face.] . . . I blamed her. . . . She represented everything that was bad and I argued with her a lot. I hit her for no good reason. . . . I hit her in the face once. . . . I feel really bad when I think about it. With precious Victoria, I get to use everything that I learned the hard way. I watch her mother make mistakes that I have made. Losing patience, you know? I don't do that with Victoria.

With her youngest daughters, Helena was calm, permissive, and tender. But, perhaps because of Helena's work schedule, Lina spent a lot of time raising her little sisters. Lina woke them up every morning to get ready for school, walked them to school, went to parent–teacher meetings, helped them with homework, and fed them. She did a lot of the daily care. During one of my visits, for example, Rosa went to the bathroom. From the bathroom, she screamed, "Lina, I need you here to help me really quick." Helena looked at me, embarrassed, and responded to Rosa, "My baby, don't you mean your mama?" Rosa contested, "I said Lina, I want Lina!" Helena looked at me and said, "Caring doesn't always mean being there [next to them] physically. . . . Look at Julio and how his life turned out. He needed my care, but not me," she said, pounding on her chest.

Helena did not hide the fact that Julio's educational trajectory during the previous ten years had been the most rewarding part of her life. She thought bringing Lina to the United States would give her daughter a better chance of succeeding in life, but in fact Lina's academic career was put on hold when she became pregnant at age sixteen. As Helena told me, "Los errores no los pagas tu, pagan los niños" [You don't pay for your own errors; your children do]. She explained that, as soon as she was able to find stability in New York City, with a paying job and a partner who was not abusive, she was able to get back on her feet. Like other migrant wage-earning mothers, it took Helena some time to be able to start remitting money home, to keep the promise she once made to her child in Mexico. Economic and emotional stability were, in her opinion, the two most important aspects of her succeeding as a mother.

THE EDUCATION OF HELENA'S CHILDREN

In the course of her ethnographic research, Oliveira had the opportunity to meet and interview Helena's son, Julio, in Mexico. He explained to her,

> In the beginning I did not understand why my mother had left me, but then I understood that she actually respected my wishes when I told her I did not want to go to the U.S. with her, I wanted to stay with my father. And then, she never abandoned me. My grandmother raised me and now I work at my uncle's pharmacy and soon I will start college. Look at everything she has given me. I wish I could have seen that when I was younger.

Julio, who was eighteen at the time of the interview, already had a child and a partner. He worked to support this new family, but he never stopped studying, because of his mother's constant pressure and the financial conditions she had imposed on him. Julio was raised by his maternal grandparents, mostly his grandmother Cecilia—Helena's mother—whom Oliveira also interviewed. Cecilia had supported her daughter's departure because she knew about Helena's difficult relationship with her ex-husband. Helena's departure was sudden, but Cecilia was quick to take Julio in before his father could take him.

BALANCING CARING ROLES

How can Helena deal with each child she cares for? Although Helena saw her work with baby Victoria as a direct conduit to the life she was providing for her children, both in New York City and in Mexico, the constant contradictions of daily life—spending long hours with baby Victoria but not being around her own daughters much—filled her with doubts and questions about how to be a "good" mother to her children. At the same time, the sadness she felt about leaving her son, Julio, in Mexico was balanced by the newfound love she had for Victoria. Her relationship with her bosses was based on the premise that she had the *knowledge* to care for baby Victoria, and that it was only with Helena's help that her boss Mayara could continue to be a busy doctor. Helena was proud of how good she was at her job, but she had doubts about how "good" she was for her own daughters.

FROM THE MICRO TO THE MACRO

Mayara was likely unaware of Helena's emotional turmoil. Helena made a point, in her words, of "trying to be professional, not ask for extra money, not tell my boss all my problems," while Mayara, for her part, did not push for more details of Helena's personal life. Thus, they maintained, apparently by mutual consent, an asymmetrical relationship. This was, of course, not the case between Yoselyn Ortega and the Krims, who seemingly refused to acknowledge the situation of their migrant employee and *her* family, even after Ortega obliquely brought it to their attention by asking for higher wages and more regular hours.

This kind of obliviousness is mirrored in the immigration policies that prevail in most immigrant-receiving countries. Like individual employers, the governments of these countries benefit from having a pool of migrants available to perform care work at low wages, thereby obviating the need to develop state-sponsored institutions to provide such services. Yet few make the effort to alleviate the trauma of separation for the migrants and their families by instituting measures such as legally allowing migrants to bring relatives, especially minor children, with them, or speeding up the family reunification process.[6]

To be sure, nations differ in this regard. At one extreme are countries like the United States, which engage in a practice we call "demand and denial"—creating a demand for migrants who are willing to work as caregivers but denying them legal entry by creating a suitable visa category—one that recognizes their skills and the need for them (Michel and Peng 2012). At the other extreme is Canada, which, in recent years, has acknowledged its need for workers by instituting a Live-in Caregiver Program that places migrants on the path to citizenship after twenty-four months of working as caregivers, and, at that point, also allows them to bring in family members (Boyd 2011; Boyd, forthcoming). But because of bureaucratic complications, the time between departure and reunion often stretches out for many years (Pratt 2012; Parreñas 2005)—so long that parents and children may have difficulty readjusting to one another, and sometimes so long that children "age out" of eligibility (Parreñas 2015). Moreover, for some children, reunion with their mothers may entail separating from loving relatives or "other mothers" who have cared for them over extended periods of time, thereby causing a second trauma, as painful as the first. To Pratt (2012, xxvi), such suffering constitutes a form of violence, or "social death."

One reason for the failure to reform may be the difficulties immigrants face in trying to articulate and communicate their situations effectively; in other words, they lack access to the popular media. The story of the Krim murders is a case in point. The mainstream media steadily and sympathetically focused on the parents' painful loss but provided only scant details about Ortega's double life, consistently referring to her in derogatory terms. The New York *Daily News*, for example, reported that Ortega "*callously* pretended she was the real victim" of the crime, and "*bizarrely whined* about treatment from the children's parents" (Jacobs 2014), while the *New York Post* referred to her as the "*killer nanny*," who was "*unhinged*" (Rosenberg 2013; emphasis added in both quotes).

The online media expressed a somewhat more complex reading of the case. In the days following the murders, participants in a string of posts on *Gawker*, for example, debated about what caused Ortega's actions (Berman 2012): "It is not beyond comprehension that people snap, which seems to be the case here," wrote "000Johanna." "We live in a culture where people are under tremendous financial pressure—and where the support networks are almost nonexistent—both emotionally and financially. There is no excuse for this horror but there are definitely explanations." Shortly thereafter, "thehoopoe3" concurred: "Well, it is clear that the woman snapped. But we also know that poverty is hugely stressful and a major contributor to mental illness. We also know that domestic help is frequently underpaid and overworked, without labor protections or legal recourse. So there seems to be a constellation of issues here." Some also blamed the lack of affordable housing in New York City and inadequate mental health care, but others were less sympathetic. Said "SnapOfAllSnaps," "OK, we all work long hours and we all have problems. But we all do not just start stabbing kids to death."

The *Daily Beast* focused on Ortega's mental condition, noting that Ortega had "begun hearing voices—and, in her family's words, 'started acting different'—back when she was 16" (Daly 2013). Reporter Michael Daly learned that Ortega "had suffered some kind of mental crisis around 2008" and had "taken a turn for the worse" once her son arrived in New York, only a few months before the murders. According to Daly, "Right up to the time of the killings, she had continued hearing voices, male and female, speaking in Spanish but still unintelligible to her save for when they urged her to hurt others." Apparently, the Krims knew nothing of this. "If only there had been some way for the parents to determine whether Yoselyn Ortega was fit to be a nanny," Daly wrote.

Ortega complained that the Krims frequently changed her schedule, causing her to miss appointments with her psychiatrist, but it seems that she did not tell them why she was so upset. "I had to do everything and take care of the kids. . . . God forgive me, so many things they made me do," she said in court papers. Despite this and other evidence of Ortega's mental instability, as well as the testimony of a psychiatrist who had examined her, the presiding judge found Ortega fit to stand trial, a decision that most of the mainstream newspapers appeared to condone.

Of course, as noted on *Gawker*, not all women in such circumstances react as Ortega did. Her actions were clearly extreme and seemingly driven by psychiatric illness, the judge's opinion notwithstanding. A Dominican nanny told Oliveira a horrendous story about one of her employers shoving her into a corner and accusing her of "making too much noise and not letting the baby sleep." Though recounting this incident in tears, she stated firmly, "I would *never* consider ending a person's life based on that incident. What happened has nothing to do with her [Ortega] being someone's nanny and everything to do with her mental issues."

Probably more common is the way Helena, the subject of Oliveira's ethnography, deals with her conflicts. While idealizing the "precious" blond, blue-eyed Victoria and taking pride in the care she is able to lavish on the child (all of this described to Oliveira within earshot of her younger daughters), Helena regrets her inability to provide the same kind of attention to her own children. She rationalizes the situation by emphasizing the educational benefits her wages allow her to bestow on them.

Although the women actually involved in this kind of two-sided maternal experience may be reluctant to articulate their true feelings, ethnographers and other scholars have not hesitated to parse the emotional complexities of women's "intimate labor," including nannying (see Zelizer 2005; Boris and Parreñas 2007; Clough and Halley 2007; Hochschild 2013). Several have shown that the tension becomes even greater when employment involves migration, as has become increasingly common for female care workers.

FROM ANALYSIS TO ACTION

It is one thing to describe and theorize about the emotional complexities of migrant care work, another to turn this into actionable principles. Pratt (2012) has sought to transform "narratives of maternal loss" into political language and to articulate a sense of shared responsibility for the consequences of maternal migration. She offers a detailed portrayal of migrant Filipina care workers in Canada, derived from extended participant observation in several British Columbia Filipina nongovernmental organizations, including a women's center, a youth group, and an experimental theater. She concludes by criticizing the "complacency around temporary labor migration" (facilitated in Canada through its Live-in Caregiver Program), which, she says, is too often presented as an unproblematic "solution to labor-market shortages in the Global North and poverty and debt in the Global South":

> Although the language of "win-win-win," costs and benefits, and labor migration as a "right"[7] suggests that migrants can be and are brought within the calculations of modern governments in mutually beneficial ways, we have shown that their lives continue to be, through the process of migration, precarious and insecure. The weight of our evidence is that this precariousness haunts the lives of their children in enduring ways. (163)

One example is the "very troubling marginalization of Filipino youths" who are the children of migrant mothers working in Canada—a finding that reminds us of the need to view the social and psychological consequences of maternal migration transnationally as well as across generations.

It is precisely in the nexus between women, migration, and family consequences that Pratt sees the potential for strategic political action. She believes that pointing to the harm done to the mother–child bond can be a strong argument against those who see migration solely as an "individual rational choice":

> Appealing to the mother–child relation works in an entirely different register . . . and it renders absurd both the notion of individual choice completely outside the bounds of economic coercion and the reduction of migration to a rational economic choice. . . . Appeals to the protection of children also calls upon strong liberal sentiments about the intimate family. . . . Excluding some families from liberal norms of familial intimacy, deeming some children unworthy of protection within our political community—these are all instances of normative

nationalism, and they provide ample grounds for ambivalence and dispute. (164)

Other scholars, however, worry that such appeals merely serve to reinscribe women in their maternal role (see, for example, Jenson, present volume).[8] They argue that focusing on the negative effect of mothers' migration on families is antifeminist because it may interfere with a woman's right to seek employment. The antifeminist implications are undeniable; in Poland and Ukraine, for example, Helma Lutz (present volume) found that absent mothers were being blamed for producing scores of "Euro-orphans."

Yet such concerns are not entirely without basis, and instead of denunciations, they call for constructive collective policies. Migration is never unconstrained. Whether they are pushed by a lack of opportunity in the home country; by difficult family or community circumstances; by national ideologies such as that of the Philippines, which emphasizes that its citizens must be willing to make sacrifices for their families or for the country; or by a more individualistic conviction that earning abroad and sending back remittances is part of their motherly duties— women leave for a reason (Segura 1994). And their leaving is rarely without consequences—sometimes positive, but too often negative.

Yet, even if the consequences of transnational maternal loss due to care worker migration are recognized and translated into political discourse, policy makers and activists still face significant challenges in seeking to address the issue. One reason is that the phenomenon is multiscalar in nature; that is, it plays out at many levels—inter- and transnationally, nationally, subnationally, locally, and within private households.

As a transnational issue, the regulation of care work migration requires a type of global governance that frequently founders on the question of state sovereignty. Although a number of relevant international conventions have been passed by the United Nations and the International Labour Organization concerning the rights of children (OHCHR 1989), migrants (OHCHR 1990), and, most recently, domestic workers (International Labour Organization 2011), key state players— often the United States—have refused to ratify these conventions on the grounds that they transgress national sovereignty. For example, the United States has ratified the United Nations Convention on the Rights of the Child, which stipulates that a child has the right to grow up in a familial environment (OHCHR 1989, preamble), but not the International Labour Organization's (2011) Domestic Workers Convention, which calls for paid annual leave (article 7 [g]), among other things.[9]

At the national level, immigration laws must be reformed to allow migrants to bring family members with them or to reduce the time required for family reunification. Canada's Live-in Caregiver Program, though not without its drawbacks, is one example of such a policy (Boyd, forthcoming; see also van Walsum 2009; Parreñas 2015). For migrants from nearby countries, temporary work visas could facilitate short-term work and circular migration—in effect, allowing intercountry commuting—so as to lessen the duration of maternal absence (Lutz 2011). For those migrating from afar, employers could be required to provide airfare to allow their employees to make regular return visits (again, this would require appropriate work visas, so they could go back and forth legally). And labor laws governing household employment could be tightened and vigorously enforced to improve components of working conditions, such as wages, hours, accommodations, and food.[10]

Because such reforms involve multiple policy domains, however, it is difficult for lawmakers—and activists—to coordinate their efforts and achieve meaningful changes. A recent report by the International Labour Organization and the United Nations Development Programme (2009, 128) proposes such sweeping measures as:

- Creating sufficient opportunities for decent work for men and women, so that people can earn enough income in their own countries to guarantee their families' financial well-being, without having to set out in search of more highly paid jobs, often of inferior quality, elsewhere, which usually require the family to separate [in other words, discouraging employment migration in the first place].
- Facilitating the return of those who migrate, helping family reunification through reintegration and training programs. . . .
- Establishing regulations that make it easier for the families of migrant workers to reunite.

- Guaranteeing that migrant workers have the same labor rights as others, and ensuring they have access to childcare. Developing information campaigns on their rights in this regard.
- Involving the employing sector as co-responsible for obeying the law and making it easier for working parents, for example, in terms of legislation regarding social protection.

But no receiving country has established these rights in full.

CONCLUSION

As long as the demand for care workers persists, and as long as "emerging economies" around the globe continue to offer few other economic opportunities, women—mothers—will undoubtedly continue to migrate to take up jobs in the rich countries. And as long as immigration restrictions impede family unification, and working conditions and expenses in destination countries make life stressful for low-paid female migrant workers, they will feel both the practical and emotional effects of their decisions. The practical consequences are relatively easy to spot; the emotional ones are more elusive—unless, as in the case of Yoselyn Ortega, they are splashed across newspapers around the world. But most, like Helena and her son and daughters, will continue to cope as best they can and suffer in silence.

NOTES

1. Most of the other newspapers followed suit; the online media were more nuanced, as will be discussed.
2. Though the circumstances are clearly different, U.S. historian Dea Boster (2015) has found examples of enslaved women becoming hysterical or even going mad in circumstances when they were separated from their children. The famous African American abolitionist Frederick Douglass once wrote, "My poor mother, like many other slave-women, had many *children*, but NO FAMILY!" (Douglass 1855, 37).
3. Starting in the 1910s, a number of states began offering mothers' or widows' pensions to lone mothers of legitimate children; these were the forerunner of the federal Aid to Dependent Children program (Goodwin 1997).

4.   Ironically, although migrants are not free to move back and forth across borders, researchers are, and thus are often asked by the migrants to serve as couriers.

5.   Data for this section stems from Oliveira's (2015) doctoral research, conducted from 2010 to 2013 in New York City and various towns in Mexico. The author employed multisited ethnographic methods to study the phenomenon of transnational motherhood and to examine transnational caregiving practices among women with mixed-status children in New York and Mexico. She interviewed and observed thirty children in Mexico (fifteen female, fifteen male, ranging in age from seven to eighteen), and thirty-seven children in New York City (twenty female, seventeen male, age four months to eighteen years). In addition, Oliveira recruited forty mothers in New York City, as well as fathers and caregivers, and more than sixty children and youths in Mexico. She surveyed 225 children, age seven to sixteen, in three schools in Puebla, to understand how maternal remittances influenced school achievement. Specifically, she compared the educational experiences and social trajectories of children who stayed in Mexico with those of undocumented children and youths brought to the United States and of those born in the United States. She refers to this arrangement as a "transnational care constellation," which is a recognizable pattern comprising the biological mother (the one who gave birth), children (in both countries), and caregivers in Mexico. The children and youths in these multifaceted relationships share the same biological mother, who has migrated to New York City, but their lives differ dramatically in terms of educational experience and familial support.

6.   In this sense, immigration laws should also be regarded as family laws (van Walsum 2009).

7.   Here Pratt has in mind the insistence on the part of international economic bodies such as the International Monetary Fund, the World Bank, and the Organisation for Economic Co-operation and Development that migration should be unconstrained and unfettered—that people around the globe should have the right to move wherever and whenever they want to in order to pursue economic opportunities and personal advancement, no matter the consequences to their families, communities, or home countries.

8.   And still others dispute Pratt's assumption that migration is, in itself, harmful. Geographer Deirdre McKay (2012), for example, argues that it is Eurocentric to impose a Western model of family formation on non-Western families. According to her, there is nothing new about Filipino/Filipina parents migrating to work; remittances "thicken" intimate ties. But Pratt (2012) argues that interview data show otherwise.

9.   Nevertheless, as Eileen Boris and Megan Undén (forthcoming) have shown, local domestic worker organizations have been able to use the International Labour Organization convention in efforts to leverage domestic workers' bill of rights legislation in several U.S. states.

10. See, for example, the initiatives of the National Domestic Workers Alliance to pass domestic workers' bill of rights legislation across the United States: http://www .domesticworkers.org/search/node/bill%20of%20rights. See also Boris and Undén (forthcoming).

REFERENCES

Badasu, Delali, and Sonya Michel. 2016. "On a Collision Course: Millennial Development Goals and Mothers' Migration." In *Women Migrant Workers: Ethical, Political and Legal Problems*, ed. Zahra Meghani, 75–100. New York: Routledge.

Berman, Taylor. 2012. "New Details Emerge About Yoselyn Ortega, the Alleged Killer Nanny." *Gawker*, October 12. http://gawker.com/5955414/new-details-emerge-about-yoselyn-ortega-the-alleged-nanny-killer.

Bettio, Francesca, Paula-Irene Villa, and Annamaria Simonazzi. 2006. "Changing Care Regimes and Female Migration." *Journal of European Social Policy* 16, no. 3: 271–85.

Boris, Eileen, and Jennifer Klein. 2006. "Organizing Home Care: Low-Waged Workers in the Welfare State." *Politics and Society* 34, no. 1: 81–108.

Boris, Eileen, and Rhacel Parreñas, eds. 2007. *Intimate Labors: Cultures, Technologies, and the Politics of Care*. Stanford, CA: Stanford University Press.

Boris, Eileen, and Megan Undén. Forthcoming. "From the Local to the Global: Circuits of Domestic Worker Organizing." In *Gender, Migration, and the Work of Care: A Multi-Scalar Approach to the Pacific Rim*, ed. Sonya Michel and Ito Peng. New York: Palgrave Macmillan.

Boster, Dea H. 2015. "No More Sick than Women Are Generally? Disability and Slave Motherhood in the Antebellum South." Paper presented at the Walter Prescott Webb Memorial Lectures, Department of History, University of Texas at Arlington, March.

Boyd, Monica. 2011. "Labour Migration for Care: Women Migrants in Canada Under the Live-in Caregiver Program." Paper presented at Rethinking Care and Migration in the Age of Low Fertility and Ageing Population Workshop, University of Toronto, March 9–10.

——. Forthcoming. "The Downward Slope: The Implications of Canada's Changing Migration Regime for Migrant Domestic Workers." In *Gender, Migration, and the Work of Care: A Multi-Scalar Approach to the Pacific Rim*, ed. Sonya Michel and Ito Peng. New York: Palgrave Macmillan.

Clark Hine, Darlene. 1989. "Rape and the Inner Lives of Black Women in the Middle West." *Signs* 14, no. 4: 912–20.

Clough, Patricia, and Jean Halley, eds. 2007. *The Affective Turn: Theorizing the Social*. Raleigh-Durham, NC: Duke University Press.

Daly, Michael. 2013. " 'Killer Nanny' Case: What the Krims Didn't Know About Yoselyn Ortega." *Daily Beast*, June 26. http://www.thedailybeast.com/articles/2013/06/26/killer-nanny-case-what-the-krims-didn-t-know-about-yoselyn-ortega.html.

Dell'Antonia, KJ. 2012. "A Neighbor's Thoughts on the Killings of Two Young Children." *New York Times*, October 26.

Douglass, Frederick. 1855. *My Bondage and My Freedom*. New York: Miller, Orton, and Mulligan. http://www.gutenberg.org/files/202/202-h/202-h.htm#link2H_4_0001.

Francisco, Valerie. 2015. "Multidirectional Care in Filipino Transnational Families. In *Engendering Transnational Voices*, ed. Guida Man and Rina Cohen, 99–116. Waterloo, ON: Wilfrid Laurier University Press.

Gillman, Ollie. 2015. "Nanny Accused of Stabbing Two Young Children to Death 'Because Their Parents Asked Her to Do More Work Around Their Upper West Side Apartment'

Appears in Court Looking Gaunt and Frail." *Daily Mail*, October 9. http://www.dailymail
.co.uk/news/article-3266903/Manhattan-nanny-accused-stabbing-two-young-children
-death-appears-court-looking-gaunt-frail.html.

Goodwin, Joanne. 1997. *Gender and the Politics of Welfare Reform: Mothers' Pensions in Chicago, 1911–1929*. Chicago: University of Chicago Press.

Hancock, Ange-Marie. 2004. *The Politics of Disgust: The Public Identity of the Welfare Queen*.
New York: New York University Press.

Hochschild, Arlie R. 2013. *The Outsourced Self: Intimate Life in Market Times*. New York:
Metropolitan Books.

Hondagneu-Sotelo, Pierrette, and Ernestine Avila. 1997. " 'I'm Here But I'm There': The
Meanings of Latina Transnational Motherhood." *Gender and Society* 11, no. 5: 548–71.

International Labour Organization. 2011. Domestic Workers Convention, 2011 (No. 189). http://
www.ilo.org/dyn/normlex/en/f?p=NORMLEXPUB:12100:0::NO::P12100_ILO_CODE:C189.

International Labour Organization and United Nations Development Programme (ILO/
UNDP). 2009. *Work and Family: Towards New Forms of Reconciliation with Social
Co-Responsibility*. Santiago: International Labour Organization and United Nations
Development Programme. http://www.ilo.org/wcmsp5/groups/public/---ed_protect
/---protrav/---travail/documents/publication/wcms_travail_pub_55.pdf.

Jacobs, Shayna. 2014. "Nanny Accused of Killing Two Children in Upper West Side Apartment
Blamed Their Parents." *Daily News*, November 15. http://www.nydailynews.com/new
-york/nyc-crime/nanny-accused-killing-children-blamed-parents-article-1.2011815.

Le Goff, Maelan. 2016. "Feminization of Migration and Trends in Remittances." *IZA World
of Labor*, January. http://wol.iza.org/articles/feminization-of-migration-and-trends-in
-remittances.pdf.

Lutz, Helma. 2011. *The New Maids: Transnational Women and the Care Economy*. London:
Zed Books.

McKay, Deirdre. 2012. *Global Filipino Migrants' Lives in the Virtual Village*. Bloomington:
Indiana University Press.

Michel, Sonya. 2014. "Care and Work-Family Policies." In *Oxford Handbook of U.S. Social
Policy*, ed. Daniel Béland, Christopher Howard, and Kimberly J. Morgan, 491–509. New
York: Oxford University Press.

Michel, Sonya, and Ito Peng. 2012. "All in the Family? Migrants, Nationhood, and Care
Regimes in Asia and North America." *Journal of European Social Policy* 22, no. 4: 406–20.

Mink, Gwendolyn. 2002. *Welfare's End*. Ithaca, NY: Cornell University Press.

Office of the United Nations High Commissioner for Human Rights (OHCHR). 1989. *Convention on the Rights of the Child*. http://www.ohchr.org/en/professionalinterest/pages/crc.aspx.

———. 1990. *International Convention on the Protection of the Rights of All Migrant Workers
and Members of Their Families*. http://www2.ohchr.org/english/bodies/cmw/cmw.htm.

Oliveira, Gabrielle. 2015. "Transnational Care Constellations: Mexican Immigrant Mothers
and their Children in Mexico and in New York City." PhD diss., Columbia University.
http://dx.doi.org/10.7916/D8RR1XBG.

Parkhurst, Jessie W. 1938. "The Role of the Black Mammy in the Plantation Household." *Journal of Negro History* 23 (July): 349–69.

Parreñas, Rhacel Salazar. 2005. *Children of Global Migration: Transnational Families and Gendered Woes*. Stanford, CA: Stanford University Press.

———. 2015. "Permanent and Transitional Guest Workers: Variations of Partial Citizenship Among Filipina Domestic Workers in the Diaspora." In *Race, Ethnicity and Welfare States: An American Dilemma?*, ed. Pauli Kettunen, Sonya Michel, and Klaus Petersen, 205–26. Cheltenham: Edward Elgar.

Poo, Ai-Jen. 2011. "A Twenty-First Century Organizing Model: Lessons from the New York Domestic Workers Bill of Rights Campaign." *New Labor Forum* 20, no. 1: 51–55.

Pratt, Geraldine. 2012. *Families Apart: Migrant Mothers and the Conflicts of Labor and Love*. Minneapolis: University of Minnesota Press.

Rashbaum, William K. 2012. "Nanny Charged in Fatal Stabbings Resented Her Employers, Law Enforcement Official Says." *New York Times*, November 5. http://www.nytimes.com/2012/11/06/nyregion/upper-west-side-nanny-resented-her-employers-police-say.html.

Rosenberg, Rebecca. 2013. " 'Killer Nanny' Yoselyn Ortega to Stand Trial, Judge Rejects Claims that 'The Defendant Is Tantamount to a Parakeet.' " *New York Post*, August 13. http://nypost.com/2013/08/13/killer-nanny-yoselyn-ortega-to-stand-trial-judge-rejects-claims-that-the-defendant-is-tantamount-to-a-parakeet.

Segura, Denise A. 1994. "Working at Motherhood: Chicana and Mexican Immigrant Mothers and Employment." In *Mothering: Ideology, Experience, and Agency*, ed. Evelyn Nakano Glenn, Grace Chang, and Linda Rennie Forcey, 211–36. New York: Routledge.

van Walsum, Sarah K. 2009. "Transnational Mothering, National Immigration Policy, and European Law: The Experience of the Netherlands." In *Migrations and Mobilities: Citizenship, Borders, and Gender*, ed. Seyla Benhabib and Judith Resnik, 228–54. New York: New York University Press.

Zelizer, Viviana A. 2005. *The Purchase of Intimacy*. Princeton, NJ: Princeton University Press.

12

EURO-ORPHANS AND THE STIGMATIZATION OF MIGRANT MOTHERHOOD

HELMA LUTZ

One of the most tenacious instances of universalism—the
belief in the universality of something—is motherhood,
doubtlessly the most intimate of relationships. The current state
of the allegedly globalized world makes this universalism both
urgently necessary and deeply problematic.

—MIEKE BAL, "FACING"

ieke Bal's (2012) statement suitably summarizes the controversy about the ambiguities of migrant women's motherhood. Feminist historians and sociologists have demonstrated that the idea and practice of motherhood has changed and shifted radically over time (Koven and Michel 1993; Michel 1999; Hochschild 2012). In this chapter, I look at the changing meanings of "good" motherhood in the context of migration. My point of departure is research on migrant mothers from Eastern Europe moving to the western and southern European Union.

Driven by the economic difficulties of their countries as a result of system transformation since the early 1990s and an ardent desire to improve their families' living conditions, millions of women have taken jobs abroad. They are working in particular as caretakers for elderly people, as child minders, or as domestic workers in private households.

A central feature of this migration is "transnational motherhood," a term that characterizes the efforts of biological mothers to perform social mothering across wide geographic distances. The particularity of this mothering practice lies in a (self-organized) rotation system, which enables the women to commute for periods of six weeks to three months rather than having to emigrate. In this way, migrant mothers remain emotionally attached to their families of origin across wide geographic distances while taking very onerous economic obligations upon themselves (see Lutz 2011; Lutz and Palenga-Möllenbeck 2010; 2011; 2012).

This chapter discusses migrant women's motherhood from a particular angle: it deals with public manifestations of moral outrage about migrant parents, and especially mothers, who leave their children behind in the custody of family members, as it is voiced in the media of the sending countries in Central and Eastern Europe. These children are referred to in a variety of ways, including "children left behind" or "home-alone children." Countries also have their preferred terms, such as "abandoned children" (Romania), "social orphans" (Ukraine), "Euro-orphans" (Poland), or "white orphans" (Moldavia). The term "orphan" is factually incorrect because the majority of the nonmigrating children stay with a relative—more precisely, with their mother, if the father migrates, or with their grandmother or an aunt, in cases where the mother is the migrant. In a few instances, fathers become caregivers. Nevertheless, the term "orphan" is used as a new label for migrants' children. It now functions as a powerful stigmatizing metaphor with far-reaching consequences for the assessment of female migration and as a label for the problematization of transnational motherhood. In some countries, the "orphan debate" has culminated in the establishment of legal measures requiring parents to ensure custodianship for their children before leaving their countries, and in social pressure calling on mothers to return "home."

I present here the results of a comprehensive media analysis of Polish and Ukrainian newspapers from 1997 to 2008, to show radical changes in perceptions of Polish and Ukrainian citizens migrating to Western and Southern Europe. This evaluation covers the time span from not long after the system transition, when these people were praised as modernizers and investors in the national economies and admired as "Euromigrants," to ten years later, when the focus changed to the presentation of migration as generating disturbing effects for the sending countries. Parents were then blamed for irresponsibility and, in particular, women were accused of bad motherhood performance.

The final part of the chapter analyzes this discourse using three different modes, which are not mutually exclusive but rather complementary. First, the "orphan debate" as an expression of moral panic is interpreted as a reaction to the sending countries' incapacity to deal with the consequences of absent working mothers, caused by feminized migration—a situation that, to a certain extent, resembles the debate about willful neglect of "latchkey children" by working mothers in the 1940s and 1950s. Second, the debate corresponds with negative evaluations and rejections of transnational motherhood in both sending and receiving countries; this form of "motherhood from a distance" is labeled detrimental to the development of children by experts (psychologists, pedagogues, and teachers), who consider caring from afar to be a deficient mothering practice. Third, the "orphan" is not only a discursive figure in (Eastern) Europe but is also now used by transnational organizations (including the United Nations Convention on the Rights of the Child, UNESCO, and others), which report that several million children worldwide are "left behind" by their migrating parents/mothers. This indicates that, disregarding the large variety of child-rearing practices worldwide, the physical absence of mothers is now globally labeled as pathological and is made the dominant element in the assessment of motherhood.

EURO-ORPHANS AND SOCIAL ORPHANS

The initial intention of this press analysis was not to find and dissect articles on "children left behind" but to collect articles about migration, transnational families, parenting, and care in a broad sense. In the context of the research project Landscapes of Care Drain, covering the years 1997 to 2008, the aim was to create a complementary and comparable collection of articles in two predominantly sending countries, Poland and Ukraine, and in one of the main West European receiving countries, Germany.[1] In Poland and Ukraine, the main issues discussed, well into the 2000s, were the recruitment of workers, work opportunities abroad, and the positive and negative consequences of migration. It was not until the late 2000s that the national debate about the abandonment of children accelerated. Therefore, our findings were unexpected. In order to locate this shift, I will give a brief overview of the collected data and then focus more closely on the "orphan" debate, starting with Poland and then moving on to the findings from Ukraine.[2]

POLAND

In Poland, labor migration has had a long tradition, since the nineteenth century. After World War II, the prototype of East–West migration was established by refugees from the socialist bloc, who left without any chance of returning, while seasonal and short-term labor migration occurred only within the socialist bloc. Following the liberalization of border regimes after 1989, this pattern changed significantly, and transnational, circular labor migration is now the dominant form of migration. Migrants no longer take their families with them to the places where they work; instead, they commute for intervals ranging from one week to several months while their families stay behind. Since the early 1990s, at least 10 percent of the population has been involved in this form of commuter migration.[3] Another new phenomenon is that of "feminized migration," which can be observed primarily in domestic and care work (Lutz 2011). In parallel with this development, Poland, like many other countries in Eastern Europe, has undergone an economic transformation toward a neoliberal market economy, which has resulted in high unemployment, affecting women more than men (Kałwa 2007).[4] During the 1990s, female unemployment increased from 54.8 percent, in 1995, to 61.2 percent, in 1997 (Fuszara 2000) and has only slowly declined.

The evaluation of migration in Polish newspapers until 2007 was dominated by positive views of its effects on the Polish economy, among which were highlighted the reduction of unemployment, the easing of the burden on social security funds and the massive deterioration of welfare state provision, money transfers plus related investment, and the extended vocational training of workers. Depending on the ideological orientation of the newspaper, labor migration was presented as an expression of entrepreneurship, as a "success story," or as an opportunity in times of crisis.[5]

With regard to gender, it is remarkable that, prior to 2007, female migration was more implicitly than explicitly addressed. Despite the huge number of women migrating during this time, the press neglected the issue. However, starting in late 2007, a major change occurred, when public discourse switched from relative silence to a very lively interest in the children of labor migrants.

The trigger of the debate, a seemingly unspectacular event, was a short documentary film produced as an assignment in 2007 by the then eighteen-year-old Aleksander Makowiak and his classmates, with the title *Alex Home Alone*. Makowiak, a computer sciences student at the Poznan Transport School, chose the theme of children whose parents migrate and work abroad, with Alex himself featured as the film's protagonist. The film was based on Alex's own experience: his father had left in 2006 to work in the Netherlands, and his mother joined him six months later. Alex's little brother, the dog, and the turtle followed a short time later. The documentary shows Alex coping with being "home alone" while staying in the family's flat. Some hilarious situations are recounted. For example, when he has to peel potatoes for the first time in his life, he cuts them into squares, and he places slips of paper around the whole flat to serve as reminders.

An article about this film in *Gazeta Wyborcza* (December 28, 2007) sparked a series of further items and, as a result, international newspapers took up the story. The Dutch daily *De Volkskrant* (June 11, 2008), for example, announced, in an article headlined "Euro-Orphan," that hundreds of thousands of Polish workers were leaving their children behind. In an interview with the Dutch journalist, however, Alex took a positive view of his parents' migration; he said it had been his own decision to stay behind and that he would follow them after finishing school.

The screening of the film coincided with the launching of a survey by two nongovernmental organizations (NGOs), Fundacja Prawo Europejskie and Instytut Europejski w Warszawie, about the effect of labor migration on families, especially children, and on so-called Euro-orphanhood, as the authors identified the problem in the title of the report (Mikuła 2008). *Gazeta Wyborcza*, in particular, took up the issue, producing items on the topic over a period of seventeen months, and was the first to use the term that has become "Euro-orphans" (*Eurosieroctwo*). The effect of this term was immense; it became the emblematic and discursive figure of the so-called Euro-orphan debate. The term quickly developed into a buzzword that was used in virtually all press articles, and also in research reports (see, for example, Majchrzyk-Mikuła 2008), without ever being clearly defined or examined. For example, a representative of the Poznan education department claimed that children living with only one parent while the other parent works abroad suffer from the same detrimental effects as those of divorced parents. In addition, scholars affirmed that such children manifest the same behavior as traditional orphans (*De Volkskrant*, June 11, 2008). The prefix *Euro-*, which was used in the press from 2003 onward in a positive way in terms like "Euro-migrants" and "Euro-labor," changed its character.

Gazeta Wyborcza's coverage of Euro-orphans during the first year of the debate was characterized by enraged headlines such as "Orphans Due to the Migration of the Parents" (December 28, 2007); "Almost 8,000 Euro-Orphans in the Province of Lodz" (January 27, 2008); "110,000 Euro-Orphans in Poland Are Expecting Help" (May 12, 2008); "Who Helps the Euro-Orphans?" (May 13, 2008); "Parents Earn Lots of Money and Their Children Are Suffering" (July 19, 2008); "Parents Are Not Replaceable" (August 12, 2008); "The Government Counts Euro-Orphans; Parents Do Not Keep Their Promise to Return" (August 16, 2008); "Do Not Forsake Your Children" (September 11, 2008); and "Read This Before You Leave Your Child" (October 3, 2008).

The indignant tone of the articles about the situation of the left-behind children is legitimated by quoting experts such as psychologists, teachers, police officers, and politicians. These professionals all describe the behavior of the children as pathological. On July 3, 2008, *Gazeta Wyborcza* covered the release of a report commissioned by the Ombudsperson for Children's Rights, "Schools Do Not Support the Euro-Orphans." The report's aim was to question schoolchildren about the effects of their parents' labor migration. The study was carried out by the sociologist Bartlomiej Walczak (2008), who polled 2,597 children in 110 schools. Walczak's findings rejected the massive number of 110,000 Euro-orphans often reported in the press, calculating that the majority of parents leaving for longer than a year were fathers rather than mothers, who were found to stay away for shorter periods. Walczak concluded that from three thousand to six thousand children ages nine to eighteen were living apart from both parents for more than one year. While their parents were away, these children usually lived with a relative such as a grandmother or aunt. However, the release of this report did not terminate the exaggeration of numbers or change the style of reporting.

Most of the articles published in the newspapers initially attribute the situation to *parents*, but as soon as a more detailed report is provided, it is *mothers* who get the blame:

> "Fifteen-year-old Maciek walked for three days through the streets, sleeping with friends. While the police, his teacher, and his father searched for him, his mother, who had left the country for work, did not" (*Gazeta Wyborcza*, May 12, 2008).
> "Bartek slips into the sleeve of a blouse that his mother had left behind and falls asleep. The soft fabric smells like Joanna. . . . He pulls on the blouse and wraps the sleeves around him, as if they would embrace him. When he feels the warmth and her smell, his stomach does not hurt anymore" (*Rzeczpospolita*, January 22, 2008).

When mothers are not directly pilloried, their absence is given an emotional significance through the description of their children's emotional problems.

Only a very small number of articles identify left-behind children as a feature of migration that might generate more positive results:

> Sabina, nineteen years old: "Father emigrated two years ago. His friend who had found himself work in Norway persuaded him. He drove away and everything improved. Previously, he always had to stay away in Warsaw or Lublin for a whole week. He would come back on a Friday night and leave again on Saturday morning. He was always tired and slept a lot. Mom worked too—up to twelve hours a day, and at night she cooked the meals. Now she no longer has to work; she is always at home, cleaning; we always have lunch together. And we talk to Dad every day via Skype; we see each other via webcam. Every two months, he comes home for two or three weeks. Then, we go for a drive and have a barbecue with Granny, walk along the Wisłok (river), and play volleyball. In Norway, he has completely changed his perspective on life, because the people there devote much time to their families, and that's what he does now." (*Gazeta Wyborcza*, May 21, 2008)

Sabina's account highlights a coping strategy that normalizes absent parenthood and evaluates it positively. Concurrently, it includes a shift toward a conservative family constellation in which the father becomes the single breadwinner and the mother is a housewife. Here, normalization comprises the establishment of a gender order that was rather exceptional in the double-wage-earner years of state socialism (see Lutz and Palenga-Möllenbeck 2014).

UKRAINE

In postcommunist Ukraine, the ideological orientation of the papers follows the divide between a pro-Russian preference and an anti-Russian position, which is generally identified as a split between the eastern (pro-Russian) and the western (anti-Russian) parts of the country. We selected newspapers representing both preferences.[6]

Compared to Poland, Ukraine was in even greater turmoil and difficulty after the transition from communist rule. The level of poverty and the scale of the economic breakdown during the transition process were significantly higher than in Poland.[7] By 2011, the number of labor migrants (*zarobitchany*) was estimated at seven million (approximately 15 percent of the population), five million of whom were considered to be staying abroad temporarily, while the remaining two million were thought to have left the country permanently (Keryk 2004; Zimmer 2007; International Organization for Migration 2011). The majority of the *zarobitchany* are believed to work as undocumented migrants in Western and Southern Europe as well as in the Russian Federation.

Although migration to Russia is dominated by male migrants from the Russian-speaking eastern part of the country, typically working in construction, migrants from the western part of Ukraine are predominantly female. Women who emigrate to Western and Southern Europe are primarily employed in domestic care work. Historically, during the communist era, short-term migration as small-scale traders to other countries of the socialist bloc was a well-known and regular income-generating activity in Ukraine, and both men and women participated. However, the majority of migrants from the Ukrainian Soviet Socialist

Republic (1922–91) to the Soviet Federation were male, organized as "working brigades" and staying abroad temporarily.

It was the increase in female labor migration from Ukraine to Poland and to Southern and Western Europe that caused strong media interest and public controversy throughout the period of our investigation. Among the themes covered by the press, human trafficking, including prostitution and white slavery, ranks high in the perils of labor migration. In total, about 30 percent of the articles dealt with this issue.

A distinctive feature of the Ukrainian press coverage, divergent from the Polish, was that female migration was explicitly addressed from 2000 onwards. In 2002, then Ukrainian president Leonid Kuchma told Italian journalists, during a state visit to Italy, that Ukrainian women migrants in Italy were prostitutes, too idle to work in Ukraine (Keryk 2004), a remark that did not make it into the Ukrainian press at the time. Only during the Orange Revolution was Kuchma quoted and shamed for this remark, during the election campaigns of the Orange Revolution leaders Yulia Timoshenko and Victor Yushchenko. Then migrants were praised as mobile, modern, and diligent citizens: "It is not the sluggards who are leaving. Only the best are leaving Ukraine, those who take over the responsibility for their families and those who are able to overcome difficulties" (*Ukraina Moloda*, September 15, 2004). With this twist, migrants became heroes instead of prostitutes and victims. After his accession to office in 2005, the new president, Yushchenko, apologized for the statements of his predecessor and asked the Ukrainian migrants abroad to return.

It is important to emphasize that, with few exceptions, until 2005 migrant women were not blamed for abandoning their children. It was *Lvivska Gazeta*, from Western Ukraine, that started the controversy, with articles such as "Abandoned Children" (March 23, 2005) and "The Orphans Whose Parents Are Alive" (July 14, 2005), and first used the term "social orphan," which originates in debates about social poverty, street children, and abandoned children in orphanages. Afterward, it took two to three years before the national press picked it up. Overall, then, *Lvivska Gazeta* is the main protagonist in this discussion. As in Poland, the metaphor of the social orphan received its force from scandalous stories, according to which migrating parents had left their children in the custody of children's homes.[8]

Lvivska Gazeta's investigations included interviews with experts such as Iryna Kurevina, a researcher at the National Institute for Strategic Studies in Lviv:

> It is important to change our legislation. For example, the passport authorities should not give permission to emigration to those citizens with minors. In Stryj, an investigation was conducted and it was found that children with parents abroad are bad performers in school, they miss school more often, but they have more money and can therefore afford more. This is a serious problem, which we call social orphaning. (August 29, 2006)

The nationwide daily *Facty i Kommentari* (June 14, 2007) picked up the issue: "Mommy, why are you working in Italy if everything you send us is drunk away by Father? Please come back, Mommy. My brother and I will provide for you." The article is about a telephone call to the *Facty i Kommentari*'s editor by a twelve-year-old girl whose mother had been away working in Rome for four years. She asked whether it was true that *Fakty* was read by Ukrainians abroad. If so, she invited the journalist to visit her village so that she could tell him about her life without a mother, in the hope that her mother would read the article and finally return. The journalist presents a gripping story, including various voices—those of children and a grandmother left behind, teachers, and regional politicians. It describes the rapidly changing environment and economy of a formerly prosperous village that has become dependent on the flow of remittances from female migrants to Italy, like a patient on an intravenous drip. Moreover, it provides a good deal of evidence about the fathers' total retreat from their responsibilities in this environment.

This article is typical of many others, declaring the mothers' migration a personal choice rather than an economic necessity for the families. As a result, aftereffects such as the misery of the children, the hardship of the grandmother who suffers from feeling that she is a bad replacement for her daughter as primary caregiver, and the descent of the father into alcoholism are all presented as the logical consequence of the mother's migration, with all contributing to the emergence of "social orphanhood." The total absence of any critical engagement with the term "orphan" on the part of the journalist means that there is no consideration of the economic or social failures of the political system, which resulted in unemployment for more than 50 percent of the population in the sending region.

From a different perspective, the same facts could be presented as a story about a highly intelligent and self-reliant young girl from the countryside who, at the age of twelve, has the courage to call a journalist and ask him to come and publish her story. She is already mature enough to tell her mother that she should get rid of a drunkard husband, showing a capacity for insight rare in most children her age. It could have been a story about a close and loving relationship between a grandmother and her two grandchildren, who are socially and emotionally extremely capable, good students in school, and diligent helpers in the household, or a story about the immense financial investment of mothers who help their children to achieve education under the most miserable of circumstances. It might have been a different story if at any point the journalist had called the mother and asked for her perspective.

None of this was done, however. The mothers are the great absentees in all of these stories. Once an article starts from the perspective of social orphanhood, it is doomed to become not only a heartbreaker of a story but also one that naturalizes the mother–child dyad and regards physical closeness between mother and children as the prerequisite for a healthy and "normal" upbringing.

By the autumn of 2007, a national debate about social orphans was in full swing, and on May 19, 2008, the theme reached the national news channel 1+1. In a three-minute report entitled "The Children of Migrant Workers," it is affirmed that the state is obliged to care for the left-behind children of migrant workers. Therefore, according to the report, Ukraine's parliament is preparing a law under which parents cannot leave the country without applying for a temporary custodian for their children during the time they are way. If relatives cannot look after a child, the child must be placed in a state institution.

Two years later, on May 12, 2010, a law entitled Legal Changes Concerning the Combat of Social Orphanage in Families of Citizens Working Abroad as Part of the Civil Code and the Family Law was passed by the Ukrainian parliament.[9]

COMPARISON OF THE TWO CASES

At first sight, it seems that the Ukrainian press targeted, in particular, *mothers* for leaving their children, whereas in the Polish debate *parents* are blamed. A closer analysis, however, demonstrates that, in the cases serving as a description of the left-behind situation in Poland, mothers and not fathers were incriminated. Thus, a trend of unequal perceptions of gender roles and expectations is visible in the press coverage in both countries.

Comparing the negative representation of migrant mothers in public discourse with the observation of practices in transnational families (Lutz and Palenga-Möllenbeck 2012) highlights the limits on economic and social citizenship rights that now exist—such as in relation to economic and social participation. During the socialist period, mothers' obligation to work went hand in hand with their care responsibilities, but currently there is no significant state support, in terms of childcare facilities, to reconcile transnational work and family life. It is also clear that, in the two sending countries, fathers are not considered responsible for the care of their children when the mother is away.

In both countries, lawmakers are in a difficult position. On the one hand, they embrace the economic advantages associated with the remittances sent by migrant men *and* women. On the other hand, they are under pressure because, although the majority of articles focus on parents and mothers, the state, in many cases, is blamed for ignoring the reality of child abandonment and for doing nothing about the problem. The highly exaggerated figures and the stories about children's misery and hardship circulating in the media of both countries, which cannot be considered the result of serious journalism, enhance the scandalization of the problem as a whole.

Ultimately, cornered by this press coverage, both governments launched restrictive responses to hamper parents' departure. But, at the same time, neither government is prepared to change direction and return to a broad provision of care facilities and support comparable to that of pretransition times. Instead, supported by NGOs and the Catholic and Orthodox churches, right-wing nationalist parties adopt educational measures and campaigns teaching a style of parenthood in which the "good mother" figure plays the leading role.

So, why has the left-behind child controversy become such an important issue in the sending countries? Why has it occurred at this particular time, and what is at stake in this debate?

MORAL PANIC

My first interpretation arises from the fact that, within a very short period of time, the orphan metaphor became a heated topic and a buzzword. It is helpful to look at the work of media analytics in relation to the creation of moral panic by using certain coverage tools, such as headlines that are relevant and significant for many members of a given society. The term "moral panic" as an illustration of social anxiety is employed when press coverage creates exaggerated attention, exaggerated events, distortion, or stereotyping (Cohen 1972). The emergence of a moral panic, however, is not just a creation of journalists; a necessary condition for the transformation of headlines into a moral outcry is a strong reaction to these stories on the part of the readership (Goode and Nachman 1994).

In the "orphan" debate, the condition of children being left behind by migrating mothers is presented as a threat not only to an individual child's upbringing but also to society as a whole, as a long-lasting and serious problem. Once a problem was identified by the use of the label "orphan," a "signification spiral" (Hall et al. 1978) was set in motion and discrete moral panics developed into a single, larger anxiety. This ensured the career of the "Euro-orphan" label and also turned it into a genre. For instance, numerous films on the subject can now be found on YouTube and other social media.

It is thus no accident that the focus of the debate is on children as symbols of the future of society. In a certain sense, the "orphan debate" can be interpreted as a legitimate way of expressing anger about everything that went wrong in the transition process. In his polemical article "Using Children as a Moral Shield," the British sociologist Frank Furedi (2013) writes, "Mention the word 'child' and people will listen. Raise the moral stakes by claiming that a 'child is at risk' and people will not just listen but endorse your demand that 'something must be done.'"

It is obvious that the feminization of migration in the sending countries was not automatically perceived as a transgression of gender norms, and thus a problem for society, in the first place, but was identified as the root cause of society's changing features after the consequences of this development were labeled as orphanhood. This label enabled people to express their concern that things were out of control, and it helped to identify the causers and the victims.

"When traditional norms and values no longer appear to have much relevance to people's lives . . . [then] they are most susceptible to moral panics. Against this background, an ordinary event like a woman leaving her children at home can assume extraordinary significance as a symbol of social chaos" (Furedi 1994). Furedi's statement, written in quite a different context, inspired me to look at earlier debates about child neglect and women's role in society. One obvious comparison is the debate about "latchkey children," which started in the 1940s in the United States. This occurred when "wartime stories published about America's 'latchkey children' were overwrought in their lamentations for the suffering boys and girls, locked in cars, scared and lonely, or wandering the street, looking for trouble" (Tuttle 1995, 93). The term is thought to have originated in an NBC television documentary broadcast in 1944, which showed the situation of children whose fathers had been called up to serve in World War II and whose mothers were working in factories. According to historian William Tuttle, working mothers had to confront hostility to the idea of mothers working outside the home, even in defense plants, like the famous Rosie the Riveter. "Feeding this sentiment were not only long-standing gender stereotypes but also a slew of wartime magazine articles and speeches by Father Edward J. Flanagan of Boys Town, J. Edgar Hoover of the FBI, and other defenders of father-led families in which the mother dutifully stays at home" (3). Extensive press coverage about neglected infants was the order of the day, and the ulterior purpose of the exaggeration of the children's misery is interpreted by Tuttle as a way of discrediting working mothers.

Tuttle's (1995, 95) example of the public's practice of shaming and blaming the mothers during that time shows amazing similarities with the present-day orphan debate: " 'Who's going to take care of me, Mother, if you take a war-plant job?' So asked the curly blond–haired boy of three or four pictured in the May 1943 issue of *Better Homes and Gardens*. The boy looked sad, but resigned to his fate." The parallel to the Ukrainian twelve-year-old is striking.

Another commonality with this debate is the private solutions mothers looked for to provide care for their children. During wartime, about 30 to 45 percent of working mothers left the care of their children to relatives other than the husband or older children. "Perhaps most importantly, grandparents filled much of the void. One grandmother even suggested, 'If anyone asks for a name for this war, it's 'Grandmother's War'" (Tuttle 1995, 96). The latchkey children panic and the orphan debate both, and in common, represent a projection of moral decay caused by working mothers.

TRANSNATIONAL MOTHERHOOD AS DEFICIENT MOTHERING PRACTICE

A complementary interpretation to the moral panic is connected to the fear that families will fall apart when mothers go transnational. This anxiety is based on the belief that, when biological mothers leave their children behind, it is to the detriment of the children.

Most scholarly work on this issue shows that researchers disagree about the idea that biological mothers are the natural and optimal caretakers for their children and cannot be replaced. Some authors focus on the disadvantages for left-behind kids and the traumatization of children caused by the migration, and therefore absence, of biological mothers (Parreñas 2005; Pratt 2012), while others show that the well-being of the children depends to a large degree on the competence of those persons who function as a care replacement (Lutz 2011; Rerrich 2012).

A quick overview of the transnational mothers debate shows that, in recent years, a growing number of studies have dealt with distant or transnational parenting, in particular with mothering from a distance and the situation of children left behind. Among these are:

- studies focusing on the relation between financial support and educational performances of children left behind (such as, for example, Nicholas 2008), the result of which is evaluated positively;

- studies that underline the negative effects of the care drain, and particularly the consequences of the absence of mothers (see, for example, Gamburd 2000; Hochschild and Ehrenreich 2003; Parreñas 2005; Phoenix 2009);
- studies that argue that the exchange of emotions and intimacy is even improved by the (virtual) co-presence of physically absent parents (while the hands-on daily care is provided by members of the extended family). Using new technologies, migrants create a sense of global connection through text messages and interface calls, showing feelings that many of them did not express before working abroad (McKay 2007; Madianou and Miller 2011); and
- studies arguing that the outcome of the care chain cannot be characterized as exclusively negative or positive (Zentgraf and Chinchilla 2012).

Some authors (Hondagneu-Sotelo and Avila 1997; Parreñas 2005) have drawn attention to the important influence of care substitution and care arrangements in transnational families. They have underlined the fact that gender relations are at the heart of these care arrangements, because the core question in care arrangements concerns the gender-specific distribution of care responsibilities. All in all, these studies suggest that the question of gender norms and ideologies in the sending country seems to be an important issue not only for care arrangements in transnational families but also at the level of the sending country's responses to the absence of mothers in their families.

Any positive perspectives are completely absent from the orphan debate in Poland and Ukraine, however, and it is likely that embracing transnational motherhood practices jeopardizes traditional gender relations and would require a public debate about new forms of parenting and fatherhood, which is a challenge these societies cannot presently face.

THE GLOBAL LEFT-BEHIND CHILD

One of the most striking discoveries I made during my research was that the debate about abandoned children is not confined to Eastern Europe but has a global dimension. Cortes (2007), for example, estimates that the number of left-behind children in Ecuador was 150,000 in 2000, while Coronel and Unterreiner (2007) estimate that 1.5 million children in the Philippines were left behind. The anthropologist and historian Annika Pissin (2013) even quotes a report that states that the number of children in China classified as left-behind children (*liushou ertong*) is as high as fifty-eight million. These are children of internal migrants moving from the countryside to the emerging factory cities, where the denial of access to housing facilities for the elderly and children is forcing parents to leave their children behind in rural areas (Biao 2007).

In a finding that confirms my analysis of the orphan debate in Eastern Europe, Pissin (2013) acknowledges that the data are not hard facts but only estimates based on guesswork. As in Eastern Europe, the term *liushou ertong* is applied not only to children whose parents have both migrated to work but also to children whose fathers alone have left— which is the majority of the cases in China. Much as in Eastern Europe, grandparents and members of the extended family are taking over the hands-on care for these children, and "in general their situation is not much worse than that of those living with other family members in the same community," writes Chinese scholar Xiang Biao (2007, 180).

Whereas Biao considers the controversy to be a reaction to dramatic social transformation in urban China, Pissin (2013) highlights the fact that the "left-behind debate" arises in countries with myriad child-rearing practices, and she argues that the global emergence of this category must have come from global organizations. She traces the debates in various organizations and actions of the United Nations, starting with the Year of the Child in 1979 and including the United Nations Convention on the Rights of the Child in 1989, which contains a standard definition of childhood and children's rights; sets idealized universal standards for all children, tailored to the Western, middle-class model; and defines childhood as the period between birth and the age of eighteen, while disregarding cultural differences and the realities of children's lives. Since then, the Western nuclear family model has evolved into a universalized ideal and has become the yardstick for the evaluation of children's well-being worldwide. Children growing up in fragmented families or in migrant families are now considered part of an "at-risk" category. UNESCO produced numerous reports about left-behind children on all five continents from 2005 onwards, later followed by NGOs like HelpAid.

These observations certainly resonate with my own research results on Eastern Europe, where, among the "players," there are many transnational, Catholic-based NGOs like La Strada, Fondazione l'Albero della Vita, and Fondazione Patrizio Paoletti, which specialize in picking up the topic, producing reports, launching campaigns, and establishing offices in the sending countries. These organizations seek to position themselves as the only advocates of children's rights in negotiations with UNESCO and UNICEF and are urging the European Union to take action to support the left-behind—via, for example, the Brussels-based union of organizations Children Left Behind.

For this reason, I agree with Pissin's (2013, 12) conclusion that the phenomenon exceeds regional or national dimensions and should instead be identified as the "global left-behind child," which is closely linked to the universal application of expert language across national borders. Pissin also identifies China's recent promotion of family policies, with a focus on nuclear families, the one-child rule, and the emphasis on good education, as an indicator of the heightened monitoring of bodies and the creation of a "quality population" (9). Although the dimensions of China's system transformation are much bigger than that in Eastern Europe, biopolitics are playing an enormous role in the creation of global capitalism in both cases (Randeria 2009).

In both cases, too, there is an element of demographic fear, albeit in different directions, because China is afraid of population growth whereas sending countries in Eastern Europe dread the loss of citizens through migration, which is seen as leading to doomsday scenarios of loss in a rapidly changing society and an upside-down world. Moreover, because mothers have always been construed as symbols of the nation, their departure symbolizes the disintegration of the state as a whole (Lutz, Phoenix, and Yuval-Davis 1995; Yuval-Davis 1997), and mothers are the first to experience this pressure.

Because migration encompasses a physical movement over geographic distances, it is understandable that a counterdiscourse against migration puts so much emphasis on physical closeness between mother and child as a psychological and social necessity for the child as it grows up. This analysis has demonstrated that, in the universal application of this belief, there is no space left for the acceptance and promotion of alternative care arrangements. Indeed, to return to the words of Mieke Bal (2012) quoted at the start of this chapter, the extent to which historically well-established models of nonbiological forms of mothering are now pathologically framed as breaches of a norm renders the universalization of motherhood deeply problematic.

NOTES

I thank Jane Jenson, Ewa Palenga-Möllenbeck, Yevgeniya Wirz, and Anna Amelina for their support and helpful comments.

1. Poland is also a receiving country of domestic and care workers from Ukraine, Belarus, and Russia. The period of inquiry was chosen against the background of the negotiations leading toward Poland's accession to European Union membership in 2004.

2. The press collection and analysis of the Polish part was done by Ewa Palenga-Möllenbeck, and the Ukrainian part by Yevgeniya Wirz. We worked on the comparison and interpretation together. For the data analysis, we used the method of critical discourse analysis established by the German scholar Siegfried Jäger (2001).

3. According to the latest microcensus (2011), out of 38.5 million Poles, about 3.6 million have been absent from their homes for three to twelve months per year (Anacka et al. 2014, 12). The feminization of migration from Poland is revealed in the fact that the number of female migrants is constantly increasing, to 52 percent in 2011 (26).

4. In 2006, the national unemployment rate was still 20 percent.

5. The analysis here draws on 316 articles (1997–2008) from the following national daily newspapers: 138 articles from *Gazeta Wyborcza* (left-liberal), 105 articles from the conservative *Rzeczpospolita*, 19 from the yellow press *FAKT*, and 54 from the Silesian regional paper, *Nowa Trybuna Opolska* (Silesia is a migrant-sending region).

6. We selected 616 articles (1997–2008) from the national papers *Fakty i Kommentary* (a populist tabloid publishing in Russian) and *Ukraina Moloda* (conservative-liberal, publishing in Ukrainian); the regional *Lvivska Gazeta Visnyk Mista* (conservative-patriotic); and the yellow press paper *15 Minut* (free-of-charge tabloid, distributed in Russian and in Ukrainian). It is important to note that *Lvivska Gazeta* focuses on the Western Ukrainian region of Lviv, a sending area for migrant women.

7. The average income level differentials are still high: 1:4 between Germany and Poland and 1:10 between Germany and Ukraine, as of January 2013.

8. Starting in 2007, the figure of 7.5 to 9 million children left behind was circulating. In an effort to trace the source of these numbers, I found a survey which estimated the number of Ukrainians working abroad at 7 million, only 6 percent of whom are said to be childless (*Lvivska Gazeta*, July 5, 2006).

9. This law is called the Feldman law after the deputy Oleksandr Feldman, a member, first, of Timoshenko's party and, later, of the Party of Regions, who was the leader of the Parliamentary Commission for Human Rights.

REFERENCES

Anacka, Marta, Jan Brzozowski, Henryk Chaupczak, Agnieszka Fihel, Grayna Firlit-Fesnak, Micha Garapich, Izabela Grabowska-Lusiñska et al. 2014. *Spoleczne skutki poakcesyjnych migracji ludnosci Polski: Raport Komitetu Badan nad Migracjami* [Social effects of post-accession migration of Polish population: Report of the committee for research on migration studies]. Warsaw: Polska Akademia Nauk.

Bal, Mieke. 2012. "Facing: Intimacy Across Divisions." In *The Global and the Intimate: Feminism in Our Time*, ed. Geraldine Pratt and Victoria Rosner, 119–44. New York: Columbia University Press.

Biao, Xiang. 2007. "How Far Are the Left-Behind Left Behind? A Preliminary Study in Rural China." *Population, Space and Place* 13, no. 3: 179–91.

Cohen, Stanley. 1972. *Folk Devils and Moral Panics*. London: MacGibbon and Kee.

Coronel, F. K., and F. Unterreiner. 2007. *Increasing the Impact of Remittances on Children's Rights: Philippines Paper*. Working paper. http://www.unicef.org/policyanalysis/files/Increasing _the_impact_of_remittances_on_childrens_rights.pdf.

Cortes, Rosalía. 2007. *Children and Women Left Behind in Labor Sending Countries: An Appraisal of Social Risks*. Global Report on Migration and Children. http://www .childmigration.net/files/Rosalia_Cortes_07.pdf.

Furedi, Frank. 1994. "A Plague of Moral Panics." *Living Marxism* 73 (November). Accessed March 3, 2016. http://web.archive.org/web/20000614173221/http://www.informinc.co.uk /LM/LM73/LM73_Frank.html.

——. 2013. "Using Children as a Moral Shield." *Spiked*, January 14. http://www.spiked -online.com/site/article/13249.

Fuszara, Malgorzata. 2000. "New Gender Relations in Poland in the 1990s." In *Reproducing Gender: Politics, Publics, and Everyday Life After Socialism*, ed. Susan Gal and Gail Kligman, 259–85. Princeton, NJ: Princeton University Press.

Gamburd, Michele Ruth. 2000. *The Kitchen Spoon's Handle: Transnationalism and Sri Lanka's Migrant Households*. Ithaca, NY: Cornell University Press.

Goode, Erich, and Ben-Yehuda Nachman. 1994. *Moral Panics: The Social Construction of Deviance*. Oxford: Blackwell.

Hall, Stuart, Chas Critcher, Tony Jefferson, John Clarke, and Brian Roberts. 1978. *Policing the Crisis: Mugging, the State, and Law and Order*. London: Macmillan.

Hochschild, Arlie R. 2012. *The Outsourced Self: Intimate Life in Market Times*. New York: Metropolitan Books.

Hochschild, Arlie R., and Barbara Ehrenreich. 2003. *Global Woman: Nannies, Maids, and Sex Workers in the New Economy*. New York: Metropolitan Books.

Hondagneu-Sotelo, Pierette, and Ernestine Avila. 1997. " 'I'm Here, But I'm There': The Meanings of Latina Transnational Motherhood." *Gender and Society* 11, no. 5: 548–71.

International Organization for Migration. 2011. *Migration in Ukraine: Fact and Figures.* http://www.iom.int/jahia/webdav/shared/shared/mainsite/activities/countries/docs/Ukraine/Migration-in-Ukraine-Facts-and-Figures.pdf.

Jäger, Siegfried. 2001. *Kritische Diskursanalyse: Eine Einführung.* Duisburg: Duisburger Institut für Sprach- und Sozialforschung.

Kałwa, Dobrochna. 2007. "'So wie zu Hause.' Die private Sphäre als Arbeitsplatz." In *Von Polen nach Deutschland und zurück. Die Arbeitsmigration und ihre Herausforderungen für Europa*, ed. Magdalena Nowicka, 205–25. Bielefeld: Transcript Verlag.

Keryk, Myroslava. 2004. "Labour Migrant: Our Savior or Betrayer? Ukrainian Discussions Concerning Labour Migration." *Migration Online,* September. http://aa.ecn.cz/img_upload/3bfc4ddc48d13ae0415c78ceael08bf5/Keryk___Labour_Migrant.pdf.

Koven, Seth, and Sonya Michel. 1993. *Mothers of a New World: Maternalist Politics and the Origins of Welfare States.* London: Routledge.

Lutz, Helma. 2011. *The New Maids: Transnational Women and the Care Economy.* London: Zed Books.

Lutz, Helma, and Ewa Palenga-Möllenbeck. 2010. "Care Work Migration in Germany: Semi-Compliance and Complicity." *Social Policy and Society* 9, no. 3: 419–30.

———. 2011. "Care, Gender, and Migration: Towards a Theory of Transnational Domestic Work Migration in Europe." *Journal of Contemporary European Studies* 19, no. 3: 349–64.

———. 2012. "Care Workers, Care Drain, and Care Chains: Reflections on Care, Migration, and Citizenship." *Social Politics* 19, no. 1: 15–37.

———. 2014. "Care-Migrantinnen im geteilten Europa: Verbindungen und Widersprüche in einem transnationalen Raum" [Care migrants in a divided Europe: Connections and contradictions in a transnational space]. *Soziale Welt* 20: 217–31.

Lutz, Helma, Ann Phoenix, and Nira Yuval-Davis. 1995. *Crossfires: Nationalism, Racism, and Gender in Europe.* London: Pluto Press.

Madianou, Mirca, and Daniel Miller. 2011. "Mobile Phone Parenting? Reconfiguring Relationships Between Filipina Migrant Mothers and Their Left-Behind Children." *New Media and Society* 13, no. 3: 457–70.

Majchrzyk-Mikuła, Joanna. 2008. *Eurosieroctwo 2008: Zapowiedź raportu* [Euro-orphans 2008: Preliminary report]. Warsaw: Studium Prawa Europejskiego.

McKay, Deirdre. 2007. " 'Sending Dollars Shows Feeling': Emotions and Economics in Filipino Migration." *Mobilities* 2, no. 2: 175–94.

Michel, Sonya. 1999. *Children's Interests/Mothers' Rights: The Shaping of America's Child Care Policy.* New Haven, CT: Yale University Press.

Nicholas, Tekla. 2008. "Remittances, Education, and Family Reunification: Transnational Strategies of Haitian Immigrant Families in South Florida." Paper presented at Transnational Parenthood and Children-Left-Behind, Oslo, November 20–21. http://africana.fiu.edu/people/faculty-grad-presentations/transnational_strategies.pdf.

Parreñas, Rhacel Salazar. 2005. *Children of Global Migration: Transnational Families and Gendered Woes.* Stanford, CA: Stanford University Press.

Phoenix, Ann. 2009. "Idealisierung emotionaler Bindung oder materielle Versorgung? Transnationale Mutterschaft und Kettenmigration" [Idealization of Emotional Bonding or Material Care? Transnational Motherhood and Immigration Chains]. In *Gender-Mobil?*

Geschlecht und Migration in Transnationalen Räumen, ed. Helma Lutz, 86–101.Münster: Westfälisches Dampfboot.

Pissin, Annika. 2013. "The Global Left-Behind Child in China: 'Unintended Consequences'in Capitalism." Working paper no. 39. Centre for East and South-East Asian Studies, Lund University. http://portal.research.lu.se/portal/files/3738266/4530030.

Pratt, Geraldine. 2012. *Families Apart: Migrant Mothers and the Conflicts of Labor and Love.* Minneapolis: University of Minnesota Press.

Randeria, Shalini. 2009. "Malthus Versus Condorcet: Population Policy, Gender, and Culture from an Ethnological Perspective." In *Between Life and Death: Governing Populations in the Era of Human Rights*, ed. Sabine Berking and Magdalena Zolkos, 25–46. Frankfurt: Peter Lang.

Rerrich, Maria S. 2012. Migration macht Schule. Herausforderungen für Care in einer rumänischen Gemeinde" [Migration teaches lessons: Demands for care in a Romanian community]. *Mittelweg* 36, no. 5: 73–93.

Tuttle, William M., Jr. 1995. "Rosie the Riveter and Her Latchkey Children: What Americans Can Learn about Child Day Care from the Second World War." *Child Welfare* 74, no. 1: 92–114.

Walczak, B. 2008. "Społeczne, edukacyjne i wychowawcze konsekwencje migracji rodziców i opiekunów prawnych uczniów szkół podstawowych, gimnazjalnych i ponadgimnazjalnych" [Social and educational consequences of the migration of parents and legal guardians of primary and secondary schools students]. Warsaw: Pedagogikum.

Yuval-Davis, Nira. 1997. *Gender and Nation*. London: Sage.

Zentgraf, Kristine M., and Norma Stoltz Chinchilla. 2012. "Transnational Family Separation: A Framework for Analysis." *Journal of Ethnic and Migration Studies* 38, no. 2: 345–66.

Zimmer, Kerstin. 2007. "Arbeitsmigration und demographische Krise" [Labor migration and demographic crisis].*Ukraine-Analysen* 20 (February 27). http://www.laender-analysen.de /ukraine/pdf/UkraineAnalysen20.pdf.

13

THE NEW MATERNALISM

Children First; Women Second

JANE JENSON

With the second wave of feminism that began in the 1960s, the dominant streams of feminism—whether radical, liberal, or socialist—framed their claims in the name of women and struggled against political discourses and policy practices that they considered too much focused on women's maternal role. In particular, they rejected patriarchal forms of gender relations that sustained a hierarchical arrangement of male power over women and that made women's childbearing and child raising the primary if not exclusive social role of women. Feminists and their allies argued, instead, for public policies and cultural practices that would sustain the autonomy of women while treating child raising as an activity that was not exclusively or even primarily mothers' responsibility. Demands for access to employment, equal pay, childcare services, and parental leaves all translated these claims into demands for public policy as well as altered family practices and gender relations.

Such movements had significant effect and made major gains in changing cultural norms as well as public policies. Commitments to gender equality as well as to the provision of supports for women's autonomy were proclaimed by international organizations as well as national governments, and these commitments did translate into policy action over a number of decades. Although one could never assert that gender equality had been achieved, numerous policy intentions and actions followed from the stance developed for the United Nations Decade for Women (1976–85). That agenda can be summarized as taking up "the major preoccupations of women around the world: improved educational and employment opportunities; equality in political and social participation; and increased health and welfare services" (Razavi and Miller 1995, 2). Another review of issues from around the globe, in the next decade, had the same list but added a fourth item: "ensuring personal safety, security, and autonomy" (Nelson and Chowdhury 1994, 11). We see, in other words, an agenda that, while never denying the place of children in women's lives, viewed those lives as multidimensional and extending beyond the family. The beneficiaries of action on this agenda would be adult women.

In recent decades, however, several of these preoccupations have been sidelined, in the Global North as well as in the Global South, as a child-centered agenda has come to dominate social and economic policy discourses and practices (Jenson 2009; Razavi 2014). As this has happened, we can observe the institutionalization of a "new maternalism."

It is "new" in contrast to an earlier version of maternalism promoted by activist women in Europe, North America, and Latin America. With respect to the Global North, "late nineteenth and early twentieth-century maternalists envisioned a state in which women displayed motherly qualities and also played active roles as electors, policy makers, bureaucrats, and workers, within and outside the home" (Koven and Michel 1990, 1077). Their maternalism was a political strategy that called for political and social rights for women because they were mothers (or motherly).[1] In Latin America, too, claims-making, well into recent decades, was often grounded in maternalism: "Motherhood became the very basis on which women staked their claims to citizenship rights and states deployed their efforts to mobilize female constituencies. At the heart of this 'civic maternalism' was the belief that women—and in particular their biological and social function as mothers—had to be recognized, valued, and protected" (Staab 2012, 303). In other words, maternalism could serve one stream of Latin American women's movements as a political strategy for empowering women.[2]

In contrast, feminists rarely invoke the "new" maternalism as part of claims-making for new rights for and empowerment of women. It is the discourse of policy communities that identifies motherhood and good mothering as the foundation for economic development and societal well-being—again, as much in the Global North as in the Global South. This focus on motherhood is the consequence of a shift in focus in social policy discourse and practices, a shift that foregrounds children's needs and even rights and defines women *qua* women primarily in terms of a maternal role, with "policies [that] recognize and reward care as a female responsibility" (Blofield and Franzoni 2015, 47). This shift brings with it a sidelining of claims for equality for adult women.

This new maternalism has not gone unnoticed. Because of the familiar resonance of maternalist discourses in Latin America, it is not surprising that feminists and social policy analysts were quick to identify and scrutinize continuities in discourses of motherhood in social policy initiatives promoted after the discrediting of the Washington Consensus and its imposition of structural adjustments in the 1990s. In such analyses (as, for example, Molyneux 2006; Tabbush 2010; Staab 2012; Nagels 2016), maternalism is understood as a political discourse that frames the accompanying policy instruments such that mothers are assigned primary responsibility for family well-being via their activities of social care. This political discourse pays little attention to economic, social, or political equality. At the same time, analyses of national and supranational policies in Europe have uncovered the ways in which increasing policy attention to social care has sidelined attention to goals and interventions in the name of gender equality in employment as well as in cultural and political life (Jenson 2008; Razavi 2014).

This chapter describes the reinscription of maternalism as political discourse, practice, and policy instruments in the social policy perspectives of much of Europe and Latin America. Although there clearly are important distinctions to be made about this emphasis on mothering and motherhood in each region, a new maternalism is visible in both. Moreover, analysts identify the same policy "culprit" for this return to a limited representation of women's roles and to writing out of gender equality: the social investment perspective (Jenson 2009; Staab 2012; Razavi 2014).

THE SOCIAL INVESTMENT PERSPECTIVE

This social investment policy perspective has reshaped a significant portion of European and Latin American social policy since the mid-1990s, particularly with regard to programs intended to reduce poverty and foster social inclusion. It is a perspective that foregrounds "the child" and places women, often in the guise of "parents," in the background. It is a perspective that places great responsibility on mothers for good parenting and child-rearing practices (Daly 2011). By extension, their practices of social care are foundations for the well-being of the economy and the future. Simultaneously, women as anything other than mothers fade from policy discourse.

When the social investment perspective is deployed, mothering, social care, and the consequences of family transformation, particularly lone parenthood, are front and center. The social investment perspective and the policies associated with it are the product of epistemic communities composed of social policy experts and decision makers seeking to "modernize" social policy after the neoliberalism of the 1980s and 1990s (Jenson and Saint-Martin 2003; Morel, Palier, and Palme 2012; Macdonald and Ruckert 2009).

Three key features of this policy perspective can be identified (Jenson and Saint-Martin 2006). First is the notion of constant learning, leading to a preoccupation with children and young adults' acquisition of human capital. In European contexts, the focus has been on early childhood education and care, the policy claim being that "defamilializing" social care can fulfill two purposes: it can provide an enriched developmental context in the early years, delivered by trained childcare workers; and it can enable parents to participate in the labor force, thereby achieving a parallel policy goal of increasing employment rates. Recognizing the importance of the knowledge economy and of human capital investments, the goal of these policies is to alter the context of childhood by breaking the intergenerational transmission of disadvantage. As one of the foundational manifestos of the social investment perspective for Europe put it in 2002, "The mainsprings of people's life chances lie in the family conditions of their childhood. . . . It is here that social advantage and disadvantage are transmitted and activated; it is here that social risks and needs find primary expression; and it is also here that the primary social safety net is found" (Esping-Andersen et al. 2002, 29). Five years earlier, the Organisation for Economic Co-operation and Development (OECD) had already begun promoting this analysis, calling for a "social investment approach" and approvingly citing "preschool interventions [that] are particularly effective in preventing disadvantage at school and thereafter" as well as "teaching 'parenting skills' to parents whose future offspring may be at risk of disadvantage" (OECD 1997, 4; 13).

In Latin America, the main goal of the social investment is "to disrupt the intergenerational transfer of poverty by building children's 'human capital'" via income transfers and, to a lesser extent, early childhood services (Razavi 2014, 11). A key policy instrument focused on human capital has been the conditional cash transfer (CCT), provided to mothers who respect the conditions imposed for caring for their children's health and education. These CCTs are generally lauded as having made significant inroads on levels of inequality as well as on extreme poverty in Latin America (Nagels 2016; Gideon and Molyneux 2012; Soares, Ribas, and Osório 2010).

The second feature of the social investment perspective is its orientation toward the future, which follows directly from its focus on children. Labeled a child-centered policy strategy, the discursive formulation is that children now are already creating the future. The policy consequences are both a constant discursive emphasis on children and a legitimation of new public spending on families with children and on education, including preschool (Daly 2011). A recent effort to measure and assess the robustness of European child-centered social policy actions, including during the time since the recent economic crisis, concludes, "Empirically the clearest shift in expenditure and the strongest increase in social spending with investment character took place in the realm of childcare service and of policies for the reconciliation of family and work. With the exception of a handful of countries, the expansion of childcare coverage was not halted by the crisis and the ensuing fiscal consolidation efforts" (Leoni 2015, 23; see also Kvist 2013).

There also has been expansion of publicly supported childcare services in Latin America (Mahon 2010). These services are often developed in parallel with the spending on CCTs as an antipoverty initiative. Although the design of policy—and therefore the consequences for mothers as well as children—varies across the region, the move toward childcare services has occurred, overall, "for several reasons: the failure of first-generation structural adjustment reforms to address problems of poverty; women's increased participation in the paid labor force (partly as a result of the structural adjustment policies promoted under neoliberalism); and the new investment social paradigm with its emphasis on the importance of human capital formation" (Lopreite and Macdonald 2014, 81). The result is that rates of participation in preschool are very similar to those in the United States (Razavi 2014).

The third feature of the social investment perspective is the idea that successful individuals enrich our common future and that ensuring success in the present is beneficial for the community and the economy as a whole, now and into the future. The social investment perspective emerged relatively early within the sectors of the development community focused on the costly effects of structural adjustments promoted by the Washington Consensus in the 1980s. With UNICEF in the lead, a shift within a number of key agencies began attributing a positive and leading role to social policy (Mkandawire 2007; Jenson 2010). Barrientos and Hulme (2009, 441) describe a "quiet revolution" in the development community that gave social protection, including social investments, a "strong 'productivist' bent." This same shift toward seeing the long-term positive economic effects of social spending percolated through the policies of the European Union in the late 1990s and early 2000s (Morel, Palier, and Palme 2012). In both regions, the focus turned to the contribution of "mothering" to the whole economy and its development.

These three features mark a break with the post-1945 approaches to economic development and social relations. The social investment perspective's macroeconomic analysis retains the focus on the supply side that neoliberalism instituted, and it is in this context that talk of social investment (rather than spending) provides discursive coherence. When one is enthusiastic about the market, it is of course natural to speak of investments. Therefore, as more activities are organized according to market principles, individuals and their families are called upon "to invest in their own human capital" so as to succeed in the labor market. At the same time, they must invest in their own futures, via savings for their retirement pensions and their children's education (Razavi 2014). But this is not neoliberalism's market fundamentalism. According to the social investment paradigm, the state is also meant to share some of this responsibility by ensuring adequate services (such as, for example, child-care) as well as through income transfers (such as CCTs, child benefits, or wage supplements, for example) to make up for the fact that market incomes are often not high enough to meet family needs.

The social investment perspective has never achieved consensus. It is most often used to frame the contemporary policy interventions of Nor-dic and liberal welfare regimes.[3] Bismarckian regimes have been slower to move toward social investment, but they are now doing so. Overall, it has spread by means of a quiet revolution that sees social spending as "an essential component of economic and social development strategies" (Barrientos and Hulme 2009, 439). International organizations, such as the World Bank, the OECD, and the United Nations and its agencies (such as UNICEF, for example) have been important to its development and spread.

THE NEW MATERNALISM IN THE SOCIAL INVESTMENT PERSPECTIVE

The growing popularity of the social investment perspective and the convergence between Latin American and European ideas has been well tracked (for one overview, see Razavi 2014). Given this convergence and the popularity of the perspective, it is reasonable to ask about the conse-quences of this focus on children, on social care, on balancing work and family, for adult women and gender equality. How does the reinscription of motherhood and maternity as women's main social role occur, and with what effects?

This reinscription, which takes the form of the new maternalism, is the work of social policy and development communities. They do not all construct their arguments in the same way, but the end result is similar. One example comes from Europe, where the process is visible in but not confined to policy transfer documents that exist at the intersection of policy analysis and policy action. Here, Gøsta Esping-Andersen's influ-ential work on social investment has been presented to, published by, and adopted by several policy communities within the European Union and the OECD world and has been taken up by his followers who are also engaged in policy transfer (see for example, Morel, Palier, and Palme 2012; Hemerijck 2013).[4] During the same time, the European Union's approach to gender differences and discrimination has dramatically changed (Jenson 2008). Indeed, this shift been described as a dismantling of the progressive gender regime constructed in earlier decades (Jacquot 2015).

Analyses developed within this framework do ultimately recognize women's central contribution to the achievement of good societal outcomes, but these contributions are confined to two roles: as workers contributing to family incomes and social protection regimes, and as mothers giving birth to the children needed to maintain Europe's well-being. Thus, driven by anxiety about demographic decline, Esping-Andersen advocates a "new gender contract" to underpin a new welfare state and support a child-centered social investment strategy via a straightforward instrumentalization of women's choices about maternity. The structure of his argument is straightforward. Postindustrial economies and modern families depend on women's employment. But women are having fewer children. This has created a new challenge: to find a balance between employment and *maternity*.[5] A new gender contract will create the conditions for this balance.

In contrast to standard feminist analysis, however, equality between women and men is not the goal. In discussing women's careers and maternity, Esping-Andersen's analysis does not even gesture in the direction of one of the most important equality claims that feminists have made for decades: equal pay. In his detailed calculations, meant to convince economists and policy makers of the payoffs of investments in nonparental childcare, he simply accepts the standard that women's wages will be 67 percent of men's (Esping-Andersen 2008). In subsequent analyses, he gives a good deal of attention to the existence of wage differentials (and their variation across countries), but the gender inequalities are treated more as causes of poverty, social inequality, and all the subsequent negative outcomes than as social relations that are themselves the product of structural discrimination—or even the long-term negative consequences of the requirement to provide social care in support of women's economic autonomy (Esping-Andersen 2009). Support for women's capacity to balance work and family is assessed primarily in terms of a policy instrument's potential for achieving a better demographic balance. In Esping-Andersen's analysis, the most important policy instrument available to achieve an appropriate balance is nonparental childcare.[6] The defamilialization of care for preschool children will, according to the policy prescriptions, allow women to successfully combine employment and motherhood and thereby avoid the demographic crisis facing Europe, as well as overcome the inequalities deriving in part from private parental investments in their children.[7]

The policy prescription is that states must spend to equalize the human capital field by investing in preschool programs as well as on education and training (Esping-Andersen 2009). Defusing this crisis will be the salvation of European social programs, as Esping-Andersen et al.'s (2002, v) child-focused and instrumentalist book dedication so bluntly puts it: "For today's children who will provide for our welfare when we are old. It is for you—and hence for ourselves—that we desire the best possible welfare state."

Not surprisingly, this new work provoked stinging critiques by feminists for treating women, their work, and their childbearing solely as instruments for societal well-being (see, for example, Gornick 2010). But why worry about the work of a few academics? The reason is simple: these same formulations of *why* social investment—*for whom* and *to what ends*—imbue the policy analysis and literature underpinning policy interventions by many actors. This child-centric reorientation of social policy (rendering even their mothers invisible) is now standard political discourse. The European Commission (2013, 13) social investment package declares, "Focusing on children is vital for a sustainable, efficient and competitive knowledge economy and an intergenerational fair society. The adequacy of future pensions depends on the human capital of those who are today children."[8] The move away from gender equality is amply evident in this document, which deals with women as simply one target group, which is suffering from higher poverty and lower employment rates. The policy package says little about discrimination or gender inequality.[9]

Gone is the post-1945 attention to social rights of citizenship, including claims for gender equality. In their place, there is attention to women, to be sure, but it deploys an instrumentalist vision. Policy communities run on ideas, and the idea that the looming fiscal crisis of social protection regimes will be fended off only by increased birthrates and more investments in human capital has gained hegemony.

A second example of this new maternalist inflection in social policy comes from another policy community. In the international development community, the instrumentalization of women's productive and reproductive lives has an even longer history, and policies have exhibited "gender awareness" for several decades (Razavi and Miller 1995, ii). It was at the foundation of the policy focus on "women in development" (WID) that took off in the 1970s.

Over time, WID proposals centered on demonstrating women's contribution to development and the ways that supporting their productive activities could be integrated into the increasingly popular "pro-poor" agenda. Within this approach, women were seen as a target group and demographic change an important goal (although in the development literature the goal was fewer and healthier babies rather than more babies, as in the recent European debates). As Shahrashoub Razavi and Carol Miller (1995, 8) explain, "When women figured prominently in the new pro-poor strategy, it was in an instrumental capacity. Female education and employment, for example, were highlighted as cost-effective means of solving the population problem. . . . Women thereby became an important 'target group.'" The primary concern became their contribution to development.[10]

Critics of the WID approach, including those who argued that structural adjustment policies were built on an assumption of the availability of women's free labor, proposed a number of gender and development (GAD) approaches. Some remained focused on an efficiency argument, while others were more concerned about social relations within the family. All, however, retained a focus on women (Razavi and Miller 1995).

By the time of the agreement on the 2000 Millennium Development Goals (MDGs), there was little doubt that agencies of the United Nations, other international organizations, and nongovernmental organizations recognized women's economic contributions as central to any successful development strategy. By 2000, however, the social investment perspective was being advocated by policy makers concerned with the Global South, producing a concomitant shift of attention toward girls.

The MDGs, for instance, did recognize that women could (and should) make a contribution to development, within a broader social investment perspective focused on education and human capital. But the needs of adult women were also, within precisely the same policy perspectives, being pushed into the shadows. For example, the third MDG was to "promote gender equality and empower women," a phrase that sounds very much inspired by a feminist perspective. The actual agreed target, however, is to "eliminate gender disparity in primary and secondary education, preferably by 2005, and in all levels of education no later than 2015" (United Nations, "Goal 3"). This goal shifted the focus toward girls, with no specific target for the empowerment of adult women or even labor market participation rates. Without targets, attention can ebb and flow. Without a target, the definition of "empowerment" itself remains underspecified and indicators could change with the times.

Of course, the place where adult women were consistently present was in the fifth MDG, to improve maternal health. The target was to reduce the maternal mortality rate by three-quarters from 1990 to 2015. Although this is a completely appropriate target, because childbirth remains potentially deadly and otherwise damaging to millions of women, maternity is only one of women's multiple social roles. Increasingly, however, as the social investment perspective spreads, explicit attention to adult women is overwhelmingly maternalist and particularly focused on the contribution of mothering healthy children. Thus, the optimism that may have been felt at the beginning of the decade of the MDG has evaporated.[11] Writing retrospectively of the goals, Razavi (2014, 122) reports, "Feminist organizations and networks have seen this as a reflection of the hegemony of the mother–child dyad . . . and the narrowing down of the much stronger gender egalitarianism of the Beijing and Cairo documents that emerged from the global conferences of the 1990s."[12]

The conditional cash transfer programs that were initiated in Latin America similarly downplay gender equality for adult women. Summarizing the gender awareness and goals of the iconic Mexican CCT program, Maxine Molyneux (2006, 439) writes, "These goals are, however, inconsistent: they represent a combination of *equality* measures (for the girls) and *maternalist* measures (for their mothers)." A similar emphasis on maternalist discourses and practices has been observed in, among other places, Peru, Chile, Argentina, Costa Rica, and El Salvador (Jenson and Nagels 2016; Nagels 2016; Staab 2010; Tabbush 2010; Franzoni and Voorend 2012).

The logic of the design of CCTs is quite similar to what we have seen for the MDG targets—equality for girls and protection for maternity. There is very little in the program design that targets women's needs and hopes for economic autonomy or security. Indeed, adult women's activities, except as mothers, are written out of the story. Writing of CCTs, Silke Staab (2010, 608) concludes, "Clearly, these efforts do not endorse equality—let alone gender equality—as a value in its own right."[13]

A third example of the way that the social investment perspective downplays equality follows from the fact that mothers have been simultaneously relabeled with the gender-neutral term "parent." One example comes from the international organization that was earliest promoter of the social investment perspective for modernizing welfare states. In its *Babies and Bosses* series, the OECD's analysis of the work-family balance nexus was originally driven by several concerns: declining fertility, poverty, and—in an earlier formulation—gender pay gaps (see OECD 2004). By the time of the synthesis report in 2007, however, the analysis had been pared down to demographic and labor supply questions, framed in a classic social investment perspective as concern with employment for all and the future of society:

> If parents cannot achieve their desired work/family life balance, not only is their welfare lower but economic development is also curtailed through reduced labour supply by parents. A reduction of birth rates has obvious implications for future labour supply as well as for the financial sustainability of social protection systems. As parenting is also crucial to child development, and thus the shape of future societies, policy makers have many reasons to want to help parents find a better work/family balance. (OECD 2007)

Although the report itself includes recommendations about gender equity, the focus is on sharing leave time (via paternity leaves) rather than on equality per se. Attention to such sharing is to be lauded, as is access to early childhood education and care services. But on-the-ground practice is less equal; the notion of "parenting" most often means "mothering." As Daly (2011, 16) writes:

The absence of attention to gender equality and the construction of many of the reforms in gender-neutral terms act to endorse familization. In the earlier discussion, we picked out the Daddy quota as an example of moves towards individualization—it was classified as such because it is constructed in such a way (in terms of payment levels and duration for example) as to target the division of unpaid work between parents and to seek change in fathers' behavior especially. This is not true for the bulk of paternity and parental leaves in place in Europe.

Thus, despite a discourse of "parenting," the actual program design reflects the reassertion of the familiar maternalism of the social investment perspective.

CONCLUSION

These examples, among others that might have been selected, document the return of maternalism to policy discourse, instruments, and practices across two large regions of the globe. This is a political discourse promoted by policy experts and within policy communities, a source of maternalism markedly different from some of its previous manifestations. If earlier versions of maternalism instrumentalized motherhood, as noted, they nonetheless were the product of one stream of myriad women's movements, which strategized that the display and recognition of motherly qualities would provide a route to women playing "active roles as electors, policy makers, bureaucrats, and workers, within and outside the home" (Koven and Michel 1990, 1077).

Now, the instrumentalization of motherhood within a child-centered social investment perspective is driven by policy communities that leave little space for women to make claims for equality or recognition of the specific and gendered inequalities and discriminations that they face. By focusing on the mother–child dyad, this new maternalism within national and international political discourses renders invisible the gender equality goals carried by national and international feminist mobilizations. This means there has been a shrinking political space for women to make claims for full citizenship, especially a social citizenship founded on equality among adult women and men.

NOTES

1. As Koven and Michel (1990) point out, many of the promoters of maternalism were well-educated, unmarried (and therefore childless) women.

2. The mobilization of "mothers of the disappeared" under the harshest Latin American dictatorships is one example. Peluffo (2007) traces the tensions within the Argentinian group Mothers and Grandmothers of the Plaza de Mayo over whether to broaden their political agenda to include claims-making about social justice more generally. Of course, maternalism was never the only wing of the women's movements in these years. Active feminist movements building on critiques of patriarchy, claims to equality, reproductive rights, and so on were present in most Latin American countries and at the regional level from the 1970s on (Sternbach et al. 1992).

3. The exception to this generalization is the United States under George W. Bush.

4. In 1996, Gøsta Esping-Andersen provided the Organisation for Economic Co-operation and Development (OECD) with a first analysis of social investment (see OECD 1997). *Why We Need a New Welfare State* (Esping-Andersen et al. 2002) was originally commissioned by the Belgian presidency of the European Council, in 2001. Note that Anton Hemerijck was one of the four authors of the 2002 book, before producing his own manifesto for the social investment perspective (Hemerijck 2013). The collection edited by Morel, Palier, and Palme (2012) is the product of a conference that brought together policy makers and academics during the Swedish presidency of the European Council, in 2010. Bruno Palier and Anton Hemerijck frequently intervened in policy discussions to promote the social investment perspective. See, for example, Vandenbroucke, Hemerijck, and Palier (2011).

5. This general argument is put forward in Esping-Andersen's own chapter in Esping-Andersen et al. (2002), with a concise summary beginning on page 66.

6. For Esping-Andersen, public spending is necessary because there is little chance of any real feminization of masculine roles. The only route to completing the "revolution" is for the state to support masculinization of women's life roles. See this, most clearly, in the conclusion to Esping-Andersen (2009).

7. For another discussion of this movement toward what Mary Daly calls a "new familism" and we call maternalism, see Daly (2011).

8. This European Commission version is a reformulation of the postulate that "good pension policies—like good health policies—begin at birth" (Vandenbroucke, Hemerijck, and Palier 2011, 6).

9. Thus, the European Commission (2013, 7) takes up the "gender dimension" in a single paragraph, pointing to higher poverty, lower wages, and the wage gap, which makes women's average earnings approximately 40 percent less than men's. However, little is said about how to reduce part-time employment or structural discrimination and, therefore, how to overcome the wage gap. For a detailed analysis of the dismantling of the European Union's commitment to gender equality across a range of programs, see Jacquot (2015).

10. Razavi and Miller (1995, 7) quote Anne Marie Goetz's (1994) criticisms of WID's emphasis on the efficiency gains of investing in women, and her comment that the emphasis had shifted from "women's needs and interests in development, to calculating what development needs from women." Women's activities had become a lever for promoting development.

11. Craig Murphy (2006, 210) writes of the Millennium Development Goals this way: "By adopting them, many powerful institutions—both governmental and intergovernmental—have come to embrace an egalitarian, human-centered view of development that was not commonplace in the 1970s. Moreover, these institutions have accepted the central role of women, and of their empowerment, in any attempt to achieve the society-wide development goals."

12. This lack of attention to gender equality and adult women has been significantly lessened in the Sustainable Development Goals that replaced the Millennium Development Goals, in 2015. Goal 5 explicitly focuses on equality in economic resources, sexual health, equal distribution of care, and so on. See United Nations, "Sustainable Development Goal 5."

13. Like Franzoni and Voorend (2012), Staab (2017, chapter 6) goes on to argue that the Chilean program that emphasizes early childhood education and care demonstrates greater potential for gender equality. However, even here there is room for skepticism. The Chilean conditional cash transfer and other programmes are not the standard conditional cash transfer being disseminated across the Global South (Ancelovici and Jenson 2013). In addition, Lopreite and Macdonald (2014) document that early childhood education and care can have quite different consequences, even for women's employment, depending on its design.

REFERENCES

Ancelovici, Marcos, and Jane Jenson. 2013. "Standardization for Transnational Diffusion: The Case of Truth Commissions and Conditional Cash Transfers." *International Political Sociology* 7, no. 3: 294–312.

Barrientos, Armando, and David Hulme. 2009. "Social Protection for the Poor and Poorest in Developing Countries: Reflections on a Quiet Revolution." *Oxford Development Studies* 37, no. 4: 439–56.

Blofield, Merike, and Juliana Martínez Franzoni. 2015. "Maternalism, Co-responsibility, and Social Equity: A Typology of Work–Family Policies." *Social Politics* 22, no. 1: 38–59.

Daly, Mary. 2011. "What Adult Worker Model? A Critical Look at Recent Social Policy Reform in Europe from a Gender and Family Perspective." *Social Politics* 18, no. 1: 1–23.

Esping-Andersen, Gøsta. 2008. *Trois Leçons sur l'État-providence*. Paris: Seuil.

———. 2009. *The Incomplete Revolution: Adapting to Women's New Roles*. Cambridge: Polity Press.

Esping-Andersen, Gøsta, Duncan Gallie, Anton Hemerijck, and John Myles. 2002. *Why We Need a New Welfare State*. Oxford: Oxford University Press.

European Commission. 2013. *Towards Social Investment for Growth and Cohesion—Including Implementing the European Social Fund 2014-2020.* COM (2013) 83 final. Brussels: European Commission.

Franzoni, Juliana Martínez, and Koen Voorend. 2012. "Blacks, Whites, or Grays? Conditional Transfers and Gender Equality in Latin America." *Social Politics* 19, no. 3: 383–407.

Gideon, Jasmine, and Maxine Molyneux. 2012. "Limits to Progress and Change: Reflections on Latin American Social Policy." *Social Politics* 19, no. 3: 293–98.

Gornick, Janet C. 2010. Review of *The Incomplete Revolution. Contemporary Sociology* 39, no. 6: 698.

Hemerijck, Anton. 2013. *Changing Welfare States.* Oxford: Oxford University Press.

Jacquot, Sophie. 2015. *Transformation in EU Gender Equality: From Emergence to Dismantling.* London. Palgrave Macmillan.

Jenson, Jane. 2008. "Writing Women Out, Folding Gender In: The European Union 'Modernises' Social Policy." *Social Politics* 15, no. 2: 1–23.

——. 2009. "Lost in Translation: The Social Investment Perspective and Gender Equality." *Social Politics* 16, no. 4: 446–83.

——. 2010. "Diffusing Ideas for After-Neoliberalism: The Social Investment Perspective in Europe and Latin America." *Global Social Politics* 10, no. 1: 59–84.

Jenson, Jane, and Nora Nagels. 2016. "Social Policy Instruments in Motion: Conditional Cash Transfers from Mexico to Peru." *Social Policy & Administration*, December. doi:10.1111/spol.12275.

Jenson, Jane, and Denis Saint-Martin. 2003. "New Routes to Social Cohesion? Citizenship and the Social Investment State." *Canadian Journal of Sociology* 28, no. 1: 77–99.

——. 2006. "Building Blocks for a New Social Architecture: The LEGO Paradigm of an Active Society." *Policy & Politics* 34, no. 3: 429–51.

Koven, Seth, and Sonya Michel. 1990. "Womanly Duties: Maternalist Politics and the Origins of Welfare States in France, Germany, Great Britain, and the United States, 1880–1920." *American Historical Review* 95, no. 4: 1076–1108.

Kvist, Jon. 2013. "The Post-Crisis European Social Model: Developing or Dismantling Social Investments?" *Journal of International and Comparative Social Policy* 29, no. 1: 91–107.

Leoni, Thomas. 2015. *Welfare State Adjustment to New Social Risks in the Post-Crisis Scenario: A Review with Focus on the Social Investment Perspective.* WWWforEurope Project, working paper 89. http://www.foreurope.eu/fileadmin/documents/pdf/Workingpapers/WWWforEurope_WPS_no089_MS08.pdf.

Lopreite, Debora, and Laura Macdonald. 2014. "Gender and Latin American Welfare Regimes: Early Childhood Education and Care Policies in Argentina and Mexico." *Social Politics* 21, no. 1: 80–102.

Macdonald, Laura, and Arne Ruckert. 2009. *Post-Neoliberalism in the Americas.* London: Palgrave Macmillan.

Mahon, Rianne. 2010. "After Neo-Liberalism? The OECD, the World Bank, and the Child." *Global Social Policy* 10, no. 2: 172–92.

Mkandawire, Thandika. 2007. "Transformative Social Policy and Innovation in Developing Countries." *European Journal of Development Research* 19, no. 1: 13–29.

Molyneux, Maxine. 2006. "Mothers at the Service of the New Poverty Agenda: Progresa/ Oportunidades, Mexico's Conditional Transfer Programme." *Social Politics & Administration* 40, no. 4: 429–40.

Morel, Nathalie, Bruno Palier, and Joakim Palme, eds. 2012. "Beyond the Welfare State As We Knew It?" In *Towards a Social Investment State? Ideas, Policies, and Challenges*, 1–32. Bristol: Policy Press.

Murphy, Craig. 2006. *The United Nations Development Programme: A Better Way?* Cambridge: Cambridge University Press.

Nagels, Nora. 2016. "The Social Investment Perspective, Conditional Cash Transfer Programmes, and the Welfare Mix: Peru and Bolivia." *Social Policy and Society* 15, no. 3: 479–93.

Nelson, Barbara, and Najma Chowdhury, eds. 1994. *Women and Politics Worldwide*. New Haven, CT: Yale University Press.

Organisation for Economic Co-operation and Development (OECD). 1997. "Beyond 2000: The New Social Policy Agenda." OECD Working Papers 5, no. 43. Paris: OECD.

——. 2004. *Babies and Bosses: Reconciling Work and Family Life*. Vol. 3, *New Zealand, Portugal, and Switzerland*. Paris: OECD. http://www.oecd.org/els/family/babiesandbosses -reconcilingworkandfamilylifevol3newzealandportugalswitzerland.htm.

——. 2007. *Babies and Bosses: Reconciling Work and Family Life—A Synthesis of Findings for OECD Countries*. Paris: OECD. http://www.oecd.org/els/family/babiesandbosses -reconcilingworkandfamilylifeasynthesisoffindingsforoecdcountries.htm.

Peluffo, Ana. 2007. "The Boundaries of Sisterhood: Gender and Class in the Mothers and Grandmothers of the Plaza de Mayo." *A Contra Corriente* 4, no. 2: 77–102.

Razavi, Shahra. 2014. "Addressing/Reforming Care, But On Whose Terms?" In *New Frontiers in Feminist Political Economy*, eds. Shirin M. Rai and Georgina Waylen, 114–34. Abingdon: Routledge.

Razavi, Shahrashoub, and Carol Miller. 1995. *From WID to GAD: Conceptual Shifts in the Women and Development Discourse*. Occasional paper no. 1. Geneva: United Nations Research Institute for Social Development.

Soares, Fábio Veras, Rafael Perez Ribas, and Rafael Guerreiro Osório. 2010. "Evaluating the Impact of Brazil's Bolsa Família: Cash Transfer Programs in Comparative Perspective." *Latin American Research Review* 45, no. 2: 173–90.

Staab, Silke. 2010. "Social Investment Policies in Chile and Latin America: Towards Equal Opportunities for Women and Children?" *Journal of Social Policy* 39, no. 4: 607–26.

——. 2012. "Maternalism, Male-Breadwinner Bias, and Market Reform: Historical Legacies and Current Reforms in Chilean Social Policies." *Social Politics* 19, no. 3: 299–331.

——. 2017. *Gender and the Politics of Gradual Change: Social Policy Reform and Innovation in Chile*. London: Palgrave-Macmillan.

Sternbach, Nancy S., Marysa Navarro-Aranguren, Patricia Chuchryk, and Sonia E. Alvarez. 1992. "Feminisms in Latin America: From Bogotá to San Bernardo." *Signs* 17, no. 2: 392–434.

Tabbush, Constanza. 2010. "Latin American Women's Protection after Adjustment: A Feminist Critique of Conditional Cash Transfers in Chile and Argentina." *Oxford Development Studies* 38, no. 4: 437–59.

United Nations. n.d. "Goal 3: Promote Gender Equality and Empower Women." Accessed February 12, 2017. http://www.un.org/millenniumgoals/gender.shtml.

———. n.d. "Sustainable Development Goal 5: Achieve Gender Equality and Empower All Women and Girls." Sustainable Development Knowledge Platform. Accessed February 6, 2017. https://sustainabledevelopment.un.org/sdg5.

Vandenbroucke, Frank, Anton Hemerijck, and Bruno Palier. 2011. *The EU Needs a Social Investment Pact.* Opinion Paper no. 5. Brussels: Observatoire Social Européen.

AFTERWORD

CROSSING INTO THE FUTURE

ALICE KESSLER-HARRIS

Why is twenty-first-century motherhood so different from that of the twentieth century and the centuries that preceded it? The chapters in this book highlight the effects of newly available technologies and of the global migrations of mothers, with or without their children, on our changing understanding of motherhood. Together, the authors argue that these changes have created a world in which the bodies of mothers (which the editors locate in chains of procreation) and the verb *to mother* (or chains of caring) are no longer in necessary agreement. The result, these essays suggest, is that identifying a "mother" is no longer simple. Motherhood is not merely a question of self-experience, measured by the emotion women feel or the labor they expend on child-rearing. It is no longer ascertainable through biological derivation of egg and semen. Far from being new, these kinds of questions have long been at issue. Here, I focus on the experience of mothers in the United States to illustrate the many facets of meaning contained in the notion of motherhood over the past two hundred years.

Identifying a mother of any particular child, we learn from this volume, is often the subject of prevailing assumptions about human rights, legal contract, and judicial decisions. As it is no longer clear what constitutes a mother, so too is it unclear who may identify as a mother, much less who is best suited to engage in the task of mothering. In these chapters, we observe surrogate childbearers, nannies, sperm donors, adoptive parents, and state authorities all participating in the "mother-ing" process, sometimes to the exclusion or marginalization of egg donors and genetically related siblings or the grandparents of the living child. We read in the daily news about quarrels over fertilized, frozen embryos, and whether putative rapists have the right to prevent their vic-tims from aborting fetuses. Hence the title of this book: how to reas-semble motherhood has become one of the central issues of the day.

These new challenges to the meaning of motherhood confront some of the most fundamental issues of human existence, including the moral-ity of creating or taking life for the satisfaction of potential parents, and whether and how embryonic life may be bought and sold. These chal-lenges remind us that questions about motherhood have been on the agenda since time immemorial. If birth mothers were readily identifiable before the advent of the petri dish and in vitro fertilization, the act of procreation was still often fraught—a product of rape or coercion rather than of desire. And the process of mothering (or of caring) often differed for women in different circumstances. Infant exposure, farming out infants to wet nurses, consigning unwanted babies to the church or to childless relatives—all actions that we now find, to some degree, repug-nant to our modern conceptions of mothering—constituted breaks in the chain of caring.

Historically, preindustrial and developing nations placed a high value on raising children to be economically useful. Religious commitment and the spread of Enlightenment thought encouraged mothers to raise virtuous individuals and good citizens as well as boys who would become soldiers. More recently, the value of a mother could be measured not so much by whether she kept or released her children but by how she cared for those who survived. Industrializing countries quickly recognized the production of a healthy labor force and a well-nurtured military as an asset.[1] They helped mothers to achieve these goals through social welfare programs that provided financial aid and simultaneously established standards of care. When manual labor became less valuable, in mature, postindustrial economies, mothers and fathers were encouraged to edu-cate their children to prepare them for skilled and professional jobs. The emotional or subjective experience of parenting then became the best argument for becoming a mother, spawning an array of family, education, and psychology specialists each bent on helping mothers to develop the full potential of every child.

The trajectory of change suggests that notions of motherhood, and especially ideas of good mothering, are embedded in complex layers of cultural and social meaning that reflect shifting demographic patterns and economic needs and also help to shape them. Several of the essays in this book suggest the specific ways in which motherhood is in dialogue with changing historical circumstance.[2] My own sense is that the commodification of everyday life, including family life and reproduction, and the dominance of market values has exacerbated painful conflicts over motherhood—conflicts that now demand legislative and judicial attention. Together, commodification and the market have removed debates over motherhood from the level of custom and produced political, legal, and normative adaptations that have turned motherhood from a structure of sentiment to a matter of negotiation and regulation. What was once a sometimes esteemed and revered role has become a legal status with defined rights and stringent obligations.

As several of the essays in the present volume suggest, the growth of modern states and the subsequent development of a global world have expanded the regulatory arena into private life, turning motherhood into a public act (see, in the present volume, Achmad, Milanich, Jenson, and Sanger). In a technologically sophisticated and borderless world, where the conception, birth, and care of a single child may involve multiple interventions by numerous people in different locations, entitlements to the rights of motherhood are often publicly contested (see Ergas, present volume). Nor is it always clear who should be called upon to fulfill the obligations.

Consider the proposition with which Martha Fineman begins her essay here. Assisted reproductive technologies and global migration, Fineman argues, are only the most recent of a long series of efforts to imagine and create modes of mothering consistent with an evolving society. Fineman's comments recall the colonial period of American history, when, in order to provide disciplined instruction for their children, mothers routinely sent them away to serve as domestics and laborers in the homes of others. In Southern colonies, orphaned children (a definition reserved for those without fathers) could be indentured until they reached the age of eighteen—mothers being thought unfit to teach them proper discipline. By the Revolutionary period and into the early nineteenth century, motherhood had come to be seen in terms of virtue. Mothers, it was thought, would convey lessons of morality to their children, even as fathers engaged in the corrupting worlds of commerce and politics. Imbued with religious principles, mothers could successfully lead their children into civic virtue, encouraging them to care for the poor and unfortunate, to avoid the sins of greed and envy, and to work hard in order to prosper (Kerber 1980; Lewis 1985; Bloch 2003). These lessons would come from women whose work was rooted in the home and who avoided the temptations and stresses of what was often known as public, or paid, work.

For these mothers, domesticity provided a value system that not only ruled the home but also guided the daily activities of women whose economic well-being generally depended on male family heads. Injunctions to obedience and submissiveness set the stage for notions of "separate spheres," which in turn promoted what can only be called domestic motherhood. Largely rural, mostly working in their own homes by taking in laundry or sewing or selling farm-produced butter and eggs, mothers participated in the household economy in crucial ways. Yet their work remained largely invisible in the larger economy. The lucky mother was one who had several children survive into adulthood. She was expected to teach them self-discipline, frugality, and the value of unrelenting work, all of which would help them to sustain their own families in the future. On a larger scale, women began to demand political and social rights *because* they were mothers.[3]

But the capacity of a mother to pass on virtue depended on economic and social circumstances beyond any individual's control. Consider the enslaved mother, for example, who gave birth and often cared for children for a few short months or years. Such mothers experienced few of the benefits of motherhood. Economically valuable for their capacity to procreate, they could not sustain chains of caring that often quickly dissolved under the economic needs of owners. Freed women found themselves coerced into field and domestic labor for others (Boster 2015). After emancipation, the motherhood of many African American women would be undermined by legislative and judicial demands for wage work and by rampant job discrimination against African American men.

Because black men could rarely afford to support families alone, black mothers, unlike most white mothers, came to be defined by their contributions to the family's economic survival, their efforts to nurture children undermined by the political and economic effects of racial discrimination (Kerber 1998). Dorothy Roberts's essay in the present volume points to some of the legacies of these patterns of law and custom (see also Roberts 2002).

But black women were not alone in struggling to sustain caring roles against the economic powers marshaled against them. If normative ideals of mothering could never be achieved by the poorest women or by enslaved women, rapid industrialization at the end of the nineteenth century challenged increasing numbers of white immigrant women as well as those who moved from rural to urban areas. When urbanization, poverty, and wage work undermined their capacity to meet required standards of mothering, more affluent women stepped in to reform the conditions under which they lived and worked. Perhaps ironically, poor mothers soon found their practical choices shaped by demands for compulsory education of their children and a new insistence on prohibiting child labor. Wage-earning mothers discovered that state intervention in the form of protective labor legislation limited their occupational choices and their incomes, even as it ameliorated the most gruesome conditions of their working lives (Kessler-Harris 1982; Woloch 2015; Muncy 1991).

Affluent women turned citizen reformers aimed to instill the values of domestic motherhood by encouraging disadvantaged women to become good mothers through the adoption of scientific practices. They provided instruction in cleanliness, nutrition, and etiquette. They established day nurseries to serve tired and exhausted mothers. Although many such nurseries served the needs of wage-earning mothers, others excluded mothers who worked for wages because wage work, in itself, was thought antithetical to mothering.[4] These constraints left many real mothers at sea. Many confronted poverty by avoiding sex or begging for access to newly developed birth control techniques (Gordon 1990). Others chose painful options like resorting to prostitution to earn a living or placing their children in orphanages to ensure they would be fed and clothed (Ramey 2012).

In the late nineteenth century and for much of the twentieth, wage work for women negated prevailing visions of domestic motherhood.

Unable to support families on a single wage, working-class men neverthe-less came to believe that a man deserved a wife who could care for him and his children and "keep" the house. Together, families and trade unions fought for a "family wage" for men, joining in an effort to provide children with two parents—one a breadwinner and the other a stay-at-home caregiver. There was nothing "natural" about this, though it quickly came to seem so.

An ideological commitment to domestic motherhood and male bread-winning shaped work and family life into an inescapable pattern. It enabled employers to refuse women good jobs and to pay them less than men, on the grounds that they were temporary or uncommitted workers. It inhibited working-class men from training women for good jobs or admitting them into trade unions, on the grounds that women would undermine their wages. Along with trade union men and religious lead-ers, employers argued that if men earned enough to keep their wives at home, women would have the opportunity to educate and train their chil-dren into the next generation's labor force. Legislative and judicial conse-quences followed on this newly installed conception of motherhood.

To preserve the virtue of women who did enter the workforce, reform-ers fought for legislation that would circumscribe the kinds of jobs women could take and their ability to work at night. By 1908, the Supreme Court had colluded in this rationale, holding that, to protect present and potential mothers, legislators might limit women's access to wage work. The protective legislation that followed in every industrial state limited the number of hours and regulated the working conditions of wage-earning women. Meant to ensure that women got enough rest to bear healthy children, the laws kept women out of harm's way during the workday and barred them from jobs considered harmful to morality. But, often, these measures so restricted job opportunities and wages that mothers turned to prostitution to provide for their children.

Even as more and more married women—and then married women with school-age children, and finally mothers of preschool children—entered the wage labor force, these strategies successfully maintained at least token obeisance to the ideal of domestic motherhood, into the mid-dle of the twentieth century.[5] By the 1920s, however, the pressures of the market were already beginning to tell. We see this in rising consumer demand for everything from ready-made clothing to automobiles and in the slowly rising numbers of married women and mothers entering the labor force.[6] Efforts to reimagine mothers as shapers of character rather than as the primary sources of affection followed soon after, leading to controversy over the strength, and even the negative influence, of the mother–child bond. The new science of psychoanalysis participated in this debate, exacerbating concerns about whether there might be such a thing as too much mothering.[7]

Still, the demand for domestic motherhood did not wane. New Deal legislation committed resources to maintaining mothers without partners in their homes through Title I of the Economic Security Act of 1935, which paid a stipend on behalf of fatherless children. By the early 1940s, a revised Aid to Families with Dependent Children program had joined a revamped Social Security program to pay mothers an additional stipend until their children turned eighteen. At the same time, the federal government stepped in to ensure the benefits of wage work (including pensions and paid vacations) to regularly employed, mostly white male workers in productive work. These policies systematically denied benefits to temporary or part-time workers, who were predominantly female, as well as to those who worked in the service and nonprofit industries, who also were disproportionately female (Kessler-Harris 2001).

Even the war did not disrupt these patterns. As hard as the War Manpower Commission worked to entice married women into the workforce, it nonetheless discouraged mothers of small children from taking jobs. In the end, its brief effort to establish nurseries for working mothers under the Lanham Act produced few spaces, and many remained underutilized (Michel 1999). When peace arrived, ferocious campaigns to drive women out of their wartime jobs, and to accuse mothers who continued to work of fostering juvenile delinquency in their children, followed (Stoltzfus 2003; Fousekis 2011).

These strategies successfully maintained the ideal of domestic mothering into the middle of the twentieth century. But the 1950s, a decade that again lauded domesticity, witnessed visible tensions. A Cold War mentality drew on women to work as teachers and nurses and as clerks and secretaries in the booming industrial sector. At the same time, rising consumer demands for housing, appliances, and higher education drove women into the workforce to provide the income that would launch their families into the middle class.

At first, the old separate-spheres ideology—the domestic code—held them back. Trade unions, still largely male dominated, sought family benefits in addition to family wages for the one-third of all American workers who were union members, instilling in their membership pride in their ability to support their families. Women, thought to be poorly committed employees who worked only for "pin money" rather than to support families, were consigned to part-time jobs, many in arenas deemed "suitable" for women. Even as expectations about home roles were daily violated by increasing numbers of women of all kinds entering the labor force, strong notions of the importance of domestic mothering persisted.

And yet the tensions grew larger.

There was, first, the pill. Effective birth control had long been understood as a necessary condition for the well-being of mothers of all kinds. The pill, introduced in 1961, provided a relatively cheap and effective mechanism that enabled women to choose not only if but also when they might become mothers. To be sure, diaphragms and other contraceptive devices had been available for decades, but they were not only inconvenient and less than perfectly effective but also, in many places, prohibited to the unmarried by law. The pill, though it was available only by prescription, placed birth control in the hands of women.

Rapid declines in birth rates for both rich and poor followed (May 2010). By the early 1970s, fiction writers and a new generation of feminists foresaw a new technology of "test-tube" babies that would permit women to avoid the procreative function while enabling men and women to choose if and when they wanted to become parents. Novelist and poet Marge Piercy (1976) foresaw a process of parthenogenesis that was liberating for women, while Margaret Atwood (1985), in a dystopian view, distinguished bearers of children from mothers.

Perhaps more important, the availability of the pill and the spread of birth control produced a change in attitudes toward mothering. Lamaze, home births, breastfeeding rather than bottle-feeding, and child-centered lifestyles redefined mothers as their own best sources of knowledge. If its early manifestations appeared in the women's health movement and in efforts to rethink women's bodies not merely as reproductive machines but also as the subjects of careful attention, this very quickly turned to efforts to naturalize childbirth. Meant to ensure the well-being of mothers during pregnancy and childbirth as much as the health of children, natural child-birth advocates tried to remove the birth process from the hands of the medical profession and the child-rearing process from the hands of experts and place both in the hands of women. As technology enabled choices about whether or not to mother, women began to imagine a new kind of motherhood—one that could more readily be integrated into lives outside the family domain.

Excitement about these new choices fueled the advent of the late-1960s women's liberation movement and produced a second fissure in the domesticity paradigm. Once women imagined themselves in control of their own bodies, efforts to achieve female autonomy followed. By the mid- to late 1960s, full-fledged efforts to attack the barriers that limited women's access to education and good jobs had begun. Some scholars identify this period as one that involved the commodification of family life—the recognition that, if individuals were shaped by the market, women's independence would require a commitment to wage labor (see, for example, Silbaugh 1997). Necessarily, this would mean a move to separate from or to reconstruct traditional, patriarchal family life, and a reconstruction of mothering. Inevitably, this produced a resistance to mothering and, in the extremes of the movement, an antimothering tone. By the early 1970s, women of all races had begun having children later in life and giving birth to fewer children. Sociologist Neil Gilbert (2008) describes this as a period in which women abandoned mother-hood, but it could equally be described as ushering in the age of the "supermom"—the woman asked to support a family while also devoting her full attention to her children.

Mothering now lost some of its sacrosanct image, its sentimentalized sheen. In the workplace, employers began to think about accommoda-tions necessary to adapt the workplace to mothers. Law firms placed mothers on "mommy tracks" that enabled them to work *only* a normal forty-hour week; some employers provided on-site childcare, only to discover that mothers took off at odd times to visit with their offspring. The U.S. military established model day care centers that included after-hours care and high-quality babysitting services (Mittelstadt 2015). Legislators pitched in by agreeing that medical insurance should cover pregnant workers as well as wives. They acknowledged the need for fam-ily leaves to care for children but for the most part neglected paid parental or maternity leaves. There was no commitment to public funding for childcare for all mothers who wanted it, as was the case in Sweden and several other countries (Jenson and Sineau 2001).

At home, nannies and au pairs took over the labor of professional mothers who could afford to replace their own labor in the home. While the affluent relied on increasing flows of migrant care workers, with or without documents, who cared for the elderly, the ill, and the young, state legislatures hesitated to fill in gaps for ordinary working people. Flexible hours for nursing mothers, paid sick leave, and mother and child clinics—benefits that European mothers have had for years—remained sparse. The struggle to mother, in the simplest sense—to adequately care for children—grew more and more bitter, even as the workday consumed ever-greater portions of time.

Lost in this transformation of domestic motherhood were the very poor, for whom wage work often meant leaving children in unsafe and unsupervised spaces. Beginning in 1967, and with increasing rapidity thereafter, mothers who had, in effect, been paid by the state (via social assistance programs) to take care of their small children faced increasing pressure to find jobs. Heedless of the aspirations of poor women to mother their own children, legislators increasingly demanded that the poorest women join the paid labor force, most of them in high-turnover, low-wage jobs that lacked the benefits of health insurance or paid parental leave time. Lawmakers failed to see that, absent job training (much less education), and without public transportation, safe housing, and sufficient subsidized day care—all the amenities that enabled middle-class mothers to go to work—domestic mothering remained a desirable alternative. Those dependent on state support argued in vain that motherhood was a job that deserved support. The ultimate result, as historian Ellen Reese (2010, 231) notes, was to create "setbacks in terms of poor mothers' rights to care for their own children at home." But Reese also tells us that pushing women into work "increased opportunities to expand and improve subsidized childcare programs" by legitimizing state support for nondomestic mothering (see also Mink 2002; Roberts 2002).

Because state funds were administered with palpable ambivalence—subject to stringent regulations on personal behavior and severe threats to parental rights—poor mothers gained little from the loss of domestic motherhood. The pattern clearly reveals the differential meanings attributed to class and race in the process of mothering. Those meanings also became evident in the rising numbers of women, many from less developed countries, who took over the household labor and childcare duties of a new generation of professional and managerial working women. The children of these care workers became products of what Helma Lutz, in the present collection, calls "transnational motherhood." Lutz, who sees in this new form of motherhood "the efforts of biological mothers to perform social mothering across wide geographic distances," details the moral outrage that has accompanied the institution of "motherhood from a distance." Sonya Michel and Gabrielle Oliveira, also in this volume, call our attention to the other side of this coin, noting in "The Double Lives of Transnational Mothers" that, in receiving countries like the United States, the mothering of transnational women tends to be devalued, just like the mothering of lower-class and minority women, with the result that policy makers and employers ignore the effects of migration on family members left behind.

Abandoning domestic motherhood has not been without pain. If the male breadwinner/domestic mothering model of motherhood limited women's opportunities in the wage labor force, the "adult worker model" has provided choice at home only for the most affluent. The assumption that every adult will earn income has produced dramatic changes in expectations of mothers, which are still being fought out. Some women have "opted out" of the labor force to care for children and have willingly (or not) paid the price in terms of losing places on career ladders. But this option works only for those with income-producing and supportive partners. For most women, the breakdown of the male-breadwinner family has meant a constant struggle between paid work and family time—a fight to make the workplace more amenable to mothering, even as fathers are urged to become more responsible.

Since 1980, Americans have been trying to imagine motherhood in a society where family labor is, in the words of sociologists, increasingly "commodified" or subject to the constraints and incentives of the market. Most mothers must earn wages in order to support their children; for the fortunate few, the temptations of the job market outweigh the pleasures of caring for children. If wage work reduces the number of women willing and eager to become mothers or to mother more than one child, it also demands a different conception of motherhood for those who join the ranks of wage earners. Increasing demands for subsidized infant care, prekindergartens, and after-school programs compete for resources against helicopter mothers and soccer moms who do not wish to be taxed for public programs. To resolve this tension, President George H. W. Bush tried to pass a law that would subsidize stay-at-home mothers as well as those who worked (Himelfarb and Perotti 2004).

The myth of the male breadwinner having exploded, the meaning of motherhood has changed dramatically. Appeals to morality and virtue can no longer sustain visions of motherhood that have collapsed under the weight of economic circumstances. How, to return to the essays in this volume, do we imagine modes of mothering under circumstances that foster a range of procreative choices even while demanding that both men and women labor in the marketplace? Will motherhood become a state-regulated by-product of human activity or a privilege for the declining numbers of women able to afford it, or the tiny number of men prepared to undertake responsibility for care? How, as Neil Gilbert (2008) asks, do we move from an effort to sustain "sentimental" motherhood to one that supports the *practice* of motherhood?

The rich and poor both love their children, but, from a practical perspective, motherhood takes on entirely different resonances for the high school dropout, the poor, or the unemployed than for the affluent, the educated, and the technically competent. Poor mothers of even the tiniest infants are pushed into meaningless minimum-wage jobs even as their better-off sisters are free to opt out of wage work for several years at a time. Lack of financial means makes it impossible for the poor to take advantage of parental leaves; their children are consigned to substandard and inconvenient childcare facilities ("warehousing") staffed by poorly paid and often untrained, unsupervised workers.

The affluent, however, benefit from a new focus on enabling mothers to continue in their jobs. Some firms now offer new parents as much as a year of almost-fully or fully paid leave; others are willing to give new mothers flexible time off. Some new mothers even rush freshly pumped breast milk home to the caretaker nanny. Under these circumstances, technological innovation in birth and caring has taken root in the vacuum created by the current debates over inequality, and debates over what motherhood is or might be are sharply embedded in class and racial conceptions. As the essays here demonstrate, with the lines of ethics and morality muddied and adequate social policies yet to be developed, technology has taken its own directions, producing some "mothers" whose virtue resides in their capacity to produce income, some who command the resources to care, and others whom, as the result of misfortune or transgression, the state deprives of their children (see Roberts, present volume).

Arguably, new technological advances and prevailing efforts to come to terms with the crumbling biological imperatives that have traditionally shored up our ideas of motherhood pose a set of problems unique to the moment. I am struck by how powerfully the essays in this book present those challenges, and how each links a particular "advance" to a new set of questions. Ergas links global surrogacy to questions of women's control of their own bodies, and hence to the right to abortion; Sanger wonders whether technological advances in egg fertilization pit the parental rights of fathers against those of mothers. Achmad, and Kahn and Chavkin, wonder how confusion over biological claims to motherhood will influence the rights of children to citizenship. As puzzling as these issues are, I am heartened by the opportunity this provides, in the words of historian Ellen Ross (1995, 413), to insert the subject of motherhood "into the many contemporary discourses where the mother as subject rightly belongs." In opening this most complicated issue to debate, these essays move us into a new and exciting intellectual project.

NOTES

1. See, for example, Davin (1978).

2. See, especially, Jenson (present volume). See also Lutz (present volume), on the issue of how changing migration patterns affect the meaning of motherhood.

3. For a comparative perspective on this issue, see Koven and Michel (1993). On this movement in the United States, see Goodwin (2007) and Skocpol (1995).

4. Historians differ on the motivation of reformers with regard to early child nurseries. Michel (1999) sees assisting wage-earning mothers as one of the primary incentives to provide childcare at the turn of the twentieth century. Rose (1999) suggests that some day care providers preferred not to serve those who earned wages.

5. Until the 1920s, as more women entered the wage labor force, efforts to keep mothers out of the wage labor force mostly succeeded. Only about 6 percent of mothers of children under school age were in the labor force before World War II, but many others

earned incomes at home by taking in sewing, laundry, or boarders. (The proportion of African American mothers in the labor force remained about triple that of white women until late in the twentieth century.) About two-thirds of white wage-earning women worked part time or part year. After World War II, 50 percent of African American wage-earning women still worked in some form of domestic service, and more than 20 percent worked in agricultural jobs. These differences suggest that mothering posed quite different challenges for black and white women. See U.S. Department of Labor, "Women in the Labor Force."

6. John Watson, who advocated withholding motherly affection, became a popular figure in the interwar period. He, along with publication of Philip Wylie's (1942) *Generation of Vipers*, did much to deromanticize mothers. They were countered by Freudian practitioners, who stressed the importance of the mother–child bond, and by G. Stanley Hall, who stimulated a shift toward child development (Plant 2010).

7. The conflict over these issues is captured in such books as *The Second Shift* (Hochschild 1989) and *Unfinished Business* (Slaughter 2015).

REFERENCES

Atwood, Margaret. 1985. *The Handmaid's Tale*. Toronto: McClelland and Stewart.

Bloch, Ruth. 2003. *Gender and Morality in Anglo-American Culture, 1650–1800*. Berkeley: University of California Press.

Boster, Dea H. 2015. *African American Slavery and Disability*. London: Routledge.

Davin, Anna. 1978. "Imperialism and Motherhood." *History Workshop Journal* 5, no. 1: 9–66.

Fousekis, Natalie. 2011. *Demanding Child Care: Women's Activism and the Politics of Welfare, 1940–1970*. Champaign: University of Illinois Press.

Gilbert, Neil. 2008. *A Mother's Work: How Feminism, the Market, and Policy Shape Family Life*. New Haven, CT: Yale University Press.

Goodwin, Joanne. 2007. *Gender and the Politics of Welfare Reform: Mothers' Pensions in Chicago, 1911–1929*. Chicago: University of Chicago Press.

Gordon, Linda. 1990. *Women's Body, Women's Right: Birth Control in America*. New York: Penguin.

Himelfarb, Richard, and Rosanna Perotti. 2004. *Principle over Politics: The Domestic Policy of the George H. W. Bush Presidency*. Westport, CT: Praeger.

Hochschild, Arlie. 1989. *The Second Shift*. New York: Avon.

Jenson, Jane, and Mariette Sineau. 2001. *Who Cares? Women's Work, Child Care, and Welfare State Redesign*. Toronto: University of Toronto Press.

Kerber, Linda K. 1980. *Women of the Republic: Intellect and Ideology in Revolutionary America*. Chapel Hill: University of North Carolina Press.

——. 1998. *No Constitutional Right to be Ladies: Women and the Obligations of Citizenship*. London: Macmillan.

Kessler-Harris, Alice. 1982. *Out to Work: A History of Wage-Earning Women in the United States*. New York: Oxford University Press.

———. 2001. *In Pursuit of Equity: Women, Men, and the Quest for Economic Citizenship in 20th-Century America*. New York: Oxford University Press.

Koven, Seth, and Sonya Michel, eds. 1993. *Maternalist Politics and the Origins of Welfare States*. London: Routledge.

Lewis, Jan. 1985. *The Pursuit of Happiness: Family and Values in Jefferson's Virginia*. New York: Cambridge University Press.

May, Elaine Tyler. 2010. *America and the Pill: A History of Promise, Peril, and Liberation*. New York: Basic Books.

Michel, Sonya. 1999. *Children's Interests/Mothers Rights: The Shaping of America's Child Care Policy*. New Haven, CT: Yale University Press.

Mink, Gwendolyn. 2002. *Welfare's End*. Ithaca, NY: Cornell University Press.

Mittelstadt, Jennifer. 2015. *The Rise of the Military Welfare State*. Cambridge, MA: Harvard University Press.

Muncy, Robyn. 1991. *Creating a Female Dominion in American Reform, 1890–1935*. New York: Oxford University Press.

Piercy, Marge. 1976. *Woman on the Edge of Time*. New York: Fawcett Crest.

Plant, Rebecca Jo. 2010. *Mom: The Transformation of Motherhood in Modern America*. Chicago: University of Chicago Press.

Ramey, Jessica. 2012. *Child Care in Black and White: Working Parents and the History of Orphanages*. Champaign: University of Illinois.

Reese, Ellen. 2010. "Who Will Care for the Children?" In *Intimate Labors: Cultures, Technologies, and the Politics of Care*, ed. Eileen Boris and Rhacel Salazar Parreñas, 231–48. Stanford, CA: Stanford University Press.

Roberts, Dorothy. 2002. *Shattered Bonds: The Color of Child Welfare*. New York: Basic Civitas.

Rose, Elizabeth. 1999. *A Mother's Job: The History of Day Care, 1890–1960*. New York: Oxford University Press.

Ross, Ellen. 1995. "New Thoughts on the Oldest Vocation: Mothers and Motherhood in Recent Feminist Scholarship." *Signs* 20, no. 2: 397–413.

Silbaugh, Katharine. 1997. "Commodification and Women's Household Labor." *Yale Journal of Law & Feminism* 9, no. 1: 81–122.

Skocpol, Theda. 1995. *Protecting Soldiers and Mothers: The Political Origins of Social Policy in the United States*. Cambridge, MA: Belknap Press.

Slaughter, Anne-Marie. 2015. *Unfinished Business*. New York: Random House.

Stoltzfus, Emilie. 2003. *Citizen, Mother, Worker: Debating Public Responsibility for Child Care after the Second World War*. Chapel Hill: University of North Carolina Press.

U.S. Department of Labor. n.d. "Women in the Labor Force." *Facts over Time*. Accessed February 6, 2017. https://www.dol.gov/wb/stats/facts_over_time.htm#women.

Woloch, Nancy. 2015. *A Class by Herself: Protective Laws for Women Workers, 1890s–1990s*. Princeton, NJ: Princeton University Press.

Wylie, Philip, 1942. *A Generation of Vipers*. New York: Farrar and Rinehart.

CONTRIBUTORS

CLAIRE ACHMAD is a doctoral candidate in the Department of Child Law, Leiden Law School, Leiden University, Netherlands. Her research focuses on the rights of the child in international commercial surrogacy. Previously, she was senior advisor to the chief commissioner, Human Rights Commission, in New Zealand, served as in-house counsel for the New Zealand government, and worked for UNICEF Nederland. She is a visiting lecturer at Auckland Law School, University of Auckland, New Zealand, and a member of the International Social Service expert group on international surrogacy and child rights.

PIEN BOS earned her PhD from Utrecht University, Netherlands, in 2008. Her dissertation analyzed the decision-making process of unmarried mothers in India with regard to relinquishment or acceptance of their children. Her postdoctoral research addressed the same subject in the Netherlands and Vietnam. In 2011, she became an assistant professor at the University of Humanistic Studies, Utrecht, and started research on the topic of meaning in life and aging well.

WENDY CHAVKIN, MD, MPH, is professor of public health and obstetrics and gynecology at Columbia University, New York. She was director of the New York City Department of Health's Bureau of Maternity Services and Family Planning, editor in chief of the *Journal of the American Medical Women's Association*, and board chair of Physicians for Reproductive Health, and is cofounder and current board member of Global Doctors for Choice. She has written extensively about reproductive health, including in *The Globalization of Motherhood: Deconstructions and Reconstructions of Biology and Care*.

YASMINE ERGAS is director of Specialization on Gender and Public Policy at the School of International and Public Affairs and of the Gender and Human Rights program at the Institute for the Study of Human Rights, both at Columbia University, New York. Her recent work focuses on the emergence of an international market in reproductive services, the transformations of "motherhood," globalization, and human rights. She also has written extensively on feminist movements and their interactions with public policy making.

MARTHA ALBERTSON FINEMAN is Robert Woodruff Professor at Emory University. She is founding director of the Feminism and Legal Theory Project and the Vulnerability and the Human Condition Initiative. Her scholarship addresses the legal regulation of intimacy and the implications of universal dependency and vulnerability. Fineman's scholarly awards include the Harry Kalvin Prize for her work in law and society and a doctor honoris causa from Lund University, Sweden, for her vulnerability thesis.

ANNE HIGONNET is professor of art history at Barnard College, Columbia University, New York. She works on art since 1400. Among her books is *Pictures of Innocence: The History and Crisis of Ideal Childhood*. Her work has been supported by grants and fellowships from the Mellon, Guggenheim, Getty, and Kress foundations and the Social Science Research Council. She is an award-winning teacher and has lectured widely, including at the Metropolitan Museum of Art, New York.

JANE JENSON is professor emerita in the Department of Political Science, Université de Montréal, Canada, where she was awarded the Canada Research Chair in Citizenship and Governance, in 2001. She has also been a senior fellow of the Successful Societies program of the Canadian Institute for Advanced Research, Toronto, since 2004. Her research focuses on comparative social policy, particularly the development of the social investment perspective, including the consequences for gender relations and women's status.

LINDA G. KAHN holds a PhD in epidemiology and an MPH in population and family health from Columbia University's Mailman School of Public Health, New York. Her research interests include predictors of pubertal development and infertility, and health outcomes of assisted reproduction in both women and children. She is currently a postdoctoral fellow in the Department of Pediatrics at the New York University School of Medicine.

ALICE KESSLER-HARRIS is the R. Gordon Hoxie Professor Emerita of American History at Columbia University, New York, where she has taught at the Institute for Research on Women and Gender. Her interests include issues of gender and wage work across time, space, race, and ethnicity. Her books include the now classic *Out to Work: A History of Wage Earning Women in the United States* and the recently reissued *A Woman's Wage: Historical Meanings and Social Consequences*.

HELMA LUTZ is professor of Women's and Gender Studies in the Department of Sociology at Goethe University, Frankfurt, Germany. Her latest books in English are *The New Maids: Transnational Women and the Care Economy* and *Framing Intersectionality: Debates on a Multi-Faceted Concept in Gender Studies*, coedited with Maria Teresa Herrera Vivar and Linda Supik. She is currently completing a monograph entitled "Behind Europe's Care Curtain: Migration and the Global Market of Care."

SONYA MICHEL is professor emerita of History, American Studies, and Gender and Women's Studies at the University of Maryland, College Park. A founding editor of the journal *Social Politics*, she is currently participating in an international project on women, migration, and the work of care. Her books include *Children's Interests/Mothers' Rights: The Shaping of America's Child Care Policy* and *Mothers of a New World: Maternalist Politics and the Origins of Welfare States*, coedited with Seth Koven.

NARA MILANICH is associate professor of Latin American history at Barnard College, Columbia University, New York. She is currently writing a book on the global history of paternity testing, to be published by Harvard University Press. Her interests include the histories of family, childhood, gender, law, and reproduction in Latin America and comparatively. She is the author of *Children of Fate: Childhood, Class, and the State in Chile, 1850–1930*, which won the Grace Abbott Prize from the Society for the History of Childhood and Youth.

GABRIELLE OLIVEIRA, from São Paulo, Brazil, is an assistant professor in the Lynch School of Education at Boston College. She received her PhD in applied anthropology from Teachers College, Columbia University, New York, with a dissertation on female Mexican migration to the United States, focusing on transnational motherhood and separated siblings. She was a Spencer Foundation dissertation fellow in 2014–2015 and a postdoctoral fellow at the University of Wisconsin–Madison School of Education in 2015–2016.

LETIZIA PALUMBO is a postdoctoral researcher in comparative law at the University of Palermo, Italy. She is also a research associate on the Addressing Demand in Anti-Trafficking Efforts and Policies project at the European University Institute, Florence. Her research interests include human rights, women's rights, reproductive rights, human trafficking, migration, and labor exploitation.

DOROTHY ROBERTS is George A. Weiss University Professor of Law and Sociology at the University of Pennsylvania, Philadelphia, with appointments in the law school and the departments of Africana Studies and Sociology. Her books include *Killing the Black Body: Race, Reproduction, and the Meaning of Liberty*; *Shattered Bonds: The Color of Child Welfare*; and *Fatal Invention: How Science, Politics, and Big Business Re-create Race in the Twenty-First Century*.

CAROL SANGER is the Barbara Aronstein Black Professor at Columbia Law School, New York, where she focuses on the law surrounding abortion, motherhood, and family. Her teaching areas include contracts, family law, and courses focusing on reproduction, the legal profession, and law and gender. Her recent scholarship addresses the regulation of maternal conduct, the regulation of abortion, surrogacy, and law's relation to culture. She is a coeditor of *Cases and Materials on Contracts* (8th ed., 2013).

INDEX

n: his spiritual development. By J. W. N. Sullivan (N. Y.: Vintage, $1.
as Man and Artist. By Ernest Newman (N. Y.: Vintage, $1.65).
niverse; the Story of Alexander von Humboldt. By Edward F. Dolan (N.
, Mead, 1959, 244 pp.).
Ranke, the Formative Years. By Theodore Von Laue (Princeton: Prince
ersity Press, 1950, 230 pp.).
Re-examination. By J. N. Findlay (N. Y.: Macmillan, 1958, 372 pp.).
e. By Walter Kaufman (N. Y.: Meridian, $1.65).
arx: his life and environment. By Isaiah Berlin (N. Y.: Oxford Univer
, $1.50).
portrait of an exile. By Stringfellow Barr (N. Y.: Holt, 1935, 308 pp.)
i. By Denis Mack Smith (N. Y.: Knopf, 1956, 207 pp.).
and the Unification of Italy. By Massimo Salvadori (N. Y.: Anvil, $1.25)
holas I. By Constantin de Grunwald. (London: D. Saunders, 1954, 294 pp
er II and the Modernization of Russia. By W. E. Mosse (London: Engl
ersities Press, 1958, 191 pp.).
lstoy. By Ernest Simmons. (N. Y.: Vintage Books, 2 vols., $1.45 each).
vsky: his life and art. By Avrahm Yarmolinsky (N. Y.: Grove Press, $2.9
Friend (Tschaikowsky). By Catherine D. Bowen and B. K. von Meck (B
Little, Brown, 1961, 484 pp.).
archist Prince: a biographical study of Peter Kropotkin. By George Woo
(N. Y.: T. V. Boardman, 1950, 463 pp.).
Bakunin. By E. H. Carr (N. Y.: Vintage Books, $1.45).
seph I, the downfall of an empire. By Karl Tschuppik (N. Y.: Harcour
., 1930, 509 pp.).
he intellectual background. By Brian W. Downs (Cambridge: Cambridg
ersity Press, 1946, 187 pp.).
aard. By Walter Lowie. (N. Y.: Harper, 2 vols., $1.75, $1.95).
George. By Thomas Jones (Cambridge: Harvard University Press, 1951
pp.).
ston Churchill. By Edgar Black (N. Y.: Monarch Books, 50 cents).
a study in tyranny. By Alan Bullock. (N. Y.: Bantam, 95 cents).
Mussolini. By Christopher Hibbert (London: Longmans, 1962, 367 pp.).
By David Shub. N. Y.: Mentor, 50 cents).
By Leon Trotsky (N. Y.: Putnam's, $1.25).
ophet Armed: Trotsky, 1879–1921. By Isaac Deutscher (N. Y.: Oxford Uni
ity Press, 1945, 540 pp.).
ophet Unarmed: Trotsky, 1921–1929. By Isaac Deutscher (N. Y.: Oxford
ersity Press, 1959, 490 pp.).
a political biography. By Isaac Deutscher (N. Y.: Vintage Books, $1.65).
who made a Revolution. By Bertram Wolfe (Boston: Beacon, $2.25).
Khrushchev. By Myron Rush (Washington: Public Affairs Press, 1958,
pp.).
on Horseback: the incredible Atatürk (Kemal). By Ray Brock (N. Y.: Duell,
an and Pearce, 1954, 408 pp.).
Maynard Keynes, economist and policy maker. By Seymour Harris (N. Y.:
ibner's, 1955, 234 pp.).
tto Croce. By Gian Orsini (Carbondale: Southern Illinois University Press,
1, 379 pp.).
By Franz Borkenau (N. Y.: Wiley, 1936, 219 pp.).

*Cervantes. By Aubrey F. G. Bell (N. Y.: Collier, 95 cents).
*Velasquez. By Margaretta Salinger (N. Y.: Abrams, Inc., 95 cents).
*El Greco. By John F. Mathews (N. Y.: Abrams, Inc., 95 cents).
William the Silent. By C. V. Wedgwood (London: Cape, 1944, 256 pp.).
*Rembrandt. By Gladys Schmitt (N. Y.: Dell, 95 cents).
*Michelangelo and Rembrandt. By Emil Ludwig (N. Y.: Ace, 50 cents).
*Rubens. By Julius Held (N. Y.: Abrams, Inc., 95 cents).
Life and Works of Grotius. By W. S. M. Knight (London: Sweet and Maxwell, 1925, 304 pp.).
*Medici. By Ferdinand Schevill (N. Y.: Harper, $1.45).
Lorenzo dei Medici and Renaissance Italy. C. M. Ady (N. Y.: Macmillan, 1952, 176 pp.).
*Leonardo da Vinci. By Kenneth Clark (Baltimore: Penguin, $1.45).
Jacob Fugger, the Rich. By Jacob Strieder (N. Y.: Adelphi Co., 1931, 227 pp.).
*Leibniz. By H. W. Carr (N. Y.: Dover, $1.35).

The Enlightenment

Montesquieu: a critical biography. By Robert Shackleton (N. Y.: Oxford University Press, 1961, 432 pp.).
The Spirit of Voltaire. By Norman Torrey (N. Y.: Columbia University Press, 1938, 314 pp.).
Jean-Jacques Rousseau: a critical study of his life and writings. By F. C. Green (Cambridge: Cambridge University Press, 1955, 376 pp.).
Bayle the Sceptic. By Howard Robinson (N. Y.: Columbia University Press, 1931, 334 pp.).
Diderot: the testing years, 1713–1759. By Arthur Wilson (N. Y.: Oxford University Press, 1957, 417 pp.).
*Les Philosophes: the Philosophers of the Enlightenment. By Norman Torrey (N. Y.: Putnam's, $1.65).
Forerunners of Darwin, 1745–1839. By Hiram B. Glass (Baltimore: Johns Hopkins University Press, 1959, 471 pp.).
Antoine Lavoisier: scientist, economist, social reformer. By Douglas McKie (N. Y.: Schuman, 1952, 440 pp.).
*Hume. By A. H. Basson (Baltimore: Penguin, 95 cents).
Adam Smith and the Scotland of his Day. By C. R. Fay (Cambridge: Cambridge University Press, 1956, 173 pp.).
Edward Gibbon. By Michael Joyce (N. Y.: Longmans, 1953, 176 pp.).
*Life of Johnson. By James Boswell (abr., N. Y.: Dell, 50 cents; N. Y.: Collier, $1.50; complete, N. Y.: Oxford Press, $3.75).
Burke and the Nature of Politics. By Carl Cone (Lexington: University of Kentucky Press, 1957, 415 pp.).
Jeremy Bentham and the Law. By George W. Keeton (London: Stevens, 1948, 266 pp.).
*John Wesley. By Francis McConnell (N. Y.: Abingdon, $1.75).
William Wilberforce and his Times. By Oliver Warner (London: Batsford, 1962, 174 pp.).
*Goethe. By Jeanne Ancelet Hustache (N. Y.: Grove Press, $1.35).
*Kant. By S. Koerner (Baltimore: Penguin, 95 cents).
*J. S. Bach. By Andre Pirro (N. Y.: Crown, $1.25).

Albert Einstein. By Leopold Infeld (N. Y.: Scribner's, $1.25).

Ernest Rutherford, atom pioneer. By John Rowland (London: Laurie, 1955, 160 pp.).

Thomas Mann. By Henry Hatfield (N. Y.: New Directions, $1.45).

Freud and His Time. By Fritz Wittels (N. Y.: Grosset & Dunlap, $1.65).

Einstein, Trotsky, Hemingway, Freud and other great companions. By Max Eastman (N. Y.: Collier, 95 cents).

Order From: THE MACMILLAN COMPANY, Department 470
60 Fifth Avenue, New York 11, New York

How to Order: Cash must accompany all orders of $5.00 or less. For larger orders we will gladly bill you or your organization

On quantity orders for single or assorted titles the following discounts are offered:

orders for $10.00-$49.99	10% discount
orders for $50.00-$99.99	15% discount
orders for $100.00 or more	20% discount

Please specify title and quantity. Make checks payable to the Macmillan Company. Quantity discounts apply only if order is addressed specifically to Department 470 of the Macmillan Company.

---

43. *Money Grows Up in American History,* by SUSAN S. BURR, 75c
44. *The Founding Fathers: Young Men of the Revolution,* by STANLEY ELKINS and ERIC McKITRICK, 50c
45. *They Were There: A Guide to Firsthand Literature for Use in Teaching American History,* by RICHARD C. BROWN, 50c
46. *Russia Since 1917,* by GEORGE BARR CARSON, JR., 50c
47. *Forty Years of Chinese Communism: Selected Readings with Commentary,* by ALLAN B. COLE, 75c
48. *The Development of American Labor,* by ALBERT A. BLUM, 50c
49. *Biography as History: Men and Movements in Europe Since 1500,* by CHARLES F. MULLETT, 50c
50. *The Indian in America History,* by WILLIAM T. HAGAN, 50c

PAMPHLETS *Published by the*

SERVICE CENTER FOR TEACHERS OF HISTORY

(Continued on cover 3)